BEETHOVEN AND HIS WORLD

BEETHOVEN
AND HIS WORLD

EDITED BY
SCOTT BURNHAM AND MICHAEL P. STEINBERG

PRINCETON UNIVERSITY PRESS
PRINCETON AND OXFORD

Published by Princeton University Press, 41 William Street,
Princeton, New Jersey 08540
In the United Kingdom: Princeton University Press,
3 Market Place, Woodstock, Oxfordshire OX20 1SY

Library of Congress Cataloging-in-Publication Data

Beethoven and his world / edited by Scott Burnham and Michael P. Steinberg.
p. cm. "Published in conjunction with The Bard Music Festival"—Half t.p. verso.
Includes bibliographical references and index.
ISBN 0-691-07072-5 (alk. paper).—ISBN 0-691-07073-3 (pbk. : alk. paper)
1. Beethoven, Ludwig van, 1770–1827. I. Burnham, Scott G. II. Steinberg, Michael P.
III. The Bard Music Festival
ML410.B4 B2812 2000 780'.92—dc21 [B] 00-038529

This publication has been produced by the Bard College Publications Office:
Ginger Shore, Director
John Isaacs, Art Director

Designed by Juliet Meyers

Composed in Baskerville by Natalie Kelly

Text edited by Paul De Angelis

Music typeset by Don Giller

The paper used in this publication meets the minimum requirements of
ANSI/NISO Z39.48-1992 (R1997) (*Permanence of Paper*)

www.pup.princeton.edu

Printed in the United States of America

1 3 5 7 9 10 8 6 4 2

1 3 5 7 9 10 8 6 4 2
(Pbk.)

Contents

Contents

PART IV
BEETHOVEN IN THE WORLD

Preface and Acknowledgments

Beethoven is forever. Beethoven in the year 2000—all millennial hype notwithstanding—is a Beethoven of the moment. In the volume we offer you here, leading scholars draw from several disciplines to produce, individually and collectively, a sense of both the current status and emergent trends in Beethoven scholarship. Of the eleven essay writers, ten are music scholars. Their contributions exemplify the trend of the last fifteen or so years to place music into dialogue with the texts and interpretive methods of literary, historical, and cultural analysis.

In this context, Reinhold Brinkmann explores the post-revolutionary milieu of Beethoven's *Eroica* Symphony, showing how music participates in the making of a new sense of time. In particular, Brinkmann's interpretation of the celebrated coda of the first movement as actually conjuring the future moves beyond the usual invocation of closure and apotheosis and serves to open up our sense of Beethoven's heroic style. By asking what "heroism" really means in the context of works like *Fidelio*, Lewis Lockwood also broadens our vision of the heroic music, offering an informed taxonomy of Beethoven's musical heroic types. Though Beethoven's heroic style is easily the composer's most public manner—it is still the prevailing soundtrack of his stature in the modern West—Brinkmann and Lockwood bring fresh nuance to our understanding of its commanding presence within our culture.

The second grouping of essays explores the emergence of Beethoven's late style, with regard to themes of temporality, memory, and voice. The late style has been the site of much recent activity in musical thought, even prompting Charles Rosen to return to his landmark study, *The Classical Style: Haydn, Mozart, Beethoven*, in order to add a new chapter. Ever drawing on the work of Theodor Adorno, critical fascination with the late style and its implied critique of Beethoven's earlier music (and indeed of the Viennese classical style) has reached a high tide. Analyses abound, particularly of the late quartets and piano sonatas, for this music seems somehow to stage the dilemmas of modern subjectivity. With its staggering disjunctions in formal process and stylistic register, its expressive intensity that is somehow both lyrical and impersonal, Beethoven's late music invites musicologists and music theorists to entertain poststructuralist and postmodern values while continuing to engage in a more traditional kind of analysis that would find and nurture an underlying coherence to this often discontinuous music. In the present volume, Elaine Sisman addresses a group of pieces written around 1815–1816 that share a preoccupation with memory, traced here in the ways that Beethoven stages the return of music from the opening movement in later movements. Sisman situates these unusual works in a post-Kantian context, linking invention and fantasia with the work of reminiscence. Glenn Stanley shows how a vexing performance problem in the first movement of op. 109 can be read as a symptom of the incursion of voices into the genre of the piano sonata—and he goes on to speculate about the nature of their conversation. Beethoven's celebrated song cycle *An die ferne Geliebte* (the locus classicus of this quintessentially Romantic genre) is Nicholas Marston's quarry in an exciting new interpretation that turns the tables on the usual way of construing the presence of the Distant Beloved and that, like Brinkmann and Sisman, reveals a Beethoven deeply engaged with the vicissitudes and possibilities of human temporality.

Moving into a more concrete world, Tilman Skowroneck peers behind the scenes into Beethoven's workshop, explaining how the young Beethoven chose his pianos, and showing along the way that the titan and the myth was also a practical worker with an interest in machinery. William Kinderman reveals a similarly workmanlike Beethoven in the process of sketching and revising his compositions; more important, Kinderman offers compelling evidence of several of Beethoven's abiding aesthetic concerns as well as keen insight into the ways that different genres come to inform and enrich each other in his music. Beethoven emerges from these two essays as a discerning musician from a specific time and place, facing the usual problems of production and dissemination, and concerned as much with the real as with the ideal.

The volume concludes with four essays engaging the broader question of reception, of Beethoven's impact on his world and ours. This emphasis represents a much worked recent trend in Beethoven studies, in line with the spread of reception theory and the related question of canon formation. Christopher Gibbs's study of Beethoven's funeral and its aftermath features documentary material appearing in English for the first time. As companion pieces to his essay we have translated some purple poems written in memory of the composer; these will never be recognized as great works, but they emerge as fascinating documents in the history of literary emotion. Above all, Gibbs shows how characteristic constructions of artistic greatness quickly gathered in the various "performances of grief" surrounding the memorialization of Beethoven. Art historian Alessandra Comini offers an illustrated discussion of Beethoven's ubiquitous and iconic frown and traces how the myth of the frown relates to the actual practices of taking life masks as well as death masks. Sanna Pederson shows how the "new musicology's" critical engagement with gender and the ideology of masculinity in fact reopens ambiguities that were crucial to the Romantic theorists of Beethoven's generation. In so doing, she deepens and contextualizes the feminist backlash to Beethoven famously broached by Susan McClary's vividly explicit suggestion of masculinist violence in the first movement of the Ninth Symphony. Can Beethoven survive without the ideology of masculinity? This is the question that rings in our ears at the end of Pederson's essay. Finally, Leon Botstein surveys the reception of Beethoven in two *fins-de-siècle*, showing how pioneering music scholars in turn-of-twentieth-century Vienna squared off on the issues of rhetoric and narrative and the question of the extramusical in Beethoven, setting the terms of an often acrimonious debate that continues in our own day.

* * * *

Beethoven and His World is the eleventh annual volume in a series to appear in conjunction with the Bard Music Festival and its reconsiderations of canonic composers. Those of us who have followed the festival over the last decade have developed an ardent respect and affection for its audiences. We imagine the readers of the volumes to have a similar profile: professionals and amateurs with a commitment to the aesthetic and cultural importance of music, eager to hear good music and to learn more about it in its various contexts. You will notice immediately that this volume is built differently from its predecessors. It contains no discrete section of primary documents. This was an editorial decision resulting from our sense of the "Beethoven difference." The man, music, and myth have remained so iconic for so long that the most telling documents and commentaries are widely known and easily available. Moreover, if there is any one thing that Beethoven can be said to have done these last two hundred years, it is to continue to confront and provoke his audiences, to demand fresh interpretations from performers, critics, and analysts. Beethoven has always been a Beethoven of the moment. We too have acceded to this demand: with a few exceptions, such as the poems of Kanne and Mayrhofer, we have filled the volume with new work, offering you eleven essays rather than the five or six of the previous volumes.

This is the first of the Bard/Princeton volumes to be co-edited—in this case by a cultural historian in addition to a music theorist. Permit us to gloat for a moment in how well we got along throughout our work on the book—a good omen for the potential of interdisciplinary work. We were supported throughout by colleagues at the Bard Music Festival, as well as at the Bard Publications Office, the Princeton University Music Department, and Princeton University Press. We would like to acknowledge in particular Leon Botstein, Paul De Angelis, Saralyn Fosnight, David Kasunic, Mark Loftin, Robert Martin, Ginger Shore, and Irene Zedlacher. We want also to thank the eleven contributors for their enthusiasm, punctuality, and intellectual generosity.

Collectively, the eleven essays that follow do argue for a symptomatic asymmetry in the politics of interdisciplinarity. They suggest as a group that music scholars are currently more eager to engage questions of cultural history than cultural historians are to think about music. As a body of work and mode of cultural experience, music remains discursively remote to historians, still much more so than word- or image-based "texts." The themes developed in this volume—such as time, memory, heroism, revolution, and gender—are prime categories for cultural analysis. The scholars engaging the themes show how music in general and Beethoven in particular participate in defining them for historical interpretation. Historians have not yet paid enough attention to music. In this respect, we hope that this book will serve as an invitation to interdisciplinary reciprocity.

BEETHOVEN
AND HIS WORLD

PART I

HEROIC
BEETHOVEN

·

In the Time of the *Eroica*

REINHOLD BRINKMANN
TRANSLATED BY IRENE ZEDLACHER

> . . . the lava of revolution flows . . .
> —Georg Büchner, *Dantons Tod*

At last, in France in the years 1788 and 1789, the volcanic movement broke forth whose fiery and bloody convulsions are yet to
be subdued. Whoever knows what I have professed before, or
who know me and what I profess today, will scarcely accuse me of
ever having been an advocate of the French and their Revolution,
or of sanctioning or acknowledging the tenets on which its leaders and advocates intended to build constitutions and nations.
But I would prove myself an extremely ungrateful hypocrite
were I not to acknowledge openly how infinitely much we owe
this wild and fantastic revolution. It has unleashed a flowing
ocean of fire for the spirit from which everyone who is not afraid
of the light is free to draw; it has planted into heads and hearts
essential ideas for the foundation of the future, which only twenty
or thirty years ago most people would have been too afraid to
conceive; it has accelerated that process of fermentation through
which we had to pass as our purgatory if we wished to reach the
heavenly gates of a new condition. It has shown how much the
human spirit may dare to desire and risk in earthly things for the
eternal call of reason within.[1]

These sentences, written in 1814 by German nationalist author and
politician Ernst Moritz Arndt, took a retrospective look at the impact of
nearly twenty years of the French Revolution in German lands. In

content and political assessment Arndt's comments hold firmly a middle ground between conservative and liberal positions, but the shape of the ideas and the vocabulary used to express them can be considered exemplary for representations of the Revolution by German intellectuals around 1800. Three aspects of this text seem typical and noteworthy.

The Revolution's spiritual dimension is emphasized over any political meaning: it has planted "ideas" in the "heads and hearts" of the people; the "fermenting process" it has promoted has been a "spiritual" one. It has pointed its contemporaries toward an "eternal call of reason." Even more striking is the form of linguistic expression, primarily the elevated style, which reveals in word choice and linguistic gesture the emotional empathy if not enthusiasm of a writer who was, as he himself declares, no supporter of the Revolution. The conspicuous use of nature metaphors to describe the revolutionary events is representative; natural events of a grand scale are summoned as comparative imagery of extraordinary force. Third and last, Arndt refers to a specific experience of time: the Revolution has "movement"; it has "accelerated" processes; it deals with an emphatically-awaited "future."

Let me first briefly discuss these three aspects as viewed against a broader documentary basis, then approach my central topic with this perspective.

I

After the democratic failure of the political revolution—however that failure be identified, with Jacobean rule or with Napoleon's self-coronation—the Revolution was increasingly viewed as a spiritual force in the history of ideas, as a historical turning point in modern consciousness. Friedrich Gentz, the constitutional conservative and German translator of Edmund Burke's treatise against the revolution, wrote as early as 1790: "[The revolution] is the first practical triumph of philosophy, the first example of a government based on principles and a coherent and consistent system."[2] And in the work of Georg Christoph Lichtenberg we find this 1790 aphorism: "The French Revolution is the work of philosophy, but what a leap from *Cogito ergo sum* to the first sound of *à la Bastille* at the Palais Royal!"[3] Such an interpretation is in line with the typical German interpretation of the revolution as it was first, and in essence, defined by Kant in the famous paragraph from his 1798 *Contest of Faculties*:

The Revolution which we have seen taking place in our own times in a nation of gifted people may succeed, or it may fail . . . but I maintain that this Revolution has aroused in the hearts and desires of all spectators who are not themselves caught up in it a *sympathy* which borders almost on enthusiasm, although the very utterance of this sympathy was fraught with danger. It cannot therefore have been caused by anything other than a moral disposition within the human race.[4]

In seemingly contemporary terms, the reception of the Revolution "in the souls of all spectators" is understood here as the realization of a philosophy of morals, as the expression of every human being's right to a civil constitution and—following from it—freedom.[5] A quarter of a century later Georg Friedrich Hegel would argue this point forcefully. In his *Philosophy of History* we read:

The French Revolution has its beginning and origin in thought. Thought, which takes the general good as its ultimate goal and seeks out all which may oppose it, has risen against existing conditions. The ultimate purpose of thought is the *freedom of will*. . . . The freedom of the Will per se is the principal and substantial basis of all Right—is itself absolute, inherently eternal Right; and the Supreme Right in comparison with other specific Rights: nay, it is, even that by which man becomes man, and therefore the fundamental principle of the spirit. . . . It may however be remarked that the same principle obtained speculative recognition in Germany, in the Kantian philosophy. . . . Among the Germans this view assumed no other form than that of tranquil theory; but the French wished to give it practical effect.[6]

In his *Lectures on the History of Philosophy* Hegel expresses this self-consciously idealistic concept with a nationalist bent that contrasts even more sharply the thinking German with the acting Frenchman:

In the *Republic* of Plato we have met with the idea that the philosophers are those who ought to reign. Now is the time in which it is said that the spiritual are to govern. . . . Thus in the French Revolution we see that abstract thought is made to rule; in accordance with it, constitutions and laws are determined, it forms the bond between man and man; and men come to have the consciousness that what is esteemed amongst them is abstract thought, and that liberty and equality are what ought to be regarded; in this the subject also has his true value, even in relation to actuality. . . . In the philosophy of Kant, Fichte, and Schelling, the revolution to which in Germany the mind has advanced in these latter days, was formally thought out and expressed; the sequence of these philosophies shows the course which thought has taken. In this great epoch of the world's history two nations only have played a part, the German and the French, and this in spite of their absolute oppositions, or rather because they are so opposite. . . . In Germany this principle has burst forth as thought, spirit, Notion; in France in the form of actuality. In Germany what there is of actuality comes to us as a force of external circumstances, and as a reaction against the same.[7]

The equation of real and spiritual events, especially the extension of the term "revolution" to include spiritual phenomena and the idealist glorification of the latter, are also the background for Friedrich Schlegel's famous "Athenäums Fragment" of 1798. The dramatic events of the "great" French Revolution, which aimed at a change of reality and a radical new beginning, here come to serve as models for the assessment and representation of trends in other fields that are directed toward the new, the future—especially in the sciences and the arts. The almost defensive elaboration of the programmatic opening thesis in Schlegel's aphorism (which is frequently quoted in truncated form) makes this clear:

> The French Revolution, Fichte's philosophy, and Goethe's *Meister* are the greatest tendencies of this era. Whoever is offended by this juxtaposition, whoever cannot take any revolution seriously that isn't noisy and materialistic, hasn't yet achieved a lofty, broad perspective on the history of mankind. Even in our shabby histories of civilization . . . many a little book, almost unnoticed by the noisy rabble at the time, plays a greater role than anything they did.[8]

In Schlegel's aphorism, a philosophical treatise and a novel are called upon not only as historical witnesses, but as historical agents whose meaning for the era is equated with the French Revolution. I will pursue this mode of thought and will later take it as an occasion to consider musical works—Beethoven's symphonies in general, and his Third Symphony in particular, composed a good half decade after the "Athenäums Fragment"—as additional representatives of those "greatest tendencies" of the age, directly linked to the French Revolution.

II

Even Friedrich Gentz had to admit in 1790 that a possible "failure of this revolution" may have to be considered "one of the severest accidents ever to befall humanity. . . . It is hope and comfort for many of the old evils under which humanity suffers. Should this Revolution die away, all those evils will be ten times harder to cure."[9] If even Gentz thought this, then it should not come as a surprise that German advocates of the Revolution often expressed their enthusiasm in somewhat dithyrambic tones.[10] In 1790 Johann Heinrich Campe, elected honorary citizen of Paris by its revolutionaries, wrote from that city:

Before long an electric and luminous stream of concepts and insights will pour forth from here to all nations of this earth; from this place where the exalted human spirit rises free and brave like an eagle from the low and dark spheres toward the sunlit ocean of truth! No, it is not delusion, it is an incontrovertible fact, . . . when I declare that human reason never before has appeared as now in a condition of such nobility, full power, activity, and promise, at least not so universally. . . . Soon this torrential and overflowing stream of ideas gushing forth from the pure spring of freedom will flood all of Europe.[11]

All the important components of contemporary German representations of the Revolution are subsumed here in one grand metaphor. The "torrential and overflowing stream of ideas" refers to the conception of revolution as an inner experience, as a philosophical idea. Campe's image of the flowing stream suggests an overwhelming natural event, defining its power in temporal terms, as "torrential" time.[12] Campe uses the imagery of flowing again in other writings, for example when he describes, in a letter of August 4, 1789, his direct and overwhelming experience of the Parisian revolutionary public:

I have freed myself from the surging flood of people that more than ever rushes through the streets toward the public squares, and I sit down now at the shore, that is: in my room, to try to sort and bring into order the innumerable new images, ideas, and emotions enveloping the spectator at every step like a swarm of young bees. In vain! The roar of the human flood breaks into my remote little room through windows and doors and walls.[13]

Georg Forster, who was labeled a German Jacobin, used the analogous image of an "avalanche" that "gains in mass as it hurls downward and destroys any obstacle in its way" to illustrate the dangerous and inescapable forces of the revolution.[14] Elsewhere Forster has the Revolution "flood all of Europe like sacred lava."[15] The image of a flaming volcanic eruption, as that of blazing fire generally,[16] is also typical for descriptions of the Revolution. Ernst Moritz Arndt even talks about the "volcanoes of revolution," thus seeking to convey its force and suddenness as well as its dangers. Other images evoked are high mountains (especially the Alps), deep abysses, oceans, thunderstorms, and hurricanes, but also the sun; dawn was the symbol for an enlightened new beginning. It is an image used very emphatically by Hegel in a late and retrospective text: "It was a glorious dawn. All thinking creatures celebrated this era. A sublime sensibility reigned in those times, a spiritual enthusiasm pervaded the world."[17] The identical arsenal of powerful natural images is employed in writings by opponents of the Revolution to communicate its horrors and dangers. Consider the poem "Die Revolution. Ein Gedicht im asklepiadischen Silbenmaße" (The Revolution. A Poem in Asclepiadic Meter) written in December 1789 by the Bonn amateur poet Apollinar (alias Bertram Maria Altstätten). Here are a few verses:

God, what is this terrible fate that pours with heavy hand
such destiny on us! What storm lies
above those mountains, brewing at the horizon!
Clouds like soot exhaled from Hell approach,
black and heavy, and move toward south and midnight,
And, where ripped apart, the sky looks red,
Red like blood. From deep in the east
Thunder sounds . . .

And see now, everywhere flare streams of sparks
Thrown into the land by rage's flame,
Burning bright.—Save us, you eternal ones!
You alone can help. Human power
Cannot control the flood which breaks the dams.[18]

And finally there is the image of fermentation, representing the idea of a natural evolutionary process. This image found in the passage by Ernst Moritz Arndt quoted above, is also used by Johannes Weitzel: "The stuff of revolution lies brewing amidst the nations."[19]

These nature metaphors are significant in that they help to stress the aspect of process in the Revolution. Above all though, they endow all political events with the force of destiny: a law that often is beyond the individual's grasp nevertheless breaks in on him/her with elemental force and nature-like consequences. The Revolution thus becomes the inevitable result of a human disposition toward reason, of the development of politics and the state, of actual conditions. Such nature imagery further suggests a radical new beginning, a beginning on a prehistorical if not on a pre-worldly basis. Franz Dautzenberg, publicist in Aachen, recognized this when he wrote in 1792 that a "nation destroys the entire ancient foundation of its constitutional structure, nearly throwing itself into Nature's arms to start afresh."[20] In contrast to the rational claims of philosophical-idealist interpretations, this kind of metaphor contains a potent irrational element, making it possible for Edmund Burke to use identical metaphors to denounce the Revolution as evil and dangerous. That this kind of metaphor is quite inconsistent and problematic shall be mentioned only in passing: nowhere is it thought—or at least openly discussed—that the emphatically invoked dawn is necessarily followed by a sunset. Reinhart Koselleck has interpreted the phenomenon of a partial contradiction in the metaphors as an indication of the inherent failure of the Revolution in both character and process.[21]

But this rhetoric of reception also builds a bridge from the French Revolution to the arts. These metaphors, images of great and overwhelming natural phenomena, are also characteristic of definitions of the sublime in contemporary aesthetic theories. By distinguishing beauty from the sublime, Edmund Burke's early treatise *A Philosophical Enquiry into the Origin of our Ideas of the Sublime and Beautiful* of 1757, Kant's *Observations on the Feeling of the Beautiful and Sublime* of 1764, his 1790 *Critique of Judgement*, and Schiller's *On the Sublime* of 1801 (which followed Kant's ideas) furnish a descriptive paradigm of the sublime which is then used to define genres and works of art. I will later return to these linkages in the descriptions of real and artistic phenomena under the rubric of the sublime, as well as to internal aesthetic parallels between theories of the ode and of the large symphonic form from around 1800, to determine the specific content of Beethoven's *Eroica* in a comparative manner.

III

Prior to that I want to discuss a third issue. It concerns a new mode of temporal experience. Again I turn to a text by Ernst Moritz Arndt, this time dating from 1804–1805, the years when the *Eroica* received its finishing touches and its first performances:

> It is regularly asserted . . . : whoever has lived through the last twenty years has lived centuries. But that just expresses mere amazement about the period. . . . The era is in flight. Its representative images pass in such quick succession that contemporaries stare and wonder, stand frozen and understand nothing. The fast succession gives them the impression of an endless period of time unfolding before their eyes, all the more so because in their ossified state they do not participate and thus have lost any measure of time itself.
>
> Time is fleeing; the wiser ones have long known it. Unimaginable things have happened; the world has suffered great transformations calmly and noisily, in the gentle passing of days as well as during the hurricanes and volcanoes of revolutions. . . .[22]

The most overwhelming effect the Revolution had on its contemporaries was indeed an entirely new mode of experiencing "time." This experience was based on the recognition that far-reaching and profound social changes were taking place, changes as extraordinary in speed as they were unforeseen. Contemporaries noted the tempo of change, the acceleration in the passage of time itself, and the "contemporaneity of the non-contemporary,"[23] the latter a result of differing levels of acceleration in disparate fields. Such experiences were frequently expressed in the wake of the Revolution. A quote from Konrad Engelbert Oelsner exemplifies the first aspect. He wrote in 1797: "The revolution has accelerated the progress of the human spirit in most extraordinary ways."[24] Georg Forster's statements regarding the "Revolution as a new and inescapable force" and the characterization of the Revolution as "an avalanche with accelerated speed" which "gains in mass as it proceeds,"[25] quoted above in a different context, belong here as well. In 1791 Karl Friedrich Reinhard, also quoted above, wrote: "The French form of government developed fast and without warning. There were moments in those past two years when it was well-nigh possible to say that the sun shone upon an entirely different nation after only one single turn around the earth."[26] And Friedrich Schlegel, in his

Viennese lectures on the philosophy of history of 1828, also considered acceleration the defining quality of the "transitional period from the age of Enlightenment to the time of revolution," though now he assessed it more critically and more conservatively: "Before long a tempo too rapid and passionate will affect the course of this event and the progress of time . . ."[27] The acceleration in temporal experience is seen as a special feature of historical progress, an intensification if not radicalization of the idea of progress.[28]

To illustrate the other phenomenon referred to above—the contemporaneity of the noncontemporary—I call upon the publisher Friedrich Perthes as witness. His diagnosis from the early nineteenth century is already distinctly inspired by historicist thought:

> In previous eras, spiritual trends and the entire world of thought and will were separated by centuries in difference; but our age has reconciled the irreconcilable within the lifetime of the last three generations alive today. The immense contrasts between the years 1750, 1789, and 1815 lack any transition and do not appear as sequences. Rather, today they exist side-by-side among all living human beings, depending on whether they are grandfather, father, or grandchild.[29]

In one brief sentence, Johanna Schopenhauer expressed the intensification of the historical moment through the experience of a compression of time: "Ten years are now so much more than a hundred used to be."[30]

Modern historians such as Reinhart Koselleck and Hans-Ulrich Wehler have pointed out the various consequences resulting from this generational experience during the decades around 1800. First of all, this change in temporal structure gave rise to the modern notion of history.[31] Johann Gottfried Herder made this clear already at the end of the eighteenth century: "The word history as we understand it does not derive from compiling and epically organizing and weaving pragmatically, but from the multifaceted and powerful term 'to happen'; I do not want anyone to be unaware of this fact."[32] "History" here clearly denotes a sequence of linear events and actions, with the idea of a movement from something to something as fundamental. The category of progress thus appears inherently accounted for. Second, after the transformations effected by the revolution, this new and radicalized experience of time helped to advance the notion of a qualitative rupture between the old and the new era.

"In the real as well as the figurative sense," wrote Johanna Schopenhauer in her 1839 memoirs, "how different, how so very different everything has become in these recent years that encompass the greater part of my existence! In express carriages and steamships, life and travel move forward at triple and quadruple speed; even the hours gallop more rapidly. What will become of arms and legs, but especially of the head, once railroads cover the earth like a net, or Mr. Green carries out his plan to reach America in his balloon in three days' time, or circles the world in only one week? This is indeed a bewildering question, and only time will tell." The author explicitly compares this new experience to the "old and honest times whose customs and lifestyles seem so distant now, as if separated from us by centuries even though scarcely fifty years have elapsed since their passing."[33] She registers the momentous experience of accelerated historical time as well as the distance contemporaries perceived between the old and the new era. At the same time, the historical progression into the nineteenth century clearly was seen as tied to a process of "denaturalization" (Koselleck) of temporal experience. The technological revolution (represented by steamship, railroad, and hot-air balloon) further added to the acceleration in life's processes, thus leading into the industrial and technological era, into modernity. But that is already beyond the scope of my topic.

At this point I would like to depart from my topic for a moment and interpolate a few thoughts on methodology and subject matter. First of all, the picture I have painted of the events of the 1789 revolution, its suddenness and the accompanying drastic changes, aspires to be neither a scientifically accurate representation nor an objective assessment of the actual events and their early history. Current historiography emphasizes the interdependence of the outbreak of the revolution and the historical events leading up to it rather than the notion of a radical break with the preceding past. Moreover, the development of a new notion of time is considered the result of a much longer historical development. But a scientifically accurate historical assessment of events is not the object of my investigation. What I wish to discuss instead are the contemporary modes of experiencing the Revolution, i.e., the subjective views handed down to us by those living under its immediate influence. Consequently, my investigation is concerned exclusively with the reception of the Revolution, particularly with the reception of the Revolution in Germany.[34] Furthermore, the radical temporalization of historical perception as it is presented here cannot be explained by the Revolution alone. Experience of the Revolution was not the only factor creating this new way of thinking, even though it had the most impact. Last, the principle of temporalization is not restricted to history alone, but is germane to other fields as well, including the sciences and the arts, and—if one considers delays, overlaps, and retrogressions as they happen well into the nineteenth century—affects the entire interconnected character of the life of each individual.

We owe much of this more comprehensive, complex, and chronologically expanded view of trends toward temporalization in the eighteenth and nineteenth century to the work of Wolf Lepenies. Lepenies shows why an accurate "chronology of transformed temporal experience is difficult to establish."[35] Particularly in the natural sciences, the "primacy of experience" and the enormous quantitative growth of knowledge—the exponentially growing accumulation of knowledge as well as the "empirical imperative" (i.e., a new understanding of science that promoted evidentiary proof and pushed toward the accumulation of a plethora of data as well as the study of the complexity of data relations that no longer could be mastered with methods of spatial categorical classification)—motivated the trend toward temporalization. Organizational structures and institutions also played an important part in this. From the academic disciplines—botany, chemistry, medicine, but also jurisprudence and philosophy, philology (with the transition from systematic grammar to historical philology), to name only some—we obtain a wide range of evidence of trends toward temporalization. A pivotal aspect of this trend is a transformation in the concept of Nature, the turn away from timeless systematic notions toward a thinking about Nature in temporal terms. Parallel with the establishment of the concept of history comes the discovery of a directed development in Nature: a "history" of Nature.[36] A particularly interesting piece of formal evidence is Chateaubriand's disavowal, in the 1826 revision of his "Essai historique, politique et moral sur les révolutions" of 1797, of "the cyclical notion of history." In descriptions of developmental stages, the image of the spiral generally begins to replace the cyclical metaphor. Lepenies, following Jauss, correctly observes, the spiral is a "metaphor of compromise," symbolizing the Janus-headed ambivalence of the nineteenth century. On the one hand it radicalizes temporalization and historization, but simultaneously creates a "re-naturalization" to counteract temporalization.[37]

We can cite two opposites from the world of art to highlight this. When the railroad line Paris–Rouen–Orléans was opened in 1843, Heinrich Heine wrote: "What changes will influence our way of seeing and our concepts! Even the basic notions of space and time have been cast into doubt. The railroad has murdered space, all that is left us is time alone."[38] In contrast, Richard Wagner's late work *Parsifal* includes the line: "Here time becomes space."[39]

Important to my discussion of aesthetic issues within the context of a change in temporal consciousness are (1) radical temporalization itself and its intensification through acceleration; (2) the direction of the temporal axis toward progress, i.e., the moment of finality within this mode of thought; and (3) the belief in the beginning of a new, superior age as the result of both. This concept, as well as the metaphors of finality with their open references to the French Revolution, will serve the analysis of a musical work of the early nineteenth century—Beethoven's Third Symphony—in its historical context. I will look both for the unique and the historically exemplary aspect of the symphony, as well as its links to the energies unleashed by the French Revolution. I chose not to look for personal allegories—the "hero" or his concrete manifestation as "Prometheus" or "Napoleon"[40]—but rather to see the historical content as sediments within the work's form and structure.

* * * *

In 1807 the secretary of the Gewandhaus, Friedrich Rochlitz, had short explanations printed on the program leaflets to prepare his Leipzig audience for the extraordinary in Beethoven's new symphony, using the following words: "Fiery, magnificent Allegro/sublime, solemn Funeral March/impetuous Scherzando/grand Finale, partially in strict style." The epithets "fiery," "magnificent," "sublime," "solemn," "grand" are identical with the adjectives used in treatises and encyclopedia articles on aesthetics that seek to define the sublime. The two principal genres defined in art as thoroughly "sublime" are, in literature, the ode, which dates back to antiquity, and in music, the more recent genre of the instrumental symphony as it was developed around 1800.

"The symphony is excellently suited for the expression of grandeur, passion, and the sublime. Its ultimate purpose in a chamber concert is to offer all the splendor of instrumental music . . . The chamber symphony . . . achieves this aim with a sonorous, polished, and brilliant style" writes Johann Georg Sulzer in his 1794 encyclopedic theory of the arts,[41] that compendium which disseminated the contemporary *communis opinio* in all things aesthetic. The first movement of the symphony is equated explicitly with the sublime effects of the ode:

> The allegros of all the best chamber symphonies contain profound and clever ideas, a somewhat free treatment of the parts [*freye Behandlung des Satzes*], an apparent disorder in the melody and harmony, strongly marked rhythms of different types, robust melodies and unison passages, concerting middle voices, free imi-

tations of a theme (often in fugal style), sudden modulations and digressions from one key to another that are all the more striking the more distant their relation, distinct gradations of loud and soft, and especially the crescendo, which when used in conjunction with an ascending and swelling expressive melody, is of the greatest effect. . . . Such an allegro is to the symphony what a Pindaric ode is to poetry: it elevates the soul of the listener, and to be successful, demands the same spirit, the same sublime imagination, and the same knowledge of art.

Certainly, Rochlitz's use of the terminology of the sublime from the encyclopedia in the concert program of the *Eroica* has strategic reasons: the *Eroica*, which was criticized by the press, particularly the Viennese press, as a problematic work, ought to be presented to the Leipzig audience—and established—as the paradigm of the symphonic genre. Obviously, the naturalistic revolutionary metaphors described earlier cannot as easily be applied to music as, for example, to painting, particularly the flourishing contemporary genre of landscape painting.[42] But in form as well as in intensity (the grand, extraordinary, overwhelming effects; the uplifting and stirring emotions evoked; the suddenness of events etc.), the rhetoric used to describe the symphony follows the same principles as the rhetoric of the Revolution. A corresponding element is also the moment of ardor, the emotional and spiritual shock created by a new and unprecedented experience. In an 1805 article for the *Allgemeine musikalische Zeitung*, the most important nonregional German music journal of the time, Rochlitz described the affective power of symphonic music from the perspective of the performer[43]:

You burn like fire, . . . you are frightened and uneasy! You play and you play well, and still—you hardly know what and how you are playing! You have to contain yourself with all your might so as not to tear into the instrument, or to rush the tempo and carry the others with you. Everything has to come out right, be it ever so terribly difficult! And you succeed—yet, without fail you feel as if you should have rushed forward ever more magnificently, more forcefully.

Around 1800 musically interested contemporaries considered the pure instrumental symphony the pinnacle of music. A *Musical Diary for the Year 1803* contains the following sentences[44]:

Purely instrumental music is the only musical genre that satisfies itself. In it alone does the art of music appear in absolute purity. Unconcerned with poetry or sculpture, this music follows its own path; it speaks solely for itself, independently and free; alone and autonomously does it reach and fulfill the highest goal. *Symphonies* are the triumph of this art. Unconstrained and free, the artist can conjure the entire world of emotions . . .

Three years later, an anonymous author in the Leipzig *Allgemeine musikalische Zeitung* praised the symphony as the quintessence of modern music, and as the model for all other genres (vocal music included). In such texts, the ascent of the symphonic principle is described in metaphors evoking a phenomenon in Nature (also interesting is how the nationalist element comes into play)[45]:

It is generally known and quite evident, thus nobody will disclaim it: the world owes to the Germans the grand, fullvoiced orchestral symphony—first to Haydn and Mozart. It is the embodiment of the supreme and most brilliant pinnacle of modern instrumental music. It rightfully rules not only its own genre, but also exercises its influence on all other genres of instrumental music, though with less justification there. Like those blessed with protean talents to reach the utmost pinnacle, the symphony reaches beyond its boundaries and gradually takes possession of all around it by right of the stronger.

As a consequence of the dominant position of the new symphonic genre, the author formulates what can be considered the claim of the symphony as instrument of culturation:

No composer who desires to keep up with the times [progress!], who does not want to become rigid, clumsy, or irritating writing pieces nobody but he himself wants to hear (at least for now); no student of music who strives after the highest, desires to educate himself with the finest models, seeks entry into the world of music and to create an audience for himself; no true if only halfway serious music lover—will be able to make do without studying or at least slightly knowing these ultimate masterworks [the symphonies].

Owing to the complexity of the new symphony, the author concludes with a demand for the printing of scores "for a twofold reason: for adequate study and comprehensive guidance" (and because of the "poverty of most musicians," the scores have to be cheap!). In a final enthusiastic salvo, he declares the almost complete dependency of present musical institutions on the new symphony:

> The symphony has assumed a more and more decisive role in all public institutions of music—especially in concerts—in direct response to its overtaking of all other musical genres. The more it was perfected to the highest degree by the greatest geniuses among composers, the more it was able to please a mixed audience. Yes, the way an orchestra now performs one of the new great symphonies is considered—generally not without reason—the measure of its ability to perform modern music at all; just as the manner of the audience's attention to and behavior toward this musical genre is taken—also largely for good reason—as an indication of the audience's ability to understand, listen to, and enjoy important new music. . . . Every manager of an orchestra who desires to achieve the best for his art, or only the best for his institution (even those who have only their reputation and their pocketbook at heart), *must* consider it of highest importance to own the best of all existing symphonies and to perform them well.

After 1800 the historical, artistic, and social status of the symphony was defined on the one hand by new artistic claims and the enlightened ideas of bourgeois society, and a new public realm and economic structure on the other. The canonization of the symphony as *the* dominant musical genre went hand-in-hand with the canonization of the sublime, the new, and progressive as principal aesthetic categories. Beethoven's canonization took place in the context of this new orientation in artistic production and reception. Revered initially as a member of the Viennese classical triad, he eventually was considered its most influential composer. Whereas early Beethoven reception had criticized the "breaking of the ode" ("Odenriß") in his work as "bizarre," as a disruption of the harmony of the classical ideal of beauty, this category from the arsenal of the sublime now became a positive and enthusiastically embraced factor in the representation of progress in musical works of art.[46] The extreme readiness of post-Revolution generations to experience the new, the extraordinary, and the progressive made this shift possible.

I do not regard Beethoven's music as music of the Revolution, just as I avoid the metaphor of a Beethovenian revolution in music. But his works, particularly those composed after 1800, mirror a shift in consciousness. They mirror the emphatic embrace of the new, of a new time, of a new century, one generally described by historians as a consequence of the French Revolution. The advocacy of a new man, a new social order, and a new mode of government—I have cited evidence for all above—led to the sensitizing of the contemporaries in other fields as well, particularly in the arts. A sensibility magnified by the experience of the Revolution entered into the rhetoric used in emphatic discussions of "the new" in texts and treatises on the arts. Even Beethoven's declaration of a "new way," of a "wholly new manner" of composition, now "sounds" different from Haydn's use of the same formula only a few decades earlier. Of course, the word is used in a letter to a publisher and refers *also* to the nascent market for music in bourgeois society, but that is part of the universal social changes and in no way minimizes its aesthetic-political thrust. Again, the enthusiasm for the new in symphonic music, for the possibility to experience something new and unheard of, as well as the subjective intensity of such experiences, are marked by a general readiness for change, by the enthusiasm for the principle of progress for which the Revolution had prepared the way. It even may be possible to argue that at the point when the failure of the Revolution had become indisputable, art began to assume the role of a surrogate. Since reality did not bring fulfillment, the sensitized individual threw him/herself into art, simulating in art what was denied by reality. And in the temporal art of music, the experience of time, of a new—in this context—revolutionary structural use of time, assumed a central role.

The historically decisive work in this regard is Beethoven's Third Symphony. Contemporaries already attested a qualitative leap beyond historical precedents in the *Eroica*. On February 13, 1805, Haydn biographer Georg August Griesinger wrote to the Leipzig publisher Härtel[47]:

> This much I can assure you: the symphony was received to great acclaim at two academies, one at Prince Lobkowitz's and the other at the house of an active music lover named Wirth. I hear it praised as a work of genius by admirers and opponents alike. The former say: it transcends anything Haydn and Mozart have created; symphonic composition has been elevated to a higher level! But the latter miss a balanced unity, and criticize the amassing of colossal ideas. In such cases everybody is right.

Indeed, the historical leap that the *Eroica* realized through sound has to do with its usage of temporal structure. It is the temporalization of musical form.[48] It seems somewhat paradoxical to use the concept of temporalization in the context of music, an art form that extends over time as time. The term does not refer to accelerando, increase in tempo (though this can be a means of temporalization, albeit a rather superficial external one), but rather to the simulation of acceleration by the compositional fleshing out of the process. A differentiation between the two polarities "form as architecture" and "form as process" will clarify the case. Form as architecture is constructed symmetry, reference to a center, the figure of the circle, being-in-itself. Form as process is directedness, dynamic forward motion, the metaphor of the arrow, and an emphasis of the finality and goal orientedness of the musical form.

Compositions of the form-as-process variety address both path and goal. As for the path, the usual descriptive models refer to composing thematically and quasi-logical extension, i.e. "developing variation."[49] More important still seems the concept of form as a chain of events which invariably refers beyond itself, a chain of events that does not conclude but progresses, continually pressing forward, in which the processes create a dynamic experience of time. The goal of a form oriented in this way lies at the end of the work, or even beyond the work itself. Finality is its organizing principle; all symphonies organized as processes are "finale symphonies."[50] In the radically constructed process form, repetition becomes problematic. In sonata form the repetition of the exposition and the beginning of the recapitulation counteract the processual character. The *Eroica* offers specific solutions for such problematic aspects: identical thematic configurations at the beginning of exposition, recapitulation, and coda are developed differently, drawing different conclusions from analogous situations that are organized in relationship to one another in terms of intensification. Added to this in specific moments on the local plane is a simulated acceleration, achieved through the unfolding of the orchestral apparatus.[51] This creates the experience of "torrential time," of a "torrential and overflowing stream of ideas" (to cite again the metaphors Johann Heinrich Campe used to illustrate the experience of the Revolution), and the immense agitation of movement (transporting player and listener alike in the manner described by Rochlitz). In musical experience "history" is thus realized as "action" (Herder). The engaged listener understands "the nearly universal yearning for a new existence" (Dautzenberg on the effects of the revolution, 1792) as the "defining moment" of his era. What Friedrich Schlegel formulated in 1828 as a diagnosis of the early nineteenth century here can be heard symbolically transformed into musical language: "Never before was there a time so deeply, so directly, and so exclusively and universally directed toward the future as ours."[52]

Concrete musical analysis becomes indispensable at this point.[53] I will primarily focus on four striking formal moments in the first movement: the opening (mm. 1–45); the end of the development and the start of the recapitulation (mm. 382ff.); the end of the recapitulation and the beginning of the coda (mm. 551ff.); and finally the end of the movement itself (mm. 631ff.). Transitional sections, so for example the additional appearances of the chromatic degree C♯/D♭ during the development (compare mm. 178ff. with C-C♯-D; mm. 346ff. with C-D♭-D-E♭), are not considered in the somewhat condensed presentation below.[54]

1. Two chords are played by the full orchestra at the beginning: harsh, almost undomesticated, thoroughly violent in sound. They define tonality, meter, tempo, orchestra, musical space, the intense "tone" of the whole. The thematic entry follows, from below, building the orchestral texture from the cellos up and creating musical space. The thematic idea, a simple broken triad over a spirited pulsating eight-note figure, appears in three configurations without ever achieving classical unity, i.e. without being fully realized in the sense of periods. In its first appearance, the idea is unexpectedly interrupted by the foreign chromatic note C♯ (m. 7), a note which suggests an objection, effecting syncopated crescendos (first violins) and sforzati, orchestral restlessness, indications of a breakup of the movement, which then returns to the native key of E-flat major. Only the strings are involved in the central event. Then the woodwinds join in. (As always in classical movements, the horns are considered part of the woodwind section, functioning as a link to the strings.) At the second entry, now with thematically employed woodwinds, analogous chromatic steps (D♭ and E in m. 18, later A and C♭ in m. 22) lead to harmonic shifts (m. 19, F minor), and in conjunction with the strings, to the splitting off of motifs. Once again, no complete theme is developed. The F-minor key (the relative to A-flat major) pulls the movement "down" into the subdominant region, opening the harmonic ambitus and producing more pronouncedly than before a pressure toward new regions. Orchestral space and dynamics expand, the sforzati intensify to hemiolic accumulations within the entire movement, which "gains in mass as it proceeds" (to use Forster's rhetoric); then the third thematic entry breaks forth, again with a crescendo, in the full orchestra, fortissimo, with timpani and trumpets (m. 37). Again, no complete theme appears. The modulating transition of sonata convention follows immediately. But from the start the entire main part of the exposition was itself a "transition"— exemplary proof of a radical strategy of development, driven by a "new irrevocable propulsive force" (again citing Forster).

2. An adequate compositional means to emphasize focal points of interest within their context is to precede them with unusual or extraordinary elements. The first movement of the *Eroica* does so to an

extreme degree at the entry of the recapitulation. This important formal caesura is given additional meaning through the so-called cumulus, the superimposition of tonic (horn) and dominant (strings) in mm. 390ff. Following Rochlitz's review, this extraordinary and rule-breaking moment was considered a misprint and was—as existing orchestra materials prove—smoothed over in the early nineteenth century. And it is the horn that is emphasized here. The recapitulation with the thematic configuration of the beginning follows. The foreign chromatic tone interferes again, but it is reinterpreted here: as Db it leads over to C, opening up the harmonic space, C major, then F major, and not F minor as in the beginning. That is, the subdominant shift is replaced by a rise to a double dominant, just as if (to use revolution rhetoric again, this time by Ernst Moritz Arndt) after passing through "purgatory," the "heavenly gates of a new condition" were opening up. And the thematic idea is now (m. 408) played by the horn (*sic*), marking a half-step upward from the sustained and repeated C to Db (*sic!*). The basic form of the mirroring (Goethe's "wiederholte Spiegelung"!) is identical, its partial reformulation opens up new ways—an equally simple and subtle procedure, the hurdle of the repeated caesura is used to drive the formal process emphatically forward. The recurring color of the horn, its prolonged standing on the fifth and the pronounced Db form a strategic bill of exchange drawing on the future. The D-flat major step is played out in the lyrically intermittent combination of flute and violin color, before the main theme appears once again in E-flat (in m. 430) and in fact displays a "state of nobility, full power, activity" (Campe), while powerfully augmenting the orchestral tutti of m. 37 and anticipating the coda (m. 655).

3. The coda (mm. 551ff.) once again takes up the thematic configuration, but now almost didactically and directly, and separating the individual elements. This configuration is reduced to its harmonic essence. Unconnected but thematically penetrated E-flat major, D-flat major and C major sound fields are juxtaposed, each four measures long and with a decrescendo after a loud entry; the C major with the tremolo of the strings appears plebeian, crude even, and can be experienced almost physically. The important final phase of the formal process develops out of it. And now, in the coda, the function of the horns reaches its fulfillment. At first the horn calls appear seemingly from behind the stage (mm. 615ff.), but ultimately (from m. 631 on) the horn takes over, as a solo instrument, the thematic figure in its final form. The disruptive function of the chromatic half tone C♯/Db is spent with the confrontation of the three harmonic levels E-flat-D-flat-C and the key of C major, accentuated by the orchestra. In the solo horn call, the melodic

fragment now not only stops on the fifth (compare the introduction of this element after the recapitulation, also in the horn!) but the chromatic disruption fails to appear. However, this cleansing does not result in a rounded structural theme.[55] Scott Burnham has shown correctly that this "last version" of the so-called main theme remains "harmonically open-ended" and that its direction is derived exclusively from the enormous increase in orchestral dynamics.[56] The conclusion drawn from this position is that the first movement of the *Eroica* lacks a "theme" in the classical sense; there is no theme that first appears in incomplete form and then, in the coda, comes into its own.[57] Rather, as Carl Dahlhaus has correctly stated, the thematic figure remains at the end of the movement what it was from the beginning: a function of the formal process, a sign of the passage of time, a vehicle of temporality. Toward the point of culmination of those processes, thematic four-bar phrases oscillating between tonic and dominant, resting on the fifth and the octave, respectively, as highest notes, are strung together, "propelling each other," while the orchestral apparatus becomes "productive" through a steadily increasing expansion (Gülke's description of Beethoven's Fifth). Thus the tendency to intensification increasingly takes over the entire orchestral collective and creates the apex of the movement, which far exceeds the third orchestral moment of intensity at the beginning of the exposition and the analogous section in the recapitulation (mm. 430ff.) This is followed now by the formulaic ending of the movement.[58] The movement virtually could go on forever. Its telos is the future.

4. But beyond that, this passage—introduced by the solo horn and providing the goal and fulfillment of the formal process—speaks a clear language. It is the musical image of a certain and concretely identifiable situation. There, in m. 631, the first horn enters, in a challenging fashion, with oboe and second horn joining in. Added is a rhythmically contoured counter-subject in the first violins that traverses back and forth across the tonal space—a swift counterpoint while the second violins accompany with typical chordal figurations. This constellation lasts for four measures—two times two—supplying first the tonic, then the dominant. This eight-measure model is repeated with an increasing orchestral apparatus (mm. 639ff): the thematic figure in the first violins and the three horns, a rapid counterpoint in the second violins, dissolved chordal accompaniment in the cellos (distinct from the bass line) and the second clarinet, harmonically filled out by the oboes, the first clarinet, then the flutes. The process is continued in a third eight-measure section (mm. 647ff.) using an expanded apparatus. The thematic figure now is played by all lower strings, from violas to bass, the counter subject

by the entire woodwind section, supplemented by the horns and the syncopated first violins, the trumpets and timpani supply the rhythmic impulse with upbeat triads. All this is played in continuous crescendo. Finally, with m. 655, the intensification process leads into the fourth eight-measure section: full orchestra with expressive violin tremolos, the thematic figure shatteringly played above the timpani roll in the trumpets and horns, partially including the woodwinds, the running counterpoint in the heavy basses, everything now forte, with sforzato accents. It is noteworthy that the figurative aspect in the measures on the dominant (mm. 659ff.) recedes behind the sound of the full orchestral tutti. It is the orchestra as such, the collectivity and its unfolding, that functions as the agent and goal over 800 measures of this gigantic movement. In those four times eight measures and their concrete content, the "radical developmental form" reaches its first fulfillment.

What functions here as the sound language of a symphonic orchestra can be described as revolutionary rhetoric, as a process of a collective coming together. After a long journey through many transitional stations, one important individual voice (the horn, m. 631) steps to the fore, as if challenging and pronouncing a thesis. Gradually, more and more voices and groups join in, agreeing, amalgamating, becoming part of a universal overarching whole. The idea of a grand, emphatic departure, of a "spiritual enthusiasm" (Hegel), seizes the orchestral collective. It is as if the music were speaking with a thousand tongues and, by doing so, becomes one single voice. The orchestra as allegory of the Revolution is what this symphony aims for at the end of the first movement; "the lava of revolution flows" here too, but as an idea, as a musical idea.[59] From our perspective, looking back into history, it is no "delusion" to claim for the symphony, and especially for this one, that an "electrical and luminous flood of concepts and insights will pour forth from here to all nations of this earth, from here where the exalted human spirit rises free and brave like an eagle from the low and dark spheres toward the sunlit ocean of truth" (Campe). And so I add to Friedrich Schlegel's *Athenäum Fragment* and declare Beethoven's Third Symphony one of the "great tendencies of the era." The symphony is this great tendency in its time and through its time: *in* the time that entered into it as its era and whose historical example it represents as *Sinfonia Eroica*; and *through* the time which forms this work of art in a processual manner as (to use again Campe's words) a "torrential and overflowing stream of ideas."

NOTES

1. Ernst Moritz Arndt, "Über künftige ständische Verfassungen in Deutschland [1814]," in *Ernst Moritz Arndts Schriften für und an seine lieben Deutschen*, vol. 2 (Leipzig, 1845), pp. 83–84.

2. Letter from Friedrich Gentz to Chr. Garve, 5 December 1790; quoted in Hans-Ulrich Wehler, *Deutsche Gesellschaftsgeschichte*, vol. 1 (Munich: 1987), p. 350.

3. Quoted in Claus Träger, *Die französische Revolution im Spiegel der deutschen Literatur* (Leipzig, 1975). See also Karl Friedrich Reinhard in his essay "Übersicht einiger vorbereitender Ursachen der französischen Staats-Veränderung," published in 1791 in Schiller's *Thalia*: "France's current reinvention, watched by all of Europe with incredulity and bewilderment, is in more ways than one the work of the Enlightenment and the triumph of philosophy. Its most effective propelling forces were publicity and public opinion." (Quoted in *Die französische Revolution. Berichte und Deutungen deutscher Schriftsteller und Historiker*, Horst Günther, ed. (Frankfurt, 1985), p. 220.

4. Immanuel Kant, *The Contest of the Faculties*, from *Kant's Political Writings*, ed. with an introduction and notes by Hans Reiss, trans. H. B. Nisbet (Cambridge, 1971), p. 182.

5. See also Johannes Weitzel, "Die Revolution," in Weitzel, *Über die Bestimmung des Menschen und des Bürgers* (Mainz, 1798): "The stuff of revolution was brewing amidst the nations. The bourgeois, incensed by the wantonness of despotic governments, opposed the claims of hereditary rule with those far more ancient rights integral to human nature. . . . Philosophy has revealed the legal origin of the state and has returned to man his eternal rights." Quoted in Zwi Batsche and Jörn Garber, eds., *Von der ständischen zur bürgerlichen Gesellschaft* (Frankfurt, 1981), p. 382.

6. Georg Friedrich Wilhelm Hegel, *Philosophy of History*, with prefaces by Charles Hegel and the translator, J. Sibree, and a new introduction by C. J. Friedrich (New York, 1956), p. 443.

7. Ibid., *Lectures on the History of Philosophy*, vol. 3, Medieval and Modern Philosophy, trans. E. S. Hildane and Frances H. Simson (Lincoln and London, 1995). Reprint of 1896 translation, pp. 48, 409.

8. Friedrich Schlegel, "Athenäums-Fragment (1798)," in *Philosophical fragments*, trans. Peter Firchow, foreword by Rodolphe Gesché (Minneapolis, 1991), p. 46. In *Gespräch über die Poesie* from 1800, Schlegel considers the above-mentioned expanded concept of the revolution exemplary (ibid., p. 202).

9. Quoted in Wehler, *Deutsche Gesellschaftsgeschichte*, p. 350.

10. See Heinrich Steffen's assessment in *Was ich erlebte. Aus der Erinnerung niedergeschrieben*, vol. 1 (Breslau, 1840), p. 364. Steffen, who later turned a conservative, wrote: "It was a wonderful time. It was not only French, it was a European Revolution! It appeared and took root in millions of souls; clear-headed great men recognized its general force and even revered it. Judgment was held over corrupt times and victory achieved over wicked and hollow conditions. The Revolution lived in all truly free European souls, even where it did not break to the fore. The first moment of enthusiasm, though it may be doomed to evolve into a terrible future, has something pure and almost sacred about it that never shall be forgotten." See also the memoirs of Johanna Schopenhauer who speaks of the "glowing enthusiasm" that news of the revolutionary events inspired in her and her friends: "La Fayette! Mirabeau! Péthion! Bailly! and so many more whose names are forgotten now but who were on everybody's lips! How I burned with joyous excitement when during peaceful evening hours I read their speeches, which were so faithfully reported to us by the *Moniteur*, to my husband and two or three of his most trusted friends! How exhilarated we were in our certain anticipation of a golden era which, though it was

approaching thunderously at the time, most certainly would bring liberty, peace, and civic happiness in the end." Johanna Schopenhauer, *Jugendleben und Wanderbilder* [1837], (Danzig, 1884), pp. 177, 180.

11. Quoted in Alfred Stern, *Der Einfluß der französischen Revolution auf das deutsche Geistesleben* (Stuttgart and Berlin, 1928), p. 22. The analogies contemporary experience drew between an elementary, grand nature and revolutionary politics is emphasized by Ernst Ludwig Posselt: "If suddenly in a renewal of the first scene of creation, the Alps would collapse from the Montblanc to Istria, if all of England would be swallowed by oceans, if the sources of the Rhine and the Danube would be covered up, and if through a outbreak of a land mass Africa would be joined with Spain: such a revolution in the physical world could not be greater, nor would the familiar shape of Europe suffer more from change than the Revolution, which we have been witnessing since 1789, brought to the political world." (*Die Weltkunde*, 1 January 1798; quoted in ibid., p. 156).

12. On the importance of "nature" for the French Revolution, see Hans-Christian Harten and Elke Harten, *Die Versöhnung mit der Natur. Gärten, Freiheitsräume, republikanische Wälder, heilige Berge und Tugendparks in der französischen Revolution* (Reinbek, 1989), though I have some reservations because of the somewhat one-dimensional and reconciling representation which at times neglects to consider the historical moment.

13. See Werner Hofmann, ed., *Europe 1789. Aufklärung, Verklärung, Verfall.* Exhibition catalogue, Hamburger Kunsthalle (Cologne, 1989), pp. 185ff.

14. Georg Forster, *Parisische Umrisse* (1793–1794), in *Werke in vier Bänden*, ed., Gerhard Gerhard Steiner, (Leipzig, n.d.), vol. 3, p. 732.

15. See Hofmann, *Europe 1789*, p. 14.

16. See Franz Josias von Hendrich, "Vergleichung der Reformation mit der französischen Revolution," in Hendrich, *Über den Geist des Zeitalters und die Gewalt der öffentlichen Meinung* (n.p., 1797): "In the beginning the Reformation was considered a fire that had broken out unexpectedly and spread with unimaginable speed. . . . The same holds true for the French Revolution. It also broke out fast and suddenly and immediately threw bright flames. . . . " (quoted after Batsch/Garber, *Von der ständischen*, pp. 373ff.). The experience of accelerated time plays a role here as well.

17. Quoted in Wehler, *Deutsche Gesellschaftsgeschichte*, p. 350.

18. Quoted in Joseph Hansen, *Quellen zur Geschichte des Rheinlandes im Zeitalter der französischen Revolution 1780–1801*, vol. 1 (Bonn, 1931), pp. 523–25.

19. See Weitzel, "Die Revolution," *Über die Bestimmung*.

20. Franz Dautzenberg, "Über den Geist unserer Zeit," *Aachener Zuschauer* 1792, no. 1, 2ff; quoted in Joseph Hansen, ibid, vol. 2 (1933), p. 34.

21. Reinhart Koselleck, "Anmerkungen zum Revolutionskalender und zur 'Neuen Zeit,'" in *Die französische Revolution als Bruch des gesellschaftlichen Bewußtseins*, ed. Reinhart Koselleck and Rolf Reichart (Munich, 1988), p. 63.

22. Ernst Moritz Arndt, *Geist der Zeit*, vol. 1 (1804–1805), in idem, *Sämtliche Werke*, ed. Karl F. Pfau, vol. 8 (Leipzig, 1905), pp. 53–54. See also on p. 218 the more general statements: "The first years of the revolution are still fresh and lively in my mind, just as if it were happening today. In those days the spirit of excitement and activity was boundless, and boundless were enthusiasm and participation, both internally and externally. How many who were part of this storm and tidal waves were conscious of what they were doing or suffering?" Or: "Our time considers ordinary what is most inconceivable or improbable, what is seemingly impossible or incredible in the order of things. What previously appeared terrible, brave, or great does not live up to the things we have been witnessing in these last twenty years. And where the past world knew of deeds in any way comparable to the present ones, those nevertheless pale because of the length of time that was

necessary to bring them to fruition." (Arndt, *Briefe über die neuesten Zeitereignisse, ihre Ursachen und Folgen*, [Germanien *(sic)* 1814], p. iii.)

23. Reinhart Koselleck, "Fortschritt und Beschleunigung. Zur Utopie der Aufklärung," in *Der Traum der Vernunft. Vom Elend der Aufklärung*. A program series of the Akademie der Künste Berlin (Darmstadt and Neuwied, 1985), p. 87. Koselleck, who has described and interpreted the phenomenon in several important publications, writes elsewhere: "A constant inspiration for progressive comparison was the recognition that individual peoples and nations, individual continents, sciences, orders or classes were ahead of others, so that finally by the eighteenth century the thesis of acceleration was formulated. The fundamental experience of progress as it was defined around 1800 focussed on a singular notion, and was rooted in the recognition of the non-contemporary that happened at chronologically the same time." ("'Neuzeit.' Zur Semantik moderner Bewegungsbegriffe," in *Studien zum Beginn der modernen Welt*, ed. R. Koselleck [Stuttgart, 1977], p. 281.)

24. Konrad Engelbert Oelsner, *Luzifer oder Gereinigte Beiträge zur Geschichte der französischen Revolution. Auswahl*, ed. Werner Greiling (Leipzig, 1987), p. 35. See also Pierre Bertaux, *Hölderlin und die französische Revolution* (Frankfurt, 1969), pp. 20ff.

25. Forster, *Parisische*.

26. Quoted in Günther, *Die französische Revolution*, p. 190.

27. Quoted in Träger, *Die französische Revolution*, p. 405.

28. See also F. Schlegel's 1828 remark: "Never before was there a time so deeply, so directly, and so exclusively and universally dependent on the future as ours is now." (*Philosophie der Geschichte*, in: *Kritische Friedrich Schlegel Ausgabe*, vol. 9 [Munich, 1971], p. 417.)

29. Quoted in Wehler, *Deutsche Gesellschaftsgeschichte*, p. 546. In the same context Wehler also refers to a note by the historian Berthold Georg Niebuhr from the 1820s, saying that already during the eighteenth century people had begun "to live faster and more intensely than before; at the time of the Revolution this was just beginning and developed mainly afterwards."

30. Quoted in ibid., p. 546.

31. "From the second half of the eighteenth century on we have an increase in the already numerous indications that refer emphatically to the notion of a new time. Time no longer is only the structure in which all history takes place, time itself becomes historical. History not only is realized in time but through time. Time becomes a dynamic force of history. But this new formula of experience presupposes a new idea of history, namely the collective-singular of history which since 1780 can be thought of without a connected object or preordained subject—as history for history's sake alone." Koselleck, "'Neuzeit.' Zur Semantik moderner Bewegungsbegriffe," *Studien zum Beginn*, p. 279.

32. Johann Gottfried Herder, *Werke*, ed. B. Suphan, vol. 3, p. 469. Quoted in G. Scholtz, "Geschichte," ed. J. Ritter, *Historisches Wörterbuch der Philosophie*, vol. 3 (Basel, 1974), p. 359.

33. Schopenhauer, *Jugendleben*, pp. 1f, 3. Such qualitative and distancing differentiation between the "old" and the "new" era is expressed also in the programmatic title of a journal first published in 1800: "The old and new century or General Chronicle of past and present times" (see Rudolf Wendorf, *Zeit und Kultur. Geschichte des Zeitbewußtseins in Europa* [Opladen, 1983], p. 305). Franz Dautzenberg's remark belongs here as well: "The defining moment of present times is the almost universal desire for a new existence." (1792. Quoted in Hansen, vol. 2 [Bonn 1933], p. 30.)

34. Over long stretches, Georg Büchner's *Dantons Tod* is a montage of quotations from contemporary writings on the revolution.

35. Wolf Lepenies, *Das Ende der Naturgeschichte. Wandel kultureller Selbstverständlichkeiten in den Wissenschaften des 18. und 19. Jahrhunderts* (Munich, 1976), p. 10. The thoughts and quotes which follow are from pp. 16ff., 27, 82, 106ff.

36. See also the summary in Wendorf, *Zeit und Kultur*, p. 309, based on the theories of Koselleck and Lepenies.

37. I describe this ambivalence in Wagner's *Ring* in my essay "Mythos—Geschichte—Natur. Zeitkonstellationen im *Ring*," in *Richard Wagner. Von der Oper zum Musikdrama*, ed. Stefan Kunze (Bern and Munich, 1978), pp. 61–77.

38. Quoted in Wolfang Schivelbusch, *Geschichte der Eisenbahnreise. Zur Industrialisierung von Raum und Zeit im 19. Jahrhundert* (Munich, 1977), pp. 38ff.

39. Looking at the plethora of evidence and arguments from all fields that Lepenies and Wendorf have assembled (in their popular summary of scholarly research), it is striking how few discussions of temporalization there are in the field of the "temporal art form" of music. Musicology has neglected to its peril this topic so particulary interesting for its subject matter.

40. See for example Constantin Floros, *Beethovens Eroica und Prometheus-Musik, Sujet-Studien* (Wilhelmshaven, 1978); Martin Geck and Peter Schleunig, *"Geschrieben auf Bonaparte": Beethovens "Eroica"—Revolution. Reaktion. Rezeption* (Reinbek, 1989); also Claude Palisca, "French Revolutionary Models for Beethoven's 'Eroica' Funeral March," *Music and Context. Essays for John M. Ward*, ed. Anne Dhu Shapiro (Cambridge, Mass., 1985), pp. 198–209.

41. J. G. Sulzer, *Allgemeine Theorie der schönen Künste*, vol. 4, (Leipzig, 1794), col. 479a. Translation from *Aesthetics and the Art of Musical Composition in the German Enlightenment. Selected Writings of Johann Georg Sulzer and Heinrich Christoph Koch*, ed. and trans. Nancy Kovaleff Baker and Thomas Christensen (Cambridge, 1995), p. 106.

42. See Hofmann, *Europe 1789*, p. 15.

43. F. Rochlitz, "Über den zweckmäßigen Gebrauch der Mittel der Tonkunst," *Allgemeine musikalische Zeitung* 8, 1804/5, col. 351.

44. "Übersicht über den jetzigen Stand der Musik," in *Musikalisches Taschenbuch auf das Jahr 1803*, ed. Julius Werden and Adolph Werden, (Penig, n.d.), pp. 71ff. Translated by Mark Evan Bonds.

45. "Merkwürdige Novität" *Allgemeine musikalische Zeitung* 8, 1805/6, col. 616ff.

46. The recourse to the philosophical idea of the sublime for the characterization of a symphonic work is rather unusual since the experience of natural events that can be called "sublime" cannot be compared directly and convincingly to the aesthetic experience of a musical composition. The application of theories of the sublime for art, and for music in particular, may signal a dilemma that until now has not been addressed sufficiently in aesthetic discussions of symphonic theory. This will have to be discussed in a broader contextual investigation. An exception to this deficiency is a passage in Peter Gülke's most recent book on Mozart. See Peter Gülke, *"Triumph der Tonkunst." Mozarts späte Sinfonien und ihr Umfeld* (Kassel, 1998), pp. 128ff.

47. Quoted in Otto Biba, *"Eben komme ich von Haydn . . . " Georg August Griesingers Korrespondez mit Joseph Haydns Verleger Breitkopf & Härtel. 1799 bis 1819* (Zurich, 1987), p. 236. See also the review in the *Allgemeine musikalische Zeitung* 7 of the same day (1804/5, col. 312): "A new symphony by Beethoven . . . is written in an entirely novel style."

48. In an article little noticed by recent Beethoven scholarship, Carl Dahlhaus has convincingly defined the "new" in Beethoven's "new way" in compositions after op. 30 as a "formal idea" (in contrast to an external humanitarian pathos). In the *Eroica* musical form appears "emphatically as a process, as a driving, unstoppable movement." Carl Dahlhaus, "Beethovens 'neuer Weg,'" in *Jahrbuch des Staatlichen Instituts für Musikforschung*

Preußischer Kulturbesitz 1974 (Berlin, 1975), pp. 49, 54. A specific form of temporal processes in Beethoven (later also in Mahler) is described by David B. Greene, *Temporal Processes in Beethoven's Music* (New York, 1982).

49. Carl Dahlhaus has argued convincingly for a substitution of the traditional thematic definition by a "thematic configuration" created from pre-thematic material for Beethoven's works of the "new way" (Dahlhaus, "Beethovens 'neuer weg,'" p. 51).

50. Following a remark by Robert Schumann from 1836, this concept is discussed in Reinhold Brinkmann, *Late Idyll. The Second Symphony of Johannes Brahms* (Cambridge, Mass., 1995), pp. 203ff.

51. Peter Gülke has described it for the Fifth Symphony. See his essay "Zur Bestimmung des Symphonischen bei Beethoven," *Deutsches Jahrbuch der Musikwissenschaft für 1970*, p. 71.

52. Already Arthur O. Lovejoy described the "temporalization of the great chain of being." See his *The Great Chain of Being* (Cambridge, Mass., 1936), chapter IX.

53. In an oral presentation I would give the subsequent analytical remarks substance through the repeated playing of musical examples. In a recording of the Südwestfunk Symphony Orchestra, Michael Gielen realizes the fast tempo (later) asked for by Beethoven (dotted halfs = 60) quite flexibly and avoids the usual heavy, agitated fortissimo of the late nineteenth century in favor of a graceful energetic forte, which, in contrast to "late Romantic" interpretations, brings to the fore the "classical" form of the work. Verbal description cannot replace the active aural engagement, i.e., direct artistic experience as the basis of judgment.

54. For this, see the fine presentation inspired by the metaphor of the "hero" in Scott Burnham's *Beethoven Hero* (Princeton, 1995), pp. 21ff. For the entire conceptual apparatus, see ibid., pp. 9ff.

55. The formulation by Egon Voss that the "main theme achieves its final form" in the coda is wrong if it means that. See "Beethovens 'Eroica' und die Gattung der Symphonie," *Kongreßbericht Bonn 1970* (Kassel), p. 601.

56. Burnham, *Beethoven Hero*, pp. 19, 53.

57. This is another reason why I avoid the allegorical figure of the "hero" in my interpretation of the *Eroica*.

58. For the function of this passage, see Lewis Lockwood, "'Eroica' Perspective: Strategy and Design in the First Movement," *Beethoven Studies*, vol. 3, ed. Alan Tyson (Cambridge, 1982), pp. 85ff.

59. In the *Eroica* this occurs primarily in the first and last movements. Strategies that encompass the middle movements as well are developed in the fifth and ninth symphonies.

Beethoven, Florestan, and the

Varieties of Heroism

LEWIS LOCKWOOD

> Even as you plunge here into the whirlpool of society, so it is possible for you to write operas despite all social handicaps—let your deafness no longer be a secret—even in art.

This diary entry from a sketchbook of 1806 carries us into the inner world from which *Leonore* emerged.[1] It is one of those pensive reflections that appear from time to time in Beethoven's sketchbooks, long before the period of his *Tagebuch* (1812–1818) when his deafness was far worse and becoming absolute.

This entry of 1806 speaks of risk and isolation. It tells of his continuing struggle to come to terms with his deafness, a struggle that had come to the surface as early as 1800 and which he had confided at first only to close friends and in his private confession, the Heiligenstadt Testament of 1802.[2] Now four years later he not only confirms his determination to thrive as an artist despite his solitude but reconfirms his dream of writing operas, of all genres the most difficult for him, demanding perpetual contact with the business world of music and theater—"der Strudel der Gesellschaft"—with singers, stage directors, impresarios, audiences, the box office—the busy world of money and prestige that only opera could bring a composer in the Vienna of his time. The deeper implication of revealing his deafness and releasing his inhibitions about opera also suggests his readiness to risk moving from the abstract and metaphorical domain of instrumental music to the operatic world of direct revelation of feeling in concrete human situations, the very stuff of operatic discourse.

Among the major genres that Beethoven pursued all his life—sonata, quartet, symphony—opera remains an only partially fulfilled desire, a marriage that he perpetually imagines but consummates only once. His "shadow career" as an opera composer runs from early to late. In Bonn in the 1780s he had grown up in a musical atmosphere in which Mozart had been a demigod.[3] Beethoven knew the major Mozart operas, all comparatively recent works, before he ever left Bonn for Vienna in 1792, and the proclamation of his avid supporters—that he would become a "second Mozart"—always implied that, like Mozart, he would become a universal artist for whom all genres would be worlds to conquer, even if his signs of genius were clearly most obvious in keyboard music.[4] But Beethoven never gave up on opera, and even though *Leonore/Fidelio* remained his only finished work—obsessively rewritten several times and with four different overtures—he dreamed of glory with other projects that never got off the ground. They ranged from a few sketches for an opera on *Macbeth* in 1808 to works on historically exotic or romantic subjects, including an opera on Romulus in 1815 or romantic fairy tales such as *Drahomira* and *The Fair Melusine* on a libretto by Grillparzer (1823). Over the years there were many such abortive ideas, and what the world lost, or never had, included a Beethoven opera on a truly exotic subject, "The Arrival of the Pennsylvanians in America."[5] How much he felt this attraction, and what fantasies it stimulated, is suggested by another sketchbook entry, of 1815, for a possible opera from Greek myth, *Bacchus*. On this Beethoven writes himself the following memo:

> Perhaps the dissonances should not be resolved throughout the whole opera, since for those primitive times our more refined music would not be appropriate. Yet the whole subject must be treated in a pastoral way. [6]

Florestan

Leonore is always seen primarily as a tale of female loyalty and heroism. It is that and much more. It is about personal suffering and redemption; about a political context in which freedom can be crushed by tyranny; about the social meanings of imprisonment and liberation. In moral terms, as Beethoven would have felt them, it is about good and evil. Whether or not J. N. Bouilly's original French libretto had been based on an actual incident during the Reign of Terror, as he later claimed it was, what's important for Beethoven is that in 1805 he could perfectly well believe that it was, and could throw himself into a work celebrating heroism in a political context in which the ideals of love and sacrifice are the central theme.[7] The revolutionary background enabled Beethoven to persuade himself that he was applying his powers as an artist not to a frivolous operatic story but to a work that directly reflected contemporary realities; not a mere stage fiction but a work with political and moral significance. And in fact it is a quality of *Fidelio* that it has continued to have this meaning for every successive generation including our own. Its inner strength has never failed to be evident to audiences, despite the limitations imposed by its stark design as a parable of good overcoming all obstacles to triumph over evil. Its shortcomings largely derive from the libretto's blunt portrayal of characters: Leonore's pure virtue versus Pizarro's implacable villainy. The minor characters, Rocco, Marzelline, and Jacquino present little beyond immediate plot responses: Jacquino insists on marrying Marzelline, who won't have him; Marzelline is infatuated with the more attractive Fidelio; father Rocco does his duty and follows orders but turns out to have a soft heart for a dying prisoner. Not that Beethoven's delineation of character is less adept than that of most of his operatic contemporaries, who are certainly lesser composers, as we see from the *Leonore* setting by Ferdinand Paer. But as great as Beethoven's *Leonore* music is in the crucially serious parts of the opera, it lacks the deftness of touch in the domestic scenes that a Mozart would have brought to such a theme. That Mozart's skill in such matters was playing on the edge of Beethoven's awareness is evident from a number of passages in the domestic scenes in which virtual quotations from Mozart quietly slip into the score, as indeed some commentators have observed.[8]

We turn now to the imprisoned hero, Florestan. It's been often remarked, as if in criticism, that he does not appear until the second act of this two-act work. But present or not, he is the central subject of the first act as well. This is clear for several reasons. First, because the action takes place entirely in the castle-fortress where he is imprisoned. Unlike other rescue operas, the rescuer doesn't need to travel to reach the victim; when the curtain opens the disguised Leonore is already onstage. Thus the prison itself, in all its starkness and power, is not only the mise-en-scène of the action but is the dominating condition of its meaning as a dramatic work. The stage setting presents the issue of imprisonment—not just Florestan's—as central to the work from the very opening, no matter what domestic byplay takes place in the courtyard. The action then unfolds on three levels—on open level ground, where the keepers live; on a first prisoners' level, probably in cells just belowground, since the prisoners when they emerge are blinded by the sunlight; and on a lowest level, the dungeon, deep in the bowels of the prison, where, as Rocco explains, "prisoners of state" are kept.[9] At one point Fidelio says about the prisoner, "He must have done terrible things"—to which Rocco replies, "Or else he has powerful enemies—it comes to the same thing." And thus the first act, playing in the courtyard on level ground, betrays constant preoccupation with the lower levels, especially the deepest dungeon, where, the libretto tells us, Florestan has been kept in solitary confinement for more than two years, in virtual darkness, chained to the wall, freezing and starving. Rocco explains that, on Pizarro's orders, for the past month he has gradually been reducing Florestan's already meager rations, that the prisoner has barely any light and no more straw to lie on. Clearly Pizarro is trying to starve him to death as painfully as possible. Accordingly, since everything in Act I implies that Florestan may die at any moment, the urgency of Leonore's reaching him becomes unbearable; and this point is then intensified by the domestic byplay between her and Marzelline-Jacquino, since Rocco wants to arrange for the marriage as quickly as possible.[10]

In Act I the physical levels of the action are dramatized through "descent"—from the sunlit world of everyday to the dark squalor of Florestan's cell. And it seems clear that the very opening of the famous Leonore Overtures nos. 2 and 3, with their stepwise descent through a ninth, beginning on an opening emphatic G, groping slowly downward for a footing and at last landing on an unexpected F♯ that now tonicizes the dominant of B minor—all this suggests exactly such a descent. In this context the differences between the two openings, of Leonore no. 2 and no. 3, take on some further importance. (See examples 1 and 2.)

In no. 2, the opening Adagio figure presents first the three-note downward figure G-F-E (with an astounding dynamic of *ff* then immediate *p* to give a different color to the downward motion) then a pause, then the same figure again with the same dynamics, opening into the full-octave descent. In Leonore no. 3, in contrast, Beethoven eliminates the double starting gesture, now holding the opening G for five beats in the winds with a decrescendo to *p*, then adding the strings and giving the long descent as one integral phrase. It is as if in no. 2 the fearful descent to the dungeon begins, then stops, recoils two steps, then continues downward; while in no. 3 the descender pauses on the threshold, then resolutely proceeds downward. In both overtures, once arriving on the F♯ as dominant of B minor (= C♭ minor), the harmony moves to A-flat major and immediately to Florestan's soliloquy of hope and memory. It could not be clearer that both overtures open with a move from the normal world to the dungeon and to the immediate, centrally important revelation of Florestan as the imprisoned hero. Beethoven's familiar tendency, especially in middle-period works, to employ register as an essential compositional dimension, here uses the scalar descent to the lower octaves as a musical analogue that has powerful formal and structural consequences for the overture and later parts of the opera. The analogy of registral levels and physical levels of stage action gives the opera some of its significance as a true middle-period work, related in various ways to the Fifth and Sixth Symphonies, the Piano Sonatas opp. 53 and 57, and the op. 59 Quartets. Especially relevant is the analogy to the downward groping, but now intensely chromatic descent that governs the Introduction to the first movement of op. 59 no. 3.

As Act II opens, we have moved from the upper to the lowest level, the dismal pit in which Florestan lies suffering. Who is this man? The text discloses that he is a nobleman, unjustly imprisoned by Pizarro two years earlier apparently because he had told the truth about Pizarro's crimes, whatever they had been. He says in his soliloquy that he had "dared to speak the truth, and chains are my reward." He is, accordingly, all of these things: a victim of political injustice; a faithful husband, who dreams of his beloved wife; a man who had always tried to do what was just and right; a man resigned to die for his beliefs if need be. He is a suffering protagonist—a hero not for what he conquers but for what he endures. In that sense he is often seen as a projection of Beethoven's sense of his own affliction in deafness and his will to overcome, forcibly uttered in his letters and statements to friends, in the Heiligenstadt Testament, and in his *Tagebuch*. As he had written to his old friend Wegeler in 1801, "Already I have cursed my Creator and my existence. Plutarch has shown me the path of resignation. If it is at all possible, I will bid defiance to my fate, though I feel that as long as I live there will be moments when I shall be God's unhappiest creature. . . ."[11] But while Beethoven could resign himself to his deafness yet muster his strength to "seize Fate by the throat," as he wrote in another letter to Wegeler, Florestan is in a different condition. Victimized not by nature but by human agency, he is helpless to end his imprisonment and has nothing to sustain him but his sense of his own worth and his love for his Leonore, who remains a faraway vision.

In 1805 the starving Florestan opens Act II with a long recitative followed by a heartfelt aria, then a quiet coda in which, while looking at a portrait of Leonore, he remembers their earlier joys together. The text for this coda is almost a farewell to Leonore; he ends it, speaking to Leonore, "Tell your heart, Florestan did what was right." And the music for this coda is a quiet F minor conclusion to the previous impassioned recitative and aria, sinking down to its conclusion as Florestan himself sinks down to the ground in his misery.

In the 1814 version Georg Friedrich Treitschke persuaded Beethoven to compose an entirely new ending in which Florestan sees a vision of

Example 1. Overture Leonore no. 2, mm. 1–19

Example 1 continued

Example 2. Overture Leonore no. 3, mm. 1–13

Example 2 continued

Leonore and, instead of sadly resigning himself to his fate, imagines her coming to rescue him and lead him to freedom, much like Egmont. Now the key word *Freiheit* recalls the Prisoners' Chorus and the basic theme of the whole work. It is now as if Florestan wills Leonore's arrival, or at least imagines it in his delirium. Treitschke takes the credit for this new idea of Florestan in his memoirs, claiming that Beethoven composed the new coda in one night. Now Florestan, who is to sing this coda "in a quiet ecstasy, bordering on madness," has an Allegro section in high and even higher register than anything earlier in the scene; he reaches to a high A and B♭ in his manic dream of *Freiheit* and the vision of Leonore before him in his cell. The inner determination of the artist and singer to win his way beyond all tortures and obstacles is written all over this section, and it brings out an intensity in Florestan to match that of Leonore in her earlier aria of hope for his salvation.

In a valuable literary study entitled *The Romantic Prison*, Victor Brombert traces the image of the prison in literature and thought in the nineteenth and twentieth centuries.[12] The prison image grew in literary prestige and importance in the later eighteenth century, especially in

France, first as the taking of the Bastille became the symbol of the Revolution, later as the fearful jails of the Terror confirmed contemporary fears that the libertarian slogans of the Revolution were to be paid for in blood. Many tales were told of torture during incarceration, and when Pizarro fears that he is in danger of being revealed as a prison governor who used "arbitrary force," contemporary audiences could not help being aware of contemporary social movements aimed at reforming the brutal treatment of prisoners. The European conscience regarding prisons had been awakened by Cesare Beccaria in Italy, whose great essay on prison reform, issued originally in 1764, was widely read and highly influential.[13] Beccaria was quoted with approval by writers and heads of state throughout the later eighteenth and down into the nineteenth century.[14] But in a larger sense, for many writers of this and later times, the prison image is not simply hell on earth. As Brombert notes, the romantic sensibility focused on the prison because the basic theme of the contemporary artist was and is freedom—freedom of expression, freedom of thought, which "can be attained only through withdrawal into the self. It is the turbulence of life that the poet—a 'spiritual anarchist'—comes to view as exile or as captivity."[15] In this sense Florestan's confinement joins with that of other imprisoned heroes of romantic fiction, from the Gothic novel down through novels of social awareness and to the enlarged domain of psychological imprisonment that plays through the work of Dostoyevsky and Kafka. In the real world it also holds a place in the long tradition of political prisoners, from those of the Terror down through the decades to our own time—the recent example of Wei Jing-Sheng in modern China can stand for countless others.

"Heroic Period," "Heroic Phase," "Heroic Style"

Despite the avalanche of critical thought on Beethoven and the "heroic," the many meanings of the term have not yet been adequately explicated or contextualized—no Lovejoy has yet come along in Beethoven studies. The current uses are varied, e.g. "heroic period," "heroic phase," "heroic style." By a kind of synecdoches what used to be generally called the "Second Period" is now quite frequently referred to as the "Heroic Period," thus naming this highly differentiated sector of Beethoven's works, many of them as different from one another as he can make them, after what is taken to be the most prominent, most pointedly revolutionary, of its aesthetic dimensions. "Heroic Period" is in fact the term employed for the years from about 1803 to 1812 by Maynard Solomon in his major biography, while William Kinderman in his one-volume general portrait divides the years 1803–1809 into two phases, called "The Heroic Style I" and "II," followed by a phase of "Consolidation, 1810–1812."[16] Obviously "Heroic Period" is more lively and memorable than "Second Period," but I must admit, without going further into it here, that if there is to be a generally accepted substitute my own preference would be "Second Maturity," which carries a still wider range of biographical and developmental meanings, and also suggests that the "First Period" has its own framework, its own trajectory of promise and fulfillment. It further suggests a revision in the critical understanding of Beethoven's development by which the First Period is not displaced, improved, or superseded by the Second, just as both are not by the Third—but rather that the achievements of each earlier period provide a set of necessary and fruitful conditions for the next, provide sustenance and new perspectives on which Beethoven could then draw as he developed and transformed his art. It is as if the Second Maturity (changing to my terminology) is built upon the First, just as the stages of a man's or woman's life are successive but connected, as we have learned from modern studies of the human life cycle.

As to "heroic phase," Alan Tyson coined this term in an influential article, using it to refer to the period from Beethoven's first overt reports of the deafness crisis (1801) to 1803–1804, years that witnessed the completion of the *Eroica* in 1804 and the beginning of his concentrated work on *Leonore*.[17] As Tyson saw it, this phase also significantly included the oratorio *Christus am Oelberge*, another product of 1803, which, he says, shares not only musical resemblances with *Leonore* but dramatic similarities as well. "The figure of Christ in the oratorio foreshadows that of the operatic hero: he might be called an '*Ur*-Florestan.' Both . . . are under the threat of a painful death but are resigned to the will of God: Florestan is lying in the dark, Christ (according to Beethoven's stage direction, which never found its way into the published score) is on his knees."[18] Thus these three works, for Tyson, reflect psychologically and artistically Beethoven's "complex reactions to the onset of deafness." As he puts it further, in a challenging remark, "There even seems to be some parallel between his preoccupation with his infirmity and his involvement with the stage: if one likes, between the heroics of dramatic song and the stoicism of isolation and silence."[19] This is a striking and vivid argument, and only on reflection does one see that it reflects and elaborates a long-established viewpoint in Beethoven biography, namely that the rise of the "heroic"—we are still focused on the heroic "phase" but are gradually closing in on the "heroic style"—finds its origins in Beethoven's deeply moving acceptance of his deafness and his determination to overcome it and to triumph as an artist, as the letters of 1801 and the Heiligenstadt

Testament make clear. Among many biographers and critics writing in English who espoused this view before Tyson were, most conspicuously, J. W. N. Sullivan and Joseph Kerman.[20] Sullivan made the deafness crisis the centerpiece of his celebrated portrait of Beethoven's "spiritual development," thus binding the life to the work by claiming that the great and powerful works (again, the *Eroica* and the Fifth) embodied his will to overcome his afflictions and come through to a personal victory—not only this, but with the further claim that the other works of this time that do not share these features—for example, the Fourth and Sixth symphonies—are "less significant." Thus Sullivan says:

> Beethoven did not always plumb the depths. He was not always busy with major problems and the most significant spiritual experiences. Such works as the fourth, sixth, and eighth symphonies depict states of mind that require no such intensity of realization. It is significant that they were all written comparatively quickly. . . . They are not in the main line of Beethoven's spiritual development.[21]

Somehow one feels that this statement is both true and untrue. It seems true in the sense that the "heroic" works, which are certainly pathbreaking, may well have partly emerged as responses to the composer's personal crises; it seems untrue in insisting that the "other" works are of a lesser order of importance because no similar claim can be made for them. Interestingly, Kerman in his book on the quartets quoted a similar passage from Sullivan on the Quartet op. 74, which, needless to say, is also an outsider to the main line for Sullivan.[22] But as for accepting Kerman's view that op. 74 "is not [a work] to raise deep questions and great issues," I disagree completely; for here the "deep questions and great issues" are not those of despair and triumph, but of the quiet subtlety and beauty of ideas that belong to a contemplative state of mind. In a similar vein Tyson quotes an eloquent paragraph from Kerman on the ways in which the *Eroica*, the opera, and the "Waldstein" and "Appassionata" are "heroic." As Kerman wrote, "with these works Beethoven made his revolution . . ."[23]

That the "heroic phase" should expand into the "heroic period" is hardly surprising, and it follows that there should be, as indeed there certainly is, a "heroic style" that indelibly stamps some of Beethoven's most famous works of this broad period. At the same time, however, the exact identity of these works in the commentaries by various writers is less secure than one would like. To start with, the "heroic style" is ascribed by many, first of all and understandably, to the "Heroic" Symphony, to the Fifth Symphony, to the *Leonore* overtures; by some, also to the two great piano sonatas op. 53 and op. 57. Beyond this, however, which works belong and which don't depends on choices not easily understood. Thus Scott Burnham in his book, *Beethoven Hero*, centers attention primarily on the *Eroica* and the Fifth, with some remarks on the Coriolanus and the *Leonore* no. 3 overtures, and somewhat more on the Egmont Overture.[24] But for Burnham's exegesis, which vividly elucidates the content, significance, and cultural meaning of this "style," the question of inclusion or exclusion of other works remains marginal if it is dealt with at all. Thus, *Christus am Oelberge* is not mentioned anywhere, and there is only one minuscule reference in the book to *Leonore/Fidelio* as an opera.[25] There is also one passing reference to the Seventh Symphony as also being "heroic," but otherwise this work is not discussed.[26] Clearly there is an oblique, imperfect relationship between Tyson's "heroic phase" and Burnham's "heroic style."[27] Understandably. Tyson is dealing primarily with personal and conceptual issues that essentially belong to biography; Burnham is focused primarily on issues of musical content (above all in the Third and Fifth Symphonies, plus a bit more) and explicitly omits biographical considerations in favor of stylistic matters and reception history.[28] Whom Burnham does cite, though in my view too briefly, is Michael Broyles, whose book, *Beethoven: The Emergence and Evolution of the Heroic Style*, not only accepted this style as an established historiographic premise but explored its origins in French Revolutionary music and its presence in a number of significant works, including not only the Third and Fifth symphonies but also several overtures and some other works.[29] But unless I misread, much of what Broyles has to say about later middle-period works after the *Eroica*, much of it very interesting and well developed, largely drops the question of whether or not they embrace the "heroic style," despite grouping symphonies Four through Nine and other works under the heading "The Evolution of the Heroic Style."

More recently some signs of restlessness have surfaced over the current uses of "heroic" as a period term and as a style-defining term. In his recent book on the concertos, Leon Plantinga argues that

> the popular and pat name "heroic" is a very poor designation for Beethoven's middle period as a whole. While most of us easily associate that term with *Fidelio*, the "Waldstein," the "Appassionata," and the Third and Fifth symphonies, there is no ignoring that this was also the period of the "Pastoral" Symphony, the Violin Concerto, the String Quartet op. 59 no. 1, the first movement of the Fourth Piano Concerto, the Sonata op. 54, and the sacred songs after Gellert, op. 48.[30]

I cannot agree more. True as it is that a number of works of epic size, dynamic trajectory, and dramatic power composed in this period constitute a genuine revolution in musical thought, the tendency to ascribe to them a fully defining role in characterizing the period as a whole has severe limitations. The worst aspect of this tendency is to overshadow or even conceal the other aesthetic principles that Beethoven mastered and drew upon in the same era. Such principles can be found in works that are primarily lyrical, intimate, and expansive, such as the first movements of the Violin Concerto; the Fourth Piano Concerto; the A Major Cello Sonata, op. 69; the Trio op. 70 no. 2; and the "Archduke" Trio op. 97; in works displaying tight concentration of content within minimal spans, such as the F Major Piano Sonata, op. 54, or the F-sharp Major Sonata, op. 78; in a work such as the "Pastoral" Symphony, explicitly devoted to celebrating the restoration of the human experience of nature and of God in nature; or in a work of profound exploration of the sense of holiness, as in the Mass in C, op. 86. Still other major works reveal forms of expression for which we barely have names and terms but for which we could readily get a consensus that "heroic" would not do. This in turn suggests the idea that a better understanding of Beethoven's modes of expression, in the full sense of the term, could be achieved by seeing him not as a "primarily heroic" composer who sometimes lapsed into the use of other aesthetic models, but rather as a composer seeking all his life to be a universal artist, who could control tragedy, comedy, and an infinite number of expressive modes that fall somewhere between. That he was at least latently conscious of possessing such power is not only clear from the vast variety of the major works themselves, but from the many eyewitness accounts of his extraordinary capacities as an improviser, from his earliest to his last years. One in particular stands out, told by his pupil Czerny and published in 1852:

> His improvisation was most brilliant and striking. In whatever company he might chance to be, he knew how to produce such an effect upon every hearer that frequently not an eye remained dry, while many would break out into loud sobs; for there was something wonderful in his expression in addition to the beauty and originality of his ideas and his spirited style of rendering them. After ending an improvisation of this kind he would burst into loud laughter and banter his hearers on the emotion he had caused in them. "You are fools!" he would say. Sometimes he would feel himself insulted by these indications of sympathy. "Who can live among such spoiled children?" he would cry, and

only on that account (as he told me) he declined to accept an invitation which the King of Prussia gave him after one of the extempore performances above described.[31]

In the light of such considerations, a new historicization of the term "heroic" as Beethoven used it and knew it in his time might give us grounds for reestablishing a baseline from which further critical thinking can proceed.

Beethoven and the "Heroic"

To begin with, it has been too little considered that in the only two works in which Beethoven actually used the term "hero"or "heroic" there is a preoccupation not only with the idea of a hero but with death and funereal commemoration.[32] His first use of the term is in the Piano Sonata in A-flat, op. 26, of 1801, of which the slow movement is a "Marcia funebre per la morte d'un eroe" (Funeral March for the death of a hero), in the unusual and dark key of A-flat Minor.[33] This "pezzo characteristica, p[er] e[sempio] una marcia in as moll," as he first planned the march in a sketched movement-plan for the work, projects the work into the world of the programmatic and depictive sonata.[34]

The great sequel to the funeral march of opus 26 is of course the C Minor slow movement of the *Eroica* symphony, also entitled "Marcia funebre," the first significant funeral march in a symphony and manifestly one of Beethoven's most profound achievements, a turning point in the history of the symphonic slow movement. Indeed, without imagining that the *Eroica* has a narrative program (though some writers have certainly thought so), it is clear that the symphony as a whole offers a spectrum of interpretations of the "heroic." One of these is the solemn celebration of the hero's death, with equal weight given to recollection of his greatness but also to his qualities in death. Beethoven could hardly make this clearer than he does when he entitles the whole work—probably doing so in 1806 as he was getting it ready for its first publication in October of that year— "Sinfonia Eroica . . . composta per festeggiare il sovvenire di un grand Uomo" (Heroic Symphony . . . composed to celebrate the memory of a great man).

The focus on death in this work, and later in *Coriolanus*, is of the essence. In *Coriolanus*, also in C minor, the death of the fallen hero at the end takes place with a famous disintegration of the opening theme exactly parallel to that of the *Eroica* slow movement.

In Plutarch, who taught him resignation, Beethoven could well have read of funeral rites for the heroes of antiquity, for whom cults existed that celebrated their status as the "distinguished dead." Neither demigods nor common men, the "heroes" were venerated as a separate class, and certain heroes in ancient Greece were worshiped as protecting the spirits of the country or state. That this could fit with op. 26 and the *Eroica* funeral march seems quite possible, as does the likelihood that Beethoven found the tragic figure of Coriolanus as Roman hero not only in Shakespeare and in Collin, but in Plutarch, who writes the life of Coriolanus side by side with that of the great Greek general Alcibiades.[35] Not only does Beethoven acknowledge Plutarch in his letters, not only was he obviously moved by the figure of Coriolanus to produce one of his most expressive and concentrated works, but his acquaintance with the figure of Alcibiades is evident in letters to and by him, and in a passage from a conversation book of 1823; all of this information has recently been brought out by E. Kerr Borthwick. As an example we find the letter from Clemens Brentano to Beethoven of either 1811 or 1813, in which Brentano refers to stories he had heard about Beethoven's eccentricities and compares them to what "the rabble always [heard] about the hound of Alcibiades . . ." about which Borthwick writes, "One has the distinct impression that Brentano fully expected Beethoven to understand the Alcibiades allusion, presumably because in conversation with him he had found that he was familiar with Plutarch's *Lives*. . . ." [36] That the figure of Alcibiades was not only ancient but also modern, and known in contemporary German literature, is clear from another letter, this time of October 8, 1811 from Beethoven to the poet Christoph August von Tiedge, also referred to by Borthwick, in which Beethoven quotes a saying attributed to Alcibiades, "After all a man has no free will."[37] Beethoven might have derived this not only from Plutarch but from August Gottlieb Meissner's *Alcibiades* (see note 37).

Beethoven's knowledge of Plutarch stands alongside his admiration for Homer as a major source for his vision of the heroic ideal—all the more so owing to the dramatic contrast that the heroes of Greek and Roman antiquity presented to Europeans of this post–French Revolutionary and Napoleonic age when disillusionment with current would-be heroes was the order of the day. In fact there is good reason to believe that Plutarch's *Lives* was deeply influential throughout Europe in the eighteenth century, not least in German literature, especially drama. According to a study by Martha Howard, two important plays from the second half of the century present protagonists who are inspired to heroic action by reading Plutarch.[38] One is Friedrich Maximilian von Klinger's *Die Zwillinge* (1776), the other is Schiller's famous revolutionary drama *Die Räuber* (The Robbers, 1781). Both center on two brothers, one of whom is fired to great ambition by reading of ancient heroes. Schiller's central figure, Karl Moor, suffers wrongs and rebels against family and society by becoming the leader of a band of robbers. Only much later does he realize that in doing so he has violated his innermost moral being and finally gives himself up to justice. When Karl Moor first appears on stage he is reading Plutarch, and his first words in the play are "How I hate this age of scribblers when I can pick up my Plutarch and read of great men."[39] The tone has a familiar ring; we might almost be hearing the voice of Beethoven.[40]

To return to the issue of heroism and death in Beethoven, in *Egmont* the imprisoned hero, about to die, has a vision of liberty as a woman, and there is a triumphant finale called a "victory symphony." Since Egmont's "victory" is at the cost of his life, the final portrayal of "triumph" is obviously not meant as a depiction but as the symbolic affirmation of a vision beyond the individual. The parallel to Florestan's vision of Leonore is clear, and in addition the Prisoners' Chorus in Act One of the opera had presented in collective terms the same ideal of freedom as a distant dream. From here the connection to Schiller's Ode and to the universal idealism of the Ninth Symphony is more than obvious.

I propose in Beethoven's work at least three varieties of heroism. (1) In the first the emphasis is on the fallen hero, his death, and the solemn celebration of his life; the funeral marches of op. 26 and the *Eroica* slow movement are the classic examples, along with *Coriolanus*. (2) In the second, the emphasis is on the visionary heroism of the triumphant inner will, as in the other movements of the *Eroica*, the Fifth Symphony, the *Egmont* "victory symphony," the Overtures *Leonore* 2 and 3, as well as in the character of Leonore and in the manic coda of the 1814 Florestan. (3) In the third category, which brings us back to where this discussion began, we find the quiet heroism of endurance. This is the deeper issue in the representation of Florestan throughout the opera, and it is one of the meanings of *Leonore/Fidelio* that has been obscured by the exclusive focus on the courage of the female protagonist. For Florestan is not only a suffering victim but is also the coequal hero of the drama. He has survived his ordeal through hope and his will to live, dreaming of freedom in the prison of his life and not succumbing to the death that, in such a situation, could have seemed a release, as it would do and has done for so many suffering victims. In that sense, I repeat, the hero as represented by Florestan is not the one who triumphs but rather the one who endures. And this accords powerfully with what Beethoven felt in the idea of the "heroic" in his life as well as in his art. The theme of endurance recurs constantly in his letters and statements, nowhere more directly than in an 1819 letter to Archduke Rudolph: "There is hardly any good thing which can be achieved without a sacrifice; and it is precisely the nobler and better man who seems to be destined for this more than other human beings, no doubt in order that his virtue may be put to the test."[41] In the deeply personal *Tagebuch* he ponders on his solitary life, without marriage, and writes, in 1812: "Submission, deepest submission to your fate . . . O hard struggle! Do everything that still has to be done to arrange what is necessary for the long journey. . . . Maintain an absolutely steady attitude." And elsewhere, stoically, "Learn to keep silent, O friend."[42] He continues in this vein, in quotations from Herder, from the Greek classics and from Oriental religious writings, including the *Rig-Veda*. The other side of acceptance and endurance is the perpetual longing for freedom, not only political but artistic, the ideal of breaking out into new territories of experience, for which the heroism of endurance strives and which gives it meaning and purpose. This is the fusion that Beethoven was obviously seeking in his artistic development, and it is nowhere better expressed than in another letter of 1819 (Anderson 955). Here he writes, now thinking much more broadly, ". . . in the world of art as in the whole of creation, *freedom* and *progress* [*Freiheit, weiter gehn*] are the main objectives."[43]

NOTES

General Note: The standard edition of Beethoven's letters is Emily Anderson, ed. and trans., *The Letters of Beethoven*, 3 vols., London: Macmillan, 1961. The original German letters can be found in *Ludwig van Beethoven: Briefwechsel, Gesamtausgabe*, ed. Sieghard Brandenburg, 8 vols. (Munich, 1996–).

1. G. Nottebohm, *Zweite Beethoveniana* (Leipzig, 1887) (hereafter cited as N II), p. 89. The entry appears on a leaf containing sketches for op. 59 no. 3.

2. See his letters of June 29, and November 16, 1801 to Franz Gerhard Wegeler in Bonn (Anderson no. 51, 54; *Briefe*, ed. Sieghard Brandenburg, no. 65, 70); also his letter of 1 July 1801 to Karl Amenda (Anderson no. 53; *Briefe*, no. 67). For the Heiligenstadt Testament see, for the original text, *Briefe*, No. 106; for a translation and interpretation, Maynard Solomon, *Beethoven*, 2nd ed. (New York, 1998), pp. 151–58.

3. For a preliminary overview of the young Beethoven's relationship to Mozart see my "Beethoven before 1800: The Mozart Legacy," *Beethoven Forum* 3 (1994): 39–52.

4. On the Mozart operas performed at Bonn in Beethoven's early years see Elliot Forbes, ed., *Thayer's Life of Beethoven*, rev. ed. (Princeton, 1967), pp. 97–8 and Ludwig Schiedermair, *Der junge Beethoven* (Leipzig, 1925), pp. 63–67.

5. On Beethoven's operatic projects a summary is found in Winton Dean, "Beethoven and Opera," ed. D. Arnold and N. Fortune, *The Beethoven Reader* (New York, 1971), pp. 381–86. For an extended discussion of these projects see the monograph by

Rudolf Pecman, *Beethovens Opernpläne* (Brno, 1981). The proposed opera on the early Pennsylvanians was an idea hatched by the writer Johann Baptist Rupprecht (1776–1846), who came to know Beethoven after 1814 and whose poem "Merkenstein" was set twice by Beethoven, as op. 100 and as WoO 144.

6. Scheide sketchbook, p. 52; quoted in N II, p. 329.

7. Bouilly's remarks are in his memoirs, published as *Mes Récapitulations* (Paris, 1836), vol. 2, pp. 81ff. Bouilly had himself served in an official position at Tours and might have been a real-life Don Fernando; see W. Dean, "Beethoven and Opera," p. 341. But Bouilly's veracity has been questioned by David Galliver, "Fidelio—Fact or Fantasy?" *Studies in Music*, 15 (1981): 82–92.

8. A small step in the direction of ferreting out reminiscences and resemblances between *The Magic Flute* and *Leonore/Fidelio* was made by Mark Brunswick, "Beethoven's Tribute to Mozart in 'Fidelio'," *The Musical Quarterly* 31 (1945): 29–32, referring to the Terzett in Act I (No. 5), which was kept intact in 1814. Particularly in the 1805 version as published by Willy Hess, we find Mozartian moments in ensemble writing that includes Jacquino and Marzelline; cf. "Ich . . . Ich" thus repeated, reminiscent of Osmin and Papageno; or Rocco in his duet with Pizarro (No. 9).

9. I am indebted here to Dr. Daniel Beller-McKenna, who prepared a paper on the "Prisoners' Chorus" for a Harvard University seminar I gave on the opera in 1990.

10. On the textual problems connected with Florestan's aria in the 1805 version see Michael Tusa, "The Unknown Florestan: The 1805 Version of 'In des Lebens Frühlingstagen,'" *Journal of the American Musicological Society* 46 (1993): 175–220. Tusa astutely points out that in the original French version of the libretto Florestan's character was somewhat differently portrayed, in that the suffering prisoner longed for release from his agony in death; in Sonnleithner's libretto for Beethoven Florestan becomes "a more stoic, resilient, and even hopeful character . . ." whose stoicism in the face of his punishment resonated well with what we know of Beethoven's acceptance of his own fate; see Tusa, p. 180.

11. See note 2, letter of July 29, 1801 to Wegeler; *Briefe*, I, p. 80. Brandenburg, *Briefe*, p. 82, fn. 6, suggests the possibility that the words, "Plutarch hat mich zu der *Resignation* geführt" refers to Beethoven's thought that from Plutarch's accounts of the lives of Greek and Roman statesmen he could infer the idea of withdrawal from public life and a flight into his inner world of music, as well as withdrawal as much as possible from city life to the countryside. It may be of interest that "Resignation" (in German) is the formal title for the curious poem "Lisch aus, mein Licht," which Beethoven set in 1817 (WoO 149); see Richard Kramer, "'Lisch aus, mein Licht': Song, Fugue, and the Symptoms of a Late Style," *Beethoven Forum* 7 (1999): 67–88.

12. Victor Brombert, *The Romantic Prison* (Princeton, N.J., 1978).

13. Cesare Beccaria, *Dei delitti e delle pene* (Livorno, Italy, 1764) plus many later editions and translations.

14. See Gary Schmidgall, "Is *Fidelio* the Saddest Opera?" *Opera News* 48 (7 January 1984): 14.

15. Brombert, *Romantic*, p. 3.

16. M. Solomon, *Beethoven*, pp. 163–72, 187–206. W. Kinderman, *Beethoven* (Berkeley, Calif., 1995), Chapters 4–6.

17. Alan Tyson, "Beethoven's Heroic Phase," *The Musical Times* 110 (1969): 139–141.

18. Ibid. 140.

19. Ibid. 139.

20. J. W. N. Sullivan, *Beethoven: His Spiritual Development* (New York, 1927; New York, 1949). Joseph Kerman, *The Beethoven Quartets* (New York, 1967).

21. Sullivan, pp. 86ff.

22. Kerman, *Beethoven Quartets*, p. 168.

23. Ibid., p. 92, quoted by Tyson, p. 139.

24. S. Burnham, *Beethoven Hero* (Princeton, N.J., 1995). See also Kerman's review of Burnham, "The Beethoven Takeover," *The New York Review of Books*, 3 October 1996, pp. 23–25.

25. Burnham, *Hero*, p. 30.

26. Ibid., p. 70.

27. Tyson's article in fact is not cited by Burnham, either in his text or bibliography, as Kerman noted in his review.

28. Burnham, *Hero*, p. xvi: ". . . I am not concerned with how the facts of his life impinge upon his work . . . but rather with how his work has impinged upon us."

29. Michael Broyles, *The Emergence and Evolution of Beethoven's Heroic Style* (New York, 1987).

30. Leon Plantinga, *Beethoven's Concertos* (New York, 1999), p. 152.

31. Thayer/Forbes, *Life of Beethoven*, p. 185; Solomon, *Beethoven*, p. 78.

32. The application of the term "heroisch" to Bacchus's dance in the *Prometheus* ballet stems not from Beethoven but from the choreographer/dancer Viganò. When Beethoven decided to use the term "eroica" for the Third Symphony is not certain; the terminal date is sometime before its use in the title for the first publication, in 1806, but how much before we cannot be sure. This was recently summarized by Thomas Sipe, *Beethoven: Eroica Symphony* (Cambridge, 1998), pp. 13 and 29. That Beethoven's use of the term belongs together with the idea of *commemorating* a hero, as in the rest of the title, is for me an essential point.

33. It is interesting to see that when Beethoven needed a funeral march in 1815 for his incidental music to the drama *Leonore Prohaska* he used this piece in an orchestral transcription, transposing it into B minor, a key that in that same year he called a "dark key" (see N II, p. 326).

34. See the movement-plan for the sonata in the Sketchbook Landsberg 7, published as K. L. Mikulicz, ed., *Ein Notierungsbuch von Beethoven* (Berlin, 1927; reprint Hildesheim, Germany, 1972), p. 52. It is reproduced in my study, "The Earliest Sketches for the *Eroica* Symphony," in my *Beethoven: Studies in the Creative Process* (Cambridge, Mass., 1992), p. 149. It is interesting that at this stage of planning Beethoven is thinking of a "marcia" as a "character-piece" but not yet of a funeral march, a decision he comes to in time. To some extent the situation in the *Eroica* seems comparable, since the earliest idea for a slow movement (1802) in the Wielhorsky sketchbook was for a C major Adagio movement in 6/8, which was displaced by the 2/4 "Marcia funebre" in 1803 when he sketched it in the "Eroica Sketchbook," MS Landsberg 6.

35. I had come to this conclusion independently from reading Plutarch when there appeared in 1998 the article by E. Kerr Borthwick, "Beethoven and Plutarch," *Music and Letters* 79 (1998): 268–72. To this article I owe the revealing references to Alcibiades by Beethoven and members of his circle, as well as its well-documented confirmation of the importance of the classics for Beethoven's moral and political outlook and his views on the proper education of his nephew Karl.

36. Ibid., p. 268.

37. Anderson no. 327; Brandenburg *Briefe*, no. 525. Brandenburg's n. 4 suggests a possible source for this quotation, though it is altered in Beethoven's usage, in August Gottlieb Meissner's *Alcibiades*, vol. 2, p. 206, citing A. Leitzmann, *Ludwig van Beethoven. Berichte der Zeitgenossen . . .*, vol. 2, p. 347. Beethoven knew or knew of Meissner and admired him, as we see from his letter to the painter Macco of November 2, 1803, in which

he hopes to receive a text (probably an oratorio text) from Meissner, "who is so honored as a writer and . . . understands musical poetry better than any of our writers in Germany." Beethoven later owned a copy of Meissner's *Skizzen*; see T. Albrecht, *Letters to Beethoven*, vol. 3 (Lincoln, Nebraska, 1996), p. 231, no. 79. Meissner's *Alcibiades* (1782), in four volumes, is a series of biographical dramatic scenes in dialogue, based on Plutarch and other ancient sources, which includes among its anecdotes the one about the dog. See Rudolf Först, *August Gottlieb Meissner, Eine Darstellung seines Lebens und seiner Schriften*, 2nd ed. (Berlin, 1900), pp. 133–52 (on *Alcibiades*). While this work was presented as a historical novel, though in verse, Meissner also wrote biographies of Masaniello, Spartacus, Epaminondas, and Julius Caesar; and also a biography of the composer Johann Gottlieb Naumann (1741–1801), who was a friend of his at Dresden in the 1770s.

38. Martha W. Howard, *The Influence of Plutarch in the Major European Literatures of the Eighteenth Century* (Chapel Hill, N.C., 1970), pp. 95ff.

39. "Mir ekelt vor diesem Tintenklecksenden Sekulum, wenn ich in meinem Plutarch lese von grossen Menschen." My translation is lightly modified from that by F. J. Lamport (New York, 1979), p.35 (act I, sc. ii).

40. Compare this to the remark about the young Napoleon by Pasquale Paoli, "This young man has the quality of an ancient [hero]; he is a man out of Plutarch"; from Arnold Schmitz, *Das Romantische Beethovenbild* (Berlin and Bonn, 1927), p. 160; Schmitz's discussion of "the concept of the heroic," pp. 152–76, though little cited by recent authors, establishes all the basic themes of this essay. In a classic formulation (p. 162) he has this to say about the renaming of the *Eroica* from the original "Bonaparte"after Napoleon's coronation: "For this symphony he [Beethoven] now chooses, instead of the name of a specific person, by whom he has been deceived, the name of an idea, by which he cannot be deceived: the 'heroic.'" Equally important is the discussion of the "heroic" in J. G. Sulzer's *Allgemeine Theorie der Schönen Künste*, 4 vols. (Leipzig, 1771–74); see Schmitz, pp. 161–162.

41. *Briefe*, No. 1292 (3 March 1819). Anderson, *Letters*, No. 948, had ascribed it to "early June 1819" but when she studied it the cut-off portion containing the signature and date was not available.

42. See Maynard Solomon's edition and translation of the *Tagebuch* in A. Tyson, ed. *Beethoven Studies 3* (Cambridge, 1982) pp. 193–285; in ibid., *Beethoven Essays* (Cambridge, Mass., 1988), pp. 293–98; and in the German edition as *Beethovens Tagebuch* (Bonn, 1990). The text appears as no. 5. Beethoven also inscribed it in Charles Neate's notebook and made a canonic setting of it (WoO 168).

43. *Briefe*, no. 1318 (29 July 1819). The italics are Beethoven's.

PART II

THE LATE
BEETHOVEN

.

Memory and Invention at the Threshold of Beethoven's Late Style

ELAINE SISMAN

This essay is dedicated to Lewis Lockwood

Beethoven's very few major works of 1815–1816 share a notable feature: The opening melody of the first movement returns either in or just before the final movement. These returns, in the C Major Cello Sonata, op. 102 no. 1 (1815); the A Major Piano Sonata, op. 101 (1815–1816); and the song cycle *An die ferne Geliebte*, op. 98 (1816), have been described in three ways: as a romantic detail, evoking nostalgia and perhaps regret; as experiments for a new kind of multi-movement work that is at once self-referential and teleological, the paradigm cases being the finale-driven Fifth and Ninth Symphonies; and as a sign of the "fantasy" element because they play with the boundaries of movements, as in the first of the two sonatas "Quasi una Fantasia," op. 27, and appear to have an inner life. The third major work of these years, the song cycle *An die ferne Geliebte*, op. 98, also returns to the melody of the first song as the last stanza of the last song. Terms used throughout the critical literature to evoke the quality of these passages are terms of memory, and include "reminiscence," "repetition," "recall," "recollection," even "flashback." Wilhelm von Lenz called the return in op. 101 a "fantastic vision"; the first Viennese reviewer called it a "rhapsodic repetition."[1] In fact the concentration of such works at the threshold of Beethoven's late style—a period Lewis Lockwood calls "the twilight stage of his career that divides the 'second' period from the 'third'"—is highly significant.[2] Beethoven's arresting means for activating memory in these pieces, especially the broadened conception of memory that I will delineate here, have never been fully explored and, moreover, have a profound impact on his late style. These works are markers in ways that go beyond their chronological placement during a period of personal turmoil and reduced productivity.

The unusual status of the two instrumental works of 1815–1816 is apparent in Table 1, which shows the layout of all of Beethoven's pieces with intermovement returns, because they are the only pieces with thematic returns that take place between movements, rather than inside another movement. (In other works the slow movement might open into a transition to the finale without such a return, like the "Emperor" Piano Concerto, op. 73, or *Les Adieux* Sonata, op. 81a, both of 1809.) All musi-

---

Table 1.
Pieces by Beethoven with "Returns" of Earlier
Movements toward the End of the Cycle

1797–1798   Op. 8. Serenade for Vn., Va., Vc., in D major

i: <u>Marcia</u>. <u>Allegro</u> ii. Adagio. iii. Menuetto. Allegretto. iv. Adagio
v. Scherzo: Allegro molto. vi. Allegretto alla Polacca.
vii. <u>Tema</u>. Andante quasi Allegretto. viii. <u>Marcia</u>. <u>Allegro.</u>

1800–1801   Op. 27 no. 1. Sonata quasi una fantasia, E-flat major

i: Andante ii. Allegro molto e vivace iii. Adagio con espr iv. Allegro vivace [Adagio] Presto
A B A$_1$ C A$_2$ →   →a$_V$ + b + a$_I$ cadenza →   a$_I$ cadenza → coda

---

1807–1808   Op. 67. Symphony no. 5, C minor

i: Allegro con brio ii: Andante con moto iii: Allegro [trans] iv: Allegro
                                   Sch—Trio—Sch*→Exp—Dev—Sch*→ Recap—Coda

---

1815   Op. 102/1. Sonata for Vc. and Piano, C major

i: Andante ii: Allegro vivace iii: Adagio → [Tempo d'Andante]→ iv: Allegro vivace
       cadenza   cadenza   trills

1815–1816   Op. 98. Song cycle "An die ferne Geliebte"

Song	1	2	3	4	5	6	
	E♭	G	A♭	A♭	C	E♭	(stanza 4 = song 1)

1816   Op. 101. Sonata, A major

i: Etwas lebhaft, mit der innigsten Empfindung   ii: Lebhaft, Marschmässig
iii: Langsam und sehnsuchtsvoll → [Tempo I] → iv: Geschwind, . . . und mit Entschlossenheit
                        cadenza   trills

1821–1822   Op. 110. Sonata, A-flat major

i: Moderato cantab ... ii: Allegro molto iii: Adagio ... → iv: Fuga. Allegro →
                                   recit., Arioso dolente   arpeggio
[L'istesso tempo di Arioso] → [L'istesso tempo della Fuga . . .]
                  arpeggio

1822–1824   Op. 125. Symphony no. 9, D minor

i: Allegro ...   ii: Molto Vivace   iii: Adagio molto ...   iv: Presto . . .
                                         fanfare, recit., recalls of i, ii, iii

---

cal compositions bring back ideas, of course, whether for coherence or unity or sheer recognition value and intelligibility, but the logic of musical forms demands returns only within a single movement. Before about 1810 it was considered daring to bring back the first movement's slow introduction during the Allegro at its original tempo; this innovation of Mozart (String Quintet in D, K. 593, 1790) and Haydn (Symphony 103, "Drumroll," 1795) was then strikingly exploited by Beethoven with multiple returns in the first movements of the "Pathétique" Sonata in C Minor, op. 13, the Piano Trio in E-flat, op. 70 no. 2, and the late quartets in B-flat, op. 130, and F, op. 135, as well as the finale of the String Quartet in B-flat, op. 18 no. 6 (*La malinconia*). (Beethoven's youthful sonata in F minor, WoO 47 of 1782–1783, returns to the slow introduction just before the recapitulation as a kind of false reprise, beginning in the subdominant, as well as retransition.) A special case, the Serenade for String Trio, op. 8, brings back the entire opening movement, an Allegro march, at the very end, to reveal that the theme of the preceding variation movement is a variant of the march, but the return seems less a reminiscence than a bookend. Other pre-1815 works will be discussed below.

Beethoven's original title for the Cello Sonata op. 102 no. 1, "Free Sonata," can still be seen on the autograph; he did not authorize that title in the published edition.[3] The word "fantasy" comes up again and again in writings about this work and the Piano Sonata in A, op. 101; the latter has even been called a "fantasy-sonata."[4] For one thing, the first movement of op. 101 is free of repeat signs (a trait shared by only four other sonatas, the "Moonlight," op. 27 no. 2, and opp. 90, 109, and 110) and, moreover, seems to begin "in the middle"[5] (Example 1). The slow movement, placed third, opens into the return of the first theme, which immediately gives way to the finale, suggesting a certain freedom of cyclic form. Martin Zenck, in his valuable study of J. S. Bach's influence on late Beethoven, associates the fantasylike features of op. 101 with the toccatas of Bach, and reminds us that Johann Mattheson's venerable 1739 treatise *Der vollkommene Kapellmeister* pointed to toccatas as emblems of the *stylus fantasticus*.[6] The broadly pastoral aspect of the work, especially in its first movement, has been taken as further evidence both of the Bach influence and of the Romantic reimagining of genre.[7]

But this raises the question of what it means to call a piece fantasylike: Does it mean "like an improvisation" or "like the musical pieces we call fantasies" or simply "like a piece that doesn't easily fit into formal categories"?[8] Musically speaking, fantasia is a process of improvising as well as the pieces resulting from that process. According to Carl Czerny, Beethoven's improvising had three musical results: a sonata form or rondo movement with a "second section" elaborating the original motive;

Example 1. Piano Sonata op. 101/i

a free variation form (the Choral Fantasy, op. 80 or the finale of the Ninth Symphony gave "a true picture of his improvising in this manner"); and a "mixed form, one idea following the other as in a potpourri, like his Solo Fantasy, op. 77."[9] One might thus differentiate between improvisations "on" a single theme, resulting in that theme worked out in sonata, rondo, or variation form (with subsidiary themes as needed), and improvisations, which moved from theme to theme. In rhetorical terms, the former requires invention (*inventio*) but emphasizes formal arrangement (*dispositio*) and elaboration (*elaboratio*), while the latter keeps invention in the forefront, and all arise in performance (*actio*), requiring that the improviser's memory (*memoria*) be well-stocked with retrievable material: thus all five of the essential parts of the orator's activity are accounted for.[10] Czerny's own treatise on improvisation explicitly compared performer and orator; the latter "strives to develop a subject as clearly and exhaustively as possible on the spur of the moment."[11]

But by 1816 Beethoven's days of improvising in public were over. His single remark about *fantasieren* at the keyboard seems wistful: an ambiguous *Tagebuch* entry of that year reads "Only as before again at the piano [to make] my own fantasies—despite all my hearing [problems]."[12] He seems to want to impel himself back to the keyboard or to mourn for lost possibilities.[13] The immediately preceding entry mentions a notice in the *Wiener Zeitung* of August 1816 about a concert to benefit invalids; perhaps Beethoven was wishing he could resume that part of his previously public musical life. As far as we know his last public appearances were in April and May 1814 to play the Archduke Trio, and in January 1815, when he accompanied a singer at a concert for the Russian empress.[14] Such a remark confided to his diary, with its implication of an engagement with the past, may have colored the composition of his subsequent works for piano.

A musical fantasy and perhaps by extension those pieces that are "fantasylike" thus focus attention on the act of creation as well as on the sources of the composer's ideas, from "feelings" to ordinary "topics" of musical discourse to specific "characteristic" elements to the more esoteric "objects" or "visions and images" or "poetic ideas" that Beethoven was reported to have in mind when composing.[15] Charles Neate, the English pianist with whom Beethoven spent some time in the summer of 1815—the period of composition of op. 102—recalled many years later that Beethoven said "I always have a picture in mind, when I am composing, and work up to it."[16]

What does it mean to have a "picture in mind"? The idea of the mental image, picture, or object is not only part of imagination, the faculty that creates such images, but also part of memory, the ability to recall those images for use in the present. Both are conjoined in the powerful rhetorical figure *phantasia*, in which a speaker uses an image to make an absent thing appear to be present, to call an experience vividly to mind. Phantasia brings the audience into the world of the speaker or composer in order to sway them, to move their passions. For the composer, such an image may be a locator in memory that stimulates the composition of thematic material, which in turn implants images in the minds of the listeners. In this sense, rhetorical phantasia is a two-way street: It stirs the appropriate images in the composer's own memory in order to create new or newly alive memories in his listeners.[17] Many kinds of musical gestures may be identified with image creation, for example the three-note descending "motive of farewell" marked "Lebewohl" in Beethoven's *Les Adieux* sonata, op. 81a; indeed, even some pure, unmarked figurations—cadenzalike arpeggios and runs, for example— may stir up "clouds of memory," as I will discuss below.

In its larger sense, fantasy was originally virtually synonymous with imagination, and before the eighteenth century fantasy was valued more highly; James Engell remarks that the Greek term *phantasia* "carried with it the suggestion of creativity and play of mind . . . [while] the Latin *imaginatio* [with its] blocklike Roman solidity derived from the primary word 'image' (a mental concept as much as a visual 'image') . . . was related to 'imitation' and carried with it a sense of fidelity and accuracy."[18] By the end of the eighteenth century, though, fantasy was taken to mean a less potent form of imagination, as suggested by the English word *fancy*, with its connotation of arbitrary caprice. John Dryden had already suggested that imagination comprised "invention, fancy, and elocution," and by 1792, in Dugald Stewart's *Elements of the Philosophy of the Human Mind*, fancy was simply a method of associating ideas or images in a lively way, rather than creating them.[19] Samuel Taylor Coleridge's famous distinction between imagination and fancy, set out in the *Biographia Literaria* of 1817, saw fancy as not only a lesser, but also a fundamentally different thing. To him the primary and secondary imagination represent, respectively, the creative power of the deity and its "echo" in human beings, which "dissolves, diffuses, dissipates, in order to recreate . . . to idealize and to unify. It is essentially *vital* . . ."[20] Fancy, on the other hand, is "no other than a mode of memory emancipated from the order of time and space; . . . equally with the ordinary memory the Fancy must receive all its materials ready made from the law of association." Thus, fancy does not create, but stitches together out of memory. It sets memory to work. Coleridge's contemporaries and most twentieth-century critics have found his distinctions obscure, but have cited them over and over as signs of the emergent romantic imagination and its consciousness of creativity.[21]

German writers like Johann Georg Sulzer and Johann Christoph Adelung, on the other hand, resisted the attempt to create a hierarchy and instead equated imagination and fantasy. Adelung in particular, in a widely read book on German literary style (four editions between 1785 and 1800), offered the terms as synonyms (*Die Einbildungsgkraft, oder mit einem Griechischen Wort die Phantasie*), describing rhetorical "figures for the imagination" as those that could help "to stir that power of the soul to create images in ever stronger gradations until the image fills the mind."[22] These figures operate in three ways: they make what is absent appear to be present, they intensify ideas, and they represent the abstract as sensual. Making the absent appear to be present is thus a recurring motif in the creation of artistically potent and moving images. Immanuel Kant also underscored the idea that imagination and fantasy draw their power from memory: "the imagination either engages in fiction (that is, it is productive), or in recall (that is, it is reproductive)." But even when it is productive, the imagination does not create anything actually new to the senses, but rather "we can always show from whence the imagination took its material."[23] To Kant, fantasy is the involuntary, spontaneous component of imagination, and both are elements in perception and judgment as well as creativity and memory.

Giambattista Vico drew a particularly vivid link between imagination and memory earlier in the eighteenth century. For other writers I have cited, imagination was the umbrella category, but for him it is memory that is central in the construction of human history: "Memory has three different aspects: memory (*memoria*) when it remembers things; a maker's imagination (*fantasia*) when it alters or imitates them, and invention (*ingegno*) when it gives them a new turn or puts them into proper arrangement or relationship."[24] As Donald Verene summarizes this aspect of Vico's thought, "Fantasia as memory is the ability to reorder what has been recalled."[25] What this offers us is a metaphor for the twin processes of improvisation and composition; both will call on mental images and order them either spontaneously or by a process of revision.

A wonderful model for the spontaneous ordering of mental images— a case of freeing the imagination of control—is given by Heinrich von Kleist in a little essay of 1805 called "On the Gradual Readying of Ideas While Speaking." Kleist suggests that often the best way to figure out what one thinks about a particular subject is simply to begin speaking to someone; just as "l'appétit vient en mangeant," the appetite comes while eating, he claims, "l'idée vient en parlant," the idea comes while speaking.[26] The notion of simply starting anywhere may come from a more venerable slice of oral culture in Horace's description of the epic poet who in a fine disregard for temporal sequence "hastens into action and precipitates the hearer into the middle of things."[27] The beginning of op. 101 has just this sense of plunging *in medias res*.

Memory is implicated in fantasy and imagination, but its rhetorical status is problematic. While the power of memory was venerated as a creative force akin to that of invention in the ancient and medieval worlds, its reputation began to attenuate in the Renaissance, and by the time of eighteenth-century rhetorics memory was often dispensed with entirely or considered a merely mechanical process.[28] In large part this was a result of the turn from primary rhetoric—instruction in eloquence for actual speaking situations—to secondary rhetoric, when manuals were chiefly concerned with literary style.[29] Yet when one reads discussions of the parts of rhetoric—invention, arrangement, elaboration (style), memory, and performance—one is struck by the very similar ways that invention and memory are conceived: Each consists in *places* where the eloquent speaker either finds or stores arguments and ideas. Impressive feats of both invention and memorization were celebrated as exemplars of a creative as well as recreative mental geography. Among the earliest self-help books, books on how to improve memory advocated systems that took their cue from a famous event of the ancient world recounted by Cicero, in which Simonides's memory made him a hero: at a lavish dinner, the ceiling suddenly fell in, and Simonides, the only one to survive, was able to remember who had been there (and who was now crushed beneath the rubble) because he could conjure up a mental picture of where each person had been sitting.[30] The idea of thus "walking" through a mental image had profound implications and led to the development of memory systems based on a "spatial geography," in which one would associate the people or things to be remembered by associating them with a room in a house, a color on a wheel, a square on a grid. To make the absent appear to be present one needed to control both space and time.

The notion of the pastness of memory and the presentness of recollection or reminiscence goes back to Aristotle, and its distinctions are crucial to my argument.[31] Memory must be of the past, said Aristotle, just as judgment and prediction are of the future, and perception is of the present. Memory is a state or affection connected with either perception or conception, once time has elapsed. Recollection is the "recovery of knowledge or perception that one had before."[32] However, one needs a starting point, because the images are likely to return to mind in the same order as the original events. Medieval commentators on Aristotle, like Albertus Magnus, described recollecting as "tracking down" what has been "set aside" through the memory, and as a conscious process that occurs through association: it is not "mere" rote memorization for that is not true memory.[33] Moreover, the recollector was frequently referred to as composing while recollecting. Thus we are back to Vico's "fantasia as memory," an essential connection among inventing and recollecting and ordering ideas. Finally, memory images themselves are emotionally charged—this aids in their recollection. Wordsworth's famous remarks in the Preface to the second edition of the *Lyrical Ballads* (1800) brings all this to the cusp of Romanticism: that a poet "is affected more than other men by absent things as if they were present" so that poetry, the "spontaneous overflow of powerful feelings . . . takes its origin from emotion recollected in tranquility." His source for this remark has been shown to be Schiller's 1791 review of Bürger's poetry, in which Schiller set out a theory of the poet distancing himself, through a passion for form, from the passions he wishes to portray, in order to write poetry out of "gentle and distant recollection [*Erinnerung*]."[34]

* * * *

The overlapping domains of fantasy, image, invention, and memory are situated to activate a wide hermeneutic field at the threshold of Beethoven's late style. They give force to precisely those elements in Beethoven's works of 1815–1816 that were and are perceived as striking, new, Romantic. The returns of the opening themes in op. 102 no. 1 and op. 101 offer a way in: the cello sonata introduces these issues, the piano sonata fully realizes them. Example 2 shows the Andante opening movement of the cello sonata, with its contemplative and idyllic melody. Among the issues in determining the status of thematic recall in this work is the problematic character of not one but two slow movements, the first and third: Is either an independent movement or is one or the other or both a slow introduction? Despite the unmistakable full cadence in the tonic in mm. 24–27 and the fact that the following Allegro is in a different key (the relative minor), a number of commentators call the opening Andante a slow introduction. This view, to my mind mistaken, arises from its *fantasia* elements: declamatory opening, cadenza, lack of a double bar before the Allegro, and a striking amount of repetition, both of motives and phrases. But the subtleties of phrase structure only slightly obscure a symmetrical closed form with an unusual disposition of phrase repetitions: while one might expect *a-b-a* or *a-a-b-a* or even *a-a-b-b*, the actual arrangement is *a-b-b-a* with unusual rhyming extensions (i.e. the first *a* and first *b* have the same one-bar extension to a V^9 chord and fermata). In fact, the first *a* and *b*, without their extensions, make a completely closed $4_V + 4_I$ period; it is the delight in questioning motivic play that renders this mysterious, and the resultant harping on the dominant that makes the whole seem introductory. The four-measure phrases are divided into two-measure incises, as marked on Example 2:

mm. 1–5 a_1 (cello—to cad. on V) a $_2$ (piano—ends with *x*, to half cad.)
    ext. on *x* (3 statements, to V9)

mm. 6–10 b_1 (cello—to IV) b_2 (piano—ends with *y*, to I)
    ext. on *x* (2 statements, to V9)

mm. 11–16 b_1 (piano—to IV) b_2 (cello—ends with *y*, to I)
    trans on *y* (3 statements, to vi, V)—trill

mm. 17–27 a_1 (cello—to V via IV) a $_2$ (piano—ends with *x*, to I imperfect)
    ext. with *x* to cadenza (to I)

In addition to motives *x* and *y*, the linear pattern of the cello's opening *a* melody gives rise to a number of identifiable motives that affect not only the first movement but the rest of the sonata as well: these include the $\hat{1}$–$\hat{5}$ descent (motive *m*), its immediate retrograde as a $\hat{5}$–$\hat{1}$ ascent (motive *n*), as well as the pattern of the last three notes played by the cello in m. 2 (motive *o*, immediately picked up by the piano in m. 3).[35] These turn out to be especially important in assessing the status of the slow movement as introduction and the return of the first movement's theme before the finale.

Example 2. Cello Sonata op. 102 no. 1/i, Andante

Example 2 continued

Beethoven suppressed the autograph's direction "attacca il seguente" between the scalar A-minor Allegro and the following Adagio (Example 3), which consists of flourishes—a kind of "sprung" version of the Andante's motive *x*—followed by motive *o* (mm. 1–3), after which a brief cello arpeggio-cadenza opens into chord progressions featuring an anguished turn to minor with diminished seventh chords (mm. 3^3–6). When an actual melody breaks out in the cello (m. 7), it has features in common with the first movement: it is marked *teneramente*, concludes with motive *o*, and is then echoed in the piano (m. 8). In the one-measure extension (m. 9), comparable to the one at the end of the first movement's phrase a_2, successive trills replace the successive statements of motive *x* (in the same order: cello, right hand, left hand). A final bit of fantasia or pensive cadenza by the cello expands on motive *o* and ruminates for just a moment on motive *x*, ending with its two repeated notes. This proves to be the correct cue, the right place in memory for the first movement to return in accordance with the association of ideas. The

Example 2 continued

Tempo d'Andante is a solid arrival, a successful recollection, more fully scored than the original, in the light of day.

What we are hearing, then, is a recollection or reminiscence of the opening movement. That movement is in the past: we cannot recollect something from the current movement, because it is still "in the present." Just as we don't consider it "recollection" when we keep in mind the topic of a current conversation, we recognize but do not recollect themes that recur within a movement because of music's temporal unfolding and structural requisites; it is not a question of recovering knowledge we once had. Thus we now hear the process of finding the "right place" so that the images will "fall into place." Of course the Tempo d'Andante, as a figure of memory, is no mere echo of the Andante. It consists of two more variations of a, the first of which (mm. 10–14) resolves all the original dominant extensions with the x motive heard in the tonic over and over, conflating a_1 and a_2 from the final segment of the Andante and removing motive o. The final return to a_1 is but a single incise with trill (mm. 15–16, like the Andante's mm. 16–17), ending with a simultaneous trill on the dominant that paradoxically resolves the successive trills of m. 8–9 that led into the Tempo d'Andante. Indeed, in retrospect the opening movement seems a taste of something whose meaning we don't grasp until we hear it again. The Adagio now appears to be an introduction to the Tempo d'Andante itself, not to the finale.

That finale is part and parcel of the fabric of the first movement and its return, given that it begins with a principal motive (n) of the Andante, the ascending $\hat{5}$–$\hat{1}$ from m. 1, in a sharply pointed yet almost jocular formulation. The triggering images and associations continue to generate a skein of related ideas in a seamless exposition. But their rhythmic evocation of present time offers an idealized version of itself in the development section and coda, in a passage I call a *vision* (Example 4). *Vision* is the Latin equivalent for the Greek *phantasia*, and I apply it to those instances in which the dominant *image* is etherealized, as here (and as we will see, in two movements of op. 101 as well).[36] After the exposition, the cello sets out as fundamental a set of tones as ever illuminated the Rhine gold (m. 75). Over it, the piano has virtually the first imitative texture in the movement, leading to a contrapuntal development that includes a learned-style passage with suspensions; the recapitulation, influenced by this topic, offers the motive in stretto. The vision makes briefly present an absent idyllic *locus amoenus*—the "pleasant place" of pastoral, a topic Beethoven develops more fully in op. 101. This blurred, shimmering vision is like a mirage, and may reflect an absent texture: Beethoven originally intended to make this movement a fugue (Example 5a), a plan

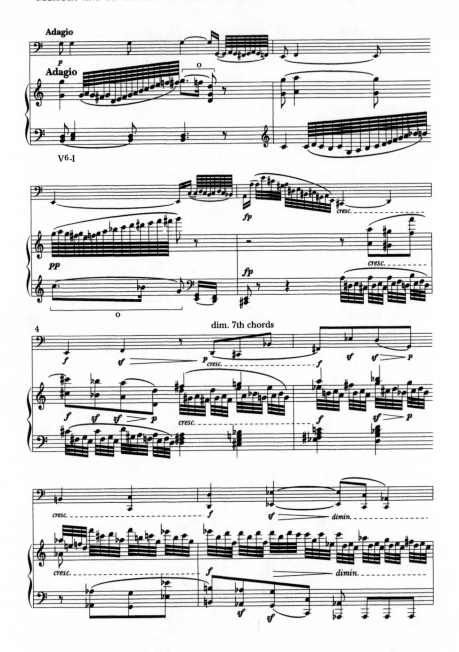

Example 3. Op. 102 no. 1/iii, Adagio-Tempo d'Andante-Allegro.

Example 3 continued

Example 4. Op. 102 no. 1/iv, end of exposition, beginning of development (*vision*), mm. 70–95.

he delayed putting into action until the finale of op. 102 no. 2 and the development section of op. 101's finale. Thus, the vision incorporates an originary impulse, the biography of the work, the source of invention. In a final twist several years later, that fugue subject, transformed, became a Handelian topic in the overture to *Die Weihe des Hauses* of 1822 (Example 5b).

The beginning of the first movement of op. 101 (Example 1, which we now see has op. 102's motive *o* similarly at the end of the first phrase) is recollected in the same place as in op. 102 but the effect is rather different (Example 6). The slow movement, with its elegiac tone and exploration of a single figure, is played *una corda*. Marked *sehnsuchtsvoll*,

Example 5a. Op. 102 no 1, sketch of theme of mvt. iv as a fugue subject (Nottebohm)

Example 5b. *Die Weihe des Hauses*, op. 124, fugue subject, mm. 89–90.

full of longing—the only such marking in the sonatas[37]—it yearns for some future state, becoming ever more harmonically fraught with its descending series of diminished seventh chords, each activated by a brief sustaining pedal, moving to a dominant pedal in A minor. The final chord now dissolves into a cadenza, toward the end of which Beethoven gives the signal to shift the pedal gradually back to *tre corde*. At the height of this emergent tone color, the first movement theme resumes its tentative, fragmentary, and tonally indecisive existence. But now there are gaps. Each phrase is separated by a rest and fermata. After the second phrase it cannot go on, stuttering once and then in a sudden access of enthusiasm racing up the tonic triad, trilling up the scale, much as the Archduke Rudolph's return was greeted at the beginning of the finale of the "Lebewohl" sonata, or as the convalescent feels new strength in the Heiliger Dankgesang movement of the A-minor quartet op. 132. Trills are heraldic signs that welcome present time.

Once again, we hear a recollection or reminiscence of the opening movement after a process of finding the "right place": the lengthy descending diminished passage that lands on an E chord at the same register of the opening,[38] the dissolution of the chord into "clouds of memory," and the yielding of the experientially more remote *una corda* to the enriched tone color of the present. But the rests between phrases and the stuttering demonstrate that although the recollection is in the present—the "absent thing" momentarily with us—this *phantasia* figure, motivated by the association of ideas, has moved on quite literally from one place of invention and memory to another: from the evocation of a pastoral topic, the hallmark of the first movement, to a more assertive, even modern, idiom far from the idyll.

The entire sonata in fact reveals a tension between gentle pastoral and the vigorous rhythms of march and fugue subject. The swaying rhythms and drone bass of the first movement signal its evocation of the pastoral world.[39] This transformation of tone from the opening movement of op. 90 (1814), with its complex and high-minded gestures and echo of the opening chords from the *Egmont* overture, to the "middle style" of pastoral, reminds us that a different sort of memory operates in pastoral compositions: an imaginary memory of an imagined golden age, a sense of nostalgia for the never-was.[40] Opus 101 eschews the classic siciliano rhythm (♩♫) in favor of the trochaic *pastorale* of Corelli's "Christmas" Concerto (♩♪♩♪) and the chorus "Giovani liete, fiori spargete" in Act I of *The Marriage of Figaro*.[41] Some of the elements in what Michael Beckerman calls the "pastoral set" are present—drone bass, harmony in thirds or sixths, and a largely noncontrapuntal style—lending an effect both dreamy and timeless.[42] But because the second and fourth movements of the sonata vehemently disrupt the idyllic pastoral mode, while the third presents sorrowing versions of it, the sonata sits squarely within the pastoral tradition, as the images collected by Simon Schama in his wide-ranging *Landscape and Memory* attest: the late eighteenth and early nineteenth centuries saw representations proliferate of both the idyllic side and the bleak side of nature.[43] Even in the golden age depicted in Virgil's *Eclogues*, the outside world and its suffering must sometimes be confronted.[44] The simplicity of pastoral always carries with it an awareness of or tension with a more complex mode of life; this opposition may also be conceived as one between the imaginary and the real or between nature and art. After all of the idylls as well as self-conscious satires and "anti-pastorals" that flourished during the eighteenth century, at century's end Schiller called for a "modern" pastoral, an idyll whose "character subsists in the complete reconciliation of *all opposition between actuality and the ideal.*"[45]

Written discussions of pastoral music in the late eighteenth century, however, show nothing of the same critiques, recognition of oppositions, nor evidence of idealism, even though pastoral operas had always incorporated some of the oppositions inherent in the genre.[46] When J. F. Reichardt described the musical idyll (or the "musikalische Komposition des Schäfergedichts") in articles of 1777 and 1782, he limited his remarks to the Lied, and argued that the principal characteristic should be gentleness, that everything heavy and vehement should be banished, and that the instrumentation should be limited to flutes, oboes, bassoons, and horns.[47] This seems to accord with the unruffled quality of Salomon Gessner's *Idyllen*, which, when published in 1756, reinvigorated the genre. Heinrich Christoph Koch's dictionary of 1802 reiterated the "tender "character" and "melody of the idealized shepherds' world" of the *pastorale*, slower than the musette and with fewer dotted rhythms than the siciliana.[48]

Example 6. Op. 101/iii–iv.

Example 6 continued

Composers themselves seemed far more aware of the extent of the pastoral mode than did the theorists' limited definitions of it as a musical topic. Beethoven clearly understood the breadth of pastoral, as his "Creatures of Prometheus" ballet, D Major Sonata op. 28 (nicknamed "Pastoral" as early as 1804 or 1805), and *Pastoralsinfonie* attest, including the religious pastoral of Christian Sturm, whose works Beethoven

Geschwinde, doch nicht zu sehr, und mit Entschlossenheit
Allegro

Example 6 continued

owned and annotated.[49] And the Pastoral Symphony was subtitled "Recollections of Country Life," making explicit the absent thing. But only the late works reveal his awareness of the contrast or conflict "between pastoral life and some more complex type of civilization."[50] Even Beethoven's invocation of God in the forest, on a sketchleaf of 1815, implies the arenas in which a more alienated existence obtains: "Almighty in the forest! I am happy, blissful in the forest: . . . In such a woodland scene, on the heights there is calm, calm in which to serve him."[51] And his sketch notation in the last movement of the Missa Solemnis—"pacem pastoralisch"—affirms that the "Prayer for inner and outer peace" will offer pastoral as a palpable alternative to the warlike incursions that peace must overcome.

Pastoral may thus be seen as a "place" both literally and figuratively, a topic of invention that becomes an activator of memory, setting the temporally and spatially "removed" against the active and "modern."[52] It is interesting in this regard that fugue is sometimes the antithesis to pastoral in the late style, despite its being anything but modern; its complexity is the perfect problematic to oppose to the pastoral. One may also hear such contrasts in the Heiliger Dankgesang, whose remote, otherworldly chorale and variations in *stile antico* are offset by the vigorous *stile moderno* sections labeled "Neue Kraft fühlend."[53]

The second movement of op. 101 (Example 7a) sets its vivid, even raucous, ascending march theme over the old descending chromatic-tetrachord bass; modern style is grounded in the past, but without the connotations of lament that this bass line often carries, as in the motive

Beethoven labeled "Lebewohl" in *Les Adieux*.[54] The specifically musical function of the descending bass is to revisit the contrary motion of the first movement theme and forecast the descending pattern of the third movement. But this vivid rhythmic evocation of present time is once again countered by an idealized *vision* in the second section (mm. 32–34, Example 7b), comparable to the finale of op. 102 no. 1. The ethereal effect of this passage derives from several features in combination: the high register, luminous but mysterious flat-six tonality, legato writing, canon, piano dynamics, and especially the pedal, the only time in the movement it is called for. Indeed, in a strange reversal, it seems to make the present virtually, if not absolutely, absent, in setting it at such a distance. Moreover, these measures are the only ones in the movement where the dotted motives resolve upward. Hence the dissolution of this vision in the following measures (making a retransition to the tonic and the character of the March, if not actually a return) requires a decisive pull downward from D♭ to C (marked with a bracket); the pedal is lifted on the first C, as we return to reality (the dominant chord marking that return with its own gravitational pull outside the flat-six).

The Trio (Example 7c) uses this left-hand oscillating figure as its principal idea and the source of canons that cascade from it. Walter Riezler rightly remarks on the Trio's "strangely reflective" character.[55] The source of this quality, I believe, is the return of the pastoral topic, alive within a thicket of overtly Bachian counterpoint, dissonance, and the recall of the March's figure of dissolution, on the same pitches (marked with a bracket in Example 7d), in a passage that makes abundantly clear the motivic relationship between March and Trio (indeed, the 5̂-6̂-5̂ figure appears in the first group of the Finale as well). Perhaps the "pure form" of the contrapuntal-pastoral allusion may be seen most strikingly in the Finale of op. 109—a topically rich set of variations—and especially in var. 4 (Example 8). The intersection of pastoral with non-fugal counterpoint is a fruitful avenue for the expansion of pastoral musical referents culled from earlier music, given the association of both with temporally distant locations, mythical and historical respectively.

Temporal distance in the slow movement, enhanced by the *una corda* pedal and the marking "full of longing," refers similarly to a historical past. The rekindling of Beethoven's interest in Bach and Handel, a well-known trope of his "late-years" persona, enlarges the concept of the kinds of memory operating in the piece: a piece may collect and recollect different historical styles, as a mode of display, a rhetorical formulation based on a specific locus of invention, in this case the past. In fact, the historical past might be viewed as the equivalent of "long-term memory"

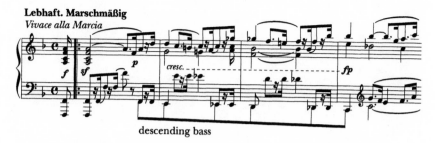

Example 7a. Op. 101/ii, March.

Example 7b. Op. 101/ii, *vision*, mm. 30–34, and trans.

Example 7c. Op. 101/ii, Trio.

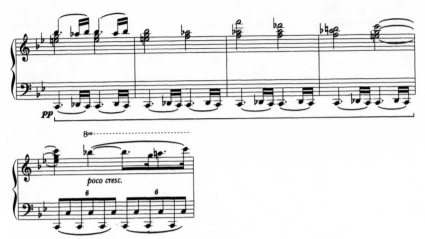

Example 7d. Op. 101/ii, Trio dissolution, mm. 87–90, and trans.

Example 8. Sonata op. 109/iii, var 4.

against which intermovement recalls might be considered "short-term" memory.[56] The fifth Goldberg variation, with its comparable turning figure (Example 9a), offers an example of this.[57] Together with echoes of that ultimate Baroque precursor, these figures may be mediated by more recent music. Two other possible sources for the slow movement are given as Example 9b and 9c; each of these Haydn sonatas, in D major (Hob. XVI:37/iii, 1781, another *attacca* movement) and in C major (Hob. XVI:48/I, 1789, one of only two movements in the Haydn sonatas marked *con espressione*), has an obsessive figure, the one in the latter strikingly similar to that in op. 101. In 1814 or 1815 Beethoven noted in his *Tagebuch* that "Portraits of Handel, Bach, Gluck, Mozart, and Haydn in my room . . . can promote my capacity for endurance."[58]

Another piece of historical memory might be operating in the chain of diminished seventh chords (invoked to a much lesser extent in op. 102 no. 1). The venerable precursors here—and these by no means exhaust the array of pieces in which such chains are to be found—are the end of the recitative in Bach's Chromatic Fantasy and the fantasylike coda of Haydn's F minor piano variations. Beethoven had already explored image-charged versions of these chords, all in pieces that

Example 9a. Bach, Goldberg Variations, var. 25.

Example 9b. Haydn, Sonata in D, Hob. XVI: 37/ii.

Example 9c. Haydn, Sonata in C, Hob. XVI: 48/i, mm. 1–2, 27–29.

invoke melancholy: in the Largo e Mesto slow movement of the Piano Sonata in D, op. 10 no. 3, in his original sketch for the slow movement of the "Lebewohl" sonata, titled "Absence,"[59] and in the labyrinthine portions of *La malinconia*.[60] And the diminished seventh is implicated in the "pathetic accent" described by Rousseau, at work in the Grave of the "Pathétique."[61] But in op. 101 the Bach reference is the strongest (perhaps mediated by the sketch for "Absence") because the chain descends while the principal motive ascends; one has the very strong sense that by literally "sinking," Beethoven is fostering the conditions for reverie.

The Finale of Op. 101 contains one tiny moment of *vision* (mm. 87–88) in the brief second group (Example 10). This passage begins with the dotted version of a turning motive that has just been played in imitative contrary motion in sixteenth notes. Now the dotted motive is imitated in descending registers in mm. 81–87, and finally appears pianissimo, in a higher register, made to shimmer with pedal. Most tellingly, the dotted turn has acquired horn fifths, which had a fairly specific meaning; as Charles Rosen writes, "Horn calls are symbols of memory—or, more exactly, of distance, absence and regret."[62] In *Das Lebewohl*, Beethoven's horn fifths accompanied an emblem of farewell as musico-verbal "utterance," the syllables "Le-be-wohl" written over the first three notes.[63] That landscape of farewell is one of imminent and imagined absence, invoking both time and space. In the op. 101 finale, the horn fifths call up the absent pastoral landscape for a moment of imagined *presence* that slips by almost before it is noticed. The develop-

Example 10. Op. 101/iv, second group with *vision*, mm. 87–88.

ment section spends all of its time in the fugal present, remnants of the idyll banished by the forte octaves.

How different are these pieces from their predecessors, the E-flat Sonata "Quasi una Fantasia" and the Fifth Symphony? The former was Beethoven's first to rearrange and make permeable the movements in a cycle, as befits its designation: an "attacca subito" appears at the end of every movement, and part of the Adagio con espressione returns just before the coda of the sonata-rondo finale in place of a final refrain.[64] The Adagio is not a slow introduction but rather a closed structure (a_V –b—a_1) in A-flat major with three added measures of cadenza/transition, yet its return (a_I only, in E-flat, with a less elaborate cadenza/retransition) toward the end of the Allegro vivace is marked "Tempo I." Of all the compositions listed in Table 1, op. 27 no. 1 has the most literal return of earlier material, moreover a return that is quite unprepared. We may speak of a recall, perhaps, but while the result is formal freedom, a recognition of relationship, and a nod to both the first movement (an Andante rondo with an Allegro second episode) and Mozart's multi-tempo rondos, it is not a revelatory process of recollecting.

With the Fifth Symphony the situation is more complicated, for here Beethoven strove for palpable musical links among all four movements. The return of the Scherzo unprecedentedly transformed into a ghostly echo subsequently collects itself into a run-up to the brilliant finale, thus intensifying the narrative trope of "struggle to triumph" and even rehearsing the sublime turn from darkness and obscurity to blazing light so well known from the opening of Haydn's *Creation*. So powerful was this passage that, even after a lengthy dominant preparation and half-cadence at the end of the development, Beethoven still chose to recall it and echo its burst of energy in the retransition to the recapitulation.[65] Is there a memory trigger at work here? A slight but insistent one, yes, in the thread of a personal voice in this symphony, beginning with the voice of a solitary fantasist—the oboe's poignant intrusion into the recapitulation of the first movement with a cadenza at the first half-cadence with a fermata, leading from the highest note in the chord (g^1).[66] The solo oboe speaks again in the crucial four-note motive during the whispered scherzo's return in the third movement. But the big half-cadence in the finale has the same top note as the half cadence in the first movement, and the recollection of the scherzo that intrudes upon the integrity of the finale begins with the famed four-note motive, calling again on the oboe for one of its presentations. Thus, there is a subtle chain of associations that the half cadence in the finale engenders, from improvisational fantasy, in the first movement, to phantasia, in the last, mediated by the oboe. The music remembers its past as part of a narrative teleology.

Linking the last two movements structurally by a recall of the third during the fourth differs from a longer-range recall, as the works of 1815–1816 demonstrate. And it is in this context that *An die ferne Geliebte* may be considered with its contemporaries, even though its text and succession of strophic variation structures render it not fully comparable to instrumental works. Here all the songs are linked by tonal transitions, as well as transformations of the first song's melodic motives.[67] The lover offers the imagery of beautiful nature to his distant beloved in order to underscore his sense of loss because it is just these hills and trees that separate them. In this work the pastoral is the present, so that exceptional means are called for to render distance musically. As Charles Rosen has eloquently discussed, the singer's inward musing on a single pitch, in the second stanza of song 2, shows him to be "lost in the act of recollection."[68] In the last song, after he sings "Take these songs, then," the final stanza returns to the first song's melody after he imagines his beloved singing his songs back to him, in a kind of echo (or perhaps boomerang) effect. The spatial distance of the beloved is mirrored in the temporal distance between the first and last songs, and the hope that sharing these songs will somehow join the lovers adds the final cyclic touch. (Perhaps because of the afterlife of "Nimm sie hin denn, diese Lieder" as a quotation in several works by Schumann, especially the Fantasy and the Second Symphony finale, and in the first version finale of Brahms's B-major Piano Trio, op. 8, the melody of Beethoven's closing song has more emotional resonance to present-day listeners than does the return of the first song.) But a textually based symmetry in a form already designed to emphasize cyclic resemblance has a different effect from a thematic return between the later movements of an instrumental cycle; the former seems designed to underscore certainty, the latter ambiguity. As a reminiscence, the return of the first song in the last has a specific meaning elicited by the sense and spirit of the text and genre. The thematic returns in the two instrumental works of 1815–1816, on the other hand, activate a *process* of memory, interacting with image, fantasy, and invention in ways that differ tellingly from *An die ferne Geliebte*, their exact contemporary, and from earlier returns, and that resonate with works of the late style.

Beethoven never again triggered explicit memory with intermovement recalls the way he did in these two works, but every subsequent work with an invocation to past time reflects at least in part their dynamic. In the introduction to the finale of the *Hammerklavier* sonata, he used fantasia-style trills and chords to move literally through the places of invention, but the images conjured up were not recollections of earlier movements but rather strange evocations of earlier toccata-based styles, and thus indicators of a recreative historical memory.[69] In the sonata op. 110, the return of the Arioso dolente and fugue are virtually part of the same movement, they exist in the present, so that their cyclic sweep, however close in technique and emotional tone to fantasia, is localized to recurrence rather than recollection. The increasingly triumphant energy of the final fugue emerges as the goal of the sonata, in a way comparable to the Fifth Symphony, whose third movement is also recalled in the fourth; indeed, if the A-flat major fugue cannot end without first cycling back to the Arioso dolente, the Fifth Symphony finale cannot even recapitulate (that is, *start* the ending) without the same power that brought the finale theme to light in the first place.

In the Ninth Symphony finale, the celebrated recalls of the first three movements are elicited by a "rememberer," the agent of memory, who is, uniquely, *inside* the piece: the cellos and basses appear to reject or reconsider the previous movements in their recitative, whose meaning becomes verbal with "Nicht diese Töne."[70] But the rhetorical voice of the rememberer allows an interpretation based on the conjuring up of absent things by means of phantasia. I would argue that the cello/bass recitative voice, like Kleist's speaker who tries to find an idea while speaking, needs to recollect past ideas in order to find the source of a subject that can be *used*. We are hearing the process of invention and investigation going through the "places" of stored mental images. Mary Carruthers similarly describes reminiscence as "an act of interpretation, inference, investigation, and reconstruction."[71] Finally the usable theme is triggered by the Adagio, the quotation most similar to its original presentation and the only one to interact with and influence the rhythm and direction of the bass line. It is this lyrical source from a variation movement that immediately gives way to the foretaste of the Ode itself, a lyrical theme for variations (Example 11). Thus, the terror fanfare's dissonance comes from the sudden shock of being forced to begin before the idea has been born, and the realization that only by searching memory for appropriate images can the idea be found. Czerny's statement that the finale of the Ninth gives a "true picture" of Beethoven's improvising can thus be seen in a new light, and links invention and memory.

Finally, in the process of planning out the relationships among the seven movements of the C-sharp minor quartet, op. 131, Beethoven rejected his original idea of bringing back the theme of the first movement (the fugue subject) right before the finale—the first time such a thing would have occurred since 1816—in favor of presenting a theme

Example 11. Ninth Symphony, iv, mm. 63–80.

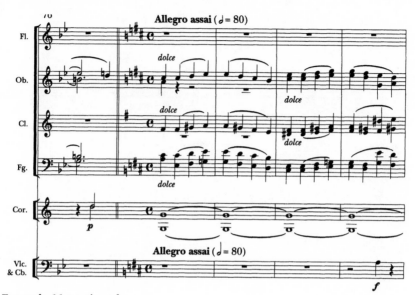

Example 11 continued

within the finale that can be seen as a version of that fugue subject (mm. 22–29, Example 12). His aim here is perhaps what Edward Cone calls "epiphany," the revelation of relationship that in drama is given the Aristotelian term "recognition," with the "recognizer" standing outside the work. [72] It is also possible to see in op. 131 what Daniel L. Schacter calls "implicit memory," which refers to being influenced by a past experience without any awareness that one is actually remembering, because certain cues "prime" the memories.[73] It is perhaps not coincidental that there is a quasi-recitative movement in op. 131, the third, giving way to a set of variations.

In his study of "The Four Introductions in the Ninth Symphony," Lewis Lockwood concluded, "In Beethoven's work, more than for any other composer up to his time, we observe a lifelong consciousness of the creative process itself. . . . [In some works] he seems deliberately to use the process of musical creation *within* the finished work."[74] I have argued that we can also see Beethoven activating the process of recollection by calling on the resources of phantasia, which links invention and memory. These processes, by setting the present against the past, inevitably complicate the often-heard suggestion that Beethoven developed teleological approaches to the multimovement works. The force of recollection impels the music into a new set of relationships both

Example 12. String Quartet op. 131. a. mvt. i; b. mvt. vii, mm. 22–25.

triggered and underscored by dynamics, by declamatory recitative, by trills, by pedals, by cadenzas. Entries in Beethoven's *Tagebuch*, copied from Kant's *Universal History of Nature and Theory of the Heavens* (an early treatise from 1755), suggest that teleological issues were on his mind in 1816. While several of these passages concern Kant's sometimes bizarre speculations about "the inhabitants of other planets"—in particular, his thesis that living beings are both spiritually and materially improved the farther away their planets are from the sun—the first ideas copied by Beethoven concern Kant's ultimate conclusion that the universe has divine purpose, wisdom, and reason behind it; that, in fact, the very order and beauty of the world, which prove they are the result of natural laws, also prove the existence of God:

> When in the state of the world order and beauty shine forth, there is a God. But the other is not less well founded. When this order has been able to flow from universal laws of Nature, so the whole of Nature is inevitably a result of the highest wisdom.[75]

One key to Beethoven's late style, then, is offered by the works that, as it were, swing open its door. By linking invention, which speaks of present and future, with memory, which invokes the past, Beethoven's new, complex teleology moves cyclic works not in a straight line toward a goal, but through a process of finding the right places for revelatory recollections. The thematic recollections in op. 101 and 102 reveal Beethoven "reordering what has been recalled," making present what had been absent, and suggesting that "the whole of Nature is inevitably a result of the highest"—*phantasia*.

NOTES

1. Wilhelm von Lenz, *Beethoven et ses trois styles* (St. Petersburg, 1852; Paris, 1909; reprint New York, 1980), p. 243; anon., *Allgemeine musikalische Zeitung Österreichs* 1 (1817), pp. 65–66, reprint in *Ludwig van Beethoven: Die Werke im Spiegel seiner Zeit: Gesammelte Konzertberichte und Rezensionen bis 1830*, ed. Stefan Kunze (Laaber, 1986), p. 341.

2. Lewis Lockwood, "Beethoven's Unfinished Piano Concerto of 1815: Sources and Problems," in *The Creative World of Beethoven*, ed. Paul Henry Lang (New York, 1970), p. 124.

3. Georg Kinsky and Hans Halm, *Das Werk Beethovens. Thematisch-Bibliographisches Verzeichnis seiner sämtlichen vollendeten Kompositionen* (Munich, 1955), pp. 282–84.

4. Paul Bekker, *Beethoven* (Berlin, 1912), p. 130; Martin Zenck, *Die Bach-Rezeption des späten Beethovens*, Beihefte zum Archiv für Musikwissenschaft 24 (Stuttgart, 1986), p. 152, is one of the more recent purveyors of this idea. It is not surprising that Beethoven dedicated his A-major sonata to Dorothea von Ertmann, a poetic pianist celebrated for her performance of the "Moonlight" sonata and of Bach's music. Johann Friedrich Reichardt commented on a performance of op. 27 no. 2 in Nicolaus Zmeskall's apartment in 1809, that in this "Fantasia by Beethoven . . . a beautiful Streicher piano was made to sound like an entire orchestra." See *Vertraute Briefe, geschrieben auf eine Reise nach Wien, ende 1808 und Anfang 1809*, letter of 7 February 1809 (I, 309) trans. in H. C. Robbins Landon, *Beethoven: A Documentary Study* (London, 1970), p. 195.

5. Charles Rosen, *The Classical Style: Haydn, Mozart, Beethoven* (New York, 1971), p. 403: "in the middle of a paragraph"; Joseph Kerman, "Beethoven," in *New Grove* 2:387: "begins quietly on the dominant as though the movement were already in progress." Richard Kramer frames this somewhat differently, as a "fragment": "Before 1819, examples of truly epigrammatic musical speech—of the spontaneity inherent in *fragment*—are rare. One thinks of the opening of Beethoven's Sonata in A, op. 101, the Bagatelles, op. 119 . . . , and very little else." Kramer, *Distant Cycles: Schubert and the Conceiving of Song* (Chicago, 1994), p. 199.

6. Zenck, *Die Bach-Rezeption*, 177. The third chapter in Part II is titled "Bachsche Form-, Ausdrucks- und Spielcharaktere in op. 101."

7. Robert Hatten, *Musical Meaning in Beethoven* (Bloomington, 1994), pp. 92 and 309 n.2, applies the term "pastoral" to the first movement of op. 101 and broadly to the entire sonata; Zenck also used the term extensively in 1986, associating it with the Bach *Präludienton* of the Preludes in A and E from *The Well-Tempered Clavier*, Books II and I, respectively, and the Prelude to the English Suite in A (Zenck, *Bach-Rezeption*, pp. 153–55).

8. I discuss some of these issues in "After the Heroic Style: *Fantasia* and the 'Characteristic' Sonatas of 1809," *Beethoven Forum* 6 (1997): 67–96. Hatten asserts that Fantasy as a genre is defined by its lack of adherence to sonata-style expectations; *Musical Meaning in Beethoven*, p. 68.

9. Carl Czerny, from "Reminiscences of Beethoven," in *On the Proper Performance of All Beethoven's Works for the Piano*, ed. Paul Badura-Skoda (Vienna, 1970), p. 15. On

Beethoven's improvisation in general, see Helmut Aloysius Löw, *Die Improvisation im Klavierwerk L. van Beethovens* (Ph.D. diss., Saarland; Saarbrücken, 1962).

10. For a convenient summary of the "divisions of rhetoric," see Richard A. Lanham, *A Handlist of Rhetorical Terms*, 2d ed. (Berkeley and Los Angeles, 1991), chap. 2. Among many other lengthy discussions, the best recent books on the subject are Brian Vickers, *In Defence of Rhetoric* (Oxford, 1988) and George A. Kennedy, *A New History of Classical Rhetoric* (Princeton, 1994).

11. Carl Czerny, *A Systematic Introduction to Improvisation on the Pianoforte*, op. 200, trans. and ed. Alice L. Mitchell (New York, 1983), p. 42.

12. "Nur wie vorhin wieder auf dem Clavier in eignen Phantasien—trotz allem Gehör." Maynard Solomon, "Beethoven's Tagebuch," *Beethoven Studies* 3, ed. Alan Tyson (Cambridge, 1982), entry 102, p. 260. My thanks to Ernest Sanders for his advice on translating this sentence.

13. Maynard Solomon translates this to mean that Beethoven is *already* improvising as before: "Just as some time ago [I am] again at the piano in my own improvisations, despite my hearing [deficiency]"; ibid.

14. Thayer, Alexander Wheelock, rev. Elliot Forbes, *Life of Beethoven* (Princeton, 1967), pp. 578, 610.

15. Ries said he was inspired by "specific objects" (Wegeler, Franz Gerhard, and Ferdinand Ries, *Biographische Notizen über Ludwig van Beethoven* (Coblenz, 1838), p. 78; Czerny described what each piece expressed as "some particular and well supported idea or object" and what inspired him as "visions and images, drawn either from reading or created from his own excited imagination" (Czerny, *Complete Theoretical and Practical Pianoforte School*, op. 500, vol. IV, chap. 2, in *On the Proper Performance*, pp. 31, 60). I give a lengthier account of these descriptions in "After the Heroic Style": 78–81.

16. Thayer/Forbes, *Beethoven*, p. 620. Neate was originally to receive the dedication of the op. 102 cello sonatas, which subsequently went to Countess Erdödy; see Kinsky-Halm, *Das Werke Beethoven*, p. 284.

17. I have discussed *phantasia* from this perspective in "After the Heroic Style": 88, and "Pathos and the *Pathétique*: Rhetorical Stance in Beethoven's C-minor Sonata, op. 13," *Beethoven Forum* 3 (1994): 103–105. See also Gregory G. Butler, "The *Fantasia* as Musical Image," *Musical Quarterly* 60 (1974): 602–24. The figure is discussed in Quintilian, *Institutio oratoria*, trans. H. E. Butler, Loeb Classical Library (Cambridge, Mass., 1920), VI.ii.29 and VIII.iii.88. I will maintain the distinction in spelling between *phantasia* as a rhetorical figure and *fantasia* or fantasy in other senses.

18. James Engell, *The Creative Imagination* (Cambridge, Mass., 1981), p. 173.

19. Ibid., p. 175.

20. Samuel Taylor Coleridge, *Biographia literaria* (London, 1906), pp. 159–60.

21. See M. H. Abrams, *The Mirror and the Lamp: Romantic Theory and the Critical Tradition* (New York, 1953), pp. 168–70.

22. Johann Christoph Adelung, *Ueber den Deutschen Styl*, 4th ed. (Berlin, 1800), I, 272. The figures are discussed at length on pp. 272–396.

23. "Anthropology from a Pragmatic Point of View" (1798, Kant's last major work), in *Kants gesammelte Schriften* (Berlin, 1902–), vol. 7 (1917), pp. 167–68, cited by Werner S. Pluhar, ed., Kant's *Critique of Judgment* (Indianapolis, 1987), p. 94 n. 73.

24. Giambattista Vico, *La scienza nuova seconda*, ed. F. Nicolini, par. 819, quoted in James Robert Goetsch, Jr., *Vico's Axioms: the Geometry of the Human World* (New Haven and London, 1995), p. 40.

25. Donald Phillip Verene, *Vico's Science of the Imagination* (Ithaca, N. Y., 1981), p. 104, cited in Goetsch, *Vico's Axioms*, p. 41.

26. Heinrich von Kleist, "Über die allmähliche Verfertigung der Gedanken beim Reden," in *Sämtliche Werke und Briefe* II, p. 319. My thanks to Robert Hymes for pointing out Charles Larmore's citation of this passage in *The Morals of Modernity* (New York, 1996), p. 197.

27. Horace, *Ars poetica*, lines 148–49, quoted by Walter J. Ong, *Orality and Literacy: The Technologizing of the Word* (London and New York, 1982), p. 142.

28. See Mary Carruthers, *The Book of Memory: A Study of Memory in Medieval Culture* (Cambridge, 1990), introduction.

29. On this change, see George Kennedy, *Classical Rhetoric and Its Christian and Secular Tradition from Ancient to Modern Times* (Chapel Hill, 1980), pp. 4–5.

30. Frances A. Yates, *The Art of Memory* (Harmondsworth, Middlesex, 1969), p. 17.

31. Aristotle, *Parva Naturalia*, "On Memory and Recollection," trans. W. S. Hett, Loeb Classical Library 288 (Cambridge, Mass., and London, 1936), 449b–53b (pp. 289–313); as *De Memoria et Reminiscentia*, trans. in Richard Sorabji, *Aristotle on Memory* (Providence, 1972), pp. 47–60.

32. Yates, *The Art of Memory*, p. 33.

33. Carruthers, *The Book of Memory*, p. 20. On Albertus Magnus's idea of reminiscence as "investigation," see Yates, *Art of Memory*, p. 80.

34. L. A. Willoughby, "Wordsworth and Germany," *German Studies Presented to H. G. Fiedler* (Oxford, 1938), pp. 432–58, cited in Elizabeth M. Wilkinson and L. A. Willoughby, Introduction to their translation of Schiller's *On the Aesthetic Education of Man* (Oxford, 1967), p. clxvii. Walter Frisch adduces ideas about memory of c. 1800, as well as later trends in psychology, in "'You Must Remember This': Memory and Structure in Schubert's G-Major String Quartet, D. 887," a paper given at the Annual Meeting of the American Musicological Society, October 1998, together with others by Beate Perry, John Daverio, and John Gingerich in a session on memory and Schubert.

35. See Lewis Lockwood's admirable discussion of these motives in "Beethoven's Emergence from Crisis: the Cello Sonatas of Op. 102 (1815)," *Journal of Musicology* 16 (1998): 308. His system of letter-identification differs slightly from mine.

36. My use of the term thus differs from that of Robert Hatten, who applies it to the brief high register G-major passage mm. 14–15 in the slow movement of the "Hammerklavier": "a vision of grace in the midst of tragic grief" (ibid., 16).

37. Kenneth S. Drake, *The Beethoven Sonatas and the Creative Experience* (Bloomington, 1994), p. 140.

38. William Kinderman makes this point in *Beethoven* (Berkeley and Los Angeles, 1995), p. 196.

39. See my somewhat more extensive discussion of pastoral in "Genre, Gesture, and Meaning in Mozart's 'Prague' Symphony," in *Mozart Studies* 2, ed. Cliff Eisen (Oxford, 1997): 73–84; the following discussion owes something to that account.

40. The association of pastoral and middle style, reasonably secure by the eighteenth century after Boileau's careful placing of it, was by no means a given throughout its history; in the 'Virgilian wheel' attributed to John of Garland, pastoral was the lowest style, with georgic (the scene of the farm) the middle and heroic (the battle) the highest; Alastair Fowler, *Kinds of Literature: An Introduction to the Theory of Genres and Modes* (Cambridge, Mass., 1982), pp. 240–41. Paul Alpers has recently argued that the pastoral is not about a golden age but about "the lives of herdsmen" and the senses of disruption and even tragedy in their lives. See *What is Pastoral?* (Chicago, 1996).

41. Some pieces begin with one pastoral rhythm and then break into another, as for example the "Pifa" in Handel's *Messiah*, which begins in the *pastorale* mode and then introduces siciliano rhythms.

42. Michael Beckerman, "Mozart's Pastoral," *Mozart-Jahrbuch* 1991: 94.

43. See, for example, the moral and spiritual Arcadia attempted by Rousseau's patron Girardin, which reflects the idyllic side of the first movement of op. 101; Friedrich's dispiriting tree in winter shows its bleak side, as in the slow movement. Simon Schama, *Landscape and Memory* (New York, 1995), pp. 544–45 (Girardin) and 195–96 (Friedrich).

44. For a vivid description of the melancholy aspects of these works, see D. M. Rosenberg, *Oaten Reeds and Trumpets: Pastoral and Epic in Virgil, Spenser, and Milton* (Lewisburg, Penna.; London; and Toronto, 1981), pp. 20–35.

45. Friedrich Schiller, *Über naive und sentimentalische Dichtung*, trans. as *Naive and Sentimental Poetry* by Julius A. Elias (New York, 1966), p. 153 (emphasis in original): "Let [the modern poet] undertake the task of idyll so as to display that pastoral innocence even in creatures of civilization and under all the conditions of the most active and vigorous life, of expansive thought, of the subtlest art, the highest social refinement, which, in a word, leads man who cannot go back to Arcady forward to Elysium." See also Lore Metzger, *One Foot in Eden: Modes of Pastoral in Romantic Poetry* (Chapel Hill, 1986).

46. Geoffrey Chew finds that twentieth-century literary theory offers some suggestive ways for framing an approach to the pastoral in music; "Pastoral," in *New Grove Dictionary of Opera*, vol. 3 (London, 1992), p. 910.

47. Johann Friedrich Reichardt, "Ueber die musikalische Komposition des Schäfergedichts," *Deutsches Museum* 2 (1777): 270–88; "Ueber die musikalische Idylle," *Musikalisches Kunstmagazin* 1 (1782): 167–71.

48. Heinrich Christoph Koch, *Musikalisches Lexikon* (Frankfurt am Main, 1802), s.v. "Pastorale."

49. Christoph Christian Sturm (1740–86), *Betrachtungen über die Werke Gottes im Reiche der Natur*, new ed. (Reutlingen, 1811); see Ludwig Nohl, *Beethovens Brevier* (Leipzig, 1870).

50. W. W. Greg's *Pastoral Poetry and Pastoral Drama* (1906), quoted by Bryan Loughrey, *The Pastoral Mode: A Casebook* (London, 1984), p. 20. Loughrey claims that "almost all modern critics have accepted this point."

51. Solomon, "The Quest for Faith," *Beethoven Essays* (Cambridge, Mass., and London, 1988), p. 219.

52. Hatten, *Musical Meaning in Beethoven*, devotes a chapter to the workings of the "pastoral expressive genre" in op. 101. My application of the idea of pastoral in op. 101 as a complex blend of image and locus topics differs from that of Hatten's plot archetype governing the details of a multimovement work.

53. I make this point in "Tradition and Transformation in the Alternating Variations of Haydn and Beethoven," *Acta musicologica* 62 (1990): 180.

54. The descending tetrachord bass appears in its chromatic form in op. 81a/i and in its diatonic form in op. 79/iii, op. 109/i, and op. 132/iii ("Neue Kraft fühlend").

55. Walter Riezler, *Beethoven*, trans. G. D. H. Pidcock (New York, 1972; first ed. 1937), p. 225.

56. On long-term, short-term, and echoic memory, see Jonathan Kramer, *The Time of Music* (New York, 1988), pp. 369, 443 n. 61.

57. Zenck points to this resemblance in *Die Bach Rezeption des späten Beethovens*, p. 163, and to others on pp. 153–85, passim.

58. *Tagebuch*, Entry 43.

59. Gustav Nottebohm, *Zweite Beethoveniana* (Leipzig, 1887), p. 99, printed also in Sisman, "After the Heroic Style": 89.

60. I am at work on a study of the image of melancholy in Beethoven, an expansion of my unpublished paper "Melancholy, the Enlightenment, and C. P. E. Bach," given at the conference "C. P. E. Bach, German Orpheus," Cornell University, February 1999.

61. Sisman, "Pathos and the *Pathétique*": 91, 101.

62. Charles Rosen, *The Romantic Generation* (Cambridge, Mass., 1995), p. 117, in the course of a lyrical description of Schubert's song "Der Lindenbaum," in which Beethoven's *Les Adieux* is also invoked.

63. Discussed in Sisman, "After the Heroic Style": 87–90.

64. On the importance of "attacca" designations to the meaning of *fantasia*, see Paul Mies, ". . . quasi una Fantasia," *Colloquium Amicorum: Joseph Schmidt-Görg zum 70. Geburtstag*, ed. Siegfried Kross and Hans Schmidt (Bonn, 1967), pp. 239–49.

65. James Webster discusses a comparable reuse of third-movement material in the fourth movement of Haydn's Symphony no. 46 in B major (1772), as well as broader issues of musical reminiscence, in *Haydn's "Farewell" Symphony and the Idea of Classical Style: Through-Composition and Cyclic Integration in His Instrumental Music* (Cambridge, 1991), pp. 267–87.

66. Karol Berger classes the oboe cadenza with those "moments of distraction in which the mind of the protagonist wanders off and gets lost in 'another world'"; "Beethoven and the Aesthetic State," *Beethoven Forum* 7 (1999): 23.

67. Christopher Reynolds, "The Representational Impulse in Late Beethoven, I: *An die ferne Geliebte*," *Acta Musicologica* 60 (1988): 43–61; idem, "Liederkreis *An die ferne Geliebte*," in *Beethoven: Interpretationen seiner Werke*, ed. Albrecht Riethmüller, Carl Dahlhaus, and Alexander Ringer (Laaber, 1994), pp. 99–108.

68. Rosen, *Romantic Generation*, p. 169.

69. Rosen calls them "evidence of the gradual creation of a new contrapuntal style" (*Classical Style*, p. 428), while Hatten labels them toccata, prelude-toccata, and invention-toccata, and argues that the final cadenza recalls a similar downward figuration in the first movement (*Musical Meaning in Beethoven*, p. 201). Richard Kramer also asserts that "the process of memory is engaged here, but it extends beyond the piece itself, to genre in some historical sense." See "Between Cavatina and Ouverture: Opus 130 and the Voices of Narrative," *Beethoven Forum* 1 (1992): 165–89.

70. The "rememberer" is an idea of Endel Tulving, *Elements of Episodic Memory* (Oxford, 1983), cited by Daniel L. Schacter, *Searching for Memory: the Brain, the Mind, and the Past* (New York, 1996), p. 161. The cottage industry of studies about the Ninth Symphony finale has been highly productive of late: a relevant selection includes Lewis Lockwood, "The Four 'Introductions' in Beethoven's Ninth Symphony," *Probleme der symphonischen Tradition im 19. Jahrhundert*, ed. Siegfried Kross (Tutzing, 1990), pp. 97–111; James Webster, "The Form of the Finale of Beethoven's Ninth Symphony," *Beethoven Forum* 1 (1992): 25–62; Nicholas Cook, *Beethoven: Symphony No. 9* (Cambridge, 1993); David Benjamin Levy, *Beethoven, The Ninth Symphony* (New York, 1995); Stephen Hinton, "Not *Which* Tones? The Crux of Beethoven's Ninth," *19th-Century Music* 22 (1998): 61–77; Michael Tusa, "*Noch einmal*: Form and Content in the Finale of Beethoven's Ninth Symphony," *Beethoven Forum* 7 (1999): 114–37.

71. Carruthers, *The Book of Memory*, p. 25.

72. Edward T. Cone, "On Syntax: Derivation and Rhetoric," *Music Analysis* 6 (1987): 246. On the theory of recognition, see Terence Cave, *Recognitions: A Study in Poetics* (Oxford, 1988).

73. Schacter, *Searching for Memory*, p. 161.

74. Lockwood, "The Four 'Introductions'," p. 111.

75. *Tagebuch*, entry 105; no. 106 concerns planet-dwellers, no. 108 the universal forces of attraction and repulsion.

Voices and Their Rhythms in the First

Movement of Beethoven's

Piano Sonata Op. 109:

Some Thoughts on the Performance and
Analysis of a Late-Style Work

GLENN STANLEY

Generations of critics and performers have stressed (and sometimes lamented) the technical and musical challenges of Beethoven's keyboard music. The composer often acknowledged that his music was difficult; once, in 1808, he even vowed to write in a simpler style for piano.[1] With few exceptions, however, he made no compromises; indeed he seemed to take pride in seeing his music was so received. While negotiating the publication of the "Hammerklavier" Sonata with Artaria in September 1819, Beethoven reputedly told the publisher: "Now there you have a sonata that will keep the pianists busy when it is played fifty years hence."[2] This terse remark is rich with implication: that his music will survive a half century, and that it will take a long time for this prodigiously difficult work to be played and understood.[3] The Piano Sonata in E Major, op. 109, is considered to be one of the more accessible sonatas among the last five; it is certainly not a pianistic challenge on the order of the "Hammerklavier." For this reason, it is fascinating to discover the complexities concealed in the apparently simple material of the first movement, which I will discuss initially from the perspective of a pianist looking at the score at the piano for the first time.

Beethoven's notation, if literally interpreted, does not always yield optimal results. I shall offer alternative readings and show that the complexity of the musical ideas in op. 109 forced him to abandon original notations that conform to these readings. I am primarily interested in problems concerning melodic line, rhythm, and meter, all of which originate in the initial motive of the first theme and are composed out across the entire movement and work. My thinking about these problems has led me to view the first movement as a dialogue, which begins with a motive exchanged by the hands and is pursued until the very last chord of the coda, which sounds in both hands simultaneously. Thus the movement is "voiced," and it possesses a lyrical quality that, to paraphrase Joseph Kerman, evokes human voices.[4] In my view, this quality, one of the underpinnings of the late style, has not been sufficiently emphasized in recent literature on the movement. However, if we are able to hear voices of this kind, we may understand the many complexities with which Beethoven confronts us as the rhetorical process of a passionate conversation.

First-Theme Motivic Voices

The idea of a dialogue depends on an interpretation of the first theme (Example 1) that associates a distinct voice with each hand. This interpretation is new: most discussions of the movement have emphasized two other kinds of voices—linear-structural and surface-melodic—that are enclosed within the motives but are not fully constituted by them. The right hand plays a series of downbeat sixteenth notes linked to offbeat dotted eighth notes. The sixteenth notes are double-stemmed to indicate quarter notes; this version of the motive has polyphonic

Example 1. Piano Sonata in E Major, op. 109, I, opening

implications, which will be developed in the course of the movement. The left hand simply plays two sixteenth notes. The hands exchange the motivic forms later in the movement.[5]

The linear-structural voices are emphasized in Schenkerian analysis; Schenker himself, Allen Forte, and other writers project a foreground two-voice succession of stepwise parallel tenths descending from $g\sharp^1$ in the upper voice and e in the bass (Example 2).[6] These tenths underlie almost all of the first theme, and there can be no question about their structural importance. But these voices are not strongly articulated, because their structural pitches fall on different parts of the motive, thus

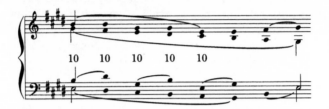

Example 2. Schenkerian reduction of op. 109, I, opening

obscuring a clear descending line. These voices are latent; they do not emerge as "speaking" voices until the development section (see pp. 100–103), where stepwise lines in both hands are spun out on the upstemmed downbeat quarter notes. The surface-melodic voices in the first theme are, on the contrary, clearly projected in the right-hand motives. Donald Francis Tovey[7] and other writers wish to bring out a line stating a sequence of rising thirds and falling fifths on the downbeat quarter notes $g\sharp^1$-b^1-e^1-$g\sharp^1$-$c\sharp^1$ etc. (Example 3a). While a literal reading of the notation supports this interpretation, it does not produce a particularly attractive line; a more elegant one can be constructed from the succession of falling fourths and rising seconds on the off beat dotted eighth notes b^1-$f\sharp^1$-$g\sharp^1$-$d\sharp^1$-e^1-b (Example 3b). This melody has a more interesting mix of intervals and is closely related to other melodies in Beethoven's late music, e.g., the first theme of the Adagio of the Ninth Symphony and the fugue that closes the Sonata in A-flat, op. 110. Moreover, a performance that brings out these fourths at the beginning highlights a melodic interval that receives extensive further develop-

Example 3a. Tovey's reduction of op. 109, I, opening

Example 3b. Alternate reduction of op. 109, I, opening

ment in the movement (see Appendix A, p. 111). But this melody seems to defy the notation, because it emphasizes pitches that are not accented; I will address this question in the discussion of the motivic rhythm.

Neither the structural voices nor the surface ones (in either guise) claim the entire two-note motive. And since the motivic presence is so strong, this seems problematic. Hugo Riemann rejects the very idea of the foreground melodic voice and emphasizes the entire figure: "The double stemming of the first notes in the right hand should not actually bring out the quarters as a melody, but rather primarily emphasize the legatissimo, the grouping of the four pitches of the chord." In his view the motive consists of the entire quarter-note *"Brechung,"* which he illustrates with a notation that stems the notes in the left hand upward to suggest a monophonic line.[8] Riemann's interpretation is shared by numerous commentators, who find in the first theme an improvisatory style based on free figurations outlining harmonies in the tradition of J. S. Bach. A. B. Marx, for example, called the first theme a "Präludium."[9]

I think this comparison is superficial and misleading: Such preludes usually present long, unbroken arpeggiated lines that are distributed between the hands. They are very different from the first theme of op.109, which is built on a short figure—a true motive—shared by two registrally and metrically distinct voices (metrically distinct in the sense that the hands are always an eighth note apart). The motive appears in ascending and descending form; it is subjected to inversional techniques in the development and recapitulation, and in its double-stemmed form possesses a polyphonic richness irreducible to a single voice. The first theme does not consist of figuration; it introduces motivic voices engaged in a dialogue that subsumes the activity of the structural and surface voices (apart from Riemann's one-voice melody, a notion that I find entirely unsupportable) that have been discovered in the motive. In light of this complex situation, we can sympathize with Jürgen Uhde's conclusion that Beethoven "wanted to disguise the line," [10] but we can also view this situation positively: Beethoven wrote a motive with several potentialities—each possessing its own expressive character—and allowed them to emerge in the course of the dialogue.

First-Theme Motivic Rhythms

In the first theme, the rhythm of the upper-voice motive seems straightforward; apart from the double-stemming of the downbeats, it indicates Lombard rhythms (often called Scotch snaps): a short accented pitch on the downbeat precedes a long unaccented one on the offbeat. (For convenience I will refer to this kind of rhythm as trochaic, which in the analysis of poetic meters denotes a pattern of one accented syllable followed by one unaccented syllable, which together comprise a poetic foot. Iambic rhythms reverse the order.[11]) Lombard rhythms have a lively, emphatic, syncopated quality, because they reverse the more customary pattern of longer durations on accented downbeat pitches and shorter ones on unaccented offbeat pitches. When I first looked at this score, I tried to play the motives as they are notated, but they seemed heavy, graceless, almost aggressive, just the opposite of graceful "arabesques" (as Hans von Bülow described them),[12] and contradictory to the dolce and piano markings and the slur marks indicating legato. Moreover, they did not correspond to my memory of performances that I had heard. I next played the motive as an upbeat figure, or an iamb, as if the sixteenth note led to a downbeat dotted eighth note.

This interpretation pleased me and satisfied my memory, but required justification, which I sought in several ways. A survey of recorded performances sheds light on the problems and different kinds of solutions.[13] Because of the quick tempo and the short durations, it was not easy to identify any accentual pattern whatsoever. After repeated hearings I did conclude that the opening rhythms are often played as iambs, but not always (e.g., Artur Schnabel's consistent trochees [EMI: F 667.808/20, 1982, first recorded in 1932]), and I also determined inconsistencies within individual performances. Some pianists play iambs for the motives that state ascending thirds and trochees for the descending fourths: von Bülow even supplies short crescendo and decrescendo marks to ensure this interpretation.[14] Maurizio Pollini (DG: 2530645) plays a regular pattern of iambs in the first phrase except on the second beat of m. 3 and the first beat of m. 4, where he shifts to trochees that emphasize the downbeat quarter-note thirds $f\sharp^1$-$d\sharp^1$ and $g\sharp^1$-e^1 that complete the cadence of the first phrase. It was reassuring that nearly all the pianists I studied sometimes played iambs, but the diversity of interpretations overshadows fundamental consensus. Because my own preference might have prejudiced my perception of the recordings, I played some of them during lectures and seminars on the movement. Often the listeners could not agree about what they had heard in one and the same performance! "Harder" evidence was required.

Beethoven began work on the sonata in the late winter of 1820; relevant sketches for the movement are found on folios 3r–5v and 6v of the sketchbook Grasnick 20b, in which Beethoven worked on the movement in the winter of 1820.[15] After some ideas for the Credo of the *Missa solemnis*, a sketch for piano in F minor (Example 4) contains intervallic content substantially different from the first theme of op. 109. However,

Example 4. Grasnick 20b, fol. 3r. st. 3–4

its texture and rhythms, including the delayed entrances of the hands, are closely related, and the notation indicates an iambic series of six-teenth- and dotted-eighth note pairs (the first eighth note was probably intended to be a sixteenth). Yet just below it on staff 5, the very first sketch (in E major) that can be unequivocally related to op. 109 fixes the rhythm of the finished piece (Example 5).[16] If the F-minor sketch pertains to the sonata, why did Beethoven abandon this notation so quickly?[17]

Example 5. Grasnick 20b, fol. 3r. st. 5–6

The rhythmic and polyphonic nature of the upper-voice motive may provide the answer. The first E-major sketch records Beethoven's attempt to achieve polyphonic motives in both hands and to link the motivic statements with ties. Although the motives of the F-minor sketch are also polyphonic, there are no quarter-note durations. In the first theme, preserving the polyphony with this notation would have required cumbersome beams and ties over bar lines, which would have been very difficult to read, particularly in the quarter-note lines of the development and the coda. (Beethoven did write beams over the bar in the slow movement of the Violin Sonata op. 23, but there he did not have the problem of notating two voices. This consideration might have persuaded him to abandon the two voices in both hands and the ties over quarter notes with which he had experimented in the E-major sketch.) The addition of the quarter note duration apparently motivated the change.[18]

Rhythmic theory provides another perspective on the problem. In his *Erläuterungsausgabe* of op. 109, Heinrich Schenker notes that the "natural relationship" for a succession of alternating sixteenth and dotted eighth notes is iambic. He advises the player to accentuate the sixteenth notes (there are no accents marks in the sketches or finished work), in order to prevent that natural relationship from asserting itself. There is a very suggestive implication in Schenker's remark: The notation is not sufficient to ensure the trochaic rhythm that he advocates.[19] The idea of a natural rhythmic relationship can be tested by applying iambic and trochaic poetic texts to the upper voice of the first theme. (To match the melody, the poems must have four metrical feet per line and two syllables per foot.)

Trochaic: "Beherzigung" (Goethe)	*Ach, was soll der Mensch verlangen,* *Ist es besser, ruhig bleiben?* *Klammernd fest sich anzuhangen?* *Ist es besser sich zu treiben?*
Iambic: "Es hing der Reif" (Klaus Groth)	*Es hing der Reif im Lindenbaum,* *Wodurch das Licht wie Silber floss.* *Ich sah dein Haus, wie hell im Traum* *Ein blitzend Feenschloss.*

The iambic text by Groth fits smoothly (at least for the first six measures, after which the cadential progression changes the number of metrical feet in the music). The trochaic Goethe text is very awkward, because the durational pattern in the music contradicts the sequence of stressed and unstressed syllables in the text. Brahms's beautiful setting of "Es hing der Reif" demonstrates that phrases based on iambic motives can accommodate a poem with this metrical structure and produce a line of "graceful arabesques." [20]

There is substantial evidence in support of an iambic reading of the motive, yet ambiguities remain. One problem arises immediately (others will be mentioned when the entire movement is discussed): If iambs for the upper-voice motives are adopted, should they also be played in the lower voice? This interpretation would result in an unaccented attack on the roots of chords E, C♯, and A, which are the first pitches of the motives in which they appear, and accented attacks on the fifths above. Some pianists play agogic accents on the first sixteenth (e.g., Paul Badura Skoda, Astree As-48, 1980). This interpretation clarifies the harmony and emphasizes the independence of the lower voice (thus supporting dialogue), but it is very mannered and disrupts the smoothness of the motivic exchange and the harmonic progression. The problem lessens when the fifths are replaced by octaves in mm. 3–4, and 7–8, and also at the beginning of the recapitulation, where the lower voice states octaves for the entire first phrase. These octaves permit an iambic performance that ensures harmonic clarity. The recapitulation is particularly interesting, because the upper member of the octave (the accented pitch in an iambic performance) is tied to an eighth note. Here, the increased length of the second note of the motive further reinforces the iambic "natural rhythm," as it is played in most of the performances I surveyed.

The iambic interpretation also enables a pianist to project motivic relationships across the movements. At the beginning of the second movement an upbeat pattern begins after the initial downbeat attack, which is developed in a two-part texture. Although the voices are not linked by a common motive, the correspondences suggest a consciously drawn link. The second variation of the third movement evokes the first theme of the first movement through a close paraphrase (with iambic notation!) of the motive and the play of the voices (Example 6).[21] A trochaic performance at the beginning of the sonata would prevent such relationships from emerging, at the cost of intermovement unity and a teleological process that has been noted in diverse readings of the movement.[22]

Example 6. Op. 109, III, var. 2, mm. 1–4

First-Theme Meter and Phrase Structure

If the voices first enter speaking iambic rhythms, they declaim naturally and gracefully. They banter softly, rather than making emphatic
trochaic declarations. But already in the second (consequent) phrase of
the theme their rhetoric intensifies—they raise their voices, gaining volume, increasing their sonority, and expanding their register. Soon their
rhythms will undergo substantial transformations. As we shall see, they
also lose control of their syntax, which is embodied by harmonic progression and phrase structure. In the first theme these elements also
help establish the initial character of the dialogue, and over the course
of the movement they also change dramatically.

Several authors, including Tovey, find it necessary to admonish
pianists to play the harmonic rhythm of the first theme according to the
notation: namely, a series of iambic quarter-note pairs.[23] I first played
the chord progression this way, but again was disappointed with the
results of a literal reading: root-position tonic and tonic-substitute harmonies are metrically weak, while dominant and passing harmonies fall
on the accented downbeats. This pattern seemed heavy and unnatural,
creating harmonic syncopations that seem out of place in the dolce-
piano context of the first phrase. The music sounded better when I
played the first E-major chord as a "phenomenal" downbeat, as if it were
the first beat of a complete measure and continued the phrase from this
point of departure.[24] This restored the grace and lightness that I missed
in the literal reading.[25] But how can it be justified?

This interpretation "normalizes" the metrical-harmonic structure of
the phrase; it is represented in Example 7 as a reduction and rebarring.
Beethoven's barring has been acknowledged by Schenker[26] and other
writers to be unusual (which might explain the admonitions to play literally). More typical barrings for music closely related to the theme are
found in the quintet from the first act of *The Magic Flute*, and the first
theme of the third movement of Beethoven's own Piano Sonata op. 79

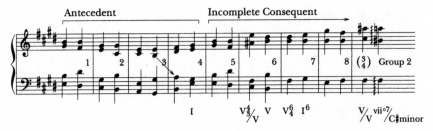

Example 7. Reduction and rebarring of op. 109, I, mm. 1–9

(see Appendix B, p. 113 Example 12b).[27] The relationship is particularly close between the two sonata themes. While the quintet moves to a half cadence on V at the end of the antecedent phrase, the harmonies of the antecedent phrase in the sonata themes are identical: I V^6 : vi iii^6 : IV I^6 : V (V^7 in op. 109) I. The only difference involves the placement of the bar lines.

Appendix B (pp. 113–15) contains a detailed discussion of Beethoven's great indecision about the harmonic structure of the first theme and its barring; here I will summarize the primary stages. The first two sketches for op. 109 that include bar lines place the first chord on the downbeat of a complete 4/4 measure; the progression unfolds metrically as in op. 79. The first sketch continues with an orthodox consequent phrase tonicizing B major on the last beat of the fourth measure. The second one replaces the arrival on dominant harmony with notations that closely anticipate the open-endedness of the final version; a♮^{2} replaces the a♯^{2} representing V/V. Only in the third sketch did Beethoven adjust the barring to make the first chord an upbeat, as it remained in all further sketches. In Appendix B, I argue that problems concerning the metrical placement of the cadence at the end of the antecedent phrase, the rejection of the conventional consequent phrase, and the desire to begin the second group on a downbeat led Beethoven to make the change. The sketches show that he did it at a late stage (and grudgingly, in my view) and provide strong evidence for a "rebarred performance" of the first theme in all its appearances. (See Appendix C, pp. 116–17 for a discussion of the transitions to the development and coda.)

If the antecedent phrase begins on a downbeat, the voices possess a regular syntax that is commensurate with the natural iambic rhythm of the motive they exchange. But just as they begin to lose their initial composure, their syntax breaks down. The consequent phrase fails to end on the expected dominant harmony; indeed it does not end at all, but rather moves without break—and without the conventional tonicization of the new key—into the second group. The process begins in the middle of the consequent phrase, when the harmonic progression "gets stuck" in mm. 6–7. Hitherto the harmonic rhythm had consisted of two chords per measure; B major and E major harmony sound for two beats in m. 6 and m. 7, respectively. The second beats of these harmonies are "extra" or redundant beats that do not advance the progression, but rather disrupt the metrical and phrase-structural regularity of the antecedent phrase. There are four and one-half measures in the consequent phrase; the voices' agitation impairs their ability to speak in well-formed sentences; at times they can only reiterate what they have already said.

After the First Theme: Voices and Their Rhythms and the Process of Dialogue

Second Group (Measures 9–15)

The second group begins by interrupting the first-theme motivic play and the expected cadence on V in m. 9. For this reason the entire group has been characterized as a "parenthetical enclosure," in which the "thematic contrast" interrupts a "continuing progression" of the first theme and delays cadential resolution until the development: "the effect is created of a suspension of time in the parenthetical section, or the enclosure of one time within another."[28] (This sense of interruption is reinforced by the shocking juxtaposition of two accented beats: the last beat of m. 8 [in the "rebarred" interpretation] and the first beat of the second group. This metrical irregularity completes the syntactical breakdown of the first-theme consequent phrase.) It is true that the tonicization of dominant harmony is interrupted by the advent of the second theme. However, B major is established at the beginning of m. 15, hence the succeeding development picks up tonally where the second group leaves off, rather than from the interrupted first group. The idea of one time being suspended within another one seems inapplicable in this context. The events of the second group are so very disruptive, and simply go on so long, that they inhibit any sense of suspended time. Dominant harmony is attained as the result of a process within the second group itself.

Moreover, while the second group undeniably interrupts, it also continues (Example 8): the lower voice waits an eighth note on the first beats of mm. 9 and 10 to respond to the upper voice; the rolled chord in the upper voice on the downbeat of m. 9 spans the octave a♮^{1}-a♮^{2} that follows immediately from (and negates the cadential implications of) the a♯^{1}-a♯^{2} octave in m. 8; the forte dynamic on the rolled chord is the goal of the

Example 8. Op. 109, I, mm. 8–10.

crescendo beginning in m. 4. (On the structural level, the descending tenths between the highest and lowest downbeat pitches in mm. 9–13 outline tenths, thus preserving the linear background of the first group.[29]) Hence the dramatic contrasts that the second group presents are all part of the dialogic process. The slow tempo and the meter change, the chromaticisms and dissonant harmony, the strongly articulated downbeats, and the trochaic sixteenth-note pairs in both voices that hark back to and negate the iambs of the first theme—these all complete the transformation of the dialogue that had begun in the consequent phrase of the first theme.[30]

Now the voices advance ideas more weighty and emphatic than the first-theme motive and increasingly assert their independence: in m. 9 the upper voice attains a^2 on the rolled chord, the lower voice moves more deliberately to its a^1 on stepwise sixteenth notes.[31] In m. 10 the upper voice again leads and the lower one follows, but after the shared pitch-class goal of the previous measure, the lower-voice $g\natural^1$ now challenges the upper-voice $g\sharp^2$. After these entrances, the trochaic stepwise lines that move primarily in contrary motions express increasing conflict. After m. 10 there are no more delayed entrances in the second group. The voices share rhythms for the last quarter of m. 10, but they maintain their independence through extreme rhythmic and textural differentiation in mm. 11 through the first beat and a half of m. 14. The left-hand sonorities in these measures are not mere accompaniment, but rather the assertions of a dissenting voice that must defend itself against the sweep and power of the declamatory arpeggio in the upper voice. The density of the lower voice has rhetorical force and foreshadows the chords spoken by both voices in the climactic mm. 75–85 of the coda.

In mm. 12–14 a sense of independent voices seemingly recedes, because the linear melodies of mm. 9–11 are replaced by arpeggios, scales, and other figurations. However, in m. 12 the upper-voice arpeggio flows from the fast rhythms of the quintuplet and sextuplet in m. 11, while the lower voice's octaves build upon its previous sonorities. And the textural and rhythmic contrasts that mark m. 10 do not diminish. In m. 13 the arpeggio occurs in both hands (Example 9), but even here the voices retain their independence. The first and last pitch of each sixty-fourth-note group in the left hand is a $D\sharp$ (in different octaves) prolonging the first-beat octave $D\sharp$ until the lower register is restored. In the right hand the downbeat $f\mathsf{x}^3$ is similarly prolonged (on the first pitch only, in the descent on the first quarter, and subsequently on the first and last pitches in the ascent).

Moreover, the left-hand $D\sharp$ on the downbeat of the second quarter prevents the upper voice from descending to the $F\mathsf{x}$, its expected goal.

Example 9. Op. 109, I, m. 13

The lower voice interrupts its conversational partner. Yet the upper voice reasserts itself immediately thereafter, and, during the ascending arpeggio, the short exchanges recall the explicit dialogue character of the first theme but with second-group intensity. The stemming of the sixty-fourth-note groups distributes the material between the voices as described.[32] The voices join for a fleeting one and a half beats of parallel motions at the end of m. 14; this is the first of several attempts over the course of the movement to reach conversational agreement through homorhythms. It leads to the B major harmony of m. 15, in which the voices part ways once again, but the establishment of the new stable tonality and the ritardando and diminuendo provide the appropriate dolce context (at the last quarter of m. 15, see Appendix C, p. 116, Example 13a) for them to begin their initial conversation again.

Development (Mm. 15, last quarter–48, first quarter)

Now the voices exchange the first-theme motives: the lower voice leads and the upper follows, stating a new idea, the 7–6 suspensions b^1-$a\sharp^1$ and $c\sharp^1$-$b\sharp^1$ on the first beats of mm. 16 and 17.[33] This reworking of the motivic pitch content transforms the rhythm: the suspended b^1 and $c\sharp^1$ must be played as the accented pitch of the pair. Here the upper voice speaks in trochaic rhythms, which, along with the dissonance in the suspension, imparts an edge to the first theme lacking in its initial statement. This tension is felt in the phrase structure as well: the voices are now unable even to complete their antecedent phrase. The expected close on B major harmony in m. 19 (the fourth measure of the phrase) is neither achieved nor even prepared; instead, a single phrase extends for six measures until the downbeat of m. 21, closing on the dominant of C♯ minor, which had been tonicized in the preceding measures.

The quarter-note melodic lines in this section and in the coda constitute the most substantial composing out and transformation of the motive; their emergence is one of the subtly wonderful features of the movement.[34] The downbeat trochaic rhythm—strongly opposing the iambs of the exposition but related to the second group—and the forward thrust of the long stepwise lines articulate the increased passion of the voices. For, despite their attempt to restore tranquility at the beginning of the development, they have not been able to overcome the "destructive force"[35] of their utterances in the second group. First they engage each other in phrase-long statements comprising four measures: the lower voice again leads (mm. 17, second quarter–m. 21, first quarter) and the upper voice responds (m. 21, second quarter–m. 25, first quarter). The upper voice answers with an urgency embodied by two-measure phrases and a determination to dominate the dialogue that is heard in the three-part sequence of ascending stepwise fourths in these phrases (m. 25, second quarter through m. 31, first quarter). (See Example 10, which includes the beginning of the recapitulation.) Another ascending fourth begins, but now the sequence is broken: the line reaches b² (m. 33) over B⁶₄ harmony (V/E). This arrival forecasts the beginning of the retransition (m. 36), and at this critical juncture in the movement, metrical and phrase structure ambiguity has reached its peak.[36]

The lower voice attempts to stand its ground in several ways. As of m. 24, second quarter, it vehemently repeats octaves; octaves had been part of its vocabulary since the very beginning of the movement, but prolonged reiterations were reserved for moments of increasing intensity (mm. 6–9 in the first theme, and 12–14 in the second group). Now the octaves continue without interruption for almost thirty measures, extending into the recapitulation. Moreover, the voices had always moved together metrically, even when conventional phrases broke down. But in mm. 33–48, the lower voice speaks in insistent harmonic rhythms that oppose the upper voice: three measures of F♯ octaves (mm. 33–35) followed by three measures of B octaves and a three-measure descent from the upper register B octave to the lower octave. These phrase groups not only diverge from the two-measure groupings of the sequence, but also begin on downbeats, creating a conflict with the upper-voice phrases that begin and end on second beats. [37] The upper-voice phrase structure has a momentum that carries over even when the sequence breaks down; it is still a presence in mm. 33–42, although the upper voice no longer states regular phrase groups.[38]

Example 10. Op. 109, I, development, mm. 16–52

Example 10 continued

Here the voices achieve their maximum metrical independence, and the dialogue has turned into an angry debate. The metrical conflicts, the lack of regular groupings in the right hand, the insistent left-hand repetitions of octaves in groups of three measures represent voices losing control of their ability to speak. They come together in dramatic fashion at m. 42, the climax and final stage of the retransition, where both hands state downbeat B octaves.[39] Metrical regularity is restored, but the voices seem to be locked in combat rather than enjoying consensus. The harmonic rhythm of the dominant prolongation in the retransition prepares for the recapitulation to begin on a notated downbeat. Two groups of two-measure dominant prolongation establish this expectation (mm. 42–43 and 44–45), but it is strikingly negated. A third prolongation introduces an "extra beat," the C$\sharp^7$ sonority on the second beat of m. 47 (enclosed in a circle in Example 10), which delays the V$^6_5$/I, pushing it over the bar line onto the notated downbeat. The recapitulation begins a beat "late." After the regularity of the dominant prolongation, this is a jolting change that places two strong beats next to each other, as in the transition from the first to the second group. Orderly syntax breaks down once more.

Recapitulation (Group 1, mm. 48–57; Group 2, mm. 58–65)

The metrical disruption combines with a long crescendo (mm. 42 ff.), extremes of register, and insistent heavily voiced motivic reiterations of dominant harmony to prepare the reappearance of the first theme in a highly transformed state. The upper voice shouts two octaves above its original register, in a forte dynamic and no longer dolce; the lower voice, an octave below its position in the exposition, still proclaims the emphatic octaves of the development. These reworkings imbue the theme with a power that contrasts starkly with statements in both the exposition and the development, but which appears as the inevitable consequence of the turbulence of the latter part of the development. Only at the beginning of the consequent phrase (m. 52) do the voices calm down, when the original registers and intervallic content and the piano dynamic are restored. But they quickly lose their composure, as the upper voice reascends and the lower voice reverts to octaves (mm. 54 ff.), and they again fail to complete a regular consequent phrase.[40]

The second group conforms closely to the exposition, but it is expanded and further dramatized by the unexpected C-major and G-major harmonies (in the F♯ minor context) that are introduced when the voices move in arpeggios (mm. 61 and 62). These foreign harmonies further strengthen the declamatory force of the arpeggios, which were already the climactic expressions of the second group in the exposition. From this highest point of rhetorical intensity in the movement, the voices slowly recover, needing more time in parallel motion (mm. 63–64) than in the exposition to restore their tranquility. The arrival of stable tonic harmony in m. 65 (see Appendix C, p. 116, Example 13b), which is equivalent to the B major of m. 15, does not signal a triumphant overcoming (upper register, prepared by a crescendo) of second group conflict as in the exposition, but rather a reflective relinquishing of the will to fight. The voices seem to pause and meditate, as the upper voice arpeggio in m. 65 suspends time and the lower voice simply rests, until they find themselves and each other in the first-theme material of the coda.

Coda (Mm. 65–99)

The coda begins more like a codetta than the relatively expansive coda (with respect to the overall proportions of the movement) that it becomes.[41] The voices reminisce over closing ideas with the utmost regularity, stating two groups of paired two-measure phrases (mm. 65, last quarter–m. 73), in which the second phrase of each group is a varied inversion of the first one and the voices exchange the motive and a quarter-note line. The voices speak in tranquil subdominant harmony at the beginning and the upper register etherealizes them. All the phrases close V-I, with the tonic harmony on a notated (= metrically weak) downbeat. A third group, beginning in m. 73, fails to attain I (see Example 11, which begins on the second part of the second group), where it is expected on the downbeat of m. 75. This beat is occupied by a quarter rest, followed by the first two chords of the previous progression separated by quarter rests and then moving to vii°7 of C♯ minor, which is tonicized without delay. (C♯ minor is the primary disrupting harmony in the movement; previously it has been present when the first-theme consequent phrase in the exposition and development breaks down and as the "extra beat" in the retransition.) At this point, a quarter note has been "lost" and all sense of metrical regularity and harmonic closure is gone. Once again the voices have failed in their quest for consensus and therefore cannot close.

The melodic contours of the phrase in mm. 78–86, second quarter recall the stepwise quarter-note lines of the development (mm. 17 ff.), while its slower rhythms and thicker textures are related to the second group. Regular two-measure groupings begin at the second beat of m. 81, but the disruptions following m. 75 still have not been completely overcome. The harmonies prepare a tonic chord on the second beat of m. 85, but a suspension delays the resolution until the first beat of m. 86. Thus the "lost" quarter is regained in a way that places tonic harmony in root position on a notated downbeat for the first time in the movement. With respect to the dialogue, the music of this phrase presents a paradox: the voices recall the conflicts of the second group but speak in one homophonic voice, suggesting that they have resolved their differences. To do so, they must interrupt themselves: after failing to reach the tonic cadence on the first-group material in mm. 73–74, they resort to second-group textures with first-theme developmental lines, but resolve the cadence on the first-group motivic material of m. 86.[42] The integration of material from both groups harks back to the conflicts of the exposition and recapitulation and, at the moment of cadence, overcomes them. (The descending tenths in mm. 79–82 reconfirm this structural linear relationship between the groups.)

The notated downbeat tonic harmony in m. 86 may be understood as the notational clarification of the meter—Beethoven's last word on the subject. It is not: After two regular two-measure groups and a series of one-measure groups on the suspension figure in the upper voice (trochaic emphasis!), we expect a notated downbeat tonic chord in the final measure. But the intervening quarter rest shifts it to a notated weak beat that is heard as unaccented; the metrical openness of the conclusion

Example 11. Op. 109, I, coda, mm. 71–end

complements the weakened sense of harmonic closure produced by the upper-voice b in the final sonority.[43] The last motivic statement by the lower voice (m. 97, last sixteenth) also implies a shift: the $g\sharp^1$-b^1 motive opened the movement as the first motive of an exchange on the down-beat of the first quarter. The rhythmic and metrical questions posed at the beginning of the movement are raised once more at its (non)conclu-sion. Hence measures 86–99 can be heard as a final remembrance; the voices are free to resume their motivic play, because they have achieved a consensus. But the sense of resolution is undermined by the metrical and melodic openness of the final measures and the brusque intrusion of the second movement.

Human Voices?

Beethoven originally called the theme of the third movement "Gesang mit innigster Empfindung;" in the first edition, the autograph "Gesang" was changed to "Gesangvoll." The implications of the change—from the designation of a specific genre to a quality—have been found significant; [44] but this significance pales in light of the com-mon root "song," the emphasis on "Empfindung," and most important, of the music itself—the style and structure of the hymnlike theme and first-variation aria. Only a handful of Beethoven's instrumental move-ments bear explicit vocal genre designations: the Cavatina in the String Quartet op. 130, the "Heiliger Dankgesang" of the String Quartet, op. 132, and the Recitativo and Arioso dolente of the Piano Sonata, op. 110; but it is common knowledge that the wide variety of styles recognized as vocal are not confined to these movements. Among the late works, Kerman compares the Adagio of the Ninth Symphony and the second movement of the String Quartet, op. 127 to cavatinas, and he locates recitatives in the String Quartets, opp. 131, 132, and 135.[45] The earlier music is replete with vocal styles as well; within the piano sonatas alone, the dirgelike slow movement of op. 10, no. 2, and the first movement of the "Moonlight" Sonata, which draws on chant and diverse styles associ-ated with laments,[46] provide two compelling examples of vocal idioms transferred to the keyboard. And the examples are not confined to slow movements, as the concluding Rondo of the "Waldstein" Sonata in C, op. 53, eloquently attests.

How does the presence of a movement that evokes a human voice—with or lacking a generic title—impinge on the meaning of its neigh-bors? The recitative and lament in op. 110 are followed by a fugue. In oratorios and other liturgical genres, fugues often express the sentiments of the group. In op. 110 we experience the overcoming of this voice's iso-lation, its finding respite and salvation in the reestablishment of the social relationships that the commingling of voices portrays and, in the coda, celebrates.[47] Song is established in the first movement, whose first theme is as *liedhaft* as any Beethoven composed. And the idea of friendship at the beginning of the piece—the first movement is to be played "con ama-bilità"—already hints at the social meaning of its concluding sections.

Not all cases are so clear-cut, and we must not always insist on this kind of unity.[48] But we should not overlook its presence. Several critics have viewed the first two movements of op. 109 as moving toward the goal of the last-movement song. Jürgen Uhde calls the third movement the "heart of the sonata." It "concentrates the energy" of the previous move-ments and "grows" from their "plenitude of musical ideas."[49] Uhde hears intimations of song in the first movement. Other writers have discerned specific vocal idioms: Wilhelm von Lenz describes the second group as a recitative; it is the center of gravity of the movement; its "yearning" char-acter is taken up and intensified by the second movement and resolved in the third.[50] For Wilfred Mellers, the "second subject recalls Bach's arioso style."[51] Neither Lenz nor Mellers specifies which ideas of the sec-ond group he has in mind, but the stepwise lines of the first section (mm. 9–11) certainly suggest vocal idioms. The arpeggios and scales that follow are less clearly vocal; indeed they have often been viewed as intrinsically pianistic and improvisational. But Beethoven incorporated such material in vocal music with a strong rhetoric; in the course of their arias both Leonore and Florestan resort to these ideas when they express the increasing intensity of their feelings in this way. Beethoven himself con-ceived of the second group as a "Fantasie"; he used this verbal notation in the first continuity draft in Grasnick 20b.[52] C. P. E. Bach, the eigh-teenth-century master of this genre who was revered by Beethoven, emphasized its highly personal nature and its rhetorical character: in the fantasy, "the keyboard player (more than anyone else) can practice the *declamatory style* [emphasis added], and move . . . from one affect to another."[53] Beethoven owned a copy of the *Essay on the True Art of Playing Keyboard Instruments*, in which this description appeared.

The first theme has also been characterized as improvisational, but as I have already argued, this view overlooks the complex nature of the motivic material and its distribution between the hands and voices. I have shown in the discussion of text underlay that a good song melody can be composed on this kind of motivic material. The lyrical quality of the first theme has been recognized: Czerny wants it to be played "very legato and singing"[54]; Reinicke hears both the second group and the development, where the quarter note lines implicit in the first-theme motive emerge, as "songlike." Although he does not characterize it in terms of song, Lenz hears in the first theme a "pleasant play" of voices that introduces the serious second group.[55]

The natural home for voices at play is *opera buffa*; in dialogue recitative and in duet, voices exchange motives as they engage in the banter that is the stuff of comedy. Ascending motives, often thirds or fourths, ask questions, descending motives respond. Octave leaps in *opera buffa* and *seria* make emotionally charged declamatory statements. The voices at the beginning of op. 109 speak in this vein. Their use in the sonata does not constitute a literal modeling: in the opera such exchanges are very brief; they are not spun out to make phrases of four and more measures as in the sonata. Nor do they take place within a single beat on the same harmony. Moreover, operatic motives often contain more than two pitches in order to accommodate the number of syllables required for a complete thought, although quick questions and answers, especially at the conclusion of a conversation, often require only two pitches with cadential functions. (Rossini's operas, which much to Beethoven's chagrin were the rage of Vienna circa 1820, represent a *locus classicus* for such techniques at this time.) Nonetheless, the first-theme voices in op. 109 possess a buffa spirit whose essence is distilled into the pianistic style of the genre through which they speak.

Writers on the aesthetic properties of the sonata in the Classic and early Romantic periods emphasized its unrivaled ability to capture the essence of speech. "In a sonata," wrote J. A. P. Schulz, "the composer might want to express through the music a monologue marked by sadness, misery, pain, or of tenderness, pleasure and joy; using a more animated kind of music, he might want to depict a passionate conversation between similar or complementary characters; or he might wish to depict emotions that are impassioned, stormy, or contrasting, or ones that are light, delicate, flowing, and delightful."[56] Schulz wrote almost a half century before the appearance of op. 109 and op. 110, but rarely are his attributions as clearly realized as in these works, which demonstrate that the speech analogy for the sonata and other instrumental genres was not always mere metaphor. Less than a decade after the publication of these sonatas, Mendelssohn brought out his first *Lieder ohne Wörter* (op. 19b, 1829–1830). The new generic name, however poetic and appropriate, should not conceal that the underlying idea was anything but new. Sonatas also sing without words. Voices can be heard in the first movement of op. 109; their complex motivic and rhythmic life expresses the revolutions of their feelings.

Coda Quasi una Fantasia Biografica

If we hear human voices in op. 109, we may ask if we hear specific ones. As we know, Schumann wrote himself into the piano part of some of his songs. The piano was the composer's voice. Can we hear Beethoven's voice in op. 109? And to whom is he speaking? The composer dedicated the sonata to Maximiliane Brentano, the daughter of Franz and Antonie, the probable "Immortal Beloved" of 1812. The family lived in Frankfurt; Beethoven had met them during a long stay in Vienna. He informed Maximiliane of the dedication in a letter of December 6, 1821.[57] It appears that Franz, who had recently advanced the composer money, was surprised and somewhat annoyed about the dedication. In an assuaging letter of December 20, Beethoven assured him that the dedication was not a form of payment or thank you for the loan, but rather an expression of the warm sentiments he held for the entire family. [58] (He had expressed similar sentiments in the letter to Maximiliane.) A dedication to Antonie was unthinkable; but the mother (to whom Beethoven several years earlier had sent highly personal news about his struggle for custodianship of his nephew Karl[59]), reflecting on the meaning of "Gesangvoll, mit innigster Empfindung," could have drawn her own conclusions. It is generally agreed that the composition of the song cycle, *An die ferne Geliebte*, op. 98 (1815), was a vehicle through which Beethoven worked through his loss of the "Immortal Beloved."[60] Was op. 109 a further coming to terms? The hypothesis must remain conjecture. But we can recognize in the first two movements a narrative course that conforms to personal history—engagement and the disaster of separation. And the last movement embodies the only kind of reconciliation Beethoven could hope for—deep feeling that sublimates passion.

APPENDIX A

Melodic Fourths

A performance that brings out the line b^1-$f\sharp^1$-$g\sharp^1$-$d\sharp^1$-e^1-b at the beginning highlights the interval of a fourth. Even if the motive is not played as an iamb, these pitches, which fall on the dotted-eighth notes, have a stronger melodic presence than the downbeat quarters. They sound for their full three-sixteenth duration before the next pitch in their register. The downbeat quarters last only one sixteenth note before each new attack. The interval of the fourth receives extensive elaboration in the movement:

m. 14, both voices: descending fourths framing the triplet figure in sequence

mm. 15–21, lower voice: ascending fourths (and seconds) as inversion of right hand m. 1ff.

mm. 25–33, upper voice: ascending stepwise fourths in sequence

mm. 48–52, lower voice: two descending fourths=octave

mm. 67–72, lower voice, upper voice: alternating descending and ascending stepwise fourths.

The stepwise fourths are prepared linearly, but not rhythmically, by the bass descent in the first phrase of the first theme, which descends an octave bisected by two fourths, the second of which skips over the penultimate F♯. (An octave bass descent divided into two complete linear fourths begins the second movement; this is another example of ideas projected over movements.) The downbeat is introduced in the right hand at the cadence in mm. 3–4. These foreshadowings illustrate how the structural and surface voices are mutually dependent: the structural voice can emerge in the development only because it assumes the rhythmic properties of the foreground melodic voice; the melodic voice achieves its greatest prominence when it takes over the line of the structural one.

Example 12a: Rebarring and reduction of op. 109, I, mm. 1–9

Example 12b: Op. 79, I, mm. 1–8

Example 12c: Reduction of Grasnick 20b, fol. 3r, st. 10/11–12

Example 12d: Reduction of Grasnick 20b, fol. 3r, st. 13–14

Example 12e: Reduction of Grasnick 20b, fol. 4r, st. 4–5

Example 12f: Reduction of op. 109, I, mm. 1–9, Beethoven's barring, r.h. only

APPENDIX B

The Barring of the First Theme and the
Beginning of the Second Group

The first two sketches for op. 109 that include bar lines place the first chord
on the notated downbeat of a complete measure. (Both these sketches are continuity drafts including work on the second group and beyond.) The first theme is
sketched on folio 3r, st. 10/11–12 and folio 3r, st. 13–14 respectively. [61] They begin
in 4/4 meter (see the reductions in Example 12c and 12d) instead of the final 2/4,
but this does not affect the basic question of the placement of the first accented
harmony. If each of their 4/4 measures were divided into two 2/4 measures, the
harmonic progression and barring of the first phrase would be identical with op.
79 and rebarred op. 109. The first sketch continues with an orthodox consequent
phrase tonicizing B major. It is followed by several measures of work implying a
modulation to C♯ minor, the key of the beginning of the second group, but lacking
the meter change and bearing little relationship to it otherwise.[62] The consequent
phrase is comparable to op. 79 in that it tonicizes dominant harmony, but it takes
longer to do so, and arrives on B on a weak beat (fourth quarter of m. 4), while
op. 79 establishes V on the downbeat of its m. 8.[63]

The second sketch begins like the first, but it also reveals even more
concerning Beethoven's uncertainty about how to continue: the second measure
now contains only three beats, and it is followed by a two-beat measure that
contains the conclusion of the antecedent phrase and the beginning of the
consequent one. The bar line concluding the two-beat measure is the last one
Beethoven wrote in the first theme, but the new metrical pattern is evident: six
quarter notes precede a 3/4 sign that marks the beginning of the second group;
these quarter notes clearly fall into three 2/4 measures. In this sketch, the tonic
conclusion of the first phrase is shifted to a notated downbeat (m. 3), and the
tonicization of V at the end of the consequent phrase is replaced by the shift
from a♯² to a♮². This crucial change directly anticipates mm. 8–9 of the final version. Despite the departures from the regular phrasing of the previous sketch,
Beethoven retains a notated downbeat for the beginning of the first phrase.

A third sketch (folio 4r st. 4–5/6, reduction in Example 12e) contains a
decisive change: the initial tonic harmony is now notated as an upbeat to a 4/4
measure, and the tonic conclusion to the first phrase now falls on the third beat,
which in the 2/4 meter of the final version is a notated downbeat. Beethoven's
indecision about meter continues: a 3/4 measure is again present, now in the
middle of the second phrase, and bar lines are again omitted for considerable
portions of the sketch, which also moves into the second group. All future
sketches of the first theme retain this barring.

What could have motivated Beethoven to notate the first tonic harmony as an upbeat? Schenker explains it by arguing that this solution allows the cadential tonic chord in m. 4 to fall on a strong beat.[64] But his reasoning begs a question: Why is the strength of the cadence more important than the strength of the first tonic articulation? There is no a priori reason to favor the former; indeed it may be argued that a metrically strong cadence on the tonic would be inappropriate so early in the movement. Nicholas Marston shares Schenker's views about the metrical strength of the first cadence, but he also recognizes the importance of the sketch Example 12d, in which he interprets the bar line after only three beats in m. 2 as Beethoven's attempt to ensure the strong metrical placement of the cadential tonic chord *and* preserve a strong initial tonic chord by retaining E major on the downbeat.[65] This is a more subtle view, in that it acknowledges the "correctness" of notating the initial tonic harmony as the downbeat. But this attempt—apart from the infelicity of introducing a 3/4 measure in the middle of a phrase—displaces the tonic harmony of the beginning of the second phrase that begins as an orthodox consequent phrase. Because tonic harmony falls on a notated upbeat at the beginning of the consequent phrase in the sketch, this barring disrupts the symmetry with respect to the first phrase, which Beethoven surely wanted to preserve at the beginning—if only as the basis for its negation at the end of the consequent phrase.

Although there is no sketch that unequivocally supports my view, I feel that the change in barring resulted from three compositional decisions: the elimination of a true consequent second phrase in the first theme and asymmetrical structure (4 1/2 measures), the avoidance of a 3/4 measure in the middle of the first group, and the placement of the first attack of the second group (presented by the $a\natural^2$ in the rebarred Example 12a, and the sketches 12d and 12e) on a notated downbeat. If Beethoven had worked further with the barring and phrase structure of sketch 12b, the substitution of $a\natural^2$ for b^2 on the last quarter of m. 4 (representing the beginning of the second group) would have occurred at the end of a measure and thus deprived it of the harmonic weight that it receives in the final version.[66] In sketch 12d, the $a\natural^2$ after the 3/4 sign is the first of six quarter notes before a bar line. It is clearly intended to be the first quarter of a 3/4 measure. Although there is no 3/4 sign in sketch 12e, the rhythms following the $a\natural^2$ are clearly suggestive of triple meter. If the three-beat measures in these sketches are converted to 4/4 measures, $a\natural^2$ falls on the fourth beat of 12d, because the consequent phrase contains seven quarters, and the second beat of an incomplete measure in 12e, which contains six quarters. The second phrase of the final version contains nine quarter notes; assuming a uniform two beats per bar (after the opening notated upbeat) in the first theme, if one counts backward from the notated downbeat a^2 at the beginning of the second group, the first quarter must come before the first bar line. This also holds for the recapitulation.[67]

Why should Beethoven favor an unequivocal downbeat notation for the beginning of the second group? Several reasons may be brought forth. It is more usual to introduce a meter change at the beginning of a measure and it helps to dramatize the shift; changing the meter in the middle of a measure would obscure and thereby deemphasize it. Moreover, the first sonority of the second group is heard as an arrival, the conclusion of a process beginning in mm. 5–8 that includes a crescendo and a move into the upper register of the right hand. The sonority itself is far more emphatic than the opening chord of the sonata: it is much thicker in both hands, the dynamic is forte, and the registral space spanning the chord has expanded substantially. Finally, if, despite the barring in the finished version, the first attack is played as the strong beat, this would produce a very dramatic juxtaposition of adjacent strong beats: the V/V harmony on the second beat of m. 8 is strong, only to be followed by a still stronger viiº⁷/C# chord that decisively negates the tonicizing implications of the previous harmony. Alfred Brendel plays the passage in this way.

The compositional process and the phrase structure of the two primary groups expose the problems Beethoven grappled with and support an interpretation that seems to contradict his notation. But there are problems and ambiguities that defy easy solution. For example, it has been pointed out that my metrical analysis and rebarring of the first theme places the cadential B $^6_4$ chord in m. 8 of the reduction on the weak beat of the measure, where it is not usually found. It is a good point; it could be explained by arguing that a "metrical modulation" takes place in the phrase at the tonicization of B in m. 6 of the reduction. Here B harmony gains strength in the middle of the phrase. This of course deprives the F-sharp harmony in m. 8 of its strength, unless we allow for another metrical shift as in m. 6. However one views the phrase-structure of the first theme, the consequent phrase contains substantial metrical and phrase-structural conflict, which Beethoven builds into the movement as an essential element of the dynamics of the dialogue.

APPENDIX C

The Transitions to the Development and to the Coda

The transitions to the development and coda help clarify the "phenomenal downbeat" beginning of the first-theme material that appears at these points in the form. [68] The last measure of the second group (m. 15, Example 13a) contains six beats. The first three conform to the group's prevailing 3/4 meter and

Example 13a: Op. 109, I, m. 15

the regular pattern of stressed and nonstressed eighth notes, after which the rhythmic shift to right-hand sixteenth notes establishes a pair of quarters. (I have added a quarter rest in parentheses under the a#¹ that clarifies the beats.) The first one can be heard as a clearly strong downbeat of a 2/4 measure, even though Beethoven writes the 2/4 sign only after these quarters. In this interpretation, the return of the motive falls on a phenomenal downbeat, a reading that is reinforced by the ascending B-major scale resolving to its upper octave over V-I harmonies, thus prolonging the metrically strong B harmony that had begun the measure as a notated downbeat.

The beginning of the coda (m. 65, Example 13b) is similar, but slightly more complex. Three beats of sextuplets continue the straightforward 3/4 meter of

Example 13b: Op. 109, I, mm. 64–65

the second group; they are followed by a quintuplet figure that comprises the first eighth note of an expected quarter note. But the quarter does not receive its concluding eighth; instead the figure leads to a complete quarter consisting of two eighth notes before the meter change. The quintuplet provides one of the most evocative moments in the movement; the meter seems suspended and with it the entire arpeggiated figure, thus completing (by remaining incomplete!), a process of etherealization that begins with the diminuendo in m. 64.[69]

Although these eighth notes continue the E major prolongation that began on the first beat of the measure, the change in the figuration rhythms allows us to hear them as part of a group that includes the two eighth notes after the 2/4 sign. They lead to these eighths by inverting the previous ascent and relaxing by descent into the first eighth note (b2) after the meter change. The ritardando further reinforces the sense of a discrete grouping, setting it apart from both the fast figurations of the first 3 1/2 beats and the return of the first-group motive at the Tempo I. They can be played effectively as a complete 2/4 measure prolonging E major as V/A, the harmony that begins the coda. In this interpretation the first A chord can be heard as an accented beat. In this context, let us note that, in the first sketch of the coda (folio 3r, st. 15–3v, st. 1), Beethoven barred the first-theme material so that the first chord is a notated downbeat of a complete measure.

NOTES

1. In a sketchbook of 1805 (Mendelssohn 15, p. 291), Beethoven wrote "Finale ever simpler—all the piano music too—God knows why my piano music still makes the poorest impression on me, especially when it is badly played." See Gustav Nottebohm, *Zweite Beethovenia* (Leipzig, 1887), p. 446; Nottebohm guesses that the citation was made in 1804, but for the chronology of the sketchbook, see Douglas Johnson, Alan Tyson, and Robert Winter, *The Beethoven Sketchbooks: History, Reconstruction, Inventory* (Oxford, 1985), p. 150. Beethoven made his remark on a leaf containing work on the beginning of the second act of *Leonore*.

2. Cf. Wilhelm von Lenz, *Beethoven. Eine Kunst-Studie*, vol. 5 (Hamburg, 1860), p. 32. Cited in Maynard Solomon, *Beethoven*, 2d rev. ed. (New York, 1998), p. 392. For further discussion of Beethoven's views on the difficulty of his piano music see my "Genre Aesthetics and Function: Beethoven's Piano Sonatas in Their Cultural Context," *Beethoven Forum* 6 (1997): 13–15.

3. Beethoven was overly pessimistic. A publication announcement of September 15, 1819 in the *Wiener Zeitung* described the sonata as the product of Beethoven's "richest and greatest fantasy," which inaugurates a new period in his piano music. Liszt played it in Paris in 1836, and Berlioz wrote an "ecstatic" review of the performance and the work. And it came to be considered the sonata of sonatas by many critics. On the other hand, the sonata was not often published; the second edition by Artaria did not appear until 1856, and it was not one of the more frequently performed sonatas in the nineteenth century.

See William S. Newman, *The Sonata in the Classic Era* (New York, 1972), pp. 50–53 and *The Sonata Since Beethoven* (New York, 1972), pp. 12–13, and Georg Kinsky and Hans Halm, *Das Werk Beethovens. Thematisch-Bibliographisches Verzeichnis seiner sämtlichen vollendeten Kompositionen* (Munich, 1955), pp. 295–96.

4. Joseph Kerman, *The Beethoven Quartets* (New York, 1979), pp. 191–222 (in his discussion of "Voice," in the late quartets). See also his recent *Concerto Conversations* (Cambridge, Mass., 1999), in which dialogue character is advanced as a basis for the entire genre and voices are personified in many suggestive ways.

5. The left hand states the polyphonic form in mm. 15, last quarter, through m. 21 of the development, mm. 52–54 of the recapitulation, and mm. 67–69 and 71–73 of the coda.

6. See Heinrich Schenker, *Die letzten Sonaten. Sonate E Dur Op. 109. Erläuterungsausgabe*, (Vienna, 1971), p. 3; Allen Forte, *The Compositional Matrix* (New York, 1961), p. 30; .and Nicholas Marston, *Beethoven's Piano Sonata in E, Op. 109* (Oxford, 1995), p. 51.

7. Donald Francis Tovey, *A Companion to Beethoven's Pianoforte Sonatas* (London, 1931), p. 257.

8. Hugo Riemann, *L. van Beethovens sämtliche Klavier-Solosonaten. Ästhetische und formal-technische Analyse mit historischen Notizen*, vol. 3, p. 383. Hans von Bülow thinks more subtly: "The melodic essence is represented exclusively neither in the ascending and descending arabesques (which should always be given expressive shading) nor in the pitches marked as quarter notes (whose duration should always be respected) but rather in the union of both elements." *Instruktive Ausgabe Klassischer Klavierwerke* Part 3: *Sonaten und andere Werke für das Pianoforte*, vol. 3 (Stuttgart und Berlin, 1883) p. 75.

9. *Berliner allgemeine musikalische Zeitung* 1 (1824): 37–38; cited in Stefan Kunze, ed., *Ludwig van Beethoven: die Werke im Spiegel seiner Zeit: Gesammelte Konzertberichte und Rezensionen bis 1830* (Laaber, 1987) p. 359. Marx had mixed feelings about the first movement, admitting to his failure to find a "leading idea" and suggesting that the sonata properly begins with the second movement.

10. Jürgen Uhde, *Beethovens Klaviermusik*, vol. 3 (Stuttgart, 1974), p. 476.

11. Discussions of rhythm in music often fall back on this terminology, although it has certain problems. In Latin poetry accent was based on length of syllable; long syllables were accented. In the modern European languages the number of syllables per word also plays a role. For example, in German the first syllable of two-syllable words is accented. (See Doris Fulda Merrifield, *Praktische Anleitung zur Interpretation von Dichtung* [Lanham, 1982], pp. 38–51.) For this reason very different kinds of musical rhythms fall into the same category. For example, if the durations of the motive in op. 109 were reversed to read dotted eighth-sixteenth, the rhythm would still be classified as trochaic, because the pattern begins with an accented downbeat. Moreover, the specific durational relationships within a foot are not fixed: in op. 109 the relationship is 1:3 within the quarter-note foot. Other relationships are common and other metrical units are possible. For example, the Brahms song "Es hing der Reif" scans in a 1:2 relationship and the foot comprises three beats overlapping a bar line.

12. Bülow, *Instruktive Ausgabe*, p. 75.

13. I conducted an unscientific survey of recordings readily available to me.

14. Bülow, *Instruktive Ausgabe*, p. 75.

15. Grasnick 20b consists of pages that were detached from the end of the Wittgenstein sketchbook, which Beethoven used from approximately May 1819 through June 1820. Additional sketches are found in two pocket sketchbooks, BH 107 and BSk 27/75. Transcriptions of the sketches for the movement have been made by Kevin Bazzana,

Glenn Stanley

"The First Movement of Beethoven's Opus 109: Compositional Genesis and Structural Dialectic," *Canadian University Music Review* 12 (1992): 1–34; Allen Forte, *The Compositional Matrix* (New York, 1961); Nicholas Marston, *Beethoven's Piano Sonata in E, Op. 109* (Oxford, 1995); and William Meredith, "The Sources for Beethoven's Piano Sonata in E Major, Opus 109," 2 vols. (Ph.D. diss., University of North Carolina, 1985). There are many differences in detail among them, but they do not have an impact on the issues that are discussed in this essay. Only Meredith transcribes all the sketches in all three books; see vol. 2, pp. 118–36.

16. In this sketch the pitches of the motive occur in the reverse order of the final version—b^1-$g\sharp^1$ instead of $g\sharp^1$-b^1. This was "corrected" in the next sketch, on folio 3r, st. 10–11. The change had profound implications for the movement. Numerous authors have traced the composing out of the motive in its final form. See Bazzana, "Structural Dialectic": 3, for a survey and references to work by Schenker, Forte, Marston, and Kevin Korsyn.

17. Meredith transcribes the F-minor sketch and calls it "the first idea for the beginning of the piece" ("Sources," vol. 1, p. 268), but concludes that Beethoven simply changed his mind about the accentuation pattern. Neither Bazzana nor Marston transcribe this sketch; Marston (p. 46) concludes that it "was not pursued further."

18. An interesting corollary of this decision may be seen at the cadence in mm. 3–4, which, with its added thirds, is intimated in Example 5. In this sketch the pitch sequence is the retrograde of the final version (the directions are also inverted but that is not the issue here), for which reason the thirds fall on notated offbeats and do not have quarter note durations. In the next sketch the sequence is adjusted so that the cadential progression is given proper weight. I do not want to claim that this was the only motivation for the change in the sequence and direction of pitches, but it might have played a role.

19. What would happen if the pianist played the motive without accenting either pitch? Might Schenker's "natural rhythm" emerge as a consequence of the pattern of short and long durations that the right-hand motive presents? Interestingly, Schenker warns that the accent should only apply to the sixteenth note, not to the upward-stemmed quarter. This is, perhaps, a valid theoretical distinction, because the quarter note stands apart from the succession of sixteenth and dotted eighth notes, but it is impossible to execute and also contradicts the rhythms of the quarter-note melodies that emerge later in the movement.

20. The motivic rhythms of the first theme of Brahms's Fourth Symphony are very similar.

21. This variation recalls more than just the first motive. It is a double variation: the second statement of the first part of the two-part theme does not simply repeat the first statement, but is based on entirely new ideas. These new ideas reappear in the second statement of the second part. (The form is A B A' B' instead of the theme's |:A:| :A':|.) In the second statements, the texture thickens, stepwise melodic lines emerge, and the expressive intensity increases significantly. In the context of the motives of the first statement, the second statement recalls the second group of the first movement. The contrast between the first and second groups of the first movement is thereby presented *en miniature*; and the dialectic of the entire first movement is revisited.

22. The composing-out of the initial g$\sharp$-b motive has been a focus of Schenker's, Forte's, and Marston's work. Uhde and Wilfred Mellers are interested in the flowering of song in the last movement and the seeds planted for it in the first two movements. I elaborate on Uhde's idea in my discussion of "Human Voices?" in the last section of this essay.

23. Tovey calls for "a clear accent on the first of every 2/4 bar" (*Beethoven. Sonatas for Pianoforte* Vol. 3, ed. Harold Craxton [London, 1931], p. 191), and Carl Reinecke even

writes in accents over the downbeats in order to reinforce this reading (*Die Beethoven'schen Clavier-sonaten* [Leipzig, 1917], p. 112). See also Riemann (*Klavier-Solosonaten*, p. 384), who connects the paired chords with slurs.

24. This term, and others such as "extra beat" and "metrical modulation" are taken from the extensive literature on metrical problems. Some of the principal recent writings that focus on Beethoven include Richard L. Cohn, "The Dramatization of Hypermetric Conflict in the Scherzo of Beethoven's Ninth Symphony," *19th-Century Music* 15 (1992): 188–206; Andrew Imbrie, "Extra Measures and Metrical Ambiguity in Beethoven," in Alan Tyson, ed., *Beethoven Studies* (New York, 1973), pp. 45–66; Roger Kamien, "Conflicting Metrical Patterns in Accompaniment and Melody in Works by Mozart and Beethoven," *Journal of Music Theory* 37 (1993): 311–48; William Rothstein, "Beethoven with and without Kunstgepräng': Metrical Ambiguity Reconsidered," *Beethoven Forum* 4 (1995): 165–93. See also Rothstein's book, *Phrase Rhythm in Tonal Music*, (New York, 1989). Some of the issues that interest me have been discussed by these authors in terms of "hypermeter," but for reasons of simplicity I worked with the more traditional concepts of phrase and phrase group.

25. A survey of recorded performances yielded results as inconclusive as those concerning the rhythm of the first motive.

26. *Die letzten Sonaten. Sonate E Dur Op. 109. Erläuterungsausgabe* (Vienna, 1971), p. 4.

27. See Meredith, "Sources," pp. 271–73, for further discussion of the relationship between op. 109 and op. 79.

28. See William Kinderman, "Thematic Contrast and Parenthetical Enclosure in the Piano Sonatas, op. 109 and 111," in *Zu Beethoven*, vol. 3, ed. Harry Goldschmidt and Georg Knepler (Berlin, 1988), especially pp. 43–48. Bazzana, "Structural Dialectic," uses Kinderman's idea as the basis for his thinking about the relationship between the second group and the first theme. See also Kinderman's essay in the present volume, p. 210.

29. Uhde, *Klaviermusik*, p. 479, also views the second group as a continuation of the first and discusses its polyphonic nature.

30. Bazzana, "Structural Dialectic," p. 10, juggles ideas emphasizing both process and discontinuities; he likens the second group to a "dramatic agent" that "expands and comments on this argument [of the first theme], and just as a Greek chorus must not take part in the action, so this section, by an extreme shift in mood, tempo, and texture, is set apart."

31. In the upper voice the descending half step from the $a\sharp^2$ on the second beat of m. 8 to the $a\natural^2$ of m. 9 recalls the half step e^1-$d\sharp^1$ and whole step $g\sharp^1$-$f\sharp^1$ in mm. 5–6 and 7–8. At the same time it inverts and denies the expected ascending resolution to b^2, and thus preserves yet transforms the relationship with the cadential $f\sharp^1$-$g\sharp^1$ in mm. 3–4.

32. A pianist can emphasize this interpretation by giving the first sixty-fourth of each group a slight emphasis or by playing agogic accents. (One could even repedal, although this would contradict Beethoven's instructions.)

33. The suspensions are prepared by the first notes of the previous motive; this can be heard despite the eighth rest that intervenes.

34. These lines create interpretative problems. After the first two quarters in mm. 17–18, which are double stemmed, the quarter notes almost always state a different pitch or pitches (dyads beginning in m. 22) from the sixteenth notes. The texture thickens, giving more emphasis to the voice stating the line. But how does a pianist bring out both voices in the same hand? The downbeat quarters are strong through their melodic continuity. But should the pianist endeavor to preserve the independence of the original two-note motive by introducing accents on the second note of the motive, thus preserving

an iambic quality? Schnabel does this, but the result seems mannered and overarticulated; the primary line moving in quarters loses momentum. On the other hand, Pollini allows the motive to succumb to the strength of the quarter notes and recede into an accompanying figure, and this interpretation deprives the motive and the entire texture of its polyphonic richness. There is no solution that satisfies all the claims made by Beethoven's complex musical ideas.

35. Uhde, *Klaviermusik*, p. 367.

36. As Jürgen Uhde has noted, attempts to determine the phrase structure of the upper-voice quarter notes after the sequence breaks up have produced widely divergent solutions that select different four-beat groupings and also include extensions, and a comparison of performances yields little agreement as well. Heinrich Schenker went so far as to criticize Beethoven for the lack of clarity. (Perhaps that was Beethoven's intention!) Compare Uhde's own attempt (*Klaviermusik*, p. 481) with Schenker's (*Erläuterungsausgabe*, pp. 14–16), and Hugo Riemann's (*Klavier-Solosonaten*, p. 390).

37. This kind of metrical conflict between parts has been discussed by Rothstein ("Kunstgepräng'") in terms of "true" and "shadow" meters and hypermeters. A single part can also contain its own shadow.

38. Both Schenker (*Erläuterungsausgabe*, pp. 15–16) and Uhde (*Klaviermusik*, vol. 3, p. 481) construe four-beat groups in this pattern whenever possible, although both must acknowledge elisions and beats that do not fit into any grouping. See also Riemann, *Klavier-Solosonaten*, p. 390.

39. Marston places the beginning of the retransition at m. 42 (*Beethoven's Piano Sonata*, p. 46), when the right hand completes its ascent to b^3 which is then repeated until the recapitulation begins in m. 48. This is an event of signal importance in the movement, yet I prefer to view it as the climax of the retransition, which begins when the left hand begins to prolong dominant harmony in m. 36.

40. The second phrase contains $5^1/2$ measures: the first two measures correspond to the exposition, followed by the unexpected appearance of subdominant harmony, which begins a cadential progression anticipating the beginning of the coda. But it sounds like a non sequitur after the first two measures. The close on V/I mirrors the V/V in m. 9, and the transition to the second group negates the dominant as it did in the exposition.

41. The thirty-four measures of the coda and the thirty-three of the development comprise more than two-thirds of the total. Even if the slow tempo of the second group is taken into account, these sections dominate the form and the passage of time. Lengthy developments and codas are prevalent in Beethoven's music, but the proportions in this movement are unusual, because the thematic groups are so short. However, the emphasis on process, which is present throughout the movement but is particularly strong in these sections, makes perfect sense in the context of dialogue.

42. This passage qualifies as a parenthetical enclosure; the sense of suspended harmonic resolution is much stronger than at the beginning of the second group.

43. See Marston, *Beethoven's Piano Sonata*, especially pp. 79–80, whose analysis of the entire sonata focuses on the tension between G♯ and B introduced in the initial motive and its harmonic implications. Citing Schenker's idea of an "unvollkommener Schluss," Marston also discusses the change in the barring of the conclusion from a double bar line to a "double-single barline" as evidence of Beethoven's "decision to leave the movement unfinished." Marston does not discuss the metrical aspects of the conclusion.

44. See Meredith ("Sources," p. 222) on the descriptions of the theme and Johannes Fischer's interpretation of the decisive shift in meaning, a view that Meredith shares to a certain degree.

45. Kerman, *Beethoven Quartets*, pp. 191–222.

46. See Timothy Jones, *Beethoven. The "Moonlight" and other Sonatas, Op. 27 and Op. 31* (Cambridge, 1999), pp. 78–79.

47. Martin Cooper interprets the fugue very differently, as the expression of an "abstract harmonious world . . . neither subject to human passion nor concerned with anything beyond themselves." See Cooper, *Beethoven: The Last Decade* (London, 1970), p. 194. Kinderman describes a narrative progression that emphasizes formal relationships. See Kinderman, "Beethoven's Piano Sonata in A-flat Major, Opus 110," *Beethoven Forum* 1 (1992), pp. 111–46.

48. The second-movement scherzo in op. 110 does not readily suggest vocal genres and thus represents a break in the narrative predicated on explicit vocal styles and genres. This also seems the case for op. 109, although the motivic and textural connections discussed earlier do provide strong links. The second movements may be considered as "actions" having an impact on the first-movement voices and forcing them to change their expressive modes.

49. Citations from Uhde, *Klaviermusik*, p. 465. On the idea of song as goal, see also Wilfred Mellers, *Beethoven and the Voice of God* (London, 1983), p. 200.

50. Wilhelm von Lenz, *Beethoven*, pp. 55–58.

51. Mellers, *Voice*, p. 201.

52. This quality was recognized in early reviews: an anonymous critic compared the movement to a "free Fantasia." See *Zeitung für Theater und Musik* (Berlin,1821), p. 184; cited in Kunze, ed., *Gesammelte Konzertberichte*, p. 357. Carl Czerny found it to be "more Fantasia than Sonata." See Czerny, *Vollständigen theoretisch-praktischen Pianoforte-Schule op. 500*, ch. 4: "Über den richtigen Vortrag der sämtlichen Beethovenschen Klavierwerke" 1st ed. (Vienna, 1842); reprint ed. Paul Badura-Skoda, (Vienna, 1963), p. 59.

53. C. P. E. Bach, *Essay on the True Art of Playing Keyboard Instruments*, trans. and ed. William J. Mitchell (New York, 1949), p. 153. Translation modified by the author.

54. Czerny, *Pianoforte-Schule*, p. 67.

55. Lenz, *Beethoven*, p. 56.

56. Cf. Thomas Christensen and Nancy Baker, eds., *Aesthetics and the Art of Musical Composition in the German Enlightenment: Selected Writings of Johann Georg Sulzer and Heinrich Christoph Koch* (Cambridge, 1995), pp. 103–05. For further discussion of sonata aesthetics circa 1770–1840 see my "Genre Aesthetics and Function: Beethoven's Piano Sonatas in Their Cultural Context," *Beethoven Forum* 6 (1997): 1–29.

57. S. Brandenburg, ed. *Beethoven Briefe*, vol. 4 (Munich, 1996), no. 1449; E. Anderson, ed., *The Letters of Beethoven* vol. 2 (London, 1961), no. 1062.

58. Brandenburg, *Briefe*, vol. 4, no. 1451; Anderson, *Letters*, vol. 2, no. 1064.

59. The letters were written in February and September 1816. Brandenburg, *Briefe*, vol. 3, nos. 897 and 978; Anderson, *Letters*, vol. 2, nos. 607 and 660. Most of the (surviving) letters to the Brentano family were addressed to both husband and wife or to Franz alone.

60. See Joseph Kerman, "*An die ferne Geliebte*," in *Beethoven Studies*, ed. Alan Tyson (New York, 1973), pp. 123–57.

61. See Forte, *Compositional Matrix*, pp. 30–31, for another discussion of rebarring based on sketches.

62. The idea of a modulation to C♯ minor had already surfaced in the previous sketch on staves 5/6–7, which is also a continuity draft that extends until staff 9. The first theme was apparently conceived to have four phrases, but it breaks off and is followed by a verbal notation about a modulation to C♯ minor and a "Fantasie," both of which are related to the second group. See Marston, *Beethoven's Piano Sonata*, pp. 46–49.

63. The first, unbarred, sketch of the theme also implies this phrase structure, but then continues with additional phrases implying a longer first theme. See ibid., pp 47–48.

64. *Erläuterungsausgabe*, p. 4.

65. Marston (*Beethoven's Piano Sonata*, p. 53): "Beethoven adopted a downbeat opening so that the initial $g\sharp^1$ received strong metrical support. But that decision shifted $g\sharp^1$ to a weak beat at the end of the first phrase, whereas in [the previous sketch] it had occurred on a downbeat at that point."

66. In the event, after completing the first theme on staves 10 and 11 (he had begun by writing both hands), Beethoven first worked on just the upper voice of the second group, writing two eighth-note b^1s (or a $c\sharp^1$-b^1) that are upbeats to a series of barred 2/4 measures.

67. Meredith ("Sources," pp. 274–78) and I have independently reached similar conclusions about this question.

68. It could be argued that Beethoven was not compelled to begin the development or the coda on a notated upbeat, because there is no second group requiring the placement of its first note on a downbeat. Shifting the barring at this point would, however, have confused the relationship between exposition and development and thus compromised an aspect of sonata-design formal symmetry.

69. In the autograph the $g\sharp^3$ that is the first of the eighth notes was originally written as the last of a sextuplet group and then crossed out. See the facsimile edition of the autograph, *Ludwig van Beethoven: Piano Sonata Opus 109*, with an introduction by Oswald Jonas (New York, 1965), p. 8, staff 5.

Voicing Beethoven's Distant Beloved

NICHOLAS MARSTON

For Lewis Lockwood[1]

I

A masterpiece that is not at all well enough known and appreciated.
                    —Wilhelm von Lenz, *Beethoven et ses trois styles*[2]

For Alexander Wheelock Thayer, the matter was quite straightforward: "no one can hear [these songs] adequately sung without feeling that there is something more in that music than the mere inspiration of the poetry."[3] The songs in question are those comprising *An die ferne Geliebte*, op. 98, composed around April 1816 to texts by Alois Jeitteles and published in October of the same year. As for the "something more," Thayer was alluding to the likelihood that for Beethoven, the Distant Beloved of the poetic cycle signified a real woman with whom the composer had been romantically involved. To bolster his case he was able to point to Beethoven's comment, in a letter to Ferdinand Ries dated May 8, 1816, that "I found only one [woman], whom I shall doubtless never possess," and to a diary entry for September 16, 1816 by Fanny del Rio, recalling a conversation between her father Giannatasio and Beethoven in which the latter revealed that he had fallen hopelessly in love some five years earlier.[4] Few evidential complexes offer more temptation to conflate life with art: the Distant Beloved of Beethoven's song cycle has regularly been identified with the "Immortal Beloved" to whom Beethoven addressed his celebrated letter of July 6–7, 1812.[5]

The identification of a fictional woman of 1816 with a real woman of 1812 inevitably leads to temporal rather than spatial interpretations of the "distance" invoked in the title of the song cycle. In his important study, Joseph Kerman expresses himself "impatient with the young man on the hill":

If his beloved is really within "spying distance," or close to it, he might well set about crossing the intervening landscape rather than making up mawkish songs. We can perhaps take the cycle a little more seriously if we are prepared to regard space-distance as a metaphor, gradually clarified by the poet, for time-distance. The poet is celebrating a past love affair.[6]

Kerman understands the "gradual clarification" of the temporal distance between the lover and his beloved as extending across the entire poetic cycle. Songs 1 and 2 and songs 3 and 4 concentrate respectively on the distance between the lovers and those phenomena—clouds, birds, winds—through whose agency that distance is bridged; songs 3 and 4 also introduce temporal images, and these displace spatial references almost entirely during songs 5 and 6.

Detailed though it is, Kerman's close analysis of Jeitteles's poetic imagery is unaccompanied by any reflection on whether and how the gradual revelation of the essential pastness of *An die ferne Geliebte* might be marked in Beethoven's music. Almost the reverse is true of the more recent comments of Charles Rosen, who acclaims Beethoven as "the first composer to represent the complex process of memory . . . the physical experience of calling up the past within the present."[7] The focus of Rosen's claim is on song 2 ("Wo die Berge so blau"), and specifically on the setting of its second verse, where the previous vocal melody is transferred from voice to piano and the voice is relegated to singing on a monotone g^1. This exchange of roles is discussed in more detail below; for the present, it need be noted only that Rosen's interpretation of the musical specifics as markers of the lover's almost involuntary submission to the "incursion of memory"[8] sits uneasily with the lover's stubbornly visual and spatial concerns:

Dort im ruhigen Tal	There, in the silent valley,
Schweigen Schmerzen und Qual.	pain and anguish cease.
Wo im Gestein	There, where among the rocks
Still die Primel dort sinnt,	the primrose meditates silently,
Weht so leise der Wind,	where the wind blows so softly—
Möchte ich sein!	there I would like to be![9]

It would seem to be the particularly seductive biographical context for *An die ferne Geliebte*, and the trope of the loss of past happiness so native to the poetry of the early nineteenth-century song cycle, that encourages so many commentators to read Beethoven's work in this memory-laden way; though resistance is possible, as witness these remarks of Richard Kramer:

> Tellingly, this cycle that most nearly mirrors the figural notion of circle is the one least driven by the narrative impulse—no story is told, no past recapitulated. Space and landscape are its controlling media: the passage of time is minimal, unarticulated, barely perceived.[10]

But this also is overly one-sided, inasmuch as the lover identifies himself at the outset as looking out toward the distant meadows where he first encountered his beloved: "Nach den fernen Triften sehend,/Wo ich dich, Geliebte, fand"); to this extent, at least, there is a minimal past to be recapitulated and kept in play. The real temporal dimension of these poems, though, lies not in the past but in the future. In song 1 the lover makes quite clear the present physical nature of his separation from his beloved, as in these examples from the second and third verses:

Weit bin ich von dir geschieden,	Now I am far from you,
Trennend liegen Berg und Tal	mountain and valley separate us
Zwischen uns und unserm Frieden,	from each other, from our peace,
Unserm Glück und unsrer Qual.	from our happiness, from our sorrow.
. . .	. . .
Und die Seufzer, sie verwehen	and my sighs are lost
In dem Raume, der uns teilt.	in the space that divides us.

Having hit on the idea of music, and specifically Lieder, as the means of bridging the distance that separates them, the lover looks forward in the final song to that time when his beloved will herself sing the songs that he has sung:

Nimm sie hin denn, diese Lieder,	Take these songs now
Die ich dir, Geliebte, sang,	Which I sang to you, my love,
Singe sie dann Abends wieder	sing them over to yourself in the evening
Zu der Laute süßem Klang.	to the sweet sound of the lute.

Wenn das Dämmrungsrot dann ziehet	When the red glow of evening then passes
Nach dem stillen blauen See,	to the still blue lake,
Und sein letzter Strahl verglühet	and the last ray flashes to its end
Hinter jener Bergeshöh';	behind those mountain heights;
Und du singst, was ich gesungen,	And [when] you sing what I sang,
Was mir aus der vollen Brust	what issued from my over-flowing heart
Ohne Kunstgepräng' erklungen,	without an artist's ostentation
Nur der Sehnsucht sich bewußt:	(I was conscious only of my longing):
Dann vor diesen Liedern weichet	Then all that parted us
Was geschieden uns so weit,	is surmounted by these songs,
Und ein liebend Herz erreichet	and a loving heart attains
Was ein liebend Herz geweiht.	that which a loving heart has hallowed.[11]

The direction of the thought is unmistakably toward some willed, even if unattainable, future when all this will come to pass; far from lamely "celebrating a past love affair," the lover proposes that his and his beloved's former happiness can be achieved again. A telling detail is the present rather than future tense conjugation of the verbs in lines 1, 3, and 4 of the final verse. While this might be explained simply as being necessitated by the poetic meter, it might also be construed more literally, as signifying some temporal transformation whereby the future becomes realized in the present, and the thing desired becomes the thing already obtained: the longed-for realization of the past in the future is momentarily figured as present.

The music and words of this final verse of the cycle are, as is well known, closely related to those of the corresponding verse of the first song:

Denn vor Liebesklang entweichet	For sounds of love can put to flight
Jeder Raum und jede Zeit,	all space and all time;
Und ein liebend Herz erreichet	and a loving heart attains
Was ein liebend Herz geweiht!	that which a loving heart has hallowed.

This is, as Kerman points out, "the one [verse] that frankly brings together space and time."[12] Moreover, Kerman makes a persuasive case for Beethoven, rather than Jeitteles, as the author of these lines, which so suggestively predict the collapse of time *and* space ("Dann . . . weichet/Was geschieden uns so weit") at the end of the final song. But whatever his involvement with the poetry, Beethoven's setting of it throughout *An die ferne Geliebte* works toward an extraordinarily vivid yet subtle realization of the telos not only envisaged but seemingly also realized in Jeitteles's verses. It is a realization that depends above all on our willingness to entertain the notion that this song cycle is less univocal, and certainly less "artless," than it may seem. While Kerman could write, nearly a century and a quarter after von Lenz's rallying call, that "it is beyond belief how much musicologists can write . . . without looking hard at important compositions,"[13] he would doubtless agree that our gazing ("spähend") needs to be complemented by equally astute *listening* also.

II

> If music is a language, then who is speaking?
> —Edward T. Cone, *The Composer's Voice*[14]

No commentary on *An die ferne Geliebte* seems fully to have recognized the fundamental ironic self-reflexivity of Beethoven's composition. In the final song of the cycle, the disconsolate lover describes his songs as being characterized by their artlessness, their lack of the "artificial": they are "ohne Kunstgepräng' erklungen." We appreciate well enough the irony of this claim, knowing what we do of the real composer of these songs and of the "dense work on a single tune, 'Auf dem Hügel,'" revealed by the sketches,[15] let alone the compositional artifice evidenced by the overall tonal scheme, the concatenation of all six songs by means of linking transitions, the recall of the opening music in the final verse of the final song, and the rich network of motivic links among individual song melodies that has been drawn by more than one commentator.[16] But artificiality is raised to an even higher plane when we recognize that *An die ferne Geliebte* dramatizes both its own genre and its status as constructed work. In the penultimate verse of the first song, the lover hits on the means to assuage the pain of separation and to bridge the distance between himself and his Distant Beloved:

Singen will ich, Lieder singen,	I will sing, then, I will sing songs
Die dir klagen meine Pein!	that speak to you of my anguish.

Embedded within *An die ferne Geliebte* is a secondary song cycle, "composed" and sung by the lover who sits "auf dem Hügel"; to borrow a term from the work of Carolyn Abbate, the cycle contains an interior cycle of "phenomenal" songs, songs in which the protagonist becomes aware of his own singing voice. Moreover, this shift in "voice" is emphatically marked in the transition from the end of song 1 to the beginning of song 2, "Wo die Berge so blau."

Song 1 ("Auf dem Hügel sitz' ich spähend") is a fine example of what Hans Boettcher classified as "variirte Strophenlied," a formal type in which strophic repetition of the vocal melody is offset by the use of variation technique in the piano accompaniment.[17] The procedure usually results, as here, in a gradual energizing of the accompanimental figuration. Indeed, the second half of the fifth and final verse of "Auf dem Hügel" is marked *nach und nach geschwinder/stringendo*, an acceleration which leads to an instrumental postlude in which an Allegro tempo substitutes for the initial *ziemlich langsam und mit Ausdruck*. The energy (though not the tempo) subsides as the forte dynamic diminishes to a piano; and the full-voiced E♭ triad on the third beat of bar 51 is abruptly pared down to bare octaves, G over E♭.[18] Beethoven's pedaling instruction enhances the aural impression made by this new sonority, which is twice repeated during a further diminuendo from piano toward pianissimo. Finally, coordinated with the pianissimo, the left-hand E♭ falls to D while the right-hand octave g/g^1 is mediated by the addition of b♮, so as to assert a $^6_4$ triad of G major, the key of "Wo die Berge so blau" (Example 1).

It is a peculiarly marked moment, sounding exaggerated and even slightly forced in its *volkstümlich* context, and almost unparalleled in the remainder of the work. Its raison d'être resides in the fact that these two bars of music (bars 53–54) represent one of those "sites of hyperbolic musical disjunction" (Abbate's memorable phrase) by means of which music's "narrating voice" makes itself heard; we are brought up against "the boundaries of a membrane laid down by an outside voice," a boundary that marks, almost literally, "the entry of a song suddenly performed," as the protagonist of "Auf dem Hügel" now assumes the persona of a composer-singer of Lieder.[19] Also germane to the interpretation of this moment in *An die ferne Geliebte* is its scarcely veiled reference to the conventions governing the approach to the cadenza in the classical concerto: the G-major $^6_4$, complete with fermata, may be the pianissimo goal of a de-energizing process at the end of "Auf dem Hügel" rather than the loud, triumphal arrival usually associated with the concerto, but it nevertheless is imbued with the same unmistakably curtain-raising, annunciatory quality. And the onset of the cadenza itself marks a potent shift in voice as the soloist (in theory, at least) takes on

Example 1. Beethoven, *An die ferne Geliebte*, mm. 49–59: the transition from song 1 ("Auf dem Hügel") to song 2 ("Wo die Berge so blau").

the role of performer/composer, breaking free from the constraints of the notated score to "speak" in his or her "natural" voice. Whereas the cadenza thus serves to highlight the "unnatural," constructed nature of the rest of the movement, the opposite is the case in *An die ferne Geliebte*: the histrionic quality of the G-major $^6_4$ at bar 54 serves only to underscore that what follows is artificially constructed in opposition to the so-called "natural" expression of feelings in the opening song. Or such would seem to be the case at this stage of interpretation: opportunity for further refinement will emerge in due course.

Jeitteles's poetry allows us to identify the return to "natural" expression without difficulty; the lover drops his assumed persona at the beginning of the last song: "Nimm sie hin, denn, diese Lieder . . . ." Gustav Nottebohm's investigation of the sketches for *An die ferne Geliebte* long ago revealed that Beethoven, evidently noting the implications of Jeitteles's scheme, at first planned to set this last song to the music of its counterpart at the beginning of the cycle.[20] Eventually, though, he chose to restrict the reprise of the music of "Auf dem Hügel" to the final verse of "Nimm sie hin," the musical reprise thereby underscoring the textual references to the final (Beethoven-authored?) verse of "Auf dem Hügel." Commentators have frequently pointed out that the newly composed melody of the initial verses of "Nimm sie hin" is itself closely linked to this *Urmelodie*, so that the eventual return to the opening music can seem to be generated from within rather than being merely an externally imposed formal event.[21] However, one may wonder to what extent Beethoven's decision to withhold the reprise of "Auf dem Hügel" at the outset of this final song compromises the resumption of the lover's original ("natural") persona at this stage in the poetic cycle. Indeed, there is nothing in the transition from the penultimate song ("Es kehret der Maien") to "Nimm sie hin" that compares remotely with that "hyperbolic musical disjunction" by means of which the change in voice between the first two songs is announced; the emphasis is instead entirely on musical continuity. The turn to C minor in the final bars of "Es kehret der Maien" sets up both the initial c^2 and supporting A♭ (IV/E♭) harmony at the beginning of "Nimm sie hin" with transparent ease; duple meter is maintained, despite the change from 4/4 to 2/4; there is no fermata or similar marked hiatus to articulate the end of one song from the beginning of the next. It is as if the lover, having moved offstage at the end of the first song in order to don the costume of a Lied recitalist before returning (with a flourish, on the point of that annunciatory V $^6_4$/G), now sheds his disguise in full view of his audience in order to reveal that we have in fact been listening only to him all along. With the disguise shed already at the beginning of "Nimm sie hin," the reprise of "Auf dem Hügel" in the last verse of this final song can indeed be left sounding like a rather perfunctory formal gesture.

But this is not the only way in which to interpret either the beginning of "Nimm sie hin" or the transition from "Auf dem Hügel" to "Wo die Berge so blau"; we need to listen to what other voices are telling us.

III

The piano accompaniment is held down to a most unobtrusive role . . .

—Joseph Kerman, *"An die ferne Geliebte"*[22]

As Kerman noted, the autograph manuscript of *An die ferne Geliebte* suggests that "in the final song the quiet, tentative-sounding piano recollection of the single line 'Auf dem Hügel sitz' ich spähend,' just before the voice brings back the whole of the tune, was a last-minute inspiration. The two bars in question were squeezed into the space originally occupied by the following one bar." He went on to speculate that Beethoven may have "had a momentary temptation to mirror this piano statement at the very beginning of the cycle."[23] Whatever the likelihood of this latter point, no such piano statement occurs, with the result that *An die ferne Geliebte* begins with the most minimal of instrumental introductions: a bald E-flat major triad giving the singer his $b\flat^1$. It seems a neutral, purely formal gesture, one consequence of which is that the "music" begins, to all intents and purposes, with the singer, from whose voice melody first issues. The piano accompaniment, initially sparse and fragmentary, falls into step with the voice in bar 4, and the right hand then plays in unison with the vocal melody from that point until the end of the verse. Only in the two-bar interlude between successive verses does the piano seek to claim any genuine independence from the voice; and this interlude is harmonically and melodically static, the pedal tonic harmony complemented by the right hand where $b\flat^2$ rings out, seemingly impotent to realize a melodic continuation of its own.

The remaining songs demonstrate a different initial relationship between voice and piano. The melody of "Wo die Berge so blau" emerges in the piano following the V^6_4/G discussed above; the ascent g^1-a^1-b^1 is tried out in two rhythmic settings, the second of which is adopted when the singer enters. Likewise, the melody of the first poetic line in songs 3, 4, and 5 is prefigured in the piano accompaniment in each case, and in song 5 this prefigurement is itself preceded by a twelve-bar dominant pedal. Set now in the context of these other beginnings, the beginning of "Nimm sie hin" appears in a rather different light. Far from prefiguring merely the melodic setting of the first poetic line, the eight-bar piano introduction to this final song is equivalent to an entire verse, and forms a complete tonal and melodic statement. More than that: this introduction usurps the lyrical, melodic utterance hitherto associated with the vocal line; it reveals in the piano a voice that is capable of *singing*.

But this is not the first time that this voice has been heard. The anonymous reviewer of the first edition of *An die ferne Geliebte*, writing in the *Leipziger allgemeine musikalische Zeitung* for 1817, was merely the first of many commentators to remark favorably on Beethoven's special treatment of the voice-piano relationship in the middle (second) verse of "Wo die Berge so blau," and to note the importance of a sensitive vocal performance to the achievement of the intended effect.[24] As noted above, the singer recites the entire verse on a monotone g^1 while the erstwhile vocal melody passes to the right hand of the piano part. A further distinctive feature of this particular verse is Beethoven's decision to set it in the subdominant of the local tonic, G major; such tonal variation is not a feature of the other strophic songs in the cycle.[25]

How are we to understand this moment? Adolph Bernhard Marx interpreted Beethoven's departure from standard *Liedform* here as motivated by the attempt to have the singer whisper "the secret words of consolation and silent hope" while the melody sounded out from the accompaniment; for Paul Bekker there was something mysterious (*geheimnisvoll*) in the modulation to the subdominant, while the instrumental presentation of the melody could be likened to a fata morgana, and the singer's restriction to a single pitch signified "dreamy self-oblivion" (*träumerische Selbstvergessenheit*).[26] On the other hand it is, as already observed, memory rather than oblivion that lies at the heart of Charles Rosen's reading, which posits Beethoven's endeavor

> to portray the separation of present reality and past memory. The genius of Beethoven is revealed best of all by the restriction of the voice to a single note: it seems as if the lover, now completely passive, is submitting almost involuntarily to the incursion of memory.[27]

But why must this music always be associated with the mysterious, the imaginary, the (temporally) remote? Why should we not accord it greater palpability and recognize it as the incursion not of memory but of another singing voice, one which sings back the music created "auf dem Hügel" by the lover-become-singer? Rather as in the introduction to "Nimm sie hin," the incursive voice here has the effect of paralyzing, if not (as in the later case) entirely suppressing, the lover's potential for lyrical expression.

Nor does the incursive voice cease when the lover reasserts himself in the final verse of "Wo die Berge so blau." At the final cadence, the lover repeats the words "ewiglich sein" to a 5-4-3 descent, d^2-c^2-b^1. Immediately this descent is concluded, the piano imitates it in rhythmic augmentation: g^2-f^2-$e^{\flat 2}$, as though the tonal scheme were set to push flatward from G again, this time to the subdominant minor. (The bass G in fact rises by semitone to A♭, the key of the next two songs, although in a wider context it functions as an upper chromatic neighbor to the dominant of C, which eventually resurfaces as the key of "Es kehret der Maien"). The g^2 on which this imitative augmentation begins is heavily freighted, however, for it is this same pitch that forms the goal of the song's melody when heard in the subdominant in the central verse. The attainment of the g^2 in bars 79–82, above the words "[weht so] leise der Wind, möchte ich sein!" simultaneously marks the point of its furthest distance from the singer's monotone g^1, which sounds—assuming the conventional tenor or baritone performance—fully two octaves beneath the incursive voice in the piano. And it is this voice, not that of the lover, that breaks out again at the end of the song to carry the music forward.

The reversal of the G-A♭ (V↓VI/C) progression at the transition from song 4 ("Diese Wolken in den Höhen") to "Es kehret der Maien" again brings the incursive voice, with its associated g^2, within earshot. Indeed, not only the g^2 itself but the introductory phrase of the vocal melody, with its 5-4-3 (g^2-f^2-e^2) and 3-2-1 (e^2-d^2-c^2) descents in parallel thirds and sixths in the piano right hand, is a sonorous reminder of the climactic events in the middle of "Wo die Berge so blau" (Example 2). That this voice, however incursive its origins, is capable of exerting a quiet authority is to be gauged from the way the lover's vocal range is now drawn above its previous upper limit of $e^{\flat 2}$/f^2 (in songs 1–4) to its own g^2 (in song 5)—though that pitch acts here as the starting point for an immediate descent to the lower octave rather than being the goal of the melodic line.[28]

This extension upward to g^2 of the lover's range resurfaces in the final vocal phrase of the work ("was ein liebend Herz geweiht"), when the lover triumphantly reaches up again to that pitch, which acts as 3 of the 3-2-1 descent to the final (vocal) tonic. Prior to this moment, though, g^2 (and g^1) features prominently in the "soprano" voice of the accompaniment, as part of a studied emphasis on the chromaticized 5-4-3 descent in E-flat which forms the third phrase of the melody of "Auf dem Hügel" and of the concluding reprise verse of "Nimm sie hin." As Christopher Reynolds notes, this phrase (Motive 3 in Reynolds's scheme) is the only one of the source motives built into the first song to be left unaltered in the coda following the reprise: "after slighting it in the fifth song and the first stanzas of the sixth, [Beethoven] dwells on it, repeating it three times consecutively in the transition from the da capo to the coda and four more times in the coda . . . . No other motive

Example 2. Beethoven, *An die ferne Geliebte*: the central verse of song 2 ("Wo die Berge so blau") recalled in the piano introduction to song 5 ("Es kehret der Maien").

compares."[29] The phrase is used in dialogue between voice and piano, a dialogue which is instigated by the piano in bar 305, in the lover's (b♭1) register; subsequently, the piano doubles the voice in this register (bars 307–309), doubles at the octave above (bars 309–311), and in bars 323–27 conjoins both registers in answer to the lover's reiteration of this mantralike phrase. Its final appearance is in bars 337–39, where it launches a precipitous descent of two and a half octaves, from the initiating b♭2 down to e♭. This is then followed by an immediate, unmediated return to a b♭2 from which not descending but ascending motion takes off: the final gesture of the work is a rhythmically condensed version of the lover's first line of text ("Auf dem Hügel sitz' ich spähend," in song 1; "dann vor diesen Liedern weichet," in the reprise of song 6). But even here the initial rising fourth is followed by the falling sixth, which brings back g2 as the final upper-voice pitch.[30]

"A most unobtrusive role"? In the course of his study, Kerman modifies this initial assessment of the voice-piano relationship in *An die ferne Geliebte*, concluding, "the way the piano almost imperceptibly assumes more and more importance as the piece proceeds" is an index of the extent to which "Beethoven could not accept the *Volksweise* ideal in its pure form."[31] The preceding remarks have outlined how, following its almost complete suppression as an individual musical component at the very outset, the piano emerges as a competitor for lyrical utterance in the middle verse of "Wo die Berge so blau" and succeeds in suppressing the lover's voice itself at the beginning of "Nimm sie hin." But far from couching the issue purely in terms of an opposition between vocal and instrumental medium, emphasis has been laid here on the identification of a more specific voice associated with the piano part, one that speaks in a melodic space typified by the pitch g^2, a pitch to which the singer is gradually coaxed in the last two songs (see Example 3 for a summary of the presence of this voice across the cycle[32]). In the final verse of "Nimm sie hin," g^2 in the piano becomes closely associated with b^b2, as part of the reiterated 5-4-3 progression[33]; and this connection prompts an association with the b^b2 of the piano "interludes" in bars 313–15 of this verse and, by extension, their counterparts in "Auf dem Hügel" (see bars 9–10, 19–20, 29–30, 39–40, and 49–50). The b^b2 associated with these interludes in the first song was characterized above as "ring[ing] out, seemingly impotent to realize a melodic continuation of its own." It finds its voice only during the cycle, and asserts itself most forcefully in the final two bars: while the lover's g^2 yields downward to e^b2, the piano b^b2 drives triumphantly upward to e^b3 before asserting its signature g^2 at the close. It is this voice that has the last word.

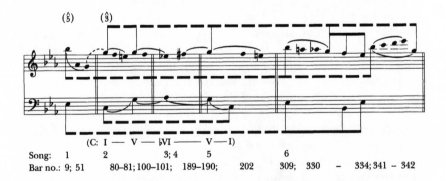

Example 3. Beethoven, *An die ferne Geliebte*: the incursive g^2-centered voice.

IV

No matter how muted or naturalized it may become, the primary fact about song is what might be called a topological distortion of utterance under the rhythmic and harmonic stress of music: a pulling, stretching, and twisting that deforms the current of speech without negating its basic linguistic shape.
—Lawrence Kramer, *Music and Poetry: The Nineteenth Century and After*[34]

Lawrence Kramer's diagnosis of the "implicitly agon[ist]ic" relationship of music and poetry in song had been anticipated by earlier studies, not least Edward T. Cone's suggestion that Schubert's setting of Goethe's *Wandrers Nachtlied*, D. 768, might be the result of "a violation of the poetic form"[35]; but it is the concept of "a topological distortion of utterance" that speaks most directly to the next interpretative crux in *An die ferne Geliebte*. "Nimm sie hin," the final song of the cycle, is the only one of the six to forgo the strophic model in favor of a more *durchkomponiert* setting. Kerman calls it "the most interesting" of the six; for Reynolds, "the synthesis of motives in the final song culminates the extraordinary synthesis of music and text that guided Beethoven throughout the entire cycle."[36] Yet despite the special attention accorded this song in the literature, evidently no one has remarked on the suggestive mismatch— the "topological distortion of utterance"—between poetry and music created by Beethoven's setting.

In the first of Jeitteles's four verses, given above in full, the lover urges the beloved to take his songs and sing them again herself. Beethoven responds to the self-contained syntax of the verse with a closed eight-bar period, the music of which has already been very closely adumbrated in the introductory piano statement. The second and third verses of the poem, by contrast, are syntactically continuous, and dependent on the initial word "Wenn" which is answered by "Denn" only at the beginning of the final verse, where the musical reprise of "Auf dem Hügel" sets in. The music of the second verse starts out from a slightly modified version of bars 1 and 2 of the first verse, but then works around the circle of fifths to cadence in the dominant. The third verse, however, recapitulates the music of the first verse entirely, and the effects of this musical reprise are powerfully disruptive of the verbal sense. In particular, the return to the initial music works to dissociate the text of the third verse from its syntactic source, the second verse, so that the implicit futurity governing Jeitteles's third verse is nullified: far from stressing its dependency on the earlier "wenn," the music creates the sense that this third verse refers to events happening in the present, that it is a straightforward statement of fact. The sense of "Und du singst, was ich gesungen" is not so much "And [at such time as] you [may/will] sing what I have sung" as "And you sing/are singing what I have [just] sung."[37]

The "presentness" of "Und du singst" is underlined by other, more dramatic musical means. The whole of the second verse is set within a slow ritardando which eventually reduces the tempo from the opening andante con moto to a single bar (Example 4: m. 283) of molto adagio immediately before the return of the tempo and melody of the first verse. This molto adagio bar functions like a huge punctuation mark: the music seems to come to a complete standstill as "Und du singst" is proclaimed independently of these same words' impending repetition as part of the third verse proper, beginning in bar 284. Kerman describes bar 283 as "one of those extraordinary compressed gestures that become more and more frequent in [Beethoven's] third period":

> The hollow, molto adagio B♭ evokes the slowly reiterated B♭s of "Auf dem Hü(gel)"; then the solemn two-part counterpoint in octaves gingerly picks out the chords of E-flat, G major, A-flat, even A-flat minor, as well as the semitone G-A♭ which had joined (or, rather, disjoined) the earlier songs. This bar seems to hold the entire tonal dynamic of the composition in a nutshell.[38]

Singular though the gesture is, it nonetheless evokes that earlier arresting moment, the transition between the first two songs in the cycle (Example 1). Here, as there, we confront the same sudden paring down of the piano texture to stark octaves; and while Kerman rightly notes the resonances of the semitone progression G-A♭, the saturation of semitone steps here—G-A♭, B♮-C, and most importantly B♭-B♮—points back to the E♭-D and B♭-B♮ moves through which the annunciatory $^6_4$ prefacing "Wo

Example 4. Beethoven, *An die ferne Geliebte*, mm. 283–285: turning point in song 6.

die Berge so blau" was achieved.[39] In addition, whereas the approach to that harmony had been marked by Beethoven's indication that the sustaining pedal be used, here in the middle of "Nimm sie hin" the textural shift from full-voiced repeated triads in the middle and lower registers of the keyboard to the bare octaves accompanying "und du singst" is further enhanced by the abrupt lifting of the pedal.

V

> Thus if we ask whose are the originating voices in opera (who, that is, do we assume is singing?) . . . we also mean "How do we conceive the origins of the sonorities—verbal and musical—that we are hearing?"
>
> —Carolyn Abbate, "Opera; or the Envoicing of Women"[40]

A well-established tradition of scholarship has it that the end (bar 295 ff.) of the first movement of Schumann's *Fantasie*, op. 17 is a thinly-veiled allusion to the melody of "Nimm sie hin, denn, diese Lieder" in *An die ferne Geliebte*.[41] As with the song cycle itself, commentators have been quick to spot the biographical resonances of the Beethoven reference: in 1836, when Schumann composed the movement, Clara was quite literally his "distant beloved"; later, in a letter of March 17–18, 1838 he wrote from Vienna to Clara, then in Paris, describing the first movement of the *Fantasie* as "probably the most passionate thing I have ever written—a deep lament for you."[42] By this time the other two movements of the *Fantasie* had been composed, and Schumann had decided to head the whole work with a quotation from Friedrich Schlegel's poem "Die Gebüsche," part of the cycle *Abendröte*:

Durch alle Töne tönet	Through all the notes
Im bunten Erdentraum	In earth's many-colored dream
Ein leiser Ton gezogen	There sounds one soft long-drawn note
Für den, der heimlich lauschet.	For the one who listens in secret.[43]

Again, much has been made of Schumann's claim, in a letter to Clara dated June 9, 1839, that she is the *leiser Ton* of the motto.[44] But if Beethoven's song cycle in some sense lies behind Schumann's piano composition—if, that is, Beethoven is "the origin of the sonorities . . . that we are hearing"—the reverse is also true: as in Jeitteles's poems—and, I shall argue, Beethoven's setting of them—past and future are collapsed into the present, and Schumann's not-yet-written composition with its appropriation of Schlegel comes to offer a key to Beethoven's work.

For Abbate's final question may be asked of song as well as of opera. In bar 283 of *An die ferne Geliebte* and the ensuing setting of the third verse of the poem, Beethoven's music "deforms the current of [Jeitteles's] speech without negating its basic linguistic shape," by drawing into the present tense words that properly speak of an imagined future (recall also the jarring effect of Jeitteles's switch to the present tense in the final verse of "Nimm sie hin"). Furthermore, the extraordinary qualities of bar 283 itself disclose its close affinity to bars 52–54 and invite us to hear it as another of Abbate's "sites of hyperbolic musical disjunction," "the boundar[y] of a membrane laid down by an outside 'voice.'" But the sense of an outside voice here is twofold. On one hand, bar 283 marks the return of a voice that has already been heard; it is the lover's natural voice, heard again for the first time since the opening song, after which it had been replaced by his assumption of the artificial persona of the Lied singer. What impels him to stop performing himself is his sudden perception of—Abbate's uncannily accurate terms again— "the entry of a song suddenly performed." "*Und du singst*": the lover becomes aware of his beloved's *singing voice*, that voice sketched in Example 3 and traced across the entire cycle. It is, as we have heard, a voice closely associated with a "soft long-drawn note," g², one that sounds "for him who listens in secret."[45] *She* is singing; *he* is listening. Only once he has stopped singing himself can he hear what we have caught, at first fleetingly, *wie aus der Ferne*, then at gradually increased length and lyricism, almost from the beginning.

To hear a distinct voice for the Distant Beloved in *An die ferne Geliebte*— a voice that is to be heard as emanating from its own source, rather than as a projection of the lover's imagination—is to recognize yet again the irony of the claim that these are songs "ohne Kunstgepräng' erklungen." It is also to understand the coda to the final song in a new way. While Kerman characterizes this part of the work in terms of "the voice [being] swept along by the piano, which behaves like the orchestra in a miniature cantata or opera finale,"[46] we may more readily hear an exchange of voices more characteristic of the operatic duet; indeed, everything from the final verse of "Nimm sie hin" to the end of the work may be construed as a final staged performance, an epilogal "phenomenal" song performed in front of the curtain, so to speak, by the lovers in concert.[47]

But to admit the Distant Beloved into one's interpretation on these terms is not entirely unproblematic. In particular, one consequence of the reading advanced so far is that the Distant Beloved increasingly calls the tune; indeed, one might say that only in the very first song, and perhaps at the outset of the second, is the lover solely responsible for what he sings; thereafter he takes his cue, albeit unwittingly, from the Beloved, who gives him his music at the start of each song, and above all at the beginning of "Nimm sie hin." All this seriously compromises the suggested assumption by the lover of the role of composer-singer of his own *Liederkreis*, beginning with song 2. And as already noted, it is the Beloved, rather than the lover himself, who has the last word.

If we feel impelled to smooth out this wrinkle in the fabric of interpretation, we may do best to return to those crucial bars 52–54 between songs 1 and 2, and to Abbate's rich account of the implications of such "sites of hyperbolic musical disjunction." Beyond the descriptions ("the boundaries of a membrane laid down by an outside voice," "the entry of a song suddenly performed") invoked above, Abbate claims that such moments may also be construed as "part of the musical sound made by *distance*."[48] Such a construal is much to the point in a work in which distance and the overcoming of distance are really the central theme. What is effected in that momentous bass shift from E♭ to D, from an E-flat major tonic that is retrospectively configured as ♭VI of an impending G major, is the simultaneous articulation of distance and of its overcoming: of distance, in that the locus of activity now shifts from the lover to the Distant Beloved—what is heard from now on is not the lover's singing voice itself, but rather the Distant Beloved's singing recall of it; of the overcoming of distance, in that from song 2 onward we are hearing the appropriation by the Distant Beloved of her lover's former songs. While the sonorities of the lover's opening song originate directly from him, they sound at a distance in both space and time between bars 55 and 282. The Beloved, in effect, is the immediate origin of *all* the sonorities heard in this stretch of the cycle, and not merely of those ascribed above to her g^2-centered voice. Songs 2–6 (prior to bar 283) are thus doubly "phenomenal" songs, in the sense that the lover's performing voice is itself "performed" by the Beloved.

A reading along these lines may also draw in the tiny but important detail of the imperfect tense of "singen" employed in the lines "Nimm sie hin, denn, diese Lieder/Die ich dir, Geliebte, *sang*," a construction that resonates with the first verse of song 1: "Nach den fernen Triften sehend,/Wo ich dich Geliebte, *fand*."[49] The consistent univocal, present-tense interpretation initially offered above—the lover sits fondly remembering his first meeting with the Beloved, and elects to use song as the means of bridging their separation (song 1); adopting the voice of singer-composer, he sings a cycle of four songs (songs 2–5); returning to his natural voice he offers the songs to the Beloved and imagines that time when she will sing them in return (song 6)—needs modification to something like the following: song 1 gives us the lover in the present, as before; but songs 2–6 take place in that future time and space, now become present and "here," envisaged by the lover in song 6, and are sung by the Beloved, for whom her lover's original singing of the songs is now in the past ("Die ich dir, Geliebte, *sang*"). The transition between songs 1 and 2 thus signifies a change in time, space, and voice: not until his moment of *anagnorisis*—"Und du singst"—in the middle of song 6 will we hear the lover's natural voice again.

VI

An die ferne Geliebte is [Beethoven's] most openly Romantic work. Even the last phrase (which is the first phrase rewritten) is both decisive and, by Classical standards, inconclusive. The end of the cycle with the return of the first phrase needs to suggest the incomplete: it is only the anguish of separation that returns. The last song is not a memory of the distant beloved but a memory of grief and of absence. Even if, as the words claim, the distance in time and space is vanquished by song, the effect of transcendence depends on our understanding that the absence persists.

—Charles Rosen, *The Romantic Generation*[50]

Memory, distance, absence: that Beethoven's song cycle engages intimately with these central themes in early German Romanticism, with what Richard Kramer calls "a poetics of the remote," is obvious enough[51]; what is at issue is the nature of the engagement, and the way in which these themes are played out. For Jean Paul Richter, writing in 1804 in his *Vorschule der Ästhetik*, the dying sound was taken as emblematic of the Romantic inasmuch as it exemplified "beautiful infinity"—a description which, as Berthold Hoeckner points out, paradoxically conflates the boundedness and boundlessness associated with the beautiful and the sublime respectively in eighteenth-century aesthetics.[52] Jean Paul's description of the "undulating hum of a vibrating string or bell, whose sound waves fade away into ever greater distances and finally are lost in ourselves, and which, although outwardly silent, still sound within" resonates with Schlegel's "soft long-drawn note/For the one who listens in secret";[53] and yet that "note" in *An die ferne Geliebte* is paradoxically one that sounds ever closer as the work proceeds. Far from "fad[ing] away into ever greater distances," it becomes increasingly more prominent and palpable.

Jean Paul was insistent that "it is more than an analogy to call the Romantic the undulating hum of a vibrating string or bell. . . . In the same way moonlight is both image and instance of the Romantic." As Hoeckner explains, what is at issue here is a "suspension of the boundary between the phenomenal and noumenal worlds" and equally the obliteration of "the difference between metaphor and event, or between the figurative and the real." As Jean Paul's subsequent expansion of these claims in relation to the dying sound in the *Kleine Nachschule* of 1825 has it, tacitly reinforcing E. T. A. Hoffmann's classic definition of music as "the most Romantic of all arts,"[54]

> Music . . . is romantic poetry for the ear. . . . No color is as romantic as a sound, since one is present at the dying away only of a sound but not of a color; and because a sound never sounds alone, but always three-fold, blending, as it were, the romantic quality of the future and the past into the present.

Hoeckner notes, "like the extension of tone into ideal space, the resolution of future and past into the present results in the unlimited expansion of time within a single instant of the temporal continuum." The interpretation of *An die ferne Geliebte* offered here makes similar claims for the role of Beethoven's music, which can be conceived as "both image and instance" not only of that "three-fold blending" of temporal categories projected by Jean Paul (and, much later, Eliot) but also of the blending of physical absence and presence: Beethoven, that is, finds the musical means to render "now" and "here" that willed future reconstitution of a past happiness that must remain always imaginary for Jeitteles's lover. Here again there is a broader context to consider:

> Of all the serious games in Romanticism, the most earnest and at the same time the most light-hearted is the quest for Paradise Lost. It concentrates the Romantic essence for us, as in a burning-glass. It is the longing for something lost; it is the sorrowful remembrance of . . . the unity, harmony, happiness and contentment that were present in a distant past but can now be evoked only in imagination. . . . In a state of longing, the imagination recreates a lost Whole out of the fragments of past happiness: that is what Romanticism demands of the arts.[55]

But just as Beethoven reconfigures the quintessentially Romantic dying sound as its opposite, so too in *An die ferne Geliebte* does he offer Paradise Regained, and—crucially, I suggest—in terms that we are invited to accept as real rather than imaginary. If all this is to suggest the extent to which, *pace* Rosen and others, *An die ferne Geliebte* might be termed a paradoxically *un*romantic work, it might, equally paradoxically, open the way to recognition of a "heroic" strain in this music. This, after all, is a work by Beethoven in *E-flat major*; are we really to hear in its ending "the anguish of separation," the persistence of absence? To do so is, as claimed earlier, to fall prey once again to the tendency to read the work as sublimated biography. Or a certain aspect of biography, at least: for the sense of the ending offered in the present interpretation also has its biographical correlative in the composer who would seize fate by the throat; who would hold fast to the transforming power of the individual will in face of the vicissitudes of life; who would disallow the possibility that things might not be so with the blunt imperative "es muß sein."

NOTES

1. An earlier version of this study was first presented at a conference, "Rethinking Beethoven's Late Period: Sources, Aesthetics, and Interpretation," held in honor of Lewis Lockwood at the Department of Music, Harvard University, November 1–3, 1996; subsequent presentations were given at the universities of Cambridge, London, Nottingham, Southampton, and Surrey. I am grateful to many colleagues, friends, and students for their constructive criticism of the ideas expressed herein.

2. In "Catalogue critique, chronologique et anecdotique de l'œuvre de Beethoven," from von Lenz, *Beethoven et ses trois styles* (Paris, 1855), vol. 2, p. 121.

3. Thayer, Alexander Wheelock, rev. Elliot Forbes, *Life of Beethoven*, (Princeton, 1967), p. 647.

4. For the letter to Ries, see Ludwig van Beethoven: *Briefwechsel: Gesamtausgabe*, ed. Sieghard Brandenburg and others, vol. 3 (Munich, 1996), no. 933, p. 257; del Rio's diary entry is quoted in Joseph Kerman, *"An die ferne Geliebte," Beethoven Studies*, vol. 1, ed. Alan Tyson (New York, 1973), p. 130.

5. See ibid., p. 131: "most biographers conclude that the letter and the song cycle were addressed to the same lady." The search for the identity of the "Immortal Beloved" has spawned not only a substantial literature of varying degrees of plausibility and scholarship but also became the impetus for a 1994 film by Bernard Rose in which concern for scholarly accuracy was scant even by the standards of this genre: see Lewis Lockwood, "Film Biography as Travesty: *Immortal Beloved* and Beethoven," *The Musical Quarterly* 81 (1997): 190–98; for the present writer, at least, the most persuasive argument for the identity of the "Immortal Beloved" remains that advanced in favor of Antonie Brentano, in Maynard Solomon, *Beethoven* (London, 1977), pp. 158–89. For the text of the letter, see Beethoven, *Briefwechsel* (Munich, 1996), no. 582.

6. Kerman, *"An die ferne,"* p. 129.

7. Charles Rosen, *The Romantic Generation* (Cambridge, Mass., 1995), p. 166.

8. Ibid., p. 169.

9. Except where otherwise indicated, German texts and translations are taken from S. S. Prawer, ed. and trans., *The Penguin Book of Lieder*, (London, 1977), pp. 25–28.

10. Richard Kramer, *Distant Cycles: Schubert and the Conceiving of Song* (Chicago and London, 1994), p. 9.

11. Translation (see n. 9) emended, both here and in the corresponding verse from Song 1 given below. Note that in the final verse of "Nimm sie hin" Prawer gives the more specific "the distance that parted us" for "was geschieden uns."

12. Kerman, *"An die ferne,"* p. 129; see pp. 126–27 for the argument in favor of Beethoven's authorship of this verse.

13. Ibid., p. 145, n. 32.

14. Berkeley, Los Angeles, and London, 1974, p. 1.

15. Kerman, p. 149.

16. See especially Christopher Reynolds, "The Representational Impulse in Late Beethoven, I: An die ferne Geliebte," *Acta Musicologica* 60 (1988): 43–61; also the derivative essay by Reynolds on *An die ferne Geliebte* in *Beethoven: Interpretationen seiner Werke*, vol. 2, Albrecht Riethmüller, Carl Dahlhaus, and Alexander L. Ringer, (Laaber, 1994), pp. 99–108. Reynolds's concluding reference to the "orphic idea that music is capable of conquering the unconquerable," and to the importance of this for both Beethoven and the succeeding Romantic generation, is germane to the interpretations offered below.

17. Hans Boettcher, *Beethoven als Liederkomponist* (Augsburg, 1928; repr. Walluf-Nendeln, 1974), p. 64.

18. Bar-number references follow the score of *An die ferne Geliebte* published in Helga Lühning, ed. *Beethoven: Lieder und Gesänge mit Klavierbegleitung* (Munich, 1990); *Beethoven: Werke*, ed. Sieghard Brandenburg, XII/I, pp. 151–64.

19. Carolyn Abbate, *Unsung Voices* (Princeton, 1991), p. 151. On "phenomenal" song, see pp. 4–10 and the further references in the index.

20. Gustav Nottebohm, *Zweite Beethoveniana. Nachgelassene Aufsätze*, ed. Eusebius Mandyczewski (Leipzig, 1887), p. 335. The sketchbook in question is the "Scheide" sketchbook, and Kerman, p. 149, cites page 73 of the book as containing "full drafts of the tunes of [Songs] 5 and 6, the latter being simply the tune of 'Auf dem Hügel' with an indication of the new words."

21. See Rosen, *Romantic*, pp. 170–72, and Kerman, ibid., pp. 145–47.

22. Kerman, p. 134.

23. Ibid., pp. 137–38. Kerman's speculation about the beginning of the work is fueled by the presence, just preceding the first note in the vocal part in the autograph, of an erased, penciled caret. This has no obvious referent elsewhere in the manuscript; the sketches for the instrumental conclusion of the cycle on page 28 of the autograph include a similar caret—not included in Kerman's transcription (his Example 1, p. 139, where the page number is incorrectly given as 26)—between staves 1–2; but this is hardly a plausible referent for the earlier sign. All these details can be seen clearly in the facsimile edition of the autograph: *Ludwig van Beethoven: "An die ferne Geliebte"* (Munich, 1970).

24. For the *AMZ* review, see Stefan Kunze, ed. *Ludwig van Beethoven: die Werke im Spiegel seiner Zeit: gesammelte Konzertberichte und Rezensionen bis 1830* (Laaber, 1987), p. 331: "Sehr artig ist der Gedanke, und, wenn der Sänger das Seinige thut, von besonderm Effect, in der zweyten Strophe, wo der Dichter eine tiefe, sinnige Ruhe schildert, der Singstimme immerfort nur Einen Ton, die Dominante, zu geben, und die Begleitung allein die Melodie und Harmonie der andern Strophen fortführen zu lassen." The review also makes special mention of the transition between songs 1 and 2, to the extent of quoting the music given in Example 1.

25. A major-minor modal shift is employed in verses 2–5 of song 3 ("Leichte Segler in den Höhen"); although the even-numbered verses of "Es kehret der Maien" commence "in" the subdominant, it is preferable to think of the musical strophe as embracing each pair of poetic verses, and thus repeating its tonally closed C-major plan three times over.

26. Adolph Bernhard Marx, *Ludwig van Beethoven: Leben und Schaffen,* vol. 2 (Berlin, 1863), p. 151; Paul Bekker, *Beethoven* (Berlin, 1912), p. 364. Kerman, *"An die ferne,"* p. 134, suggests Reichardt's *Erlkönig* as Beethoven's model for the treatment of the voice-piano relationship here.

27. Rosen, *Romantic,* p. 169. I have discussed Rosen's and Kerman's "temporal" interpretations of *An die ferne Geliebte* in "'Wie aus der Ferne': Pastness and Presentness in the Lieder of Beethoven, Schubert, and Schumann," *Schubert durch die Brille* 21 (1998): 126–42.

28. From a Schenkerian perspective, the g^2 in "Es kehret der Maien" remains active across the melodic span of each verse, representing the *Kopfton* of a 5-line *Urlinie*.

29. Reynolds, "The Representational Impulse": 53 and Example 10.

30. Kerman, *"An die ferne,"* pp. 140–41 and 145–48, stresses the importance of the mediant, G, as a melodic cadential pitch in the cycle, and also notes the prevalence of the 5-4-3 progression in "Nimm sie hin." William Kinderman, *Beethoven* (1995), pp. 192–95, remarks, "Beethoven's cadence is left open, with the final accented E♭ major chord placed on a weak beat of the triple metre"; the melodic close on 3 rather than 1 is presumably also taken as contributing to the openendedness here.

31. Kerman, *"An die ferne,"* pp. 134, 154.

32. Example 3 may be compared to ibid., pp. 141–42 and Example 4.

33. Admittedly, the appearance of this instrumental voice at the beginning of "Nimm sie hin," while it features the 5-4-3 progression in the $b^{\flat 1}$-g^1 register, completely eschews g^2. However, the autograph shows that Beethoven at first planned immediate repetitions of the 5-4-3 progression in the higher octave in the bars corresponding to 266, 274, and 292 of the final version. This latter point is also noted in ibid., pp. 146–47 and Example 14; Kerman opines, "they would certainly have sounded saccharine and flabby."

34. (Berkeley, 1984), p. 130.

35. For the "implicitly agonic" view, see Lawrence Kramer, *Music and Poetry,* p. 127; Cone's remarks on the Schubert song occur in "Words Into Music: The Composer's Approach to the Text," in *Sound and Poetry,* Northrop Frye, ed. (New York, 1957), p. 7; reprinted in Edward T. Cone, *Music: A View From Delft: Selected Essays,* ed. Robert P. Morgan (Chicago, 1989), p. 118.

36. Kerman, *"An die ferne,"* p. 145; Reynolds, "The Representational Impulse": 55.

37. Rosen, *Romantic,* likewise discusses this moment in terms of presentness; but his interpretation turns on the bringing of the past into the present rather than the making present of events properly construed as being set in the future: "this *molto adagio* is the emotional climax, the moment of most intense expression—the precise instant when past becomes indistinguishable from present. . . . It is not simply the presence of the beloved but the songs of regret and longing which are remembered and become present, and these songs are themselves already the expression of memories," p. 172.

38. Kerman, *"An die ferne,"* pp. 147–48.

39. The b♮ in the $^6_4$ chord comes from the b♭ heard on the third beat of bar 51 in song 1. Further to the resemblances noted in the main text, one might also observe the suggestion of a V→VI/C progression as G/B♮ moves to A♭/C in bar 283, a progression that both echoes the identical, and longer-range, progression governing the tonal relationship of songs 2–5 (see Example 3), and reverses the retrospective tonal sense—→VI-V/G—of the transition between songs 1 and 2 at bars 52–54.

40. From *Musicology and Difference: Gender and Sexuality in Music Scholarship,* ed. Ruth A. Solie (Berkeley, 1993), p. 235. For related concerns see also Abbate's study, "Elektra's Voice: Music and Language in Strauss's Opera," in *Richard Strauss: Elektra,* ed. Derrick Puffett (Cambridge, 1989), pp. 107–27.

41. For further references, and a rather more skeptical view of the suggested association, see Nicholas Marston, *Schumann: Fantasie,* op. 17 (Cambridge, 1992), pp. 34–42. Other recent discussions of the Beethoven connection are Berthold Hoeckner, "Schumann

and Romantic Distance," *Journal of the American Musicological Society* 50 (1997), pp. 109–32, and R. Larry Todd, "On Quotation in Schumann's Music," in *Schumann and His World*, ed. R. Larry Todd (Princeton, N.J., 1994).

42. Robert and Clara Schumann, *Briefwechsel: kritische Gesamtausgabe*, vol. 1, ed. Eva Weissweiler (Basel and Frankfurt am Main, 1984), p. 126.

43. Schumann's source for *Abendröte* could have been either *Friedrich Schlegels Gedichte* (Berlin, 1809), pp. 12–34 or the "neueste Auflage" (Vienna, 1816), 16–38. For a modern edition, see Friedrich Schlegel, *Dichtungen*, ed. Hans Eichner (Munich, Paderborn, Vienna, and Zurich, 1962), Kritische Friedrich-Schlegel-Ausgabe, ed. Ernst Behler, vol. 5, pp. 177–91; the lines quoted by Schumann are on p. 191.

44. Schumann, *Briefwechsel*, vol. 2 (Basel and Frankfurt am Main, 1987), p. 562.

45. I recognize that no g^2 is sounding in or around bar 283 itself; my point is that it is here, in bar 283, that the lover first understands who is the possessor of that other voice that he has been hearing.

46. Kerman, *"An die ferne"* p. 155.

47. Cf. Reynolds, "The Representational Impulse": 52, where he argues, "the da capo [of the music of song 1 at "dann vor diesen Liedern weichet"] is just a precondition for moving on to the coda. In terms of the text, only when the beloved has sung the lover's songs back to him can they overcome what has separated them. The resinging of the songs—namely, the da capo—makes possible the union; it is not the union itself. That emerges in the coda, as fuel for the climax." Reynolds's interpretation, however, finds no space for the Distant Beloved to speak (or sing) for herself in the sense advocated here. Barbara Turchin, "Robert Schumann's Song Cycles in the Context of the Early Nineteenth-Century 'Liederkreis'" (Ph.D. diss., Columbia University, 1981), pp. 57–58 notes, "the term da capo, with its implication of literal repeat, is perhaps not the best description of this musical return [in the last verse of "Nimm sie hin"]. Rather, Beethoven's intention is to reinterpret, poetically and musically, the opening song. . . . The final stanza thus expands to a length which is equivalent to that of the previous songs. Moreover, the increasingly condensed presentation of melodic ideas within the stanza creates a powerful, musical crescendo. In this manner Beethoven simultaneously effects a climactic recapitulation and developmental coda of great force and subtlety." The sublimated sexual connotations of the climax referred to by Turchin and Reynolds, and furthered in the coming together of the lovers envisaged in the present interpretation, are obvious enough.

48. Abbate, *Unsung Voices*, p. 29; emphasis original.

49. Italics mine in both cases.

50. P. 174.

51. Kramer, *Distant Cycles*, p. 85

52. Hoeckner, "Schumann and Romantic Distance": 60–61, from which all subsequent references and translations are taken except where otherwise identified.

53. See n. 43.

54. E. T. A. Hoffmann, "Review of Beethoven's Fifth Symphony," in *E. T. A. Hoffmann's Musical Writings: "Kreisleriana," "The Poet and the Composer," Music Criticism*, ed. David Charlton, trans. Martyn Clarke (Cambridge, Eng., 1989), p. 236; Hoffmann's review was first published in the *Leipziger allgemeine musikalische Zeitung*, 12 (1810).

55. Peter-Klaus Schuster, "In Search of Paradise Lost: Runge, Marc, Beuys," *The Romantic Spirit in German Art: 1790–1990*, ed. Keith Hartley, Henry Meyric Hughes, Peter-Klaus Schuster, and William Vaughan (London, 1994), p. 62.

PART III

BEETHOVEN
IN THE
WORKSHOP

·

The Keyboard Instruments

of the Young Beethoven

TILMAN SKOWRONECK

Introduction

The notion is almost universally assumed that Beethoven was unhappy
about his pianos throughout his whole life. His complaints concerning
the poor quality of his Erard grand[1] are widely known, as well as the
reports on the neglected state of his Broadwood piano later on[2] and his
famous remark about the piano being inadequate.[3] Yet all these comments refer to the period after 1803 when Beethoven had started to
extend the tonal range of his compositions from five to five and a half
octaves. Beethoven's early playing style is dealt with by Carl Czerny, who
states somewhat baldly:

> . . . as his playing as well as his compositions were ahead of his
> time, the extremely weak and imperfect fortepianos of that time
> (until about 1810) could often not yet support his gigantic perfor-
> mance.[4]

Assertions like Czerny's lead us to believe that Beethoven's impatience
with his pianos was perhaps even greater in his early years because they
were still more imperfect.

When William S. Newman's article "Beethoven's Pianos Versus His
Piano Ideals" appeared in 1970, even the view described above was new.
According to Newman, the hypothesis that Beethoven preferred
Broadwood's pianos and the English action had been uncritically put
forward in several major Beethoven publications. Newman seems to
have been the first who, in "re-examining the known evidence," came to
"suggest certain conclusions quite contrary to those usually stated." One

of these conclusions is that the three "Beethoven pianos" (Erard 1803, Broadwood 1817, and Graf 1825[5]) "partly for the very reason, that they are Beethoven's only extant pianos and partly because they figure specifically more than any other instruments identified with him in the early sources, have been emphasized far beyond their actual musical value to Beethoven."[6] Yet even this article seems to support Czerny's ideas. One of the questions raised at the end was "how much light knowing the pianos Beethoven actually played throws on his own music and its interpretation,"[7] because "since the piano as an instrument never seemed to come up to Beethoven's desires, we have to assume that it was not in itself a major source of inspiration for his music." [8]

A considerably more recent publication, *Fortepianos and their Music* by Katalin Komlós (1995), presents somewhat different conclusions: "From the very beginning of his Viennese career, Beethoven stretched the limits of the fortepiano. Disregard of the capabilities of the instrument is a crucial feature of Beethoven's artistic approach, which is not evident when the music is played on a modern piano . . . thus an essential aspect of the music is lost."[9] According to this line of reasoning, a positive attitude toward Beethoven's struggle with the piano can give insights into his style, which otherwise remain hidden. Still again, the existence of a struggle remains unquestioned even by Komlós.

In contrast to statements like Newman's or Komlós's, my experience has suggested that the early piano music of Beethoven gives ample proof of stretching the limits of the fortepiano *player*, partly through subjecting him to the task of *not* exposing his instrument to an excess of force in certain complex passages[10]. Also, since Beethoven in his early life made a strong impression as a keyboard virtuoso[11] this idea could not, in my opinion, have its logical explanation in any "disregard of the capabilities of the instrument."

Keeping in mind the rapid development of the fortepiano during Beethoven's lifetime, as well as his own development as a composer, it will be self-evident that we cannot speak of "Beethoven's attitude" toward "the fortepiano" of his time as a fixed entity. Trying to understand to what extent Beethoven actually stretched the limits of the instrument is an impossible task unless we limit the period of our inquiry, the instrument (or group of possible instruments), and the music in question.

This article can be seen as an attempt to discuss Beethoven's relationship to the keyboard instruments he used in his "early" period.[12]

The Keyboard Instruments of the Young Beethoven—Tradition and Choice

Clavichord, Organ, and Harpsichord

No preserved keyboard instrument has been identified as actually having been played by Ludwig van Beethoven before 1803. One exception may involve the fortepiano of Mozart. During Beethoven's first stay in Vienna in April 1787, he played for Mozart, and perhaps also took some lessons. The anecdote says that he was "taken to Mozart,"[13] so it can be assumed that he played on Mozart's own fortepiano, an instrument attributed to Anton Walter 1782,[14] which is preserved and playable today. This instrument had its normal place in Mozart's study, to be removed from the house for "all his" concerts,[15] but there are no reports of any major appearance of Mozart for that period,[16] so the instrument probably stood in Mozart's home. Obviously, the circumstances of this anecdote do not reveal anything about Beethoven's favorite instruments at that time, but it is evident that he was well acquainted with the fortepiano on this occasion, as he seems to have impressed Mozart with his playing.

Beethoven's experience with the fortepiano can be traced to 1784: The surviving part of the early concerto in E-flat major (WoO 4) bears the title: "un Concert / pour le Clavecin ou Forte-Piano / Composé par / Louis Van Beethoven / agé douze ans"[17] (his age was actually thirteen years).

Earlier than 1784 information becomes scarcer. Beethoven seems to have replaced his teacher Christian Gottlob Neefe more than occasionally as court organist (from 1781) and "cembalist" of the orchestra (1783). His interest in the organ was great at that time. Indeed, it seems that one of his first independent steps was to search out possibilities to practice on the organs of different cloisters and churches.[18]

However, what kind of instruments Beethoven used for daily practice or private performances from his seventh year—or earlier—when his musical training is supposed to have begun, to his thirteenth year, can only be guessed. There are few reasons to believe that the keyboard instruments, which are relevant for these early years, were fortepianos. Instead, it seems that our question about his relationship to that instrument should be preceded by others: Could the definite choice of the fortepiano—however "normal" in view of historical events it may seem today—have been a part of his emancipation from his early background, and what other kind of instruments suggest themselves as being pertinent to Beethoven's early training?

Apparently, Beethoven made extraordinary progress upon the keyboard right from the beginning, in spite of the harsh treatment he received from his father.[19] We can assume that the basis for his later keyboard technique was laid at this early stage, and that part of his conception of what fortepianos "should be able to do" derived from the instruments he initially had been accustomed to.

Beethoven scholarship has until very recently relied largely on the supposition that Beethoven was instructed upon the fortepiano right from the beginning.[20] A possible explanation for this belief lies in the extraordinary development and success of both instrument and composer later on. The idea of development as progress, of aesthetic transformation as a march toward a goal, of technical changes as the triumph over inferior models of the past, was largely accepted in nineteenth-century thinking. According to this view of historical change, there could be no doubt that the fortepiano, though not yet fully developed in Beethoven's earlier days, was already seen as predestined for lasting success. The few exceptions, scholars who at least admit that Beethoven *might* have played the clavichord, or "all three instruments"[21]—that is, harpsichord, clavichord, and fortepiano—do so reluctantly, partly it seems because the clavichord is a soft instrument: "The instrument [for the lessons with Neefe from around 1780] was initially probably the old clavichord, but soon already the Pianoforte,"[22] or: ". . . it would appear, that by this time [i.e. 1783], Beethoven had played the clavichord, organ, harpsichord, and presumably the piano. . . . His "Kurfürsten" Sonatas WoO 47 . . . could have been performed on a large clavichord, although with considerably less effect than on a fortepiano. . . . Beethoven was thoroughly familiar with the use of such dynamic indications as *pp, ff* (hardly for a clavichord), *cres*. . . ."[23]

Our uncertainty about his early instruments stems mainly from the—to our eyes—indistinct terminology in these documents. If we disregard conjectural substitutes of later times, as, for instance, "pianoforte" or "piano," the term clavier is used in all the sources about the young Beethoven before 1783.[24]

Clavier (or klavier; my spelling will vary, following the source at hand) represented either "whichever stringed keyboard instrument"[25] was expected in the context or, specifically, clavichord[26] or "keyboard" in general. This was the case throughout the eighteenth century.

Many eighteenth-century writers appear not to have worried much about distinctions in terminology,[27] judging from their often inconsistent use of terms such as flügel, clavecin, klavier, clavichord or fortepiano. Michael Latcham describes the typical eighteenth-century situation in an article about Mozart interpretation.[28]

During the last decades of the eighteenth century and to a lesser degree at the beginning of the next, the three instruments were thought of as members of one family, usually called "clavier." When, therefore, we ask which instrument Mozart played on or wrote for, harpsichord, piano or clavichord, we are posing the wrong question. . . . Mozart played "clavier" and wrote for "clavier." The instrument he would have used on particular occasions would have depended on suitability and availability.

Johann Nicolaus Forkel (1749–1818), on the other hand, complained in 1781 about the exclusive use of "clavier" in music editions:

The mere use of the word clavier does not suggest anything and it is indeed careless and puzzling if a composer writes: "Sonatas for clavier," without indicating at the same time to which kind they really belong. Because there is a difference whether I compose for harpsichord, fortepiano or clavichord; each composition for each of these instruments should have a different character.[29]

Clearly, Forkel's choice not to mention the specific meaning (clavier = clavichord) helps to make his point (this meaning is documented abundantly in other contemporary sources). But about the *unspecified* use of *clavier* we learn two things: there was sometimes no preunderstood context to guide even an eighteenth century "Kenner" of music, and the choice of instrument *did* matter, at least to some.

In our case, the general eighteenth-century context of keyboard lessons to a talented youngster, in a German city around 1777, with teachers born around 1739 (Johann van Beethoven) and 1708 (Gilles van den Eeden)[30] makes it possible to identify with some probability the instrument of Beethoven's early training as the clavichord. I will here give four contemporary descriptions of the merits of instruction on the clavichord, from 1753, 1768, 1773 and 1789:

Every clavierist should have a good harpsichord and also a good clavichord to be able to play all kind of pieces alternately. Who can play on the clavichord in a good fashion, will be able to do the same on the harpsichord, but not the reverse. So one must use the clavichord to learn the right expression and the harpsichord to strengthen the fingers.[31]

. . . it [the clavichord] has the advantage that one does not need to annoy oneself with [the replacing of] quill plectra, they [*sic*] also keep the tuning better . . . This is why they are used for teaching: Because anyone who has learned on it can also play on organs, harpsichords etc.[32]

I went to Mr. L'Augier's concert, which was begun by [a] child of eight or nine years old . . . who played two difficult lessons of Scarlatti, with three or four by M. Becke, upon a small, and not good Piano forte. The neatness of the child's execution did not so much surprise me, though uncommon, as her expression. All the pianos and fortes were so judiciously attended to; and there was such shading off some passages, and force given to others as nothing but the best teaching, or greatest natural feeling and sensibility could produce. I enquired of Signor Giorgio, an Italian, who attended her, upon what instrument she usually practised at home, and was answered, "on the clavichord." This accounts for her expression, and convinces me, that children should learn upon that, or a Piano Forte very early, and be obliged to give an expression to lady Coventry's Minuet, or whatever is their first tune; otherwise, after long practice on a monotonous harpsichord, however useful for strengthening the hand, the case is hopeless.[33]

For learning, the Clavichord is undeniably most suitable, at least in the beginning; because no other keyboard instrument is more suited for achieving subtlety of expression. Later, it is an advantage, if one can have a harpsichord or a good fortepiano as well; because the fingers achieve more strength and elasticity by playing on these instruments.[34]

The main source covering Beethoven's first musical steps after 1777 is the compilation of recollections of Cäcilia and Gottfried Fischer, children of the landlord of the Beethovens. In spite of the gossipy character of parts of the manuscript and the mixing up of names and events, it provides a generally reliable source of events near-at-hand: How Beethoven was treated during music lessons, what instruments he played besides the klavier, and the struggle of the landlord with too much music making, frequent visitors, or inhabitants with erratic habits (Cäcilia, eight years senior to Beethoven, showed interest in music; as a result, some of the descriptions of musical situations are quite detailed).

Compiling the information about the different activities and rooms in the house, we get the following picture: When Beethoven's clavier lessons started he was still so small that he had to stand on a little footstool in front of the instrument. This would have been in his own room, where he was seen by several persons (including Beethoven's friend Franz Wegeler who saw the "doings and sufferings of Louis" from the rear of another house), "standing at the clavier and weeping."[35] That the Beethoven boys had their bedrooms at the rear (there were four rooms at the rear of the house) is confirmed by Fischer in other contexts. Now the clavichord is a very soft instrument; if Carl Czerny's recollection of Beethoven, which relates that "in his youth he had practiced enormously, often until long after midnight"[36] is true, the clavichord would, because of its soft tone, have been the only choice to avoid constant struggle with the other inhabitants of the house.

On the other hand, the frequent music making with friends of Johann van Beethoven could be heard in the street, causing people to stop and listen.[37] Since clavichords usually are too soft for chamber music, this indicates that there must have been at least two keyboard instruments in the house, one for Ludwig's practicing in his room, and another one that stood in one of the "two big rooms towards the road." The latter instrument, "Herr Johann v. Beethoven sein Klavier," which had to be tuned by the organist Franz Joseph Mombauer,[38] was loud enough to function in chamber music and to be heard in the street. Later on, just before the Beethovens definitely moved out of the Fischer house, that is before 1787, the constant music making had become a problem for the landlord: By that time, Ludwig had a klavier at the front right above the bedroom of the Fischers. This was clearly a louder instrument than a clavichord, for it disturbed old "Master Fischer" in his afternoon sleep.[39]

What instrument Johann van Beethoven's klavier was we do not know. The title of Beethoven's first work (the Dressler variations, WoO 63, from 1782): "Variations pour le Clavecin sur une Marche de Mr. Dresler composées et dediées à son Excellence Madame Comtesse de Wolfmetternich née Baronne d'Assebourg par un jeune amateur Louis van Beethoven agé de dix ans," as well as the total absence of any dynamic signs, may suggest that they were written with a harpsichord in mind. Still, this is no firm indicator of his father's instrument. One wonders if the "Hof Tenorist" and private clavier teacher Johann van Beethoven had the means or the inclination to obtain an expensive instrument of a new kind, that is, a fortepiano.

At this point we can conclude that, according to eighteenth-century German practice, Beethoven's first instrument of daily exercise was probably a clavichord; he soon became an accomplished organist, and played harpsichord continuo in the court orchestra, and probably solo pieces on the harpsichord as well. Of all these instruments, the clavichord is the only one designed to produce dynamic shading, crescendo, and decrescendo. Despite its softness, a good clavichord can have a greater dynamic range (not level) than some early pianos, and the action is so simple that a good player can create all intended effects unhindered.[40] From a good fortepiano, keyboard players of Beethoven's generation would at least have expected qualities not inferior to this standard.

The Introduction of the Fortepiano in Bonn

We have seen that influential German writers of the eighteenth century praised the clavichord for teaching. But it was also generally acclaimed for performance, in private or for a small audience. Especially the north German school around C. P. E. Bach cultivated the clavichord as a medium for expressing the intense and spontaneous. In his autobiographical sketch, added to the contemporary German translation of Charles Burney's travel reports, C. P. E. Bach writes in 1772:

> My main study, especially in the last years, has been to play the clavichord,[41] and compose for it, as *cantabile* as possible despite its insufficient length of tone. This is not easy, if one [either] doesn't want it to sound empty, or if the noble simplicity of the melody is not to be spoiled by too much noise [i.e. probably: "by means of exaggerated embellishing"].[42]

Another musician who was positive about the clavichord was Neefe, who wrote in the preface of *Zwölf Klavier-Sonaten* (Leipzig 1773):

> These sonatas are clavichord sonatas: I would like them to be played on the clavichord only; because most of them will make little effect on the harpsichord or the fortepiano, since neither of the two is as capable of cantabile and the various modifications of tone as the clavichord.[43]

Neefe, born in 1748, had been in Bonn since 1779 and became Beethoven's teacher about 1780. As he was an admirer of Johann Sebastian and especially C. P. E. Bach, his connection with *Empfindsamkeit* and consequently the clavichord is not surprising. But ten years after the preface mentioned above, his exclusive preference for the clavichord had given way to a certain curiosity toward new developments: In a letter to Carl Friedrich Cramer's *Magazin der Musik* (2 March 1783, published on 30 March, the same letter where he mentions Beethoven as "a boy of eleven years and of promising talent" who "plays the clavier very skilfully and with power"[44]), he describes Bonn's musical life. Interestingly, he departs from the generalized use of the term clavier whenever he mentions keyboard instruments of special interest. This is the case with the collection of five historical harpsichords from between 1646 and 1664 owned by music enthusiast Hofkammerrath von Mastiaux.

We also learn that among the thirteen *Dilettanten* mentioned by Neefe (including Beethoven and six other talented youngsters) nine played clavier at varying levels, but only two persons either owned a fortepiano (or "hammerclavier") worth mentioning or were able to master it: one was Johann Gottfried von Mastiaux, who had a "large hammerclavier in the shape of a pyramid" in his collection. This clearly was a brand-new instrument, as it still had to be completed with a ped-alboard, a glockenspiel, and a stop with pipes. The other person was the obviously very talented Countess von Hatzfeld, fashionably "trained by the best Vienna masters in singing and clavier playing." She is explicitly described as a brilliant fortepiano player, and we can assume that she owned a fortepiano.

Neefe also describes the inventions by the builder of the Mastiaux hammerclavier: Gottlieb Friedrich Riedlen (born in 1749) was in Neefe's opinion a "skilled mechanicus" who, except for building "quilled harp-sichords (*Flügel*) of the ordinary kind" appears to have been very keen on innovation and experiment and certainly was a zealous promoter of his projects. His experiments with metal harpsichord plectra may not seem very extraordinary in comparison with the invention of a "means to let most clavier-instruments stay in tune, even though the climate has a strong influence on the strings" or "an instrument, which through a special mechanism prints out in notes everything that is played during the performance." Of a more serious character were probably the remaining three *Instrumente*,[45] one with "hammers of a new invention of which the player may expect nothing but satisfaction," another kind, also newly invented, with quills and hammers, and an "instrument with gut strings, with which one can make the impression of two violins, viola, cello, double bass and the flute with all ease."

It seems that Neefe was less biased against these instruments than Carl Friedrich Cramer (born in 1752) was himself. Although Cramer let instru-ment builders advertise in his music magazine,[46] reviewed the work of especially talented builders[47] and personally contributed with a lengthy report of a "Bogenhammerclavier"[48] all in the same year, at the end of 1783 he seems to have lost patience with all new tendencies, writing:

It is indeed a sad thing for music to find this sort of instrument [fortepiano] to be dominating in whole nations, and to find even in Germany, the real home of the clavier [clavichord], and especially in the southern parts, twenty good pianofortes, fortpiens [sic], clavecin-royals, and whatever else this kind of *Hackbrett* is called, for every single tolerable clavier.[49]

We need not concern ourselves with Cramer's objections against changing fashion, but the example clearly shows that the tide was definitely turning and that, especially in southern Germany, fortepianos were replacing clavichords in ever larger quantity. Equally clear, in comparison, is that in 1783 the situation in Bonn (which does not belong to the "southern parts") can be safely described as fairly provincial. Only four years later, Neefe sent another, much shorter letter to Cramer's *Magazin* in which he wrote:

The love of music is increasing greatly among the inhabitants. The clavier is especially liked; there are here several *Hämmerclaviere* [sic] by Stein of Augsburg and other equivalent instruments.[50]

adding a list of fifteen *Amateurs*[51] devoted to this instrument.

However shy Beethoven may have been when his father tried to show him off to visitors, he soon found his own ways to introduce himself to the musical scene described by Neefe in 1783. His personal contact with one of the private musical circles of Bonn in 1784,[52] when he was introduced at the house of the widow van Breuning (he soon became clavier teacher for the two children and took part in musical activities of the house) is but one example of his various connections: most officials of the court were enthusiastic musicians, and some were extraordinarily active. Johann Gottfried von Mastiaux (named above as the owner of the large hammerclavier), a devotee of Joseph Haydn, organized house concerts in his *Konzertsaal* once a week during the winter and had, apart from his many musical instruments, a huge collection of music scores. One of his five children, Caspar Anton, a good clavier player, was a friend of Beethoven's. Countess von Hatzfeld, a niece of the Elector, received the dedication of Beethoven's "Venni Amore" variations (WoO 65), composed between 1788 and 1791. She was certainly an excellent musician.

[She had been] trained in singing and clavier playing by the best masters of Vienna to whom, indeed, she does very much honour. She declaims recitatives outstandingly and it is a pleasure to listen

to her sing arias "di parlante." She plays the fortepiano brilliantly
and in playing yields herself completely to her emotions, therefore
one can often hear the "tempo rubato" without her losing the
beat. She is enthusiastically devoted to music and musicians.[53]

Countess von Hatzfeld was one of the persons who had brought
about the appointment of Neefe as court organist. Even if Beethoven
first met her through Neefe after 1780, the meeting probably took place
much earlier than 1788.

Neefe himself started an agency for fortepianos and clavichords of
Friederici and other renowned masters.[54] There was thus ample occasion for Beethoven to become acquainted with the new fortepiano once
he started to be active in public performance himself, and we can therefore assume that his possible association with the clavichord became less
important rather than being strengthened when Neefe became his
teacher, despite Neefe's earlier affinity with this instrument.

The titles of Beethoven's compositions give some evidence of this
development[55]: Of his works for keyboard instruments from the Bonn
period, two are for "clavecin ou fortepiano" (the early concerto from
1784 being the first, see above), one for "pianoforte ou orgue," and
three (from 1787) are exclusively for "fortepiano" (as compared to two
works for "clavecin" in all: the early Dressler variations and, somewhat
unexpectedly, the "Venni Amore" variations for Countess von Hatzfeld).
His chamber music is for "clavecin ou fortepiano" in one case, for
"fortepiano" twice and for "clavecin" twice. His eleven songs are all for
voice "and clavier"; five works bear no prescription at all.

The songs, primarily written for private performance, were obviously
intended for whichever keyboard instrument was available, or clavichord, but the chronology of most of the other works shows a tendency
away from the harpsichord toward the fortepiano.

As recent research on the instruments of important builders[56] has
invariably led to the postdating of important developments in fortepiano building (such as the introduction of the so-called German, or
Prellzungen, piano action by J. A. Stein), the notion that fortepianos of a
quality to satisfy professional musicians or advanced *Liebhaber* appeared
in Bonn only shortly before Neefe wrote about them in 1783 is not altogether unlikely. The exact pace of the fortepiano's introduction in
Bonn's musical circles cannot, however, be concluded from the documents. On the other hand, the Stein "grand" fortepiano type, which
only a little later turned out to be important for Beethoven's early
career as a fortepianist, certainly came to Bonn after 1783 and before
1787, as a comparison of the two letters by Neefe quoted above shows.

Towards a Personal Conception of Fortepiano Playing

If we can believe the widow Karth (whose testimony is treated some-what reluctantly in general by Thayer, Schiedermair, and others), Count Waldstein gave Beethoven a fortepiano as a present in 1788.[57] By then, Beethoven had been in Vienna for the first time, and on his way back probably visited the workshop of Johann Andreas Stein,[58] one of the most influential fortepiano builders of his time.

By 1791, Beethoven's reputation as an outstanding fortepiano player had grown considerably. A well-known description of his playing was written by Carl Ludwig Junker in November of that year. Here we find also the first testimony of Beethoven's interest in the quality of keyboard instruments (Junker had listened to the musicians of the Bonn court chapel during their stay at Mergentheim, between September and October 1791):

> I heard also one of the greatest Klavier players, the dear, good Bethofen, some compositions by whom appeared in the Speier Blumenlese in 1783, written in his eleventh year. True, he did not perform in public, probably the instrument was not to his mind. It was a Flügel by Späth and in Bonn he is accustomed only to play upon one by Stein. Yet, to my far greater pleasure, I heard him extemporize, I was even invited to give a theme for him to vary.
> . . . Even all the outstanding members of this orchestra [the Elector's orchestra] are his admirers, and all ears, when he plays. But he remains modest and free from all pretension. Nevertheless he confessed that upon the journeys, which the Elector had enabled him to make, he had seldom found in the playing of the most famous Klavier players what he supposed he had a right to expect. His playing differs so much from the usual way of treating the Klavier, that it seems as if he had made his own path towards the perfection he has reached now.[59]

Beethoven's refusal to perform on a Späth instrument deserves some explanation: Franz Jacob Späth from Regensburg (c.1714–1786) is said to have invented the *Tangentenflügel,* a harpsichord-shaped instrument with an action different from both harpsichord or forte-piano (and in fact in every way from the clavichord, despite the term *tangent* for the tone-producing device of both instruments).[60] On depressing the key in a *Tangentenflügel* a wooden strip, not unlike a harpsichord jack, is propelled through an intermediate lever called a *Treiber,* or driver, upward to the string. It then immediately falls back.

The technical difference from the early piano (of whichever sort) is that this tangent slides loosely in a channel, unconnected to any part of the mechanism. The top of this tangent is usually uncovered, and therefore produces a sharp and somewhat cymbalonlike sound, which differs considerably from the "average" fortepiano sound of that time, produced by leather-covered wooden hammers. The difference between this and the harpsichord is that the sound is produced not by plucking, but by striking the string, which allows for dynamic variation (in the case of the clavichord the tangent is in contact with the string even after the attack).

The fact that all *Tangentenflügel* preserved today were built after 1790 by Späth's son-in-law and successor Christoph Friedrich Schmahl (1739–1814),[61] has recently led to some discussion about whether common contemporary wordings referring to Späth's own production (as for example "*Flügel* from Regensburg," a "Spättisches *Fortepiano*," "*Fortepiano* in der Form eines *Flügels*") invariably mean the *Tangentenflügel*, since he may have produced other sorts of instruments as well.[62] In the case of Junker's report, however, Beethoven's refusal to perform suggests an instrument that differed in some way from a fortepiano (the term *Flügel* used here, otherwise reserved exclusively for harpsichord—and Tangenten*flügel*—until well into the nineteenth century,[63] indicates the same). It is not possible to trace the exact nature of Beethoven's problems with this Späth *Flügel*; Junker's account suggests that Beethoven improvised on that very instrument in spite of his possible reservations. He may only have been unaccustomed to its action, or it could have been acoustically unsuited for a performance before a larger audience.

The Stein Fortepiano, to which Beethoven had access in Bonn, would have been a wing-shaped, double-strung concert instrument with a compass of five octaves, a German action and light (probably solid) wooden hammers with leather covering.[64] This fortepiano may or may not have been the present from Count Waldstein mentioned earlier.[65] The idea that one or several of the Stein "grands" in Bonn that Neefe named in 1878 were easily accessible to Beethoven is certainly more appealing than the notion that such an expensive instrument would have been given to him and, indeed, been accepted by him.[66]

Although it has been observed that Junker "had much to gain from being impressed and absolutely nothing to gain from criticizing" and that his enthusiastic report might have been an attempt to "depict himself close to court society,"[67] this is the only detailed contemporary evidence of the characteristics of Beethoven's playing we have. More important still, we know exactly *when* Junker heard Beethoven play.

The most interesting information revealed by Junker is that Beethoven at twenty was already at a stage where he played markedly differently from other fortepianists, and thought about playing in a different way (his disapproval of the usual manner of treating the fortepiano recurs in his correspondence with Andreas Streicher in 1796, see pages 171–175). It is evident that Beethoven's idiosyncratic approach to the fortepiano as described by Junker was modeled on the Stein, and that the expressive potential of this type of instrument did not seriously frustrate his approach. If, as I initially stated, his conception of what the fortepiano "should be able to do" derived from the earlier types of instruments, his discovery of "what the fortepiano could do better" than other instruments has to be seen in direct connection with the characteristics and possibilities of the Stein fortepiano.

Franz Gerhard Wegeler, who also reports from the Mergentheim journey,[68] seems confident about the details,[69] but might be wrong regarding the chronology of events. Apropos Beethoven's encounter with the keyboard virtuoso Sterkel, Wegeler writes: "Beethoven, who until then had not heard any great, outstanding clavier player, did not know the finer *nuances* in the treatment of the instrument; his playing was rough and hard."[70]

By 1791 Beethoven had already been in Vienna and had certainly heard other famous keyboard players, much as suggested by Junker. Schiedermair, who discusses the passage, says that Beethoven later told Schindler that his playing had been "rough" because he was used to playing the organ at that time.[71] In addition, Wegeler's anecdote asserts that Beethoven easily adjusted to Sterkel's rather different and "somewhat ladylike" playing, a quality altogether incompatible with a rough and hard technique. Beethoven's own explanation suggests that the testimony about his rough playing simply found its way into a wrong story. As I have mentioned above, Beethoven is believed to have been especially keen on organ playing during the early 1780s rather than in 1791.

Another anecdote suggesting "rough playing" is equally difficult to date, and still more difficult to analyze. This is Anton Reicha's description of Beethoven performing a Mozart concerto at the Bonn court:

One evening when Beethoven was playing a Mozart piano concerto at the Court, he asked me to turn the pages for him. But I was mostly occupied in wrenching out the strings of the piano, which snapped, while the hammers stuck among the broken strings. Beethoven insisted upon finishing the concerto, so back and forth I leaped, jerking out a string, disentangling a hammer, turning a page, and I worked harder than did Beethoven.[72]

As pointed out above, fortepianos of a design to be used in concerto performances came to the Bonn Court after 1783, allowing us to locate this incident somewhere between 1783 and 1792, when Beethoven left Bonn.[73] But even if we knew the exact date, without knowing more about the circumstances we cannot establish any theory about Beethoven's technical approach. It is extremely hard to break strings in early fortepianos without damaging parts of the action first.[74] So even if Beethoven played too loud, or was carried away by temperament (or was unusually tense because of performing a concerto at the court), some other influence may have caused strings to break.

Actual string breakage occurs as a consequence of structural weakness of individual handcrafted strings or wrong string dimensions in certain areas of the instrument. Such structural weaknesses reveal themselves usually when other conditions change: after the instrument has been tuned up (for instance to match the pitch of an orchestra), as a reaction to changes of climate (caused, for instance, by sudden draft, candles, or the public), or at the first few occasions when a new instrument is used for an entire performance.

Disentangling broken strings during a performance on the other hand is an intricate maneuver to be performed quickly; along with the obvious pleasure Reicha has in telling this story, it might well reflect the recollection of his involvement rather than the actual number of broken strings. The fact that Beethoven played on suggests that this number may have been lower than Reicha implies.

The Early Vienna Years—the Choice Redefined

The Early Fortepiano in Vienna

Which sort of fortepiano Beethoven used privately during those first years after he moved to Vienna 1792 is not known, and may in fact be of little consequence. Directly after his arrival he rented a clavier of some sort, as several entries in his diary show, for little less than half of his monthly house rent, or the price of a pair of boots.[75] Between 1794 and 1795 he was a permanent guest of Prince Lichnowsky,[76] who was a good fortepiano player himself. I have not found any information about the instrument Lichnowsky had.

For his appearances in public or in private circles he would have used the fortepianos provided for the occasion; after 1790, the fortepiano had definitely replaced the harpsichord (and the clavichord) in Vienna.

If Beethoven during the first years of establishing his fame as a concert pianist and extemporizer made use of the different kinds of fortepianos[77] representative of Vienna during this period, no documentary evidence can be found about his personal preferences before 1796. Three documents between 1796 and 1802 name Beethoven together with a piano builder. They illustrate in due course his mastery of one type of instrument, his criticism of another, and finally his preference: the first[78] names a new Walter piano at the house of an actor named Müller, "mastered [by Beethoven] to enchantment [of the listeners]" in April 1796. The second, a letter from Beethoven to Andreas Streicher (November 1796), discusses the qualities of a Streicher fortepiano, which Beethoven had borrowed for one of his concerts.[79] The third document is the well-known reminiscence of Carl Czerny, who in the winter of 1799–1800[80] was introduced to Beethoven. The ten-year-old Czerny noticed a Walter fortepiano[81] at Beethoven's place, and remembers that these instruments were "then the best."[82]

So at the latest toward the end of 1801, Beethoven had deliberately chosen a Walter fortepiano (or at least accepted one offered to him) in spite of his friendship with Andreas and Nanette Streicher, who represented the building tradition of J. A. Stein. The next sections will investigate the process that may have led to this choice.

Beethoven's Impression on His Public

The majority of the thirty-three contemporary reports about Beethoven's playing before 1800 I have analyzed agree about its general character.[83] As soon as he started to appear in public in 1795 (if Beethoven performed much during his very first years in Vienna, not many reports of these occasions survive), his performances (for instance, of his first two piano concertos) led without exception to great acclaim. Most reports applauded the brilliancy, virtuosity, and ease of his performance. In 1795–1796, in Vienna and during concert tours, he invariably "enchanted" his public, both in performing written music[84] and in public improvisation. In 1798 and on one later occasion, his playing, and the content of his improvisations or his compositions were criticized by two writers independently, both for lacking clarity and for unevenness.

If his stage manners in 1791 had provoked a characterization of him as a "dear, good" and modest man, by 1799 his behavior was described as somewhat "haughty" (compared to the virtuoso Joseph Wölffl[85]). In 1800, the encounter with the provocative Daniel Steibelt[86] made him improvise in an offensive manner and behave rudely.

Reports about the lack of order in Beethoven's study, his neglecting to tune his own fortepiano, his quick temper, and the lack of clarity in his playing became common in the first decade of the nineteenth century. But only a trace of such eccentricities can be sensed in the early reports. So, for example, his sudden fits of temper and the rude impression he frequently made are scarcely documented before 1800. Also, of all witnesses, only Anton Reicha and Ignaz von Seyfried seem to have observed any peculiarity about Beethoven's forceful or vigorous treatment of the fortepiano before the turn of the century. Seyfried described Beethoven's playing (thirty years after the event) as follows: ". . . his playing tore along like a wildly foaming cataract, and the conjurer [i.e., Beethoven] constrained his instrument to an utterance so forceful, that the stoutest structure was scarcely able to withstand it."[87]

Seyfried may have inserted this passage in order to illustrate Beethoven's genius in a romantic way.[88] Still, even Seyfried does not go so far as to state that a fortepiano actually was damaged on any occasion. Descriptions of Beethoven breaking piano strings in fits of anger and about his lack of care for his own instruments always refer (with the exception of Reicha's anecdote discussed above) to situations after 1800.[89] Most probably, such events would otherwise have been put to paper by someone from the "enchanted audiences" or by his friends. That anything of the sort would have disturbed the generally positive musical impression made by Beethoven during this period is certain.

Two Letters to Andreas Streicher

The pianist, fortepiano teacher, and piano manufacturer Andreas Streicher is delightfully clear about the kind of virtuoso attitude that an audience in 1801 would have rejected. In his booklet about the treatment of the instruments built by his wife Nanette, the tasks and limitations of a good fortepiano player are described as follows (all italics in Streicher's texts are original):

All musical instruments, *even the human voice,* have their own range of expression, which cannot be transgressed without making a bad impression on the listeners, or provoking reproaches from the *connoisseur.*[90] . . . Neither shall [the fortepianist] tyrannize his instrument, nor is he its slave. Bravely he renders himself to all the fire of his passion; but pure taste holds the reins and prevents him from producing ugly tones. . . . *Everybody flies from rough expression.*[91]

Further on, Streicher compares the stage behavior of a "good" and a "bad" fortepianist. The latter is described like this:

> A player with the reputation: "he plays extraordinarily and such as you have never heard," sits down (or throws himself) at the fortepiano. Already his first chords are given with such strength, that one wonders if he is deaf, or thinks that his audience is. By moving his body, arms and hands he seems to want to show, how difficult the labor undertaken by him is. Getting excited, he treats his instrument like one seeking revenge, who has got hold of his hereditary enemy and is about to torture him to death slowly with cruel lust. He wants to play forte, but since he already overdone it at the beginning, it is no longer possible to produce more sound. So he *pounds*, and now the abused strings go out of tune, some of them fly among the listeners, who hastily retreat in order to protect their eyes. At this note stands sforzato! Luckily, the hammer and the string still hold. But listen, how the tone grinds, how painful it is to the ear! He transforms passionate fire to anger, and he expresses soothing feelings by *cold playing*. —Since he exaggerates everything, it is natural, that, when expressing the sensation of pain, he lets the fortepiano squeal and howl, and during quick and joyful melodies beats into lameness keys and hammers . . .[92]

Of course, this description of a fictive would-be virtuoso is somewhat exaggerated. But we can safely assume that Beethoven's difference from *serious* contemporary pianists depended upon other characteristics, or rather qualities, than those named by Streicher. Two letters from Beethoven's early correspondence show that he actively sought friendly contact with Streicher, and that they shared certain ideas about fortepiano playing. These letters represent the only authentic utterances by Beethoven about pianism (from this time), and the early Viennese fortepiano[93] (at all). As we do not know Streicher's part of this correspondence, the character of the relationship between the two men can only be sensed through Beethoven's manner of writing, so I will quote both letters in full.

In the first letter (c. July–September 1796), Streicher is addressed as piano teacher, and the remarks about piano playing have to be understood as an exchange between two fortepianists:

> Dear Streicher! I really must apologize for answering so late to your friendly letter . . . to tell the truth, I was prevented by my work piling up. Your little pupil moved me to tears, when she

played my adagio, and astonished me besides. I wish you good luck, that you are so fortunate to be able to demonstrate your insights with such a talented pupil, being equally glad for the fact, that the dear little [girl] with all her gifts obtained you as a master. Sincerely, dear Streicher, for the first time I dared to listen to my terzett[94] in performance, and this will really make me compose more for the klavier than before, I will be content, [even] if only few [should] understand me. Up till now, the way of treating the klavier is certainly still the most uncultivated of all instruments, often one believes oneself hearing only a harp, and I am glad, that you are one of the few who understand that if one can feel, one also can sing on the klavier. I hope a time will come, where the harp and the klavier are two totally different instruments. Besides, I believe that you can let her play anywhere, and, between us, she would make some of our ordinary conceited lyre-grinders ashamed.

One more thing: I hope you will not blame me, if I show just a little interest in her education? That is, that I only concern myself about her progress, because without wanting to flatter you, I would not know what to tell her more or better than you. Just let me contemplate her progress and encourage her. —Farewell now, dear Streicher and remain my friend as I am wholly

Your true friend   L. v. Beethoven

[Postscript] I hope to be able to visit you soon, and to let you know my house number, my regards to your dear wife. [95]

The main subject of this letter is Beethoven's interest in one of Streicher's gifted pupils.[96] The famous passage about piano playing fulfills two functions:

1. To create a general basis of communication. After returning from a five month concert tour to Prague, Dresden, Leipzig, and Berlin in the spring of 1796, Beethoven had to reestablish contacts with his acquaintances.

2. To flatter. Beethoven obviously feared that his interest in the girl might be taken as interference. A means to achieve a desired reaction would be to allude to items of shared interest, so Beethoven inserted a passage that represented the content of both his own and Streicher's opinions, to establish the feeling of mutual understanding. So it is no

mere coincidence that the vocabulary used in Streicher's own book, written five years later, is strikingly similar to Beethoven's:

> It is a pity, how few of all those who play the fortepiano try to treat it according to its true nature. Nothing is more common than to hear this resourceful instrument *ill-treated* in a way to produce no better effect than a tinkling harp or a miserable Hackbrett.[97]

About producing a singing tone on the piano, Streicher has this to say:

> [For the fortepianist it is important] to have an instrument which enables him to *play lightly, singing, dextrously and with expression.*[98] . . . [The good player] knows how to let the tone sing, without straining his instrument.[99]

Not very long ago, faithful replicas of historical fortepianos were still scarce and many of the extant originals had not yet undergone careful restoration, so that the sound generally associated with Beethoven's early pianos would easily have allowed for interpreting the "harp" mentioned by Beethoven as his personal implicit criticism of the instruments themselves. Reading Beethoven's lines without prejudice toward an early and "defective" instrument, we see Beethoven's commands mean nothing of the sort. He, "who can feel," can also "sing" on the klavier; so it is the fault of the *player* if the klavier sounds like a harp. Or, in Streicher's words:

> If some believe that it is far inferior to the other instruments for *expressive playing*, this accusation can only mean those fortepianos, which have an inflexible tone, *which are very heavy to play, and where the action does not support the movement of the fingers.* . . .

> But even the best action can but *prepare a good touch.* It can only *make it possible and easy* for the player *to touch in such a way*, that the tone produced is exactly of the character desired by the music or his feeling. It is *his* task to enliven the action. *He alone* is responsible if his instrument makes a better or worse impression . . .[100]

As Streicher's book was written to accompany the instruments built in the workshop of his wife (and of Streicher himself), he naturally points out later in the text that these instruments have all the qualities required. Beethoven seems to have shared this opinion insofar as he did not question their capacities for "singing" in his letter. He also borrowed Streicher's fortepianos for his concerts.

In November of the same year 1796, Beethoven writes to Streicher from Pressburg (today's Bratislava, some 50 km from Vienna), where he was to give an *Akademie*. Obviously, he had asked Streicher to send a fortepiano for this concert, and had agreed to try to sell it by negotiations not known to us:

Dear Streicher!
I received your fortepiano, which is really marvelous, the day before yesterday. Anybody else would like to have it for his own, and [should be: but] I—You may laugh, but I would have to lie, if I didn't tell you, that it is too good for me, and why?—Because it deprives me of the freedom to create my own tone. Besides, this shall not hinder you to make all your fortepianos in the same way, there will not be found many others with equal whims. Wednesday the 23rd will be my *Akademie*. If Stein [Streicher's brother-in-law Matthäus Andreas Stein] wants to come, he is cordially welcome, certainly he can sleep at my place.—

I had the same idea about selling the fortepiano before you, and certainly I will try to carry it out. Thank you very much for responding to my wishes, I only wish to be able to return some of your politeness, and [I wish] that you were convinced without me here saying so about how much I wish that the qualities of your instruments will be recognized here and elsewhere. I also wish that you will always like me and regard me

as your loving and warm friend   Beethoven

Pressburg, November 19, 1796, *post christum natum*

[postscript] Many regards to your wife and to bride and bridegroom [M. A. Stein had married seven days earlier.][101]

As the letter is adorned with many compliments it is hard to understand what Beethoven wanted to communicate with these lines. Since Beethoven agreed to promote the sale of a fortepiano, which he had borrowed for a concert, Streicher would not even have expected Beethoven to buy the fortepiano, so it seems logical at first glance to interpret the letter as a compliment (William Newman even talks about "enigmatic joshing").

Still, Beethoven's wish to "create his own tone" (a novelty in terms of eighteenth-century musicianship) bears a clear note of criticism. This criticism does not appear to be aimed at the instrument in question alone, because Beethoven states explicitly that his idiosyncratic fancies should not prevent Streicher from building "all his instruments" with the same quality. Instead, it was the *type* of fortepiano that prevented Beethoven from creating his own tone. As mentioned above, Beethoven used a fortepiano by Anton Walter in 1800. This letter may indicate that he had started to contemplate alternatives to the Streicher/Stein model already in 1796.

The Interaction of Building Concept and Performance Aesthetics

Two Viennese "Original" Builders

My interpretation of Beethoven's second letter would be difficult to verify, had not contemporary writers shown the inclination to describe the "German" (Stein/Streicher) and "Viennese" (Walter) fortepianos in terms of contrast. The most important and comprehensive description of the two traditions comes from Ferdinand von Schönfeld, also in 1796:

> It is certain that in a manner of speaking we have two "original" instrument builders, that is Walter and Streicher; all the others imitate either the former or the latter; especially Walter has many copyists, as many come from his school.[102]

The third builder named in this text is Johann Schanz, who according to Schönfeld built his instruments as copies of Stein (a characterization not supported by Schanz's surviving instruments[103]). But even if Schönfeld were not used to careful analysis or description of technical detail, he did not fail to observe the consequences that piano design could have on the manner of playing:

> As we now have two "original" instrument builders, we divide our fortepianos in two groups: those of Walter and those of Streicher. On careful observation, we can divide our greatest pianists in two groups as well. The first of these groups likes to stimulate the ear strongly, that is with a lot of noise, consequently it plays very sonorously, extremely quickly, exercises the trickiest passages and

the quickest octave-leaps. This asks for force and strong nerves,[104] by exerting these, one cannot achieve a certain moderation, so one needs a fortepiano, which does not start to jangle.

For virtuosos of this kind we recommend a fortepiano of Walter's kind. The other group of our great pianists seeks nourishment for the soul, and likes not only precise, but also sweet, melting playing. Those cannot chose a better instrument than one of Streicher, or the so-called Stein model.[105]

The reason why the first group of powerful pianists should use the Walter model is, according to Schönfeld, because other instruments (i.e., of Streicher's model) would start to "jangle" (the German expression is: "überschnappende Schwebung"). Schönfeld gives no technical explanation for this. Neither does Streicher himself give the whole explanation as to why his instruments might not support such strong attacks:

> *Strong pounding* (which cannot but spoil any fortepiano) gives in any case far less tone than is generally believed, because each string can only give a certain degree of volume. If one wants to exceed this limit by a vigorous attack, [the string] will vibrate in an unnatural way.[106]

Obviously Streicher chose consciously not to include an advanced discussion of technical detail in his book, perhaps to avoid being criticized as old-fashioned. As will be seen, the retaining of a conservative action design by the Streicher firm was no mere lack of innovative fantasy. His action was the result of a carefully judged balance of interactive mechanical elements, and was perfectly suited to his performance aesthetics.

Understanding the principles that lie behind the differences between Walter's and Streicher's fortepianos may contribute to an understanding of Beethoven's criticism of Streicher and his choice of Walter's instruments.

Streicher versus Walter

Some general differences between Streicher's and Walter's pianos during the last decade of the eighteenth century concern the weight of the moving parts of the action and the strings: the Streicher firm retained the wooden kapsels, very thin hammer shanks, and very light hammers of Stein.[107] Walter used brass kapsels and heavier hammers.

Walter's strings were generally thicker than Streicher's and the treble of his instruments from around b1 was triple strung.[108]

The main difference that explains both the two characterizations given by Schönfeld and the caution recommended by Streicher regarding "pounding," is the absence of a *hammer backcheck* in the latter's instruments. This device has the function of catching the hammer on returning from the attack, preventing it from hopping up and striking the string again. This effect would be the normal result of forceful playing on Streicher's instruments.[109] Stein, and Andreas and Nanette Streicher, relied mainly on the absorbing quality of the material that covered the *hammer rest.[110]* Walter, on the other hand, did incorporate checks in his construction,[111] enabling the pianist to play at whichever dynamic level he desired without the hammer rebounding.

The following description (again by Schönfeld) of the development of tone characteristics in Walter's instruments explain what Streicher had in mind by stating that strong pounding cannot but spoil *any* fortepiano (italics mine):

> [Walter's] fortepianos have a full bell-like tone, a clear attack and a strong, full bass. At first, the tone is somewhat dull; if one has played for some time, it becomes very clear, especially in the treble. If they are played very much, the tone soon becomes sharp and ironlike, which can be corrected by re-leathering the hammers.[112]

Streicher himself could not resist commenting upon the same phenomenon in his own words, but without actually naming Walter:

> [One can assume] that, if the separate tones as well as those played simultaneously shall please or move, they should as much as possible resemble those of the best wind instruments.

> If the tone of the fortepiano is different (a so-called *silver tone*, which soon, especially when playing strongly, becomes an *iron tone*), it already borders on the *dry, thin, meager*; and it is too far away from a resemblance to the human voice, or to those instruments that so strongly influence our feeling with their round sound that fills the whole ear.[113]

The iron tone described here is caused by the change in density of the leather hammer covering through playing.[114] Clearly, the covering of Walter's hammers wore out rather quickly, maybe because of its different material or because of the louder playing pianists associated with Walter, but also as a consequence of his heavier hammers.[115]

It appears that Streicher not only regarded the lighter construction as sufficiently efficient[116] but hesitated to change it in a way so as to make it less enduring or to tempt pianists to exceed the limits of his instruments. His description of *the string* that starts to vibrate in an unnatural way,[117] taken literally, is a clear indication of his opinion about these limits. The pianist was not even to go so far as to let the hammers bounce twice, because the limit of the strings was reached at lower dynamic levels.

Discussing Beethoven's "Own Tone"

Beethoven's letter to Streicher from Pressburg helps to define both the limits he was willing to observe in 1796 and the particular character of his preference.

We can assume that Beethoven himself had taken the initiative to borrow Streicher's fortepiano since in his letter he thanks Streicher for "responding to his wishes"; therefore it was probably not Streicher who had asked Beethoven to promote his instruments in concert. As mentioned above, Beethoven had been acquainted with Stein's pianos since his last years in Bonn, so there can be no doubt that he knew what particular features[118] he would encounter in such an instrument. Clearly, the limitations of its construction presented no serious problem to him. Performing[119] on an instrument which sounded good but deprived him of the "freedom to create his own tone," as he wrote to Streicher, neither frustrated his expressive ambitions so much as to be reflected in his letter, nor created restrictions in terms of his playing technique. In Schönfeld's terms, Beethoven may well have been a pianist of "force and strong nerves," but he was certainly capable of "a certain moderation" when necessary to perform on an instrument of a type that otherwise would have started to "jangle."

If Beethoven's "virtues," displayed in this historical performance situation—his tolerance toward instrumental limits and his flexible musicianship—reveal an unknown facet of "Beethovenian" attitude, his modest remark that he preferred to create his "own tone" seems to represent a well-known side of his character. Indeed, our previous discussion of Walter's model invites us to interpret "his own tone" as simply "more tone," which is verifiable because absolute volume turned out to become an almost *exclusive* concern of Beethoven later on. But this is a tricky discussion, as his focus through the years shifted away from aesthetics, first to a wish to hear his fortepianos better, and finally to the rather fruitless attempts toward constructions that enabled him to hear the instruments at all.[120] Beethoven's hearing had started to deteriorate somewhere around 1797,[121] so one should not confuse his later problems with whichever interpretation one gives to "his own tone" in 1796. But we can go so far as to assert that Walter's action has certain advantages for the realization of some of Beethoven's specialities. It is, for instance, easier to give long fortissimo passages (such as the closing formula in the first movement of his Sonata op. 2, no. 3) the impression of a fully engaged classical orchestra, without having to think about the limits of the instrument. Furthermore, the execution of most *sforzati* is made much easier by employing an action with a *check*, that is, without the risk of the hammers rebounding and striking twice.

Epilogue: Extension of Range in 1803

While there is a lack of information about Beethoven's own fortepiano(s) between 1796 and the beginning of 1800, when the young Czerny observed a Walter piano in Beethoven's room, his inclination toward the "Viennese" type can be reasonably sensed. Apart from the possibility that the Walter "sound" may have appealed to Beethoven, it seems likely that he preferred to use instruments that did not force him to check his spontaneous musical approach, precisely because he did *not* want to exceed the limits of the instrument. In this respect Walter's fortepianos seem to have satisfied Beethoven for some time, even though his personal relations with Walter were far less cordial than those he had with Streicher. In a letter dated November 1802, he communicates details about the purchase of a new Walter fortepiano[122] to his friend Nikolaus Zmeskall:

You may, dear Z., present to Walter my affair in a strong dose, first of all because he deserves it anyway; but also because the whole swarm of klavier builders crowds to serve me since the time they started to think I was at odds with Walter,—and that free of charge, everyone wants to make a klavier as I want it. For example Reicha has been asked urgently by the maker of his klavier to talk me round to let him make a piano forte, and he is still one of the worthier, where I already have seen some good instruments—you have to tell him, that I will pay him 30 Dukaten, when I can have it gratis from all the others, but I will only give 30 Dukaten on the condition that it is made from mahogany, and I also want to have the *una corda* stop, —if he does not agree, tell him that I will choose one of the other [builders], to whom I will tell all this. . . .[123]

Indeed, the climate between the two men seems to have been rather frosty. But it is obvious that Beethoven dearly wanted to obtain one of Walter's instruments, although he seems to be trying to dictate the price.

One of the possible reasons why Beethoven tried to purchase a new Walter piano in 1802 was that he needed a larger instrument. Viennese builders—including even Streicher—had started to add some keys in the treble by the last decade of the eighteenth century, and by 1802 Beethoven may have sensed that these novelties had come to stay. Already in early sketches for his third piano concerto from April 1800, he had exceeded the usual five-octave range with two notes, and by its premiere, April 5, 1803, he had extended the treble to c^4.[124]

The first identified larger instrument in Beethoven's possession is the "piano forme Clavecin" from Erard (preserved today),[125] which was given to him as a present on August 8, 1803. This instrument has a compass of five-and-a-half octaves and an action that is very closely related to Broadwood's grand action.[126] It is not known whether the arrival of the Erard had any influence on the planned purchase of the Walter. But from 1803 on, he in any case started to use bigger ranges in most of his compositions for piano (initially five and one half octaves of the Erard, later six octaves, as in many Viennese fortepianos after around 1805).

Conclusion

We have seen that early on Beethoven became used to the best fortepianos of his time (the Stein instruments in Bonn) and that after 1791 he used the various types common in Vienna to the general delight of his public and that he was well aware of their different characteristics, choosing the Walter for himself, but not totally rejecting the Stein/Streicher model. Obviously, he felt more need to criticize contemporary pianists than to comment upon instruments in a negative way, at least in writing.

Consequently, his sometimes extreme musical notation from this period may be seen as a faithful reproduction of what was possible for Beethoven the pianist on the instruments of the day, rather than as idealistic, visionary, or transcendent transcriptions of musical ideas (impossible to be performed literally by *any* pianist).[127]

An analysis of the relationship between Beethoven's musical notation of the early period and the characteristics of relevant fortepianos should be based on the belief that his extreme dynamics, long slurs, and awkward passage work, however provocative or challenging they may have been to the contemporary pianist, were nevertheless first and foremost intended as practical and realizable.

REFERENCES

Adlung, Jakob. *Musica Mechanica Organoedi* (Berlin, 1768). Facs. ed. Christhard Marenholz. (Kassel, 1931).

Bach, Carl Philipp Emanuel. *Versuch über die wahre Art, das Clavier zu spielen.* (Berlin, 1753 and 1762). Christian Friedrich Henning. Facs. ed. Lothar Hoffmann-Erbrecht. (Leipzig, 1957).

Barth, George. *The Pianist as Orator.* (Ithaca and London, 1992).

Beethoven, Ludwig van. *Briefwechsel Gesamtausgabe.* Ed. Sighard Brandenburg. (Munich, 1996).

Burney, Charles. *Tagebuch einer musikalischen Reise.* Trans. C. D. Ebeling. 1772. (Hamburg, 1772). Ed. Richard Schaal. (Wilhelmshaven, 1975).

Cramer, Carl Friedrich. *Magazin der Musik.* (1783–1787). Facs. repr. (Hildesheim and New York, 1971–1974).

Czerny, Carl. "Erinnerungen aus meinem Leben," from *Über den richtigen Vortrag der sämtlichen Beethofen'schen Klavierwerke.* (1842). Ed. Paul Badura-Skoda. (Vienna, 1963).

DeNora, Tia. *Beethoven and the Construction of Genius.* (Berkeley and London, 1995).

Ferguson, Howard. *Keyboard interpretation.* (Oxford, 1975).

Fischer, Gottfried. *Des Bonner Bäckermeisters Gottfried Fischer Aufzeichnungen über Beethovens Jugend.* Ed. Joseph Schmidt-Görg. (Munich-Duisburg, 1971).

Gätjen, Bram. "Das Hammerklavier—akustisches Bindeglied zwischen Clavichord, Cembalo und modernem Flügel? Untersuchungen zur Wechselwirkung zwischen Hammer und Saite." From *Zur Geschichte des Hammerklaviers.* (Blankenburg, 1993).

Harding, Rosamond E. M. *The Piano-Forte.* (London, 1933 and 1978).

Komlós, Katalin. *Fortepianos and Their Music.* (Oxford, 1995).

Latcham, Michael. "Alternatives to the modern piano for the performance of Mozart." Lecture at Institut für Aufführungspraxis Michaelstein. c. 1992.

———. 1993. "The check in some early pianos and the development of piano technique around the turn of the 18th century." *Early Music,* February 1993: 28–42.

———. "The pianos of Johann Andreas Stein." From *Zur Geschichte des Hammerklaviers.* (Blankenburg, 1993).

———. 1997. "Mozart and the pianos of Gabriel Anton Walter." *Early Music,* August 1997: 382–400.

Lelie, Christo. *Van Piano tot Forte.* (Kampen, 1995).

Newman, William S. "Beethoven's Pianos Versus His Piano Ideals." *Journal of the American Musicological Society* 23: 484–504

———. 1988. *Beethoven on Beethoven. Playing His Piano Music His Way.* (New York, 1970).

Prod'homme, J. G. 1936. "From the Unpublished Autobiography of Antoine Reicha," *Music Quarterly* 22: 339–353

Rampe, Siegbert. *Mozarts Claviermusik. Klangwelt und Aufführungspraxis.* (Kassel, 1995).

Riethmüller, Albrecht, ed. *Beethoven. Interpretationen seiner Werke.* (Laaber, 1996).

Robbins Landon, Howard C., Ed. 1990. *Das Mozart Kompendium.* Trans. Fred Büttner. (Munich, 1991).

————. *Ludwig van Beethoven. Leben und Werk in Zeugnissen der Zeit.* (Zürich, 1970, 1992, and 1994).

Rosenblum, Sandra P. *Performance Practices in Classic Piano Music.* (Bloomington and Indianapolis, 1988).

Rowland, David. *A History of Pianoforte Pedalling.* (Cambridge, 1993).

————. "Beethoven's pianoforte pedalling", *Performing Beethoven.* Ed. Robin Stowell. (Cambridge, 1994) pp. 49–69.

Schiedermair, Ludwig. *Der junge Beethoven.* (Weimar, 1925 and 1939).

Schönfeld, Johann Ferdinand von. *Jahrbuch der Tonkunst von Wien und Prag.* (Vienna, 1796). Facs. ed. Otto Biba. (Munich–Salzburg, 1976).

Solomon, Maynard. *Beethoven.* (New York, 1977).

Streicher, Andreas. *Kurze Bemerkungen über das Spielen, Stimmen und Erhalten der Fortepiano, welche von Nanette Streicher, geborene Stein in Wien verfertiget werden.* (Vienna, 1801). Facs. K. Lelieveld. (The Hague, 1979).

Thayer, Alexander Wheelock. Rev. Elliot Forbes. *Life of Beethoven.* (Princeton, 1967).

Türk, Daniel Gottlob. *Klavierschule.* (Leipzig and Halle, 1789). Facs. ed. Erwin R. Jacobi (Kassel, 1967).

Wainwright, David. *Broadwood by Appointment. A History.* (London, 1982).

Wegeler, Franz Gerhard and Ferdinand Ries. *Biographische Notizen über Ludwig van Beethoven.* (Coblenz, 1838). Facs. repr. (Hildesheim and New York, 1972).

NOTES

1. For example, in his letters to Andreas Streicher (18 September, 1810 and November 1810). Beethoven, *Briefwechsel* vol.2, p. 153ff., 161ff.

2. Most famous is the description of Johann Andreas Stumpff, who in 1824 visited Beethoven and found the treble of the piano without tone, and the broken strings entangled "as a thornbush after a storm." Kerst, F., 1913, *Die Erinnerungen an Beethoven* (Stuttgart, Julius Hoffmann), quoted in Lelie, 1995, p. 148.

3. Remark to Karl Holz 1826. Thayer/Forbes, *Life of Beethoven*, p. 984.

4. ". . . da sein Spiel so wie seine Compositionen der Zeit vorausgeeilt waren, so hielten die damaligen noch äußerst schwachen und unvollkommenen Fortepiano (bis um 1810) seinen gigantischen Vortrag oft noch gar nicht aus." Czerny, 1842, "Erinnerungen" in *Über den richtigen Vortrag*, ed. Badura-Skoda, 1963, p. 22. All translations in this paper are mine unless otherwise indicated.

5. A fourth piano, only recently rediscovered, is by Sebestyén Antal Vogel, in Beethoven's possession between 1812 and 1814. Lelie, *Van Piano tot Forte*, p. 169.

6. Newman, "Beethoven's Pianos."

7. Ibid.

8. Ibid.

9. Komlós, *Fortepianos*, p. 61.

10. Rosenblum, *Performance Practices*, p. 58, writes this about dynamics in Beethoven's piano sonatas: "Of 9,297 indications of all types, approximately 24 percent are absolute soft dynamics (*mp, p, pp, ppp*) and 15 percent are absolute loud (*mf, f, ff*), yielding the surprising statistic that Beethoven suggested only two-thirds as many absolute loud as absolute soft sounds."

11. His pianistic career was most successful during his first decade in Vienna. After 1808, he gave up playing in public, mainly because of his deafness. For documents about Beethoven's last concert in 1808, see Robbins Landon, *Ludwig van Beethoven*, pp. 140ff.

12. This article is based on my B.A. thesis at the Department of Musicology, Gothenburg University. I would like to thank Mats Krouthén and my wife Pauline for reading and discussing this text with me in great detail. Their valuable observations led to some major improvements. Also I owe thanks to Alf Björnberg and to David Yearsley, who freed this text from some flagrant Germanisms and who radically reduced the number of commas. The staff of the Artisten Library in Gothenburg has been especially helpful and effective. I also would like to thank Malcolm Bilson for his valuable comments and for his encouragement to publish this paper. Special thanks to my father Martin Skowroneck, who in uncountable discussions about organological matters freely communicated his professional insights as an instrument builder to me.

13. Thayer/Forbes, *Life of Beethoven*, p. 87, and Robbins Landon, *Ludwig van Beethoven*, 1994, p. 36. The words quoted are identical in the two slightly different readings. Schindler, on the other hand, says that the encounter took place in the rooms of Emperor Joseph. (Schiedermair, *Der junge Beethoven*, p. 118).

14. Latcham, "Mozart and the pianos."

15. According to a statement from 1855 by Carl Mozart, quoted in ibid., p. 399.

16. Robbins Landon, *Das Mozart*, p. 36.

17. Riethmüller, *Beethoven*, p. 376.

18. Thayer/Forbes, *Life of Beethoven*, pp. 61ff. We do not know exactly when this happened; Thayer relates one anecdote in which Beethoven's age is given as ten years.

19. See ibid., Chapter 3.

20. The various English translations of "clavier" are symptomatic of this observation. It may not be surprising that Thayer, writing in the last century, says that Beethoven was "destined for a more systematic instruction in pianoforte playing" (p. 60), and accordingly translates most—not all—occurrences of the word clavier into "pianoforte." But even the article on Beethoven in *The New Grove Dictionary of Music* puts "piano" in place of clavier.

21. Rowland 1994, "Beethoven's pianoforte," p. 50.

22. Schiedermair, *Der junge*, p. 96.

23. Rosenblum, *Performance Practices*, p. 27.

24. That is, mainly the so-called Fischer manuscript and other scattered recollections of later dates, and a few official documents, such as a concert *avertissement* from March 26, 1778 (reprinted and translated in Thayer/Forbes, *Life of Beethoven*, pp. 57ff.)

25. That is, clavichord, harpsichord, or fortepiano. Experimental instruments would have been named or described in most cases.

26. Rampe, *Mozart's Claviermusik*, pp. 16ff., gives a meticulous account of eighteenth-century keyboard terminology.

27. Except, of course, those who had a description of the different instruments as their main issue. This was usually the case in clavier methods, such as C. P. E. Bach's or D. G. Türk's, but also in some detailed reports, such as Burney's *Tagebuch einer musikalischen*.

28. Latcham, about 1992, "Alternatives to the modern piano for the performance of Mozart," lecture, pp. 2ff.

29. "Beym bloßem Wort Clavier läßt sich eigentlich nichts denken, und es ist unvorsichtig und sonderbar genug, wenn der Componist so oft hinsetzt: »Sonaten fürs Clavier«, ohne zugleich zu bestimmen, für welche Gattung desselben sie eigentlich gehören. Denn es ist ein Unterschied, ob ich für den Flügel, oder das Forte piano oder das Clavichord setze; Jede Komposition für jedes einzelne dieser Instrumente muß ihren abgeänderten

Charakter haben." Forkel, Johann Nicolaus, 1781. *Musikalischer Almanach für Deutschland auf das Jahr 1782*, Leipzig, p. 82, quoted after Rampe, *Mozart's Claviermusik*, p. 20.

30. Tobias Friedrich Pfeiffer, who is said to have taken over Ludwig's tuition in around 1779, was probably younger; see Schiedermair, *Der junge*, p. 75. He was, however, Beethoven's teacher only for a short period. According to B. J. Mäurer, a cellist, the lessons took place at irregular times, even at night, at Beethoven's house (ibid., p. 77). It is improbable that Pfeiffer initiated any major changes to the situation at hand.

31. "Jeder Clavierist soll von Rechtswegen einen guten Flügel und auch ein gutes Clavichord haben, damit er auf beyden allerley Sachen abwechselnd spielen könne. Wer mit einer guten Art auf dem Clavichorde spielen kann, wird solches auch auf dem Flügel zuwege bringen können, aber nicht umgekehrt. Man muß also das Clavichord zur Erlernung des guten Vortrags und den Flügel, um die gehörige Kraft in die Finger zu kriegen, brauchen." Bach, *Versuch*, pp. 10ff.

32. ". . . es [das Clavichord] hat . . . den Vortheil, daß man sich mit den Federn nicht placken darf, auch sind sie beständiger in der Stimmung. . . . Deswegen braucht man sie auch bei der Information: denn wer darauf wohl gelernet, kann caeteris paribus auch auf Orgeln, Clavicymbeln , u. d. gl. fortkommen." Adlung, *Musica*, p. 144.

33. Burney, 1773. English quotation from Komlós, *Fortepianos*, pp. 134ff.

34. "Zum Lernen ist das Klavier, wenigstens am Anfange, unstreitig am besten; denn auf keinem anderen Klavierinstrumente läßt sich die Feinheit im Vortrage so gut erwerben, als auf diesem. Kann man in der Folge einen Flügel oder ein gutes Fortepiano daneben haben, so ist der Nutzen für den Lernenden desto größer; denn die Finger bekommen durch das Spielen auf diesen Instrumenten mehr Stärke und Schnellkraft." Türk, *Klavierschule*, p. 11.

35. Fischer, *Aufzeichnungen*, p. 32, and Thayer/Forbes, *Life of Beethoven*, p. 57.

36. Czerny, 1852. Anekdoten und Notizen über Beethoven in *Über den richtigen Vortrag*, p. 22. Of course "in his youth" is not precise.

37. Fischer, *Aufzeichnungen*, pp. 46 and 50. Fischer names Tobias Friedrich Pfeiffer (who was in Bonn in 1779–1780) and Franz Georg Rovantini (1781) as chamber music partners of Beethoven, who would also be heard extemporizing ("vargieren" = variieren) on these occasions. We can thus date these occasions quite accurately.

38. Ibid., p. 53. This *may* indicate a large instrument with several stops. Most fortepianos of that time were duple strung and not more difficult to tune than a clavichord. Still, we do not know if Mombauer did not tune all the instruments in the house.

39. Ibid., p. 69.

40. Many fanciful and often faulty descriptions of the basic principle of the clavichord action can be found in the literature. The shortest and most correct description appears in Ferguson *Keyboard*, pp. 4ff.: "At the far end of each key is a small brass blade, or tangent. When the key is depressed the tangent rises and strikes a pair of unison strings, at the same time stopping them like the finger of a violinist's left hand. The section of strings to the right of the tangent vibrates to produce the note required, while the section to the left is damped by a piece of felt wound round the end of the strings. When the key is released the tangent falls back, the whole length of the two strings is damped by the felt, and the note ceases to sound."

41. Bach is one of the writers who are careful in defining keyboard instruments by terminology. By klavier he generally means clavichord.

42. "Mein Hauptstudium ist besonders in den letzten Jahren dahin gerichtet gewesen, auf dem Klavier, ohngeachtet dessen Mangels an Aushaltung, soviel möglich sangbar zu spielen und dafür zu setzen. Es ist die Sache nicht so gar leicht, wenn man das Ohr nicht

leer lassen und [should be *oder*] die edle Einfalt des Gesanges durch zu vieles Geräusch nicht verderben will." Burney, *Tagebuch*, pp. 455ff.

43. "Diese Sonaten sind Klaviersonaten: Ich wollte daher, dass sie auch nur auf dem Klaviere gespielt würde; denn die meisten werden auf dem Flügel, oder Pianoforte wenig Wirkung thun, weil keines von beyden des Kantablen und der verschiedenen Modifikation des Tons so fähig ist, als das Klavier." Komlós, *Fortepianos*, p. 37. Komlós quotes a translation from William Newman, slightly altered here.

44. C. F. Cramer, *Magazin der Musik* 1 (1783): 377–400. This translation is from Thayer/Forbes, *Life of Beethoven*, p. 66.

45. Unlike clavier, *Instrument* is used sometimes for the group of keyboard instruments with experimental actions. Those with plain hammer actions normally were called hammerclavier or fortepiano.

46. The Schleswig builder Jürgensen offered for instance a "clavecin royal" of his own invention (the clavecin royal was actually a concept of J. G. Wagner from Dresden) and a "bellsonoreal," which could imitate all possible kinds of instruments. Cramer, C. F., *Magazin der Musik* 1 (1783): 662.

47. Such as the Kassel fortepiano builder Wilhelm, who built square pianos of high quality after English models. Ibid., 666.

48. Ibid., 654. The concept may have resembled the gut-strung instrument by Riedlen, named above.

49. "Traurig freylich ists für die Tonkunst, diese Gattung Instrumente unter ganzen Nationen so herrschend zu finden, und selbst in Deutschland, dem wahren Vaterlande der Claviere, besonders in den südlicheren Provinzen, zwanzig gute Fortepianos, Fortpiens, Clavecin-royals und wie die Hackbrettart weiter heisst, gegen ein einziges erträgliches Clavier anzutreffen." Ibid., 1246ff., quoted and discussed also in Komlós, *Fortepianos*, p. 5. (As this text uses very detailed and specific vocabulary—a clavecin royal was, for example, a certain invention by the Dresden builder J. G. Wagner—my interpretation of clavier as clavichord deserves no further explanation in this case.) Obviously, Cramer regretted the decline of the clavichord as an "institution," even though the fortepianos that started to be fashionable in southern Germany were "good," and some clavichords were merely "tolerable."

50. "Die Musiklibhaberey nimmt unter den Einwohnern sehr zu. Das Clavier wird vorzüglich geliebt; wir haben hier mehrere Steinische Hämmerclaviere von Augsburg, und andere denen entsprechende Instrumente." Cramer, *Magazin der Musik* 2 (8 April 1787): 1386.

51. Including Beethoven, four Mastiaux sons and nine adult countesses. The list closes with "etc."

52. Schiedermair, *Der junge*, p. 110. Thayer/Forbes says 1782.

53. Cramer, *Magazin der Musik* 1 (30 March, 1783): 387–388; trans. based on Thayer/Forbes, *Life of Beethoven*, p. 37.

54. Schiedermair, *Der junge*, p. 49.

55. Of course, the choice of titles in printed music may have been influenced by commercial rather than musical aspects, and should not induce far-reaching conclusions.

56. For instance in Latcham, "The Pianos of . . . Stein," or Latcham, "Mozart."

57. Thayer/Forbes, *Life of Beethoven*, p. 94. Newman, *Beethoven's Pianos*, p. 486.

58. Thayer/Forbes, ibid., p. 88. Beethoven's possible visit to Stein's workshop is supported by an entry in his conversation books, in the hand of his nephew: "Frau von Streicher [Stein's daughter Nanette Streicher] says, that she is delighted that at fourteen years of age you [i.e. Beethoven] saw the instruments by her father and now see these of

her son." (quoted ibid.). Thayer points out that, however unlikely, this also may refer to the Stein pianos known to Beethoven from Bonn.

59. "Noch hörte ich einen der größten Spieler auf dem Klavier, den lieben guten Bethofen, von welchem in der speierischen Blumenlese vom Jahr 1783 Sachen erschienen, die er schon im elften Jahr gesetzt hat. Zwar ließ er sich nicht im öffentlichen Konzert hören, weil vielleicht das Instrument nicht seinen Wünschen entsprach; es war ein Spathscher Flügel, und er ist in Bonn gewohnt, nur auf einem Steinschen zu spielen. Indessen, was mir ungleich lieber war, hörte ich ihn phantasieren, ja ich wurde sogar selbst aufgefordert, ihm ein Thema zu Veränderungen aufzugeben. . . . Selbst die sämtlichen vortrefflichen Spieler dieser Kapelle sind seine Bewunderer, und ganz Ohr, wenn er spielt. Nur er ist der Bescheidene, ohne alle Ansprüche. Indes gestand er doch, daß er auf seinen Reisen, welche ihn sein Kurfürst machen ließ, bei den bekanntesten guten Klavierspielern selten das gefunden habe, was er zu erwarten sich berechtigt geglaubt hätte. Sein Spiel unterscheidet sich auch so sehr von der gewöhnlichen Art, das Klavier zu behandeln, daß es scheint, als habe er sich einen ganz eigenen Weg bahnen wollen, um zu dem Ziel der Vollendung zu kommen, an welchem er jetzt steht." Carl Ludwig Junker in Boßlers *Musikalische Korrespondenz* 47, 23 November 1791, quoted in Robbins Landon, *Ludwig van Beethoven,* p. 33. So the date of the rejection of the Späth *Flügel* and the obvious preference of Stein's fortepianos is 1791 rather than 1783, as stated in Newman, "Beethoven's Pianos," and Newman, *Beethoven,* p. 50.

60. See figure in Appendix I.

61. Rampe, *Mozart's Claviermusik,* p. 29.

62. A well known letter from Mozart (17 October, 1777) who also preferred Stein's instruments to Späth's twelve years before Beethoven, is discussed in Latcham, "Alternatives," p. 3. Latcham argues that Mozart probably did not mean *Tangentenflügel* but an "ordinary" fortepiano when he writes about Späth's claviere, because he directly compares them with the mechanically superior piano forte of J. A. Stein.

63. About the use of the word *Flügel,* see Rampe, *Mozart's Clavermusik,* p.19. That Junker fails to define the Stein instrument used by Beethoven is of no importance here, because the instruments by that builder in Bonn were identified as fortepianos earlier. (See my quotation of Neefe, above.)

64. See Latcham, "The pianos of . . . Stein," p. 41. The overall design of Stein's instruments was so successful that Stein's daughter Nanette, who moved to Vienna two years after the death of her father in 1794 and continued piano building there together with her husband Andreas Streicher, produced it virtually unchanged until 1805.

65. This notion derives from Newman, "Beethoven's Pianos," p. 486.

66. Solomon, *Beethoven,* devotes a whole chapter to Beethoven's ambivalent attitude toward financial or material support, and his general inability to show his gratitude in an adequate manner.

67. DeNora, *Genius,* pp. 68ff.

68. Wegeler-Ries, *Biographische,* pp. 17ff.

69. Although he was no eyewitness, referring to information given by "Father" Ries.

70. Ibid.

71. See Schiedermair, *Der junge,* pp. 145–47.

72. Translation from Prod'homme, "Antoine Reicha": 351.

73. And not, as has been suggested, in 1795 in Vienna (see DeNora, *Genius,* p. 175). Reicha lived in Hamburg in 1795. My dating is confirmed in Reicha's biography: Olga Šolotová, *Antonín Rejcha,* trans. Deryck Viney (Prague, 1977, 1990), p. 12.

74. Unless the strings were not very good. Apparently strings came from various sources and were of differing quality.

75. Thayer/Forbes, *Life of Beethoven*, pp. 135ff. Keeping in mind Beethoven's initial financial difficulties, this instrument may have been a compromise between quality and price, and the house rent very low.

76. Ibid., p. 258.

77. At least seven of the innumerable Viennese piano builders from this period are noteworthy. Of these, Nanette Streicher, together with her brother Matthäus Andreas Stein and her husband Andreas Streicher continued to produce the German type of fortepiano of her father J. A. Stein. Another German builder, Anton Walter, who had come to Vienna in 1780, built somewhat sturdier instruments, as a rule triple strung in the treble (as opposed to Stein, who only sometimes used triple stringing) and with a slightly different type of action, today generally known as Viennese action. Both concepts had their followers, and the "whole swarm of piano builders," as Beethoven called them in 1802, produced and sold prodigious quantities of instruments. Johann Schanz, for instance, is said to have produced 130 instruments, squares and grands, a year. The average for a little workshop would have been 4 instruments a year (Lelie, *Van Piano*, p. 110).

78. Quoted in Robbins Landon, *Ludwig van Beethoven*, p. 51.

79. This letter will be discussed in detail in the next section.

80. Czerny, "Erinnerungen," p. 10.

81. Unfortunately, this instrument has not been preserved or identified.

82. Czerny, "Erinnerungen," p. 10. The sincere attitude of Czerny's writings in general (in contrast, for example, to Schindler) has made scholars gladly accept most of Czerny's personal views as facts. I keep wishing to know what Streicher or Schanz had to say to his "Walter, damals die besten."

83. See Appendix B.

84. Including parts of the sonatas op. 2 during public concerts. This description disagrees with the commonly accepted theory that the eighteenth-century sonata was in general designed for the salon, thus offering some insight into Beethoven's contrasting conception.

85. Thayer/Forbes, *Life of Beethoven*, p. 205.

86. Wegeler/Ries, *Biographische*, pp. 81ff.

87. Quoted and trans. from Thayer/Forbes, *Life of Beethoven*, p. 206.

88. Details of Seyfried's description may also have been influenced by his later experience with Beethoven.

89. The connection between Beethoven developing certain habits and his upcoming deafness is evident. Here there is no space to investigate the underlying psychological mechanisms.

90. "Alle tongebenden Instrumente, selbst die Menschenstimme, habe ihren bestimmten Wirkungskreis, den man nicht überschreiten kann, ohne durch üblen Eindruck auf den Zuhörer, oder durch den Tadel des Kenners bestraft zu werden." Streicher, *Kurze*, p. 3.

91. "So wenig [der Fortepianist] sein Fortepiano tyrannisiert, eben so wenig ist er auch ein Sklave desselben. Kühn überläßt er sich dem ganzen Feuer der Begeisterung; allein der reine Geschmack hält die Zügel, und läßt ihn nie in häßliche Töne ausarten . . . Vor dem rohen Ausdrucke flieht jedermann." Ibid., p. 19.

92. "Ein Spieler mit dem Rufe: »er spiele außerordentlich, so etwas habe man nie gehört,« setzt sich, (oder *wirft* sich) zum Fortepiano.—Schon die ersten Accorde werden mit einer Stärke angegeben, daß man sich frägt: ob der Spieler taub sey, oder seine Zuhörer dafür halte? Durch die Bewegung seines Leibes, seiner Arme und Hände, scheint er uns begreiflich machen zu wollen, wie schwer die *Arbeit* sey, welche er unternommen habe. Er geräth in Feuer, und behandelt sein Instrument gleich einem Rachsüchtigen, der

seinen Erbfeind unter den Händen hat, und mit grausamer Lust ihn nun langsam zu Tode martern will. Er will Forte spielen, allein da er schon im Anfange die Töne übertrieben, so kann er keinen höheren Grad von Stärke mehr herausbringen. *Er haut also,* und hier verstimmen sich plötzlich die mißhandelten Saiten, dort fliegen einige unter die Umstehenden, welche sich eilig zurückziehen, um ihre Augen in Sicherheit zu setzen. Bey dieser einzelnen Note steht ein Sforzando! Glücklicher Weise hält der Hammer, hält die Saite noch aus. Aber hören Sie, wie der Ton knirrscht, wie schmerzlich er dem Ohre fällt! Leidenschaftliches Feuer verwandelt er zur Wuth, die sanften Empfindungen drückt er durch *kaltes Spielen aus.*—Da er alles auf einen höheren Grad spannt, so ist es natürlich, daß er das Fortepiano bey dem Ausdrucke des Schmerzens schreyen und heulen läßt, und beym raschen, freudigen Gesang der Musik, Tasten und Hämmer lahm schlägt. . . ." Ibid., pp. 20ff.

93. That is, with a compass of five octaves or five octaves and two extra keys.

94. Beethoven, *Briefwechsel*, p. 33n., argues that Streicher's pupil may have performed some part of a piano trio and points out that the only slow movement marked *adagio* is in op. 1, no.1.

95. "Bester Streicher! Ich habe Sie recht um Verzeihung zu bitten, daß ich Ihnen auf Ihren sehr verbindlichen Brief an mich so spät Antwort gebe. . . . wenn ich Ihnen sagte, daß mich meine mich fast überhäufende Arbeiten daran hinderten, so lüge ich gewiß nicht. Ihre kleine Schülerin lieber St. hat mich zudem, daß sie mir bey dem Spiele meines Adagios ein Paar Zähren aus den Augen gelockt, in Verwunderung gesetzt. Ich wünsche Ihnen Glück, daß Sie so glücklich sind, Ihre Einsichten bey so einem Talent zeigen zu können, so wie ich mich freue, daß die kleine liebe bey ihrem Talent Sie zum Meister bekommen hat. Aufrichtig lieber St. ich habe mich zum erstenmale getraut, mein Terzett spielen zu hören, und wahrlich es wird mich bestimmen mehr für's Klavier zu schreiben als bisher, wenn mich auch nur einige verstehen, bin ich zufrieden. Es ist gewiß, die Art das Klavier zu spielen, ist noch die unkultivierteste von allen Instrumenten bisher, man glaubt oft nur eine Harfe zu hören, und ich freue mich lieber, daß Sie von den wenigen sind, die einsehen und fühlen, daß man auf dem Klawier auch singen könne, sobald man nur fühlen kann, ich hoffe die Zeit wird kommen, wo die Harfe und das Klawier zwei ganz verschiedene Instrumente seyn werden. Übrigens glaube ich, daß Sie die Kleine überall spielen können laßen, und unter unß, sie wird manchen von unseren gewöhnlichen eingebildeten Leyrern beschämen.

"Noch eins: Werden Sie mir wohl nicht übel nehmen, bester St., wenn auch ich nur einigen wenigen Antheil an ihrer Bildung nehme?—d.h. daß ich mich um ihre Fortschritte bekümmere, denn ohne Ihnen schmeicheln zu wollen, ich wüßte ihr nichts mehr und besser zu sagen als Sie. Nur ihre Fortschritte beobachten, und sie aufmuntern lassen Sie mich.—Nun leben Sie wohl lieber St. und bleiben Sie mein Freund, so wie ich bin ganz

"Ihr wahrer Freund   L. v. Beethoven.

"Ich hoffe Sie bald selbst besuchen zu können, und dann werde ich Ihnen auch die Nummer von meiner Wohnung anzeigen, grüßen Sie mir ihre liebe Frau."

Beethoven, *Briefwechsel*, vol. 1, p. 32. Apart from obviously missing letters, Beethoven's spelling is unchanged here. Capitals are used according to modern rules, for better understanding.

96. Probably Elisabeth von Kissow (1784–1868), who had come to Vienna together with the Streichers. Ibid. p. 32ff., n.

97. "Es ist zu bedauern, daß, so viele auch Fortepiano spielen, dennoch so wenige danach trachten, es nach seiner wahren Natur zu behandeln. Nichts ist gewöhnlicher, als dieses reichhaltige Instrument so *mißhandeln* zu hören, daß es oft keinen besseren Effekt, als eine klimpernde Harfe, oder ein armseliges Hackbret [*sic*] machen kann." Streicher, *Kurze*, pp. 3ff.

98. "[Es ist wichtig für den Fortepiano—Spieler] ein Instrument zu haben, auf welchem er *leicht, singend, fertig, mit Ausdruck spielen* [kann]." Ibid.

99. [Der gute Spieler] weiß den Ton *singen zu lassen*, ohne sein Instrument anzustrengen. . . ." Ibid., p. 17.

100. "Wenn auch einige glauben, daß es *im ausdrucksvollen Spiele* den anderen Instrumenten weit nachstehen müsse: so kann diese Beschuldigung doch nur solche Fortepiano treffen, *deren Ton wenig Biegsamkeit hat, deren Tastatur-Tractament äußerst hart ist, und bey welchem die Mechanik die Bewegung der Finger nicht unterstützt.* . . ."

"Aber auch die beste Mechanik kann doch nichts weiter thun, als *den guten Anschlag vorbereiten.* Sie kann es dem Spieler nur *möglich und leicht machen, daß er so anschlagen kann,* damit genau die Art des Ton's erfolge, welche die Musik oder sein eigenes Gefühl verlangt. *An ihm also liegt es jetzt, diese Mechanik zu beleben. Auf ihm allein liegt nun die* Verantwortlichkeit der besseren oder schlechteren Wirkung seines Instruments . . ." Ibid., pp. 4 and 6.

101. "Lieber Streicher! Vorgestern erhielt ich Ihr Forte piano, was wahrlich vortrefflich gerathen ist, jeder andre würde es suchen an sich zu behalten, und ich—lachen Sie ja recht, ich müßte lügen, wenn ich Ihnen nicht sagte, daß es mir zu gut ist für mich, und warum?—Weil es mir die Freiheit nimmt, mir meinen Ton selbst zu schaffen, übrigens, soll Sie das nicht abhalten alle Ihre Forte-piano so zu machen, es werden sich ja auch wohl wenige finden, die ebenfalls solche Grillen haben. Am Mittwoch den 23ten dieses Mts. ist meine Akademie, will Stein kommen, so soll er mir herzlich willkommen seyn, Nachtlager hat er ganz sicher bei mir.—Was den Verkauf des forte-pianos anbelangt, so hatte sich diese Idee schon vor Ihnen bey mir entsponnen, und ich werde auch gewiß trachten, sie auszuführen.—Für Ihre Gefälligkeit, mir so willfährig zu sein, danke ich Ihnen herzlich lieber St., ich wünschte nur, in etwa Ihre Gefälligkeit erwiedern zu können, und daß Sie ganz davon, auch ohne daß ich es Ihnen hier sage, überzeugt sind, wie sehr ich wünsche, daß die Verdienste Ihrer Instrumente auch hier und überall erkannt werden, und wie sehr ich wünsche, daß Sie immer mich gern haben mögen, und mich betrachten mögen

"als Ihren Sie liebenden und warmen Freund   Beethowen
Preßburg am 19ten November anno 96 post christum natum

viel schönes an Ihre Frau, und an Braut und Bräutigam." Beethoven, *Briefwechsel*, vol. 1, p. 33.

102. "Überhaupt ist es aber gewiß, daß wir gleichsam zwei Originalinstrumentenmacher haben, näml. Walter und Streicher, alle Uebrigen ahmen entweder dem [*sic*] Ersteren oder dem Anderen nach; vornehmlich findet Walter sehr viele Kopisten, weil mancher derselben aus seiner Schule abstammt." Schönfeld, *Jahrbuch*, p. 90.

103. See Latcham, "Alternatives . . ." p. 10.

104. Many eighteenth-century writers use "nerves" but actually mean "muscles."

105. "Da wir nun zwei Originalinstrumentenmacher haben, so theilen wir unsere Fortepiano in zween Klassen: die Walterischen und die Streicherischen. Eben so haben wir auch bei genauer Aufmerksamkeit zwei Klassen unter unsern größten Klavierspielern. Eine dieser Klassen liebt einen starken Ohrenschmauß, das ist, ein gewaltiges Geräusche;

sie spielt daher sehr reichtönig, außerordentlich geschwind, studirt die häckeligsten Läufe und die schnellsten Oktavschläge. Hiezu wird Gewalt und Nerverstärke erfordert; diese anzuwenden, ist man nicht mächtig genug, eine gewisse Moderazion zu erhalten, und bedarf also eines Fortepianos, dessen Schwebung nicht überschnapt.

"Den Virtuosen dieser Art empfehlen wir ein walterisches Fortepiano. Die andere Klasse unserer großen Klavierspieler sucht Nahrung für die Seele und liebt nicht nur deutliches, sondern auch sanftes, schmelzendes Spiel. Diese können kein besseres Instrument als ein Streicherisches oder sogenanntes Steinisches wählen." Schönfeld, *Jahrbuch*, pp. 90ff.

106. "Das *zu starke schlagen*, (welches jedes Fortepiano verderben muß) gibt überhaupt weit weniger Ton, als man gewöhnlich glaubt, denn jede Saite hat nur ihren bestimmten Grad von Stärke, den sie angeben kann. Will man durch einen heftigen Anschlag diese Stärke noch höher treiben; so wird sie dadurch in eine unnatürliche Schwingung versetzt . . ." Streicher, *Kurze*, p. 10.

107. Latcham, "Alternatives," p. 12

108. Lelie, *Van Piano*, p. 103.

109. On most modern copies of Stein fortepianos, a check is added.

110. The function of the check is discussed in great detail in Latcham, "The Check," and Latcham, "Mozart."

The question, whether the felt bushings of the hammer pivots in the wooden Stein-Kapsel acted as a substitute for the missing check, receives contradictory answers in two of Latcham's articles. In 1993, he dismissed this notion, because adjustments of these bushings to add friction in the pivot would have led to undesired effects on the repetition, making the action "sluggish" (p. 34). In 1996 (date of publication; the article was presented in November 1993), Latcham argued *for* possible adjustments of the bushings, obviously owing to new source information.

In general, any superfluous friction in the hammer pivots would have undesired effects on the tone length, causing the hammer to stay in contact with the string even longer than normal. Not having the opportunity to experiment with a Stein action, I imitated this retarding effect with the adjustment screws in an English grand action: With screws too loose, the lateral movements of the hammer (around _ mm) made the tone slightly less concentrated in some cases. When, on the other hand, I adjusted the screws so that the hammer was only just visibly retarded, the tone became markedly dull and short at once.

111. Walter used a leather-covered rail as a check for all hammers. Some other builders had individual checks for each hammer. The heavier hammers in Walter's fortepianos made a check indispensable. With the check-rail removed, hammers of his model start to restrike already around mezzoforte.

112. "[Walter's] Fortepiano haben einen vollen Glockenton, deutlichen Anspruch, und einen starken vollen Baß. Anfänglich sind die Töne etwas stumpf, wenn man aber eine Zeitlang darauf spielet, wird besonders der Discant sehr klar. Wird aber sehr viel darauf gespielet, so wird der Ton bald scharf und eisenartig [occasionally quoted as 'eigenartig = strange", which is wrong] welches jedoch durch frisches Beledern der Hämmer wieder zu verbessern ist." Schönfeld, *Jahrbuch*, p.88.

113. "[Man kann annehmen], daß, wenn sowohl die einzelnen als zusammen klingenden Töne des Fortepiano Gefallen erwecken oder rühren sollen; sie sich so sehr als nur möglich, dem Tone der besten Blasinstrumente nähern müssen.

"Ist der Ton eines Fortepiano anders, (ein so genannter *Silberton*, der aber sehr bald, besonders bey starkem Spielen *Eisenton* wird;) so grenzt er schon an das *trockene, dünne, magere*; und ist zuweit von der Ähnlichkeit mit der Menschenstimme, oder denen Instrumenten entfernt, welche durch ihre runden, das ganze Ohr ausfüllenden Töne, so mächtig auf unser Gefühl wirken." Streicher, *Kurze*, pp. 12ff.

114. The density of the material that covers the hammers has a measurable effect on the overtones. See Gätjen, "Das Hammerklavier."

115. Wearing out faster is a logical consequence of their greater mass. We may observe that at least Schönfeld attributes the wearing out to *much* playing, not *strong* playing.

116. The lower string tension in his fortepianos (a consequence of thinner strings and a duple strung treble) enabled Streicher to retain a lighter soundboard ribbing than Walter. This resulted in better resonance (see Lelie, *Van Piano*, p. 91), partly compensating for disadvantages caused by the light construction. Four pages of Streicher's book are devoted to explaining why pianists often *think* that they are not properly heard in concerts, and to instruct players how to perform so that they are audible.

117. We cannot decide here whether Schönfeld's "jangling" alludes to this phenomenon or to the sound produced by the hammers jumping up, owing to the missing check.

118. That is, in terms of consequences for the player. There is no information about the degree of Beethoven's understanding in technical matters.

119. Unfortunately, we do not know which pieces Beethoven played at his Preßburg *Akademie*.

120. Again, some aspects of Beethoven's contact with the Stein-Streicher family can serve as an example of this development. In 1809, after a long period of experiments, Streicher seems to have found a convincing design and presented an instrument that "sounded like an orchestra," as he "had abandoned the soft, too easy yielding and the bouncing roll of the other Viennese instruments and gave his instruments upon Beethoven's recommendation more resistancey and flexibility, . . . so that they satisfy every virtuoso who not only seeks easy brilliance in his playing. . . ." (Reichardt, *Vertraute Briefe*, 7 February, 1809 quoted in Beethoven, *Briefwechsel*, vol. 4, p. 78).

In 1817, Beethoven asked Streicher in a letter to Nanette Streicher to "be so kind to arrange one of [his] pianos more after my weakened hearing," adding: "Maybe you do not know that I, although I have not always had one of your pianos, I always have preferred them since 1809— Only Streicher would be able to send me such a piano as I need. . . ." Beethoven, *Briefwechsel*, vol. 4, p. 77.

This piano was never sent, probably because of the announcement of the Broadwood piano, which Beethoven received as a present in June 1818.

In 1820, Beethoven discussed, probably with Matthäus Andreas Stein, the possibility of quadruple stringing (another Viennese builder, Conra Graf, experimented with four strings). An entry in the conversation books runs: "You should not let Graf do anything with your klavier" (from Kerst 1913, p. 309, quoted in Lelie *Van Piano*, p. 190).

Stein repaired and changed the Broadwood piano in 1823, but in 1824, Beethoven had broken all the treble strings of this instrument. See ibid., pp. 148ff.

121. His own indications (in letters and the so-called Heiligenstadt Testament) vary between late in 1796 and late in 1798.

122. Obviously this was another instrument than the one observed by Czerny. It is not likely that Czerny was mistaken about the date of his first introduction, as he names Beethoven's address, Tiefer Graben, where he lived only in 1799–1800. On the other hand, Czerny *might* have mixed up instruments and events. In another passage of the letter to be quoted presently, Beethoven alludes to a piano by another builder, Johann Jakesch (c.1763–1840), upon which he was to "show his art," at his home in November 1802. We have no information about Jakesch's pianos.

123. "Sie können mein lieber Z. dem Walter meine Sache immerhin in einer starken Dosis geben, indem er's onehin verdient, dann aber drängt sich seit den Tägen, wo man glaubt, ich bin mit Walter gespannt, der ganze Klaviermacher schwarm, und will mich bedienen—und das umsonst, jeder von ihnen will mir ein Klawier machen wie ich es will, so ist Reicha von demjenigen, von dem er sein Klawier hat, innigst gebeten worden, mich zu bereden, daß er mir dörfe ein piano forte machen, und das ist doch einer von den brawern, wobey ich schon gute Instrumente gesehen—Sie geben ihm also zu verstehen, daß ich ihm 30♯ bezahle, wo ich es von allen umsonst haben kann, doch gebe ich nur 30♯ mit der Bedingung daß es von Mahagoni sey, und den Zug mit einer Saite will ich auch dabey haben,—geht er auf dieses nicht ein, so geben Sie ihm unter den Fuß, daß ich einen unter den anderen aussuche, dem ich dieses angebe. . . ." Beethoven, *Briefwechsel* vol. 1, p. 137.

124. Rosenblum, *Performance,* pp. 33ff.

125. Thayer/Forbes, *Life of Beethoven,* p. 335.

126. If there is one fortepiano that he criticized when his hearing was at least fairly good, it was this Erard grand piano. By 1810, he wrote to Andreas Streicher that it was "utterly useless." See Lelie, *Van Piano,* p. 170.

127. Even if his self-proclaimed new way of composing after 1802 as well as his future hearing problems allow for the latter interpretation of many problematic spots, or even whole concepts in his later work.

APPENDIX A

Splith's Tangent Action
(Details of the Dampers Omitted)

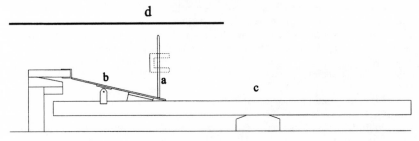

a: tangent   b: *Treiber*   c: key   d: string   (after Lelie, 1995 and Harding, 1933)

Stein/Streicher Hammer Action

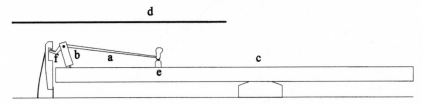

a: tangent   b: wooden *Kapsel*   c: key   d: string   e: hammer rest   f: *Schnabel* (after Streicher, 1801)

Walter Action with Hammer Check

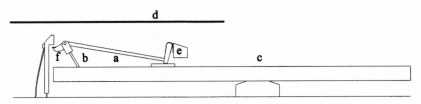

a: hammer   b: brass *Kapsel*   c: key   d: string   e: hammer backcheck f: *Schnabel* (after Lelie, 1995)

APPENDIX B

Contemporary Reports of Beethoven's Playing 1791–1800

In the Beethoven literature, the documents about Beethoven's playing usually appear in chronological order of the events in question. In order to understand the immediate impression left by his playing, I isolated the fifteen contemporary reports (between 1791 and 1800) accessible to me,[1] from the sources that were written down at a later date, and compared the content of the two groups.

Most of the contemporary sources illustrate Beethoven's qualities as pianist and extemporizer through descriptions of the impression he made on the public. Most reports originate in 1795–1796, when he debuted as a concerto pianist/composer and made his journey to Berlin. Three reviews or descriptions come from 1798–1800.

In 1791 (Junker's text, see above) and 1793, we have descriptions of Beethoven as one of the foremost players.

In 1793, Beethoven himself writes to Eleonore v. Breuning that some of the Vienna "Klawiermeister," though being his enemies, keep trying to listen to him in order to copy his style.

One (Reicha at Berlin) tells in 1796 that Beethoven was so kind to play three times, without further commenting on the event.

Eight writers name universal applause and public success; on one occasion, the public even disregarded the interdiction of applause at the concert location in question.

Four sources, even one of the critical ones, name Beethoven's mastery of technical difficulties, brilliancy, or ease of performance.

In six cases, the public was enchanted, or the artistry, taste, or feeling of the performance, or masterful improvisation is especially mentioned.

After 1798, Beethoven's playing was occasionally criticized: One review, and one newspaper article that compares him with the young virtuoso Wölffl 1799 complains about indistinct and irregular playing. (The wordings of this article leave some doubt about whether the criticism was aimed at Beethoven's playing alone or also at his compositions.)

In contrast to this group of sources, the reminiscences of eyewitnesses not written down under the direct impression of a certain event (that is after 1800 in most cases, as for instance in Wegeler's and Ries's annotations, which are quoted copiously in the literature) tend to accentuate the young Beethoven's genius or certain musical deeds of wonder.

Of seventeen of these examples (only two from before 1795), six relate some sort of special performing "trick," such as repeating a whole improvisation, fast sight-reading from complicated manuscripts, or the transposing of a half tone during a concerto rehearsal.

Four reports use strikingly eulogistic wordings about the impact of Beethoven's playing on the listener.

There are eight descriptions of brilliance, passion, or the beauty of his playing. The English pianist J. B. Cramer was "completely entranced" in 1798 on hearing Beethoven extemporize. Beethoven himself recalled in 1810 that his public in Berlin in 1796 was crying after a performance.

One source describes his playing in 1791 (at Mergentheim) as "rough and hard;"[2] another one reports broken strings during Beethoven's Mozart performance at the Bonn court.

Tomášek in Prague, though generally positive, has some criticism about the inorganic development of ideas in the music played by Beethoven (1798)[3].

Only the most exuberant (poetic would be the term in the early nineteenth century) text, by Seyfried, comes to the point of stating that the "stoutest structure (of the instrument) scarcely could withstand" Beethoven's "forceful utterances."[4]

NOTES

1. Most of this material is taken from Thayer/Forbes, pp. 105–257 and Robbins Landon 1994, pp. 33–79. Whenever possible, I compared the sources from Thayer with the original German versions, as his translations are sometimes not precise.

2. Wegeler/Ries, pp. 17ff. Date probably wrong.

3. Thayer/Forbes, p. 208.

4. Ibid., p. 206.

Contrast and Continuity

in Beethoven's Creative Process

WILLIAM KINDERMAN

For Daniel

In *The Sense of Reality,* Isaiah Berlin wrote about early Romantic aesthetics that "All creation is in some sense creation out of nothing. It is the only fully autonomous activity of man. It is self-liberation from causal laws, from the mechanism of the external world, from tyrants, or environmental influences, or the passions, which govern me—factors in relation to which I am as much an object in nature as trees, or stones, or animals."[1] Beethoven, a pivotal figure in this reassessment of artistic creation as original, autonomous activity, left an incomparable documentary record of the process itself, in the form of thousands of pages of sketches and drafts for his musical works.[2] The existence of these sources allows us to trace some of the ways in which musical conventions and ideas have been reshaped in accordance with artistic purposes and goals, some of which were envisioned only gradually by the composer himself.

The present essay is concerned with the relation between freedom and determination, or chaos and order, in Beethoven's creative process. On some level, decisions about variance and invariance were indispensable aspects of his everyday compositional activity. For instance, Beethoven's convictions about originality—that art "does not stand still"[3]—exerted severe limitations on the reuse of his own earlier ideas. A new symphony or sonata needed to be unlike his earlier ones. On the other hand, elements of invariance and consistency also applied to basic compositional features, such as the character of keys. Not only verbal comments by Beethoven but the works themselves bear eloquent witness to this phenomenon. Beethoven's celebrated "C minor mood" is just the most familiar example of similarities in technique and character that apply as well to his pieces in other keys.[4]

The conviction that artistic communication should not be entirely fixed in advance was bound up with the notion of *fantasieren*—fantasy as the spontaneous generation or reinterpretation of musical ideas. When Karl Holz asked Beethoven in 1826 which of the last quartets was the greatest, the composer reportedly stated a preference for the C-sharp Minor Quartet, op. 131, while referring to "a new type of voice-leading" and claiming that "there *is less lack of fantasy than ever before.*"[5] Subsequent commentators, such as Gustav Nottebohm, have stressed the fantasylike qualities of this quartet.[6] Beethoven's longstanding interest in merging fantasy with sonata is most familiar from the two piano sonatas "Quasi una Fantasia" op. 27, written in 1800–01. In a sketchbook dating from 1807–08, Beethoven wrote, "One improvises actually only when one doesn't pay attention to what one plays, so if one would extemporize in the best, truest way in public, it's necessary to give oneself up freely to one's inclinations."[7] It is difficult to translate adequately the German verb "fantasieren," since this term designates not only extemporization or improvisation per se but also underscores the role of the productive imagination or "fantasy" in generating the activity.[8]

Like Mozart and other virtuoso keyboard composers of his age, Beethoven embodies the ideal of an "orator in tones" whose music stirs the mind and passions of the listener.[9] In a manner not unlike literature, poetry, or drama, his musical works can display an immediate expressive character while also conveying a narrative thread, whereby a succession of expressive states come to represent a whole greater than the sum of the parts. This difference within unity, or contrast within continuity, is a fundamental aspect of Beethoven's style whose importance can hardly be overestimated. Ultimately, its aesthetic roots may lie in a synthesis of Baroque and Classical tendencies. Beethoven's highly integrated and even deterministic aesthetic stands in contrast to the art of colorful juxtaposition that was brought to its highest development by Mozart. The compelling force of the dramatic narrative continuity in Beethoven owes much to the older Baroque aesthetic of a unity of character; in this sense, his entire artistic enterprise rested on a synthesis of stylistic traditions that seemed to be independent of or even antagonistic to one another.[10] The merging of Bachian solidity and continuity with the dramatic contrasts and discontinuities of the Classical style lends to Beethoven's art a unique richness and power.

This study concerns some of Beethoven's compositional strategies for reconciling the parts and whole in pieces from various stages of his career. The works to be considered include two of the most imposing piano sonatas from his first dozen years in Vienna: the Sonata in E-flat Major, op.7, and the "Waldstein" Sonata, op. 53, as well as his opera *Fidelio* and the three final piano sonatas, opp. 109–111. Evidence from the compositional process often provides clues that can help us to interpret Beethoven's evolving aesthetic goals in these works.

* * * *

It has been known since the pioneering source study by Nottebohm that the big Sonata in E-flat major, op. 7, evolved from its third movement, the dancelike Allegro with Minore. This movement was originally conceived as one of a group of four "bagatelles" independent of the sonata.[11] It is clear, however, that this movement was no mere appendage to the work, but must have formed the emerging core in Beethoven's creative process. Like other Beethoven sonatas, op. 7 relies heavily on strong contrasts in character in which the Allegro with Minore assumes a central role. The internal contrasting section of a dance movement, or "trio," is a compact part of the formal design that can be used to expose expressive relationships present in other parts of a multimovement work. In the Trio of the Second Symphony, for instance, Beethoven juxtaposes phrases in the woodwinds in D major with an emphatic answering call in the strings on F-sharp major, thereby encapsulating a relationship that looms large in the outer movements of the symphony.

The Minore in op. 7 employs a texture of rapid, arpeggiated triplets, in a ternary meter somewhat suggestive of the galloping of a horse. At the same time, the slow harmonic rhythm and acute dissonances are reminiscent of an earlier work of tragic character in this unusual key of E-flat minor, a work with which Beethoven was familiar: the prelude from the first book of Bach's *Well-Tempered Clavier*. Particularly bleak and desolate are the last two phrases of the Minore, in which the melody is finally exposed as bare melodic pitches in the right hand, played pianissimo, over a continuation of the triplets in the left hand (Example 1a). In these measures, the grating dissonance of the diminished-seventh harmony C♭-D-F-A♭ is heard against the E♭s played above and below. Beethoven emphasizes the dissonance by holding it through two measures, placing the middle of each phrase entirely in its shadow. The Minore ends in the same register in which it had begun, but at the second resolution of the dissonance in measure 146 the rhythmic vitality of the triplet movement abates as the music comes to rest on the open unharmonized fifth E♭-B♭, marked triple pianissimo.

The despairing character of this passage makes a powerful contrast to the main Allegro section, which is of lyric character, its beginning marked

dolce. However, the most telling relationship to the extraordinary dissonance at the end of the Minore is found in the main theme of the finale
of op. 7. In fact, this connection helps explain a very striking and unusual
feature of the theme: its delicate beginning with a dominant-seventh
chord on the dominant, a sonority that is approached melodically from
above and adorned, in the first full measure, by an appoggiatura E♭-D
that exactly parallels the appoggiatura figure on these notes at the

Example 1a. Piano Sonata in E-flat Major, op. 7, III, end of Minore

Example 1b. Piano Sonata in E-flat Major, op. 7, beginning of Finale

conclusion of the Minore (Examples 1a and 1b). Beethoven's emphasis
on this expressive motive, in conjunction with the opening pedal on the
dominant and the descending contour of the four-measure phrases, all
contribute to the suspended, gracious quality of the theme. But what
gives added depth to the main theme of this rondo is its sensitive cadential resolution in E-flat major of the bleak phrases from the Minore of the
preceding movement. The coda of the rondo, on the other hand, offers

· 196 ·

another kind of resolution of tension, as robust, Baroque-style figuration from an earlier C minor episode is reshaped into more gentle accents and transparent textures. In both cases, the fundamentally gracious character of the rondo finale is underlined: strife is transformed into grace.

If the preexisting bagatelle movement exerted decisive influence on the finale of op. 7, considerations of intermovement contrast and continuity played a leading role in one of the most fascinating of Beethoven's substitutions of movements: his removal of the popular "Andante favori" (WoO 57) as the slow middle movement of the "Waldstein" Sonata in C Major, op. 53. In 1804, after completing the sonata in its original form with the Andante, Beethoven replaced this charming movement by a short but profound Introduzione. According to the anecdotal report of Ferdinand Ries, it was the overall length of the sonata that prompted Beethoven to abridge it, as he replaced the independent slow movement with a mere transition.[12] That there were other musical reasons for the change speaks for itself. Sketches for the Introduzione are lacking, but it can be postulated on the basis of the surviving manuscripts that the movement was probably composed during April–May 1804.[13] This is a period in which Beethoven was intensely preoccupied with his opera *Fidelio*, whose earlier versions completed in 1805 and 1806 are generally known by the title he would have preferred, *Leonore*. Whatever the original motivation may have been for Beethoven's removal of the "Andante favori," it is clear that some cross-fertilization from the opera had occurred by the time that he composed the new transitional slow movement for the sonata.

The "Andante favori" is a spacious, decorative rondo, whose returns of the charming main theme are always delicately varied. The contrasting episodes between statements of the theme, on the other hand, are opulently and almost operatically conceived, sometimes taking on the atmosphere and gestures of ballet music. The appeal of this ingratiating music is preserved in the most troubled of Ries's anecdotes. Ries related that when Beethoven first played the Andante for him and his musician friend Kumpholtz, they were so enthusiastic that they convinced Beethoven to repeat his performance. Subsequently, Ries infected Prince Lichnowsky with his enthusiasm for the piece, and the prince, too, learned a portion of it, which he then claimed as his own, and played for Beethoven. This turn of events was unfortunate for Ries. For, as he put it, "Beethoven was greatly angered, and this was the reason why I *never again heard Beethoven play.*"[14]

Both of the great piano sonatas on which Beethoven labored during the time of composing *Leonore*—the "Waldstein" and the "Appassionata"— partake in the key symbolism of the opera. On one side of the central schism of the opera is the F minor music of the dungeon scenes and of Florestan's aria in the last act; on the other is the brilliant C major of the three *Leonore* overtures and the finale of the last act, which culminates in the arrival of the minister of state and the release of Florestan and the other political prisoners held by the tyrant Pizarro. F minor is also the key of the "Appassionata," op. 57, which was apparently conceived at around the time that Beethoven wrote the music for these parts of the opera in 1804.[15] These two works also show some motivic and tonal similarities, such as the emphasis on the semitone D♭-C and the prominence of D-flat major in an F minor context. But if Florestan's "God!—what darkness here!" might serve as commentary on the conclusion of the "Appassionata," the choral text "Hail to the day! Hail to the hour!" at the end of *Leonore/Fidelio* might almost be the motto for the jubilant C major coda of the "Waldstein" finale.

In its original form with the "Andante favori" as slow movement, the "Waldstein" contained no sustained gaze at the dark side of this expressive duality; the tragic character that shapes the "Appassionata" throughout is absent here. However, by substituting the Introduzione, Beethoven both deepened the expressive contrast of the whole—with more than a glance at the opera—and he also strengthened the continuity between these antithetical sections by connecting the slow transition directly to the sonority heard at the beginning of the finale.

In order to place the Introduzione properly into context, we need to recognize its affinity to the F minor orchestral music marked "Grave" that begins the last act of the opera. This passage, in turn, is closely linked to Beethoven's earlier Cantata on the Death of Joseph II (WoO 87), a work written by the young Beethoven at Bonn in 1790. The crucial gesture, which was reused in all three of these works, consists of four distinct sonorities presented as pairs: mysterious low unison octaves in the bass register, against which harmonized sonorities are heard in the higher registers, first on the tonic and then on a contrasting or more dissonant harmony. In the cantata, these chords also provide the setting of the text "Todt! Todt!" ("Dead! Dead!") in the chorus, making explicit the music's desolate expressive connotations.

As the curtain opens on the final act of *Leonore/Fidelio*, we hear a transposition of this "death" topos into the dismal, F minor gloom of Pizarro's dungeon (Example 2).[16] Beethoven exploits here a variety of means—rhythmic, harmonic, linear, and motivic—to give to this music a powerful dramatic coherence that was beyond his ability in 1790. Beethoven now discards the fermate that prolonged each sonority in the opening of the cantata. He endows the music with a new rhythmic energy bound up with his characteristic device of diminution or foreshortening: the metric emphasis on two-measure units allows us to hear the three repeated chords in measure 5 as a diminution of the rhythmic shape of the entire opening gesture, with its slow articulation of three impulses spread over five bars. This process propels the music forward, generating a gradual increase in tension. The larger harmonic progression, on the other hand, is controlled by a descending bass, reaching the first significant phrase division at measure 11 on the dominant of F minor. Here Beethoven injects declamatory motives in the strings into the texture, motives strongly reminiscent of the unharmonized string phrases heard near the beginning of the "Joseph" cantata.

Example 2. *Fidelio,* Act II, beginning

Example 2 continued

But unlike the cantata, this music seems constantly to be listening to itself. The expressive gesture in measure 11 highlights the semitone D♭-C, and Beethoven's rhythmic and dynamic nuances underscore the poignant tension of the dissonance. This motive, in turn, is joined to a higher, answering inflection in the winds, with both elements combined into a sequential progression that builds in intensity. But that is not all: the D♭-C semitone figure is not only an expressive figure but a *structural* intensification—only in the merging of both functions does it take on its full aesthetic force. For the voice-leading of the opening woodwind chords—the gestures set ominously to "Dead! Dead!" in the cantata—had already exposed the interval C-D♭ in a conspicuous way. The string

Example 2 continued

motive is racked with the painful dissonance already heard at the very outset of the Grave.

Let us now consider how Beethoven employed a variant of this same topos in the substitute slow movement of the "Waldstein" Sonata. As we have seen, the substitute movement is an extended introduction to the finale, to which it is directly linked; at the same time it makes a much stronger effect of contrast in relation to the outer movements than did the original slow movement. At stake in Beethoven's decision to substitute the Introduzione were issues of balance and integration in the sonata cycle as a whole. This substitution also marked a turning-point in Beethoven's practice. After the "Waldstein" the principle of a contrasting slow movement linked to the finale in a three-movement design becomes a mainstay of his style for about six years, until 1810. Examples include the "Appassionata" and "Lebewohl" Sonatas, the Violin Concerto, and the last two piano concertos.

By juxtaposing the contrasting slow movement directly with the finale, Beethoven brings their moods into a closer relationship, setting the moment of transition to the finale into sharp relief. Many later masterpieces, from the "Archduke" Trio to the C-sharp minor quartet, follow this pattern. But most revealing in comparison to the "Joseph" cantata is the way Beethoven achieves that quality of gigantic simplicity that marks the slow interlude of the "Waldstein" (Example 3). The topos from the cantata—with a low tonic pedal in unharmonized octaves answered first by tonic harmony and then by a dissonant harmony with ascending voice-leading—is replicated in the sonata. The harmonic resolution of the dissonant sonority, however, is not to the tonic, as in the cantata, but to an E major chord, which lends a more directional impetus to the phrase, bridging the accented silence at the start of the second measure. Furthermore, the ascending seventh in the bass, from F to E, is treated by Beethoven as the starting point for a long stepwise *descending* progression, even more relentless than the one in *Leonore/Fidelio*.

The form of the Adagio molto is based on a twofold statement of this progression drawn from the topos of the cantata, blended with an expressive idiom suggestive of recitative and thematic dualism. Following the opening nine-measure phrase, Beethoven restates the initial motive in the right hand, which unfolds in a declamatory fashion, with rising echoes in a polyphonic texture. (Unlike the rest of the Introduzione, this passage is faintly reminiscent of the "Andante favori.") After only six measures, however, the passage dissipates into a hushed, enigmatic return of the beginning of the Adagio molto. The recitative-like phrases posit an alternative to the somber, static character of the opening music that recalls the cantata. This brighter, more consoling voice cannot be sustained, however; the music settles even more deeply into the pensive mood generated by the falling-bass progression and countervailing ascent in the right hand. Only after an arresting climax on a widely spaced diminished-seventh sonority and the convergence onto the dominant seventh of C do we reach a miraculous turning point: the descending bass movement is reversed as G rises to G♯, clearing the way for a cadential progression in C major that underscores the luminescent texture and vast spacing at the beginning of the finale.

Perhaps most remarkable here is the severe economy of the thematic material and tight coherence of its development. In the "Waldstein," the structural model of the solemn chord progression that opens this youthful work was sufficient to ground the entire structure of the slow introduction. At the same time, the dark-hued, mysterious character of this music creates an expressive polarity that places the brilliant C major world of the outer movements of the sonata in a new light.

Many features of the Introduzione—the uncanny accented silences, the breaking off of the recitative-like second theme, and the gradual, compelling melodic ascent in pitch to the goal on high G—shape the movement as a drama in process. Much more than the movement that it replaced, this piece seems to embody a narrative of seeking, or questing, whereby an idealized goal, once achieved, signals the end of the endeavor. As a drama, it signals an enactment in real time, and the pivotal event—the attainment of high G as the gateway to C major—closes the door on the Introduzione.

Although the key of the Introduzione is F major, not F minor, and the thematic material remains distinct from the Grave in the opera, symbolic parallels exist between these two works. At the end of his aria, Florestan deliriously envisions Leonore as an angel leading him to freedom, a dramatic idea that is embodied musically through the upward soaring of an oboe heard in F major. This passage was added to the opera only in 1814, when *Fidelio* received its final revision. The progression in the sonata is less overtly symbolic, yet more decisive, since its outcome marks a liberation from confinement. The transition yields to the sweeping main theme of the finale, which seems to unfold on a vast registral height above a deep pedal in the bass. Through Beethoven's incorporation of the Introduzione, the preexisting finale seems not to be taken for granted, but rather to be sought for and achieved.

* * * *

In 1814, while finishing the last revision of *Fidelio*, Beethoven complained that he had earned a "martyr's crown." The most frustrating, or paradoxical, of his experiences with the opera may have concerned the overtures, four in all. The trouble with the great overtures to *Fidelio*—the second and third *Leonore* overtures—is that they distill the overriding dramatic themes with such powerful concentration as to overshadow, if not annihilate, the homely opening scenes of the first act. Beethoven's very choice of C major as the key for these overtures is bound up with his anticipation of the most weighty events to follow—these are foreshadowed not only in a direct quotation from Florestan's aria and in the trumpet calls, but no less importantly in the ecstatic climax in the coda of *Leonore* No. 3 on a dominant minor ninth chord, where the musical intensity equals that of the most gripping of the later staged dramatic events. No amount of revision, including even the compression of the original three acts to two, could resolve

Example 3. Piano Sonata in C Major, op. 53 "Waldstein," II–III

Example 3 continued

the fundamental conflict between the overture and the ensuing Act I. Beethoven had spectacularly overindulged his characteristic practice of musical foreshadowing. Consequently, the greatest of all dramatic overtures—*Leonore* No. 3—had to be cut from the opera to which it is inextricably bound.

Beethoven's musical revamping of the beginning of the opera involved rearrangement of the opening vocal numbers as well. The opening duet in A major between Marzelline and Jacquino ("Jetzt, Schätzchen, jetzt sind wir allein") was originally No. 2, but was placed by Beethoven at the outset of the opera in 1814. This duet brilliantly employs his new techniques of heightened tonal contrast—as heard at the beginnings of the G major Piano Sonata, op. 31 no. 1, and the "Waldstein"—to depict psychological tension between characters. As Jacquino nervously but eagerly broaches the topic of marriage he is rebuffed by Marzelline. The disharmony between them is reflected by Beethoven's shifts from A major to B minor and back. Repeatedly, Marzelline changes the key of Jacquino's entreaties when she answers him. The rhythm of the "knocking" distractions that annoy poor Jacquino returns with a vengeance in Marzelline's emphatic cries of "No" ("Nein"). Jacquino's hope ("Hoffnung") becomes bothersome to Marzelline, since "he hopes at the slightest appearance" ("Er hofft bei dem mindesten Schein").

In connection with this new opening number Beethoven changed the key of the *Fidelio* overture to E major, dominant of the ensuing duet in A major. Tonally, the *Leonore* overtures in C major anticipate not only the finale of Act II but also the original first number, Marzelline's aria "O wär' ich schon mit dir vereint" ("Oh, were I already united with you"), which is in C minor moving to C major. A problem was lodged in the dramatic gulf between the naive sensibility of the lovestruck but deceived Marzelline, on the one hand, and the stirring moral and political implications of the *Leonore* overtures, on the other. If it seems risky for Beethoven to have overlapped these spheres of tonal symbolism, given the humble character of Marzelline and her undue prominence at the outset, the final version largely avoids such ambiguity by muting the tones of heroism in the new E major overture, which just hints at the bigger issues that lie concealed. In turn, the reference to Marzelline's love for Fidelio in the middle section of the opening duet serves to prepare her ensuing aria, which expands on this topic.

Beethoven's sensitivity to nonadjacent connections and psychological subtleties is illustrated by another passage that must surely have been added to the work in 1814, even if surviving sketches for it are lacking. This is the moment in Act II, No. 14, when the gravediggers stare at the unmoving prisoner: Rocco: "Maybe he is dead." Leonore: "Do you mean that?" Rocco: "No, no, he is sleeping." (Example 4). At the Poco Adagio, the arpeggiated oboe line in F major is a near quotation from the concluding section of Florestan's aria, heard just before. In its register and character, the quotation closely resembles the oboe phrases surrounding Florestan's text "ein Engel, Leonoren" ("an angel Leonore"), a passage in which the exchange of melodic phrases between oboe and voice makes the symbolic role of the oboe explicit.

What is the meaning of this correspondence? From the perspective of the gravediggers as they move toward the motionless prisoner, it appears that he may be dead. What has sustained Florestan's vital forces against all odds in his predicament is an idealized, spiritual experience— a sustaining vision of Leonore as angel of freedom. In a profound sense, the aria of the prisoner, and especially its culminating F major section, is inward and psychological, and not an outward display or physical performance. The oboe excerpt in the melodrama thus conveys how Florestan's life is sustained through his imagination and inner conviction; in so doing, it precisely identifies this inward state with the symbolic climax of the preceding aria. If we wish, we may even take these two events to be simultaneous rather than successive: the outward life sign that Rocco acknowledges with the words "No, no, he's sleeping" coincides with that inner vision that soon becomes more real than external reality. For the real object of aspiration and agent for change has just entered the forbidden chamber, and Florestan's imminent death is about to be circumvented.

*   *   *   *

Our last examples are drawn from the final trilogy of piano sonatas that Beethoven composed between 1820 and 1822: the Sonatas in E major, op. 109, in A-flat major, op. 110, and in C minor, op. 111. In these works, issues of contrast and continuity are pursued in unique and far-reaching ways. In their narrative designs, each of these three sonatas ultimately unfold toward a condition of lyric euphoria, which is outwardly manifested in the employment of slow variations as the basis for the finales of op. 109 and op. 111.

Like the third movement of op. 7, the opening movement of op. 109 was conceived originally as a separate, independent short piece, or bagatelle.[17] This information at first seems surprising, since the opening "Vivace, ma non troppo" is indeed intimately linked—motivically, structurally, and melodically—to the two ensuing movements. For a brief time Beethoven may have entertained thoughts of both an independent

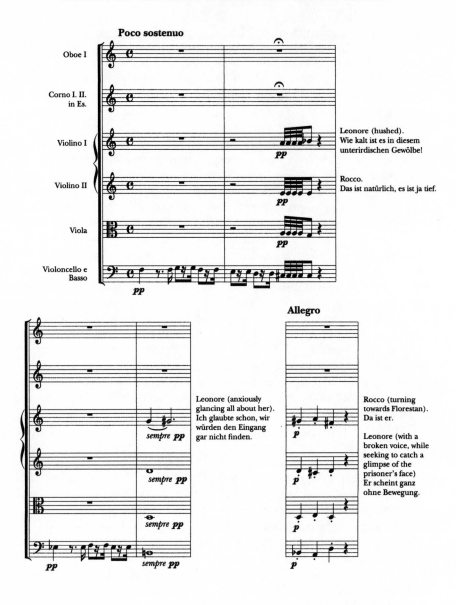

Example 4. *Fidelio*, Act II, Melodrama

Example 4 continued

bagatelle in E major—the piece that became the first movement—and of a two-movement sonata progressing from E minor to E major, as in his earlier sonata in this key, op. 90. If so, he very soon blended these ideas, establishing an especially close network of relations between the three movements of what became op. 109.

At the outset of this sonata, Beethoven introduces a sharp contrast, as the continuous, Baroque-style texture of the Vivace yields, at the threshold to a cadence in the dominant B major, to a side-stepping diminished-seventh chord at the beginning of the Adagio espressivo (Example 5). This second thematic idea was labeled by Beethoven in one of his drafts as a "Fantasie."[18] In its meter, texture, tonality, and rhetoric, this passage differs strikingly from the Vivace, resembling an impassioned meditation abounding with runs and flourishes. Although much longer than the initial Vivace, it is treated like an immense inter-polation, and when the cadence in B major is finally supplied in the same register in measure 16, the Vivace continues, creating an effect of parenthetical enclosure, or the enclosure of one time within another.

Example 5. Piano Sonata in E Major, op. 109, I

Example 6. Artaria 195 Sketchbook, Berlin, p. 35, stave 8

The first movement relies heavily on the juxtaposition of these two contrasting thematic ideas, which are finally brought into close inter-relationship in the coda.

Beethoven's sketches for the second and third movements of op. 109 are concentrated in the Artaria 195 Sketchbook held in Berlin, at the Staatsbibliothek preussischer Kulturbesitz.[19] In the middle of p. 35, stave 8, Beethoven discontinues his sketches for the "Incarnatus est" of the Credo of the Mass in favor of descending pianistic figuration in 12/8 time. In the context of the following sketches, this music is almost certainly conceived in a rapid tempo and in the key of E minor (Example 6).

Scholars who have studied this sketch have either, like William Meredith, puzzled over its possible relationship to op. 109[20] or, like Nicholas Marston, have explicitly excluded it from that sonata.[21] However, close examination of the sketch in the context of the other entries for this movement shows that it was indeed the springboard for the E minor Presto in the sketches that eventually became the Prestissimo of the work as we know it. It will be seen that the triplet figuration spells out a descending line, with the first members of each triplet group of sixteenths sounding the following notes: G-F♯-E-D-C♯-B-A-G-F♯-E-D-C-B-C. As in some passages of the finished work, C♯ in the first measure is pitted against C in the following bar. The character of the sketch suggests a spontaneous keyboard improvisation of the kind that Beethoven is known to have used as the basis for extemporization in his earlier years.

In the sketches in staves 10–11 and below, Beethoven retains the key, meter, and basic rhythm of the original sketch on stave 8, but he now replaces the sixteenth notes by eighths, in phrases that spell out a falling triadic pattern, first on the tonic triad and then as a sequence a step higher. The continuation of this draft already comes recognizably close to the work as we know it. The derivation of this material from the original sketch is nevertheless clear not only from the common use of turn figures using neighbor notes and the descending contour and register, but also from the basic rhythmic pulse. In all probability, the pulse of the rapid sixteenths was simply renotated in the later sketch as eighth notes in a swifter tempo, which is indeed confirmed in subsequent sketches, where Beethoven adds the designation Presto.

Not rarely, Beethoven would leaf ahead somewhat in his sketchbooks to find a fresh opening of pages, which consequently can appear out of order chronologically, if he subsequently filled in the intervening space with sketches. This is the case in the ensuing sketches for the second movement of op. 109. Before making many more sketches beyond the initial entries on pp. 35–36, Beethoven entered an extensive draft for the movement on pp. 41–42.[22] An excerpt from this draft showing part of the recapitulation of the second movement is provided in Example 7. As will be seen, the turn figures and stepwise descending contour of the material on p. 41 draw upon aspects of both of the sketches from p. 35 that we have discussed. In the draft, however, Beethoven has changed the meter to 6/8 time, as employed in the finished work.

Why did Beethoven remove the material of Example 7 from the evolving movement and develop the music along very different lines? Unlike the finished work, this passage shows much of the recapitulation in the tonic major, and the texture of this second theme with its patterns of stepwise descending parallel thirds found no place in the piece as we know it. Undoubtedly, the problem had to do with a too close kinship to Beethoven's first movement. A pattern of stepwise descending parallel thirds or tenths in E major is characteristic of the Vivace sections of the opening movement. It was apparently at about this point in the compositional process that Beethoven resolved to use his preexisting bagatelle as the opening movement of a three-movement sonata in E major. Consequently, the emphasis on the tonic major in the evolving second movement was purged, and that movement was cast instead consistently in the minor. In its relentless, driven character as well as its insistence on the minor mode, the Prestissimo makes an impressive large-scale contrast to the lyrical outer movements in E major.

Carl Czerny once remarked about Beethoven's improvisations that "Often a few insignificant tones were all that were needed to improvise a whole piece, for example the finale of op. 10, no. 3 in D major."[23] On occasion, as during his devastating victory in a "piano duel" over Daniel Steibelt in 1800 when Beethoven disdainfully poked out a few notes from Steibelt's quintet placed upside down as the basis for his own improvisation, he could seemingly turn almost any musical configuration into artistic coinage. Something of this quality can also be discerned in his compositional process for the second movement of op. 109, in which the rapidly descending triplet figuration of Example 6—a basic pianistic idea with a well-defined rhythmic-motoric quality—was developed, step-by-step, into forms familiar to us from the finished work. As often in Beethoven, a distinctive quality of rhythmic tension was paramount from the beginning. The imaginative, transformational process at the core of

Example 7. Artaria 195 Sketchbook, Berlin, p. 41, staves 13–16, showing part of recapitulation of second movement of op. 109 in E major

Beethoven's creative method can easily elude the grasp of analysis, if it does not take into account all parameters of the musical experience.[24]

According to the sketches, Beethoven would have composed the second movement of op. 109 during June of 1820. Shortly before, his publisher Adolph Martin Schlesinger had requested three piano sonatas from Beethoven, and the composer reported in his letter to Schlesinger of June 28, 1820, that the first sonata (op. 109) was already finished, and that the other two would be ready by the end of the following month.[25] This claim was overly optimistic, since op. 109 was not entirely finished for months to come, and opp. 110 and 111 were composed mainly in late 1821 and the first months of 1822, respectively. On the other hand, it has been often asserted in the scholarly literature that Beethoven began composition of opp. 110 and 111 only in the latter half of 1821.[26] This conclusion requires reassessment.

I have recently identified sketches from the period of June 1820 that seem to represent Beethoven's first ideas for each of these remaining members of the final sonata trilogy. At the time he ventured these sketches, Beethoven had not yet clearly differentiated his evolving sonata projects from one another. The first sketch for op. 110 is found on p. 63 of the large-format sketchbook that follows Artaria 195, namely the Artaria 197 Sketchbook (Berlin, Staatsbibliothek preussischer Kulturbesitz). Because of its position in the latter half of this source, previous scholars had regarded these sketches as stemming from 1821. The assumption was that Beethoven worked from the beginning to the end of his sketchbooks more or less in order, and that the succession of sketchbooks offers a chronological mirror of his compositional progress.

In the case of the sketches for op. 110 in Artaria 197, this assumption does not hold. Artaria 197 is one of those sketchbooks of homemade character, in which a variety of papers dating from different periods have been joined together. Close examination of the first pages of sketches for op. 110 shows that these sketches were definitely not part of a bound book when Beethoven wrote down the entries. The nonalignment of candle wax stains and ink blots, and even the distribution of doodles from Beethoven's nephew Karl demonstrate that when these pages were filled with sketches for op. 110, they were used as a collection of loose papers, and were not part of a larger bound book.[27] In this instance, as surely in some others, Beethoven gathered together his work as a sketchbook partly as a housekeeping measure, in order to impose order on work that had already been committed to paper.

A transcription of p. 63 of Artaria 197 is shown in Example 8. Since these sketches were made when the bound sketchbook did not yet exist, we must seek other evidence for dating them. This evidence is provided by the sketches for the Credo of the *Missa solemnis* that are interspersed between entries for the "next sonata" ("nächste Sonate"), as Beethoven has written at the top of the page. The entry for the bass line of a passage in the Credo on stave 7, labeled "Bass durchaus: so geht überall" ("bass throughout: this works everywhere") relates specifically to a draft for the "sedet ad dexteram" of the Credo on p. 1 of Artaria 195, and makes most sense in the context of Beethoven's work on the Credo during the first half of 1820; the same applies to other Mass sketches on the page, such as the entry for the "et vitam venturi" fugue on stave 11. Since Beethoven claimed to have begun work on more than one sonata by June 1820, there is every reason to attribute this sketch to that period.

Gustav Nottebohm associated the inscription "next sonata" with op. 109,[28] and William Drabkin, in the dissertation on the genesis of op. 111, associated it with that sonata,[29] but the sketches on p. 63 actually represent the first surviving entries for the "next sonata" after op. 109, namely op. 110.[30] These sketches outline the basic concept of the new sonata even before the thematic material and keys have been established. The sketch on system 1 is linked, through its recitative-like rhetoric and its harmonic and rhythmic inflections, to the recitative transition leading to the Finale of op. 110. The conclusion of this section on the tonic note of C-sharp minor in system 2, and the reinterpretation of that pitch as part of a rising progression in Allegro tempo in a major key, correspond to the transition from the first Arioso dolente to the Fugue in op. 110. The descending pattern on the right side of this system is associated, through its unusual pianistic articulation and vocal accentuation, with passages in the second arioso of the work as we know it. The scherzo-like entry in staves 9–10, on the other hand, has little in common with the finished sonata. The sketch at the bottom, however, contains an early version of the Arioso lament, notated here in C minor. The 6/8 meter, repeated accompanying chords, chromaticism, and rhetorical inflections of the sketch bear a tangible relation to op. 110. Furthermore, the sketches in the following pages of Artaria 197 develop some of the ideas from p. 63 so clearly that their relation to the sonata is beyond question.

As these sketches show, Beethoven seems to have begun his composition of op. 110 with the Finale, which exploits contrast in remarkable ways, its double presentation of a mournful lament in the minor balanced against fugal sections in the major. This unique design displays a kinship with the duality of the "Agnus Dei" and the "Dona nobis pacem" in the final movement of the *Missa solemnis*, which occupied Beethoven at this time.[31] In a fashion somewhat analogous to the affinity between *Leonore/Fidelio* and the "Waldstein" and "Appassionata" Sonatas,

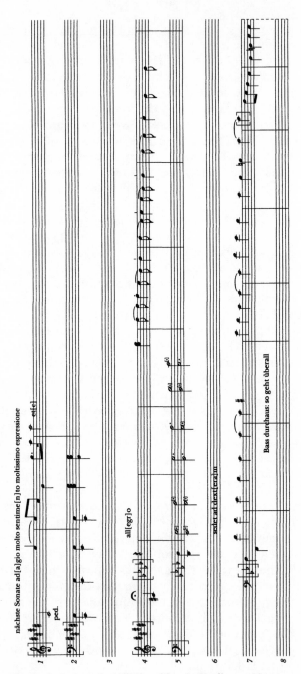

Example 8. Artaria 197 Sketchbook, Berlin, p. 63

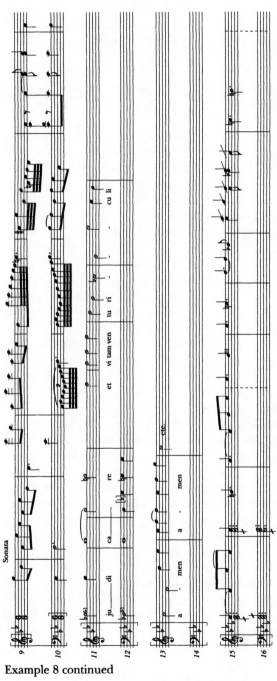

Example 8 continued

Beethoven allowed compositional preoccupations derived from the Mass to infiltrate this final sonata trilogy composed concurrently with his work on the *Missa solemnis*. The process was a reciprocal one: that is, resources drawn from his vast experience with instrumental music also found application in his major vocal compositions, such as *Fidelio* and the *Missa solemnis*.

If the initial sketches for op. 110 were masked from identification in part by their keys, with the first sketch for the Arioso dolente written in C minor rather than A-flat minor, the same applies to the initial sketch for what became op. 111. On p. 58 of the pocket sketchbook SV 82, BH 108, a source published in facsimile and transcription by the Beethoven-Haus, edited by Joseph Schmidt-Görg, Beethoven made brief entries for a Presto in connection with a "Sonata in E minor" ("Sonate in E moll"). One of the sketches is shown in Example 9a, in Schmidt-Görg's transcription. On account of datable entries in the sketchbook, these entries can be determined as stemming from early June 1820, the period immediately following Schlesinger's request for three sonatas and presumably the beginning of the period when Beethoven made all of the other sonata sketches we have discussed.[32] Once again, scholars seeking to identify early sketches with reference to the keys of the finished works have failed to find a context for Beethoven's ideas. Schmidt-Görg makes no comment on these sketches, and Marston, who reproduces the entries in his book on op. 109, concludes quite correctly that "the sketches [do not] appear to have anything to do with the second or third movement of Op. 109."[33] However, the rhythm, meter, harmony, motivic profile, and the rising sequential motion all display a conspicuous affinity with the first movement of op. 111, and particularly to that section where Beethoven constructs a fugal exposition based on his head motive beginning with longer notes on the first and third degrees in minor. The corresponding section of the finished work, beginning at measure 35, is shown in Example 9b. Beethoven's sketch for the counterpoint to the main idea also bears comparison to the countersubject in octaves in the completed sonata, as in the left hand at the beginning of measure 37, where the notes F-E♭-C are analogous to the falling thirds of the sketch. In the finished work, of course, the note values are halved, and the tempo "Allegro con brio ed appassionato" instead of Presto. It is especially the rhythmic shaping of this contrapuntal topos that reveals its affinity with what became part of the first movement of op. 111.

Thus the initial idea retained for op. 111 was a cast-off from Beethoven's attempts toward a "Presto in E Minor," whereas the early sketch for the Arioso dolente in C minor on p. 63, Artaria 197, was soon absorbed into the context of a Sonata in A-flat Major, op. 110. The keys for Beethoven's earliest sonata sketches were interchanged as the works assumed individuality and independence from one another. In the case of op. 111, further stages in the evolution of the initial contra-puntal idea can be identified in the extant sketches. Some of the subse-quent sketches in Artaria 197 refer to a "second sonata" (i.e., a sonata after what became op. 110) containing as its third movement a Presto based on a developed version of the contrapuntal topos, which is now

Example 9a. BH108, p.58

Example 9b. Piano Sonata in C Minor, op. 111, I, mm. 35–38

Example 10. Artaria 197 Sketchbook. Berlin, p. 76

virtually identical to that employed in the completed work. This sketch, on p. 76, Artaria 197, and headed by the words "3tes Stück Presto," is shown in Example 10, in Drabkin's transcription. It reveals Beethoven's intention to develop his material as a series of fugal entries, just as in the first movement of the finished piece. Yet the larger context for this idea was still to be radically altered, as Beethoven decided to cast the sonata in two movements, with the second acting both as antipode and as resolution to the first.

Much has been written about the structure, narrative design, and even the possible philosophical significance of Beethoven's last sonata.[34] In view of these speculations, it is not without interest to know that the genesis of op. 111 does reach back in some form to June of 1820, when Beethoven began to envision not only op. 109, but all three of the last piano sonatas. Much of the startling originality of these pieces lies of course not in the themes and motives themselves, but in their relation to the larger musical context. In fact, Czerny once remarked on a lack of originality of the finale of op. 109 inasmuch as he claimed that the "whole movement was in the style of Handel and Bach."[35] Undoubtedly all three sonatas draw significantly on the legacy of these two composers, the only figures of their time who in Beethoven's opinion possessed "genius." At the same time, even if the older masters were superior in their "solidity" (Festigkeit), Beethoven felt that the "refinement of our [modern] virtues has advanced matters" and that a need existed for "freedom and progress . . . in the world of art as in the whole of creation." To express this standpoint of progressive conservatism— that quality of scholarly futurism that applies so well to his late style— Beethoven even coined the term "Kunstvereinigung," or "artistic unification."[36]

The evolution and deployment of a single musical idea—such as the contrapuntal idea in C minor shown in Example 10—illustrates this double aspect, pointing as it does with a Janus-face forward and back, as visionary art and historical legacy. In its conservative, historical role, it represents a venerable C minor trope stressing the lowered sixth and leading tone, a trope that was not Beethoven's invention, but which extends back through masterpieces by Haydn and especially Mozart to at least J. S. Bach's *Musical Offering*. The redeployment of this C minor fugal kernel from a projected third movement to the first movement of the evolving sonata is richly suggestive. We cannot explore all of the implications here, but these extend even to the issues raised in Thomas Mann's Adorno-influenced "Kretzschmar" lecture in the eighth chapter of his novel *Doktor Faustus,* where reference is made to an "end without any return"—representing in this context a resolution on a spiritual plane removed from strife. In op. 111, Beethoven seemed to resolve his "C minor mood" once and for all.

As these examples show, Beethoven's process of artistic development from acorn to oak—from initial, tentative, fragmentary ideas to completed work—did indeed involve a large measure of autonomy, in Isaiah Berlin's sense, although it is most definitely not creation "out of nothing." The autonomy of the productive imagination opens up necessarily in relationship to a means of expression, a communicative language without which the process of *fantasieren* would be muted or silenced altogether. What is involved here is a dialectical relationship, in which the new—the principle of contrast and progress—grows out of the familiar—the principle of continuity understood broadly enough to embrace historical respect and a veneration of existing cultural values.

NOTES

1. Isaiah Berlin, *The Sense of Reality: Studies in Ideas and Their History* (London, 1996), p. 178.

2. For an overview of the sketchbooks, see Douglas Johnson, Alan Tyson, and Robert Winter, *The Beethoven Sketchbooks: History, Reconstruction, Inventory* (Berkeley and Oxford, 1985). More recent studies devoted to the interpretation of these sources include Barry Cooper, *Beethoven and the Creative Process* (Oxford, 1990); William Kinderman, ed., *Beethoven's Compositional Process* (Lincoln and London, 1991); and Lewis Lockwood, *Beethoven: Studies in the Creative Process* (Cambridge, Mass., and London, 1992). For a recent overview of the scholarly literature on Beethoven's sketches, see my essay "Beethoven: Sketch Studies" in Murray Stieb, ed. *The Reader's Guide to Music: History, Theory, and Criticism* (Chicago and London, 2000).

3. Alexander Wheelock Thayer, rev. Elliot Forbes, *Life of Beethoven* (Princeton, 1967), p. 982.

4. For a recent study of Beethoven's treatment of this key, see Michael Tusa, "Beethoven's 'C-Minor Mood': Some Thoughts on the Structural Implications of Key Choice," *Beethoven Forum* 2 (1993): 1–27.

5. See Thayer/Forbes, *Life of Beethoven*, p. 982. This continues the quotation in note 3.

6. Gustav Nottebohm, *Beethoveniana* (Leipzig and Winterthur, 1872), p. 54.

7. "Man Fantasiert eigentlich nur, wenn man gar nicht acht giebt, was man spielt, so— würde man auch am besten, wahrsten fantasieren öffentlich—sich ungezwungen über- lassen, eben was einem gefällt." A facsimile of the page containing this inscription appears as illustration 6 in *Beethoven, Goethe und Europa: Almanach zum Internationalen Beethovenfest Bonn 1999* (Laaber, 1999), accompanying the essay by Hans-Werner Küthen, "'Was ist, und zu welchem Ende treiben wir das virtuose Spiel?': Gedanken zum Thema *Beethoven und der Reiz des Unübertrefflichen*" (pp. 107–38). Also see Helmut Aloysius Löw, "Die Improvisation im Klavierwerk L. van Beethovens" (Ph.D. diss., Saarland University, 1962), p.12, and Elaine Sisman, "After the Heroic Style: *Fantasia* and the 'Characteristic' Sonatas of 1809," in *Beethoven Forum* 6 (1998): 76.

8. For a recent discussion of related issues, see Elaine R. Sisman, "After the Heroic Style": 67–96. Sisman cites a contemporary critic, August Wendt, who in 1815 "found it problematic that most of Beethoven's sonatas and symphonies were marred by the form- lessness of the fantasy." (p. 96) And see Sisman's contribution to the present volume,"Memory and Invention at the Threshold of Beethoven's Late Style," passim.

9. See in this connection, George Barth, *The Pianist as Orator* (Ithaca, N.Y., 1992); and Elaine Sisman, "Pathos and the *Pathétique*: Rhetorical Stance in Beethoven's C-Minor Sonata, Op. 13," *Beethoven Forum* 3 (1994): 81–105.

10. For a more detailed discussion of this topic, see my essay "Bachian Affinities in Beethoven" in *Bach Perspectives* 3 (1998): 81–108.

11. Gustav Nottebohm, *Zweite Beethoveniana: Nachgelassene Aufsätze* (Leipzig, 1887), pp. 508–11.

12. See Thayer/Forbes, *Life of Beethoven*, p. 351. This explanation is offered in many commentaries, such as the recent essay on the sonata together with the "Andante favori" (WoO 57) by Ulrich Siegele in *Beethoven: Interpretationen seiner Werke*, vol. 1, ed. Albrecht Riethmüller, Carl Dahlhaus, and Alexander Ringer (Laaber, 1994), pp. 370–79.

13. See my study "Skizzen zur *Leonore*: Der Einfluss instrumentaler Gattungen auf die Oper," in *Von der 'Leonore' zum 'Fidelio,'* ed. Helga Luehning and Wolfram Steinbeck (Bonn, forthcoming). The missing sketch source may also have contained work on *Leonore*,

numbers 3–11 and the first movements of the Triple Concerto, op. 56, and the Piano Sonata in F major, op. 54.

14. See Thayer/Forbes, p. 351. According to Carl Czerny, it was Beethoven himself who dubbed the piece "Andante favori" on account of its popularity.

15. Some sketches for the sonata are found in Mendelssohn 15, the main sketchbook for the opera, and a detailed report from Ries concerning Beethoven's work on the finale of op. 57, if accurate, would connect his intensive work on the piece to the late summer of 1804. Also see, in this connection, Theodore Albrecht, "Beethoven's *Leonore*: A New Compositional Chronology," *Journal of Musicology* 7 (1989): 165–90.

16. In the "Joseph" cantata, this music is heard in C minor, which was originally contemplated as the key for the dungeon scene in the opera and then rejected in favor of F minor, as Beethoven's sketches show. For more detailed analysis of the cantata, see my study *Beethoven* (Oxford and Berkeley, 1995), pp. 20–27, from which parts of the present discussion are drawn.

17. See in this regard William Meredith, "The Origins of Beethoven's Op. 109," *The Musical Times* 126 (1985): 713–16; and Nicholas Marston, *Beethoven's Piano Sonata in E, Op. 109* (Oxford, 1995), esp. pp. 29–37.

18. For a detailed discussion and transcription of the draft, see my articles "Thematic Contrast and Parenthetical Enclosure in the Piano Sonatas, Opp. 109 and 111," in *Zu Beethoven 3: Aufsätze und Dokumente*, ed. Harry Goldschmidt (Berlin, 1988), pp. 43–59; and "The Reconciliation of Opposites in Beethoven's Sonata in E, Op. 109," *Arietta* 1 (1999): 5–9.

19. My edition of this sketchbook will be published by the University of Nebraska Press, as *Beethoven's Sketchbook for the Missa Solemnis and the Piano Sonata in E, Op. 109* (Lincoln and London, forthcoming).

20. William Meredith, "The Sources for Beethoven's Piano Sonata in E Major, Opus 109" (Ph.D. diss., University of North Carolina, Chapel Hill, 1985).

21. *Beethoven's Piano Sonata in E, Op. 109*, p. 81. Marston writes that this entry "could hardly be called a 'sketch' for op. 109 in any strict sense; yet the implicit key and explicit time signature call to mind the second movement of the sonata."

22. Meredith rightly points out this irregularity in the sequence of sketches, but Marston treats the sketches as if they were in order. He writes about the draft that "one is taken aback by its content, much of which is quite new," and adds "Nothing on pages 35–40 gives any warning of the extensive draft of nearly 130 bars which begins here." (*Beethoven's Piano Sonata in E, Op. 109*, p. 125.) Actually, the material on p. 35 has much in common with the draft on pp. 41–42.

23. Czerny, "Anecdotes and Notes about Beethoven," in Paul Badura-Skoda, ed., *On the Proper Performance of All Beethoven's Works for the Piano* (Vienna, 1970), p. 15.

24. For instance, Schenkerian voice-leading analysis in itself, for all its value, is not an adequate basis for approaching Beethoven's style, in which issues of rhythm, phrasing, and expressive rhetoric assume such importance.

25. *Beethoven Briefe*, vol. 4, ed. Sieghard Brandenburg (Munich, 1996), L. 1397.

26. See, for instance, Robert Winter's remarks in *The Beethoven Sketchbooks*, pp. 268–69; and Brandenburg's commentary to Beethoven's letter to Schlesinger from June 28, 1820, on p. 406 n. 7, where he claims, "At the time of the letter in question, [the two sonatas] were not yet begun."

27. A detailed discussion of this evidence is contained in the commentary to my forthcoming edition of Artaria 195. The doodles in Karl's hand were drawn to my attention by Lynn Matheson, who is currently writing a dissertation on op. 110 at the Hochschule der Künste Berlin.

28. Cf. Nottebohm, *Zweite Beethoveniana*, p. 463; also Johnson, et al., *The Beethoven Sketchbooks*, pp. 266–67.

29. "The Sketches for Beethoven's Piano Sonata in C Minor, Opus 111" (Ph.D diss., Princeton University, 1976), vol. 2, p. 1.

30. See in this regard also Karl Michael Komma, *Die Klaviersonate As-Dur Opus 110 von Ludwig van Beethoven* (facsimile edition with commentary, Stuttgart, 1967), p. 5; and Klaus Kropfinger, "Streichquartett B-Dur op. 130" in *Beethoven: Interpretationen seiner Werke*, vol. 2, ed. Albrecht Riethmüller, Carl Dahlhaus, and Alexander Ringer (Laaber, 1994), p. 301, note 4.

31. For a detailed study of this sonata and its affinities to the *Missa solemnis*, see my article "Integration and Narrative Design in Beethoven's Piano Sonata in A-flat Major, Opus 110," in *Beethoven Forum* 1 (1992): 111–45. Also see Birgit Lodes, *Das Gloria in Beethovens Missa Solemnis* (Tutzing, 1997), esp. pp. 261–68.

32. Beethoven accepted Schlesinger's proposal to write the sonatas in a letter from May 31, 1820 (*Beethoven Briefe* vol. 4, L. 1393); in his commentary to this letter, n. 4, Brandenburg states that "Beethoven composed the Sonatas op. 110 and op. 111 only in 1821/22."

33. *Beethoven's Piano Sonata in E, Op. 109*, p. 36.

34. The dichotomy embodied in the two movements of op. 111 has been variously described in terms of "Samsara and Nirvana" (Hans von Bülow), the "Here and Beyond" (Edwin Fischer), and "Resistance and Submission" (Wilhelm von Lenz); studies of a speculative cast treating op. 111 include Philip T. Barford, "Beethoven's Last Sonata," in *The Beethoven Companion*, ed. Thomas K. Sherman and Louis Biancolli (New York, 1972), pp. 1040–50 (this essay originally appeared in *Music & Letters*), and Wilfrid Mellers, *Beethoven and the Voice of God* (New York and London, 1983), pp. 254–84.

35. Carl Czerny, *On the Proper Performance of All Beethoven's Works for the Piano*, p. 56 [66].

36. The preceding quotations stem from Beethoven's important letter of July 29, 1819 to the Archduke Rudolph (*Beethoven Briefe*, vol. 4, L. 1318). For detailed commentary that explores the notion of "Kunstvereinigung," see Hans-Werner Küthen, "*Quaerendo invenietis. Die Exegese eines Beethoven-Briefes an Haslinger vom 5. September 1823*," in *Musik-Edition-Interpretation: Gedenkschrift Günter Henle*, ed. Martin Bente (Munich, 1980), pp. 282–313; see also my book *Beethoven*, esp. pp. 1–7, 13–14, 201–10, 225–37, 277–78, and 335–36.

PART IV

BEETHOVEN
IN THE
WORLD

.

Performances of Grief:

Vienna's Response to the Death of Beethoven[1]

Christopher H. Gibbs

In the winter of 1827, as Beethoven lay dying in Vienna, the musical world paid court. London's Philharmonic Society sent a generous gift of £100 "to be applied to his comforts and necessities during his illness."[2] An especially rewarding present had already arrived from England: the new forty-volume Arnold edition of Handel's works, given by Johann Andreas Stumpff, who had resolved to send the composer the lavish offering after a visit two years earlier.[3] Beethoven's friend and onetime landlord, Baron Johann von Pasqualati, provided champagne and rations of stewed fruits.[4] Publisher Anton Diabelli presented a print of Haydn's birth house, which Beethoven enthusiastically showed composer Johann Nepomuk Hummel, exclaiming "the cradle of a great man."[5] From Mainz, the publisher Johann Joseph Schott dispatched a case of Beethoven's beloved Rüdesheimer Berg Wein, 1806 vintage, four bottles of which arrived on March 24; "pity, pity—too late!" the composer lamented, allegedly his final words before slipping into unconsciousness.[6] A steady stream of friends and admirers came to pay last respects, some of whom left moving accounts of these encounters.[7] Anton Schindler, Beethoven's factotum, gave his assessment of the scene in a letter written shortly after Beethoven's death: "His last days were extremely remarkable, and he prepared himself for death with a truly Socratic wisdom."[8]

At four-thirty on the afternoon of Monday, March 26, violinist Ignaz Schuppanzigh, the foremost champion of Beethoven's chamber music for nearly the past thirty years, presented the third concert in his latest subscription cycle at Zum rothen Igel (the Red Hedgehog) on the Tuchlauben in the inner city. String quartets by Mozart and Haydn opened the program, and then Schuppanzigh and cellist Josef Linke were joined by Carl Czerny, Beethoven's former student and another ardent promoter of his music, to perform Beethoven's Piano Trio in G Major, op. 1, no. 2. Outside, a violent storm was raging.[9] As his music resounded in the small hall, Beethoven lay on his deathbed not far away, in the so-called Schwarzspanierhaus on the *glacis*, or ramparts, just outside the city walls. Suddenly at about a quarter to six,[10] according to Anselm Hüttenbrenner, who was at his side, "[A] loud clap of thunder accompanied by a bolt of lightning illuminated the death chamber with a harsh light. . . . Beethoven opened his eyes, raised his right hand and, his fist clenched, looked upward for several seconds with a very grave, threatening countenance, as though to say, 'I defy you, powers of evil! Away! God is with me.'"[11] With that, he fell back, dead.

Within the year of Beethoven's death at age fifty-six, and particularly during the first six months, countless people across Europe and beyond mourned and honored him. These performances of grief, as they might be called, found all manner of expression. An extraordinary funeral (Schindler likened the scene to the Praterfest at the Congress of Vienna), numerous ceremonies and services, obituaries and memorial articles, reminiscences, poems, musical tributes, concerts, and the announcement of a project to erect a suitable monument—all bear witness to the depth of feelings aroused.[12] Mozart's funeral in 1791 had barely registered in public awareness, and even Haydn's in 1809 had proved a surprisingly modest affair.[13] Schubert's death, which as we shall see became intimately linked to Beethoven's, attracted far more public attention than the resilient myths about the supposedly neglected young composer would suggest; yet in no way did it elicit the magnitude of response that Beethoven's had just twenty months earlier.[14]

Reactions to Beethoven's death reveal a society enthralled not only by the greatness of the artist, but also, as so many commented at the time, by the man himself. The present essay surveys the scope of the Viennese responses by examining documents from the time, many of which are unfamiliar and previously untranslated. Although these materials possess an immediacy that later accounts and biographies cannot, they are nonetheless often contradictory in small but intriguing ways. Even the most apparently straightforward facts, information that does not involve interpretation or commentary, present the biographer with problems. As is commonplace in the retelling of events, be they in the distant or immediate past, people see, remember, and record the same things differently. The most familiar accounts of Beethoven's death and its aftermath, which have been repeated endlessly for generations, are not necessarily the most accurate. Sometimes corroborating testimony or documentary evidence can help to resolve discrepancies, although not always. In any case, a more significant issue may be the degree to which so much crucial information has been treated as transparent, as if all the details were known, agreed upon, and not interpreted in any manner. Such thinking has only helped accommodate the use of Beethoven's image to a wide variety of aesthetic, cultural, and political ends.

The emphasis here will be on trying to reconstruct some of what happened around the time of Beethoven's death and during the following year, and on considering what was known, and how it all became known, in his own time and after. In other words, a principal concern will be the historical events themselves, as well as the ways in which these events were initially represented in history—ways that frequently led to mistakes, misunderstandings, and myths. While the belief that it is possible to arrive at definitive answers to historical questions is no longer held as unproblematic, the issue of how Beethoven's image has been constructed during the past two centuries has gained greater attention. Ultimately, beyond documenting the Viennese performances of grief in 1827–28, a certain redoubling will be suggested throughout this essay between recurring themes in Beethoven's biography—such as his struggles with fate, his long search for an understanding wife, his financial difficulties, and his political allegiances—and the narratives of his death. Many of the stories about his last days and hours perform—enact—larger biographical concerns. What is at stake so often in these accounts in and around his death is, I believe, the enduring image of Beethoven the man.

"Plaudite, amici, comoedia finita est": Beethoven's Death

Beethoven's death came as little surprise. During his final four-month illness, friends and admirers kept one another updated about his condition, and these reports gradually filtered out to the general population. His was a particularly public death, especially in view of the magnitude of his funeral and the detailed descriptions of his final days that soon appeared in the press. As Beethoven's health deteriorated during his later years, it became increasingly clear that he would not live to old age, and by late 1826 people suspected the end was near.[15] The summer had proved especially trying as the shock of his nephew Karl's botched suicide attempt confronted Beethoven in the last week of July. In late September, a few days after Karl's release from the hospital, the two traveled to Gneixendorf, some fifty miles from Vienna, to stay with Johann van Beethoven. The nine-week residence with his brother's family was sometimes tense, although not unproductive, as Beethoven worked on his last completed works, the String Quartet in F, op. 135, and the new finale to the Quartet in B-flat, op. 130. Beethoven and Karl returned to Vienna at the beginning of December, supposedly by open carriage, and spent an ill-advised night at a cold, damp tavern on the way that only worsened the composer's fragile condition. Back at the Schwarzspanierhaus, Beethoven was tended to by family and friends, including the publisher Tobias Haslinger; editor Johann Schickh; and Stephan von Breuning, Beethoven's childhood friend from Bonn; Stephan's second wife, Constanze; and their thirteen-year-old son Gerhard, who nearly fifty years later recorded his reminiscences in an invaluable book called *Aus dem Schwarzspanierhause* (1874).[16] Schindler, back in Beethoven's good graces after several years' absence, took care of countless practical matters, as various doctors, including Johann Malfatti and Ignaz Andreas Wawruch, tried to alleviate the composer's deteriorating condition.[17] The stated cause of death was dropsy or retention of fluid (*Wassersucht*), but dropsy is a symptom of various illnesses, not a specific disease, and the term was often used generically in the absence of a more specific diagnosis.[18] Shortly before Beethoven lost consciousness, he received last rites from a priest,[19] then everyone waited for the inevitable.

The most vivid contemporary accounts of Beethoven's death are to be found in letters from Vienna to London, especially ones written by Schindler, Sebastian Rau, and Johann Baptist Streicher to either Stumpff or Ignaz Moscheles. On March 24, Schindler described the dire state of affairs to Moscheles in a letter soon to be widely known when published in the English music journal the *Harmonicon*. I have retained the spelling and punctuation of Johann Reinhold Schultz's translation as it appeared in print less than two months after Beethoven's death:[20]

> . . . By the time you read these lines, my good Moscheles, our friend will be no longer among the living. His dissolution approaches with rapid steps; and, indeed, it is the unanimous wish of us all to see him soon released from his dreadful sufferings. Nothing else remains to be hoped for. One may, indeed, say, that for the last eight days he has been more like a dead than a living man, being able only now and then to muster up sufficient strength to ask a question, or to inquire for what he wants. His condition appears to be very similar to that which was endured by the Duke of York. He is in an almost constant state of insensibility, or rather of stupor; his head hanging down on the chest, and his eyes staring fixed for hours upon the same spot. He seldom recognizes his most intimate acquaintances, and requires to be

told who stands before him. This is dreadful to behold, but only for a few days longer can such a state of things last: since yesterday all the natural functions of the body have ceased. He will, therefore, please God, soon be released, and we from the pain of witnessing his sufferings.

Crowds of people flock to his abode, to see him for the last time; though none are admitted, except those who are bold enough to molest the dying man in his last hours. . . .

He feels his end approaching, for yesterday he said to me and Mr. Breuning, "*plaudite, amici, comoedia finita est.*"

This letter, as printed in the *Harmonicon*, ends with a description of the course of Beethoven's illness, including Schindler's harsh condemnation of nephew Karl, that was in fact drawn from an earlier letter of his to Moscheles of February 22. The final paragraph then returns to the text of the March 24 letter:[21]

It will, perhaps, not be uninteresting to you, to learn from what period the melancholy epoch dates itself. It was on the 3rd of December last year, that Beethoven came with his ungrateful and depraved nephew from the country to Vienna. On this journey he was obliged, owing to the bad state of the weather, to pass a night in a wretched inn; the consequence of which was, that he caught so severe a cold, that an inflammation of the lungs immediately took place, and he arrived here in that state of health. No sooner was the inflammation subdued, than all the symptoms of dropsy appeared, which increased to such a degree, that it became necessary, as early as the 18th of December (1826), to perform, for the first time, the operation of tapping, or he really must have burst. On the 8th of January, 1827, the second operation took place; on the 20th the third, and on the 27th of February the fourth. Now, my friend, figure to yourself Beethoven, with his impatience, his irritable temper, under such a dreadful malady. Only think that, in addition to this calamity, the ill-treatment and mortifying conduct of his own and nearest relations should be superadded! Both his physicians, Malfatti and Wawruch, attribute the cause of his disease to the dreadful agitations of mind to which the excellent man was long exposed, on account of his nephew, and to his lengthened stay in the country during the wet season. He exposed himself to these discomforts entirely on account of this young man, because the police had interdicted the residence of the latter in the capital; and Beethoven wished to enter him in some regiment.

[*Pause of some hours.*]

I have just left Beethoven. He is now certainly dying; before this letter is beyond the walls of the city, the great light will have become extinct for ever. He is now in full possession of his senses. The inclosed hair I have just cut from his head. I hasten to despatch this letter, in order to run to him. God bless you.

> Your most sincere friend,
> A. SCHINDLER

On March 26, with Beethoven's end imminent, Schindler and Breuning went off to make funeral arrangements in the district cemetery in the suburb of Währing, where the latter's first wife Julie was buried.[22] While Schindler and Breuning were away, the last visitor arrived: Anselm Hüttenbrenner (1794–1868), a young composer who had been living in his native Graz since 1821.[23] Although his presence at Beethoven's deathbed is confirmed by contemporary reports, some three decades elapsed before Hüttenbrenner recounted his own version of the course of events.[24] His letter to Beethoven's biographer Alexander Wheelock Thayer (August 20, 1860) has been quoted frequently ever since its first publication in the *Graz Tagespost* on October 23, 1868, shortly after Hüttenbrenner's death. Less familiar are Thayer's notes concerning a personal meeting in Graz earlier that summer (June 5, 1860).[25] After relating some background information about his first encounters with Beethoven in the late 1810s, during the time he and Schubert were fellow students of Salieri's, Hüttenbrenner recalled to Thayer his last meeting with the composer (all comments in parentheses are apparently Thayer's, and those in brackets are my own):

In the winter of 1826–27 his friends wrote him from Vienna that if he wished to see Beethoven again alive he must hurry up thither from Gratz [*sic*]. He hastened to Vienna, arriving a few days before Beethoven's death. Early in the afternoon of March 26 Hüttenbrenner went into the dying man's room. He mentioned as persons whom he saw there Stephen v. Breuning and Gerhard, Schindler, Telscher [*sic*] and Carl's mother. (This seems to be a mistake, i. e., if Mrs. v. Beethoven is right.) Beethoven had then long been senseless. Telscher began to draw the dying face of Beethoven. This grated on Breuning's feelings, and he remon-

strated with him, and he put up his papers and left (?). Then
Breuning and Schindler left to go out to Währing to select a grave.
(Just after five—I got this from Breuning himself—when it grew
dark with the sudden storm, Gerhard, who had been standing at
the window, ran home to his teacher.) Afterward Gerhard v. B.
went home, and there remained in the room only Hüttenbrenner
and Mrs. van Beethoven. The storm passed over, covering the
Glacis with snow and sleet. As it passed away a flash of lightning
lighted up everything. This was followed by an awful clap of
thunder. Hüttenbrenner had been sitting on the side of the bed
sustaining Beethoven's head—holding it up with his right arm. His
breathing was already very much impeded, and he had been for
hours dying. At this startling, awful peal of thunder, the dying man
suddenly raised his head from Hüttenbrenner's arm, stretched out
his own right arm majestically—"like a General giving orders to an
army." This was but for an instant; the arm sunk back; he fell back.
Beethoven was dead. . . .

Another talk with Hüttenbrenner—It seems that Beethoven was
at his last gasp, one eye already closed. At the stroke of lightning
and the thunder peal he raised his arm with a doubled-up fist; the
expression of his eyes and face was that of one "defying death"—
a look of defiance and power of resistance.

H. must have had his arm under the pillow. I must ask him.

I did ask him; he had his arm around B.'s neck.[26]

Thus, when fate knocked at Beethoven's door for the last time,
Hüttenbrenner was present to witness and record the encounter. There
is ample reason to be suspicious of a story related more than thirty years
after the fact, even though Hüttenbrenner's presence at Beethoven's
death and the outbreak of an unusual storm are independently documented. The scene Hüttenbrenner presents has proved irresistible to
biographers.[27] "Defiance," "power," and "resistance," after all, are words
that loom large in the Beethoven mythology and have since played a
central role in nearly every retelling of his end. The heroic composer,
"like a General"—like Napoleon?—made one last stand during the last
moments of his life. Responding with clenched fist, as Hüttenbrenner
put it in his letter to Thayer, it "seemed as though he were calling like
a valiant commander to his faint-hearted troops: 'Courage, men!
Forward! Trust in me! The victory is ours!'"[28]

We might want to consider the powerful appeal of Hüttenbrenner's dramatic oral and written accounts in light of the ways that they seem to relate to the two most famous letters Beethoven ever wrote, both of which were apparently never sent and were thus only discovered immediately following his death: the Heiligenstadt Testament of 1802 and the letter to the "Immortal Beloved" of 1812.[29] The ultimate recipients of these unsent letters were not Beethoven's brothers, both named and absent,[30] or the unknown woman whose identity has inspired voluminous study and speculation to this day, but, rather, posterity, which continues to be fascinated by the dual images of heroic suffering and vulnerable romance contained within them.[31] If Hüttenbrenner's representation of the dying Beethoven shaking his fist at fate has left an indelible trace on the composer's image, the more specific interest of his account today concerns the continuing mystery of the identity of the person in the room with him at the precise moment of Beethoven's death.

We know from other accounts that Stephan von Breuning, his son, and Schindler where present when Hüttenbrenner arrived in the middle of the afternoon on March 26.[32] The artist Joseph Teltscher is mentioned in both Hüttenbrenner's oral account and his letter to Thayer, and his three drawings of the dying (or perhaps dead) composer survive (see Fig. 1).[33] Gerhard von Breuning mentions that Beethoven's faithful housekeeper Sali was present.[34] Within the transcription of Hüttenbrenner's oral account, as we have seen, Thayer inserts his own doubts that Karl's mother was there, and he later notes further, "Mrs. Beethoven says that Karl's mother could not have been present at Beethoven's death, as it was a matter of complaint with her that no news of his dying condition reached her until after all was over. Dr. Breuning also thinks she could not have been there, for he has no recollection of ever having seen either of the sisters-in-law of Beethoven."[35] In any case, Hüttenbrenner's letter to Thayer later that summer mentions only Therese: "When, on 26 March 1827, at about three o'clock in the afternoon, I entered Beethoven's bedroom, I found him with Herr Hofrat von Breuning, his son, Frau van Beethoven, the wife of Johann van Beethoven, and also my friend, Joseph Teltscher, portrait painter. I believe that Professor Schindler was also present."[36]

All of the most compelling evidence suggests that Karl's mother was not present at Beethoven's deathbed, and indeed her fraught relationship with Beethoven would have made any such final encounter unlikely. Maynard Solomon, the preeminent Beethoven biographer of our time, nonetheless places her there, and later in a position of prominence at the funeral.[37] The repercussions of this confusion, which has baffled Beethoven's biographers for so long, have recently been

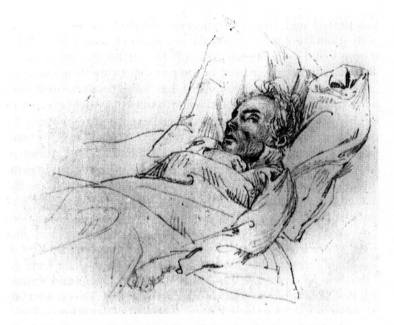

Fig. 1: *Beethoven on his Deathbed*. Pencil drawing by Joseph Teltscher.

enshrined in popular culture: Johanna is revealed as Beethoven's "Immortal Beloved" and Beethoven becomes the "true fleshly father" of Karl in Bernard Rose's fanciful movie *Immortal Beloved* (1994).[38] If the story of Beethoven's raising his fist against fate at the end exemplifies, and satisfies, one central aspect of the Beethoven myth—the defiant, struggling, heroic artist—the presence of a mysterious woman reflects another component, namely his long and fruitless search for a loving and understanding wife. Hüttenbrenner's colorful representations of Beethoven's death thus symbolically perform crucial biographical issues that Beethoven poignantly expressed in the Heiligenstadt Testament and the "Immortal Beloved" letter.

Marcia Funebre

Many matters required attention in the three days before Beethoven's funeral. The autopsy, conducted by Johann Wagner on March 27, was of immediate interest, given understandable curiosity about the causes of Beethoven's deafness and final illness.[39] As Johann van Beethoven, Breuning, Schindler, and Karl Holz searched Beethoven's apartment for valuables, some unpleasantness arose when Johann hinted that money had disappeared and Breuning allegedly stormed out of the room. Eventually seven bank notes, worth the not inconsiderable sum of 7,000 florins, were found in an unseen drawer.[40] During Beethoven's last days there had already been comment in the press about the magnanimous gift of £100 (equivalent to 1,000 florins) that had recently arrived from London,[41] and after news about the bank notes became public even more attention was paid to the whole issue of Beethoven's alleged poverty. In the months that followed there was annoyance in England that the composer had clearly not needed the money and continuing defensiveness in Vienna over charges that he had been neglected by prominent persons in his adopted city. The debates in the domestic and foreign press, the impassioned letters back and forth between Vienna and England, and threatened legal action against the estate, display a good deal of nationalist partisanship and mistrust.[42] Schindler wrote to Moscheles that Beethoven was being "insulted in the grave" and regretted that "well-meaning friends should be publicly attacked for their noble endeavors."[43] Beethoven's reputation was clearly at stake in Vienna and abroad; some felt he had acted dishonestly in seeking help when he was not truly in need, especially from outside Vienna. The best explanations offered, which may well be accurate, are, first, that he regarded the bank notes, which he had put aside years earlier, as money for Karl's future, not for his own present; second, that he did not know how much longer he might live and feared he might no longer be able to earn an income from composing; and, third, a statement from Breuning that Beethoven was "perfectly helpless in all economic and financial matters."[44]

To complicate matters further, there were complaints that the English money was being used to pay for Beethoven's funeral expenses, as if the Viennese could not take care of the appropriate honors themselves.[45] Once again, damage control was required from Beethoven's advocates to mitigate what was quickly becoming a widely publicized scandal. A codicil to Beethoven's will—dated March 23, the last complete document from his hand—had stipulated that the capital should go to Karl's "natural or testamentary heirs" and that Karl would have to live from the income.[46] As a lawsuit would ultimately have been costly and embarrassing for everyone involved, all claims on the money were withdrawn after more than a year and the remaining funds eventually went into the estate.[47]

As with the passionate interest in the Heiligenstadt Testament and the Immortal Beloved mystery, the controversy over Beethoven's late finances and burial costs calls for some explanation. Even if we cannot fully understand Beethoven's personal motivations, such as his continual fear of poverty and of being cheated, nor all of the overdetermined causes of the heated public debates, we should note that these (over)reactions themselves recall two central components of Beethoven's biography: his curious and often dubious financial arrangements and, more important and subtle, claims to Beethoven as a universal composer, the property of all mankind ("alle Menschen werden Brüder"), in contrast to the nationalist claim of Beethoven as specifically and uniquely German. The contest between England and Vienna performs this debate in striking ways. The obituary in *The Gentleman's Magazine* of London closed with this observation, "In their neglect of living genius the feelings of the Germans appear to assimilate too closely with those of their brethren the English; for, although Beethoven was allowed to languish and expire in poverty, his remains were honored with a splendid and ostentatious funeral."[48]

On March 27, Breuning requested Schindler's permission for a death mask to be made the following morning by the artist Josef Danhauser:

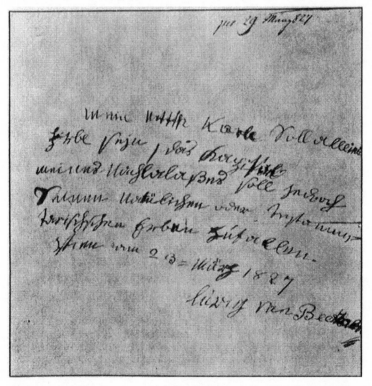

Fig. 2: Codicil to Beethoven's Will, dated March 23, 1827. (Municipal Archive, Vienna.)

"Such casts are often permitted in the case of famous men, and not to permit it would later be grieved as an insult to the public."[49] Together with his brother Carl and another artist, Danhauser cast the mask, but as this was done after the autopsy, during which "the petrous portion of the temporal bone" had been cut out, Beethoven's face was severely deformed.[50] Danhauser also drew his head and made separate oil sketches of the head and hands. A lithograph of the drawing, dated March 28, was offered for sale to the public.[51]

Preparations for the funeral, which had begun even before Beethoven's death, assumed new urgency. As Sebastian Rau informed Moscheles on March 28, "Beethoven will be buried on the 29th. An invitation went out to all the artists, orchestras, and theaters. Twenty virtuosos and composers will accompany the body with torches; Herr Grillparzer has prepared a most touching address, which Herr Anschütz will deliver at the grave. On the whole, preparations are being made for a solemn funeral worthy of the deceased."[52] Franz Grillparzer, Vienna's foremost literary figure, had been at work on the address for some days already. As he recalled years later, "I had got to the second half when Schindler entered once more to fetch what he had ordered, for Beethoven had just died. At that moment there was a terrible commotion within me, tears poured from my eyes and—as was usually the case when I was overwhelmed by genuine emotion—I could not complete the oration as weightily as I had begun it."[53]

Breuning composed the funeral notice, which Haslinger printed:

Invitation
to
Ludwig van Beethoven's
Funeral
*which will take place on the 29th of March at 3 o'clock in
the afternoon*

The company will assemble at the house of the deceased,
Schwarzspanierhaus, No. 200, on the glacis outside the
Schottenthor
The Procession will move on from there to the Trinity
Church in the Alsergasse

The musical world suffered the irreparable loss of the
celebrated musical poet on the 26th of March 1827 toward 6
o'clock in the evening. Beethoven died from the consequences
of dropsy, in the 56th year of his age,
after having received the holy sacraments.

> The day appointed for the obsequies will be made known
> subsequently among
>
> **L. van Beethoven's**
> Admirers and Friends
>
> (This card will be distributed at Haslinger's music store.)

Breuning also helped attend to the newspaper announcements. In his letter to Schindler inquiring about the death mask, he noted that on March 28 or 29 the *Oesterreichischer Beobachter* and perhaps the *Wiener Zeitung* would state the time of the service.[54] The first obituaries appeared in the following days, including a surprisingly prompt one, on March 28, by Friedrich Rochlitz in Germany's most prestigious musical journal, the Leipzig *Allgemeine musikalische Zeitung*.[55] The *Wiener Zeitschrift für Kunst, Literatur, Theater und Mode* ran an obituary on March 29 that was probably written by its editor Johann Schickh. Schickh was well positioned to write the piece—a longtime friend of Beethoven's, he had visited early in the afternoon on the day the composer died and was one of the people actively involved with the funeral preparations. Given this context, it is significant that Schickh spends so much space discussing the English gifts of the Handel edition and the £100:[56]

> Ludwig van Beethoven, the Michaelangelo of German musical art and the last of its heroes, those who brought glory to the previous century and carried forth that glory into the present century, is no more! He died on 26 March at the age of 56 years, 3 months, and 10 days, after a lengthy and painful illness, that of common dropsy. Van Beethoven was born on 17 December 1770, not 1772, as reported in the *Conversations-Lexicon*.
>
> As one of the most brilliant composers of every genre of music, from the Lied to the symphony, and to opera and sacred music, his loss is sure to be deeply felt in general, and also in particular because he will not complete the great oratorio he began, nor will musical literature have his profound spirit and character to thank for a Requiem, since that too was part of his plans as a composer. Van Beethoven the composer will be as unforgettable and immortal as Mozart, the Raphael Urbino of composers; as a man and a friend, Beethoven will live forever in the memory of all those who were lucky enough to know him more closely, because of his childlike simplicity, his exacting honesty and love of truth, and his benevolence, fidelity, and loyalty. In its 12th number, this newspaper mentioned the magnanimous gift of the London edition of

Haendel's complete works that was sent to Beethoven by Mr. A. Stumpff, a German living in London. When the departed thanked the aforementioned bearer of this gift by means of the pen of his friend, Mr. Schindler, who stood at his side with friendly devotion during his entire illness, he made general mention of the great expense of his illness and expressed the wish that an earlier offer from the London Philharmonic Society—to give a concert for his benefit—might now be put into action, since he could soon find himself in need. In accordance with the desires of the departed, Mr. Stumpff shared this disclosure with Sir G. Smart and Mr. Moscheles, members of the Philharmonic Society. They then brought this news to a meeting of the Committee of the Society, where they found such general assent that the Society, of the opinion that swift aid was called for, immediately made payable the amount of 100 pounds sterling through the banking houses of Rothschild in London and Vienna. As splendid and appreciative this rapid granting of our unforgettable van Beethoven's wish may seem as a sign of London's full recognition of his excellent merit, it must not however be presumed that some urgent need of the great man was thus being ameliorated with this, since Mr. van Beethoven found himself in the possession of a pension and enough of a ready fortune that he could have gone without outside aid for a long time to come. And were things the other way around, the recognition of the extraordinary merit and the noble character of the departed would have found in Vienna as well the means to assist every need of this fascinating man through similar arrangements. Thus the rumors about this event need to be set right for the sake of the truth. Arrangements are now being made to ensure a decent gravesite for the departed. In addition, an academy concert planned by the professors of music for the defrayal of the cost of a monument promises such success that this monument will soon be raised as a worthy memorial of the veneration accorded Beethoven, and it will speak of this veneration to coming generations.

Not all the published information was accurate. The report in Vienna's *Der Sammler* the same day is typical in its reverence and in the way it mistook the identity of the one in whose arms the composer died:

Notice: Music has lost its ornament and Vienna its most prominent resident. On 26 March, towards 6 P.M., Ludwig van Beethoven died of dropsy, in his 57th year, in the arms of his brother. Today, the 29th of this month, his mortal remains will be brought to Währing and laid to rest there. News of this loss will be lamented by artists and art lovers in all parts of the world. He cannot be replaced.[57]

On March 28, Beethoven's body lay in state. The composer's unruly hair, which must have seemed to many contemporaries emblematic of his eccentric and revolutionary persona, especially in comparison with the powdered wigs of his most illustrious predecessors, immediately became a treasured relic. As was common practice in courtship and remembrance, Schindler had sent Moscheles some strands of hair on March 24, while Beethoven was still in agony.[58] On March 26, Hüttenbrenner helped himself ("Frau van Beethoven, at my request, cut off a lock of his hair, and gave it to me, as a sacred remembrance of Beethoven's last hour"). On March 27, the singer Luigi Cramolini talked the old woman minding the body (he thought her the maid) into letting him lift the cover and quickly clip off some hair.[59] On March 28, Danhauser and associates did the same while making the death mask: "We had cut off two locks from the temple where it grew thickly, as a memento of the celebrated head."[60] In his diary that day, Schubert's good friend Franz Hartmann recorded his success in getting some strands from the attendant: "We gave the old man a tip and begged him for a few of Beethoven's hairs. He shook his head and motioned to us to be silent. We were going slowly and sadly down the steps when the old man softly called from the balustrade above that we should wait at the gate . . . the old man came out the door, his finger on his lips, and handed us the hair in a bit of paper." Hartmann's older brother Fritz did likewise later that day.[61] By Thursday, March 29, the date of the funeral, young Breuning came to collect his treasure: "I went with my father to Beethoven's dwelling and wanted to cut off a lock of his hair. Father had not allowed me to do this before the lying-in-state ended, in order not to spoil his appearance; but now we had found that strangers had already cut off all his hair."[62] Private collectors and prominent public institutions, such as the Beethoven-Haus in Bonn, the American Beethoven Society, Vienna's Gesellschaft der Musikfreunde, the Library of Congress, and the British Library today boast possession of some of the prized locks.[63] As we shall see later, these relics continue to fascinate.

Descriptions of Beethoven's imposing funeral differ about how many mourners joined the procession from Beethoven's house to nearby Trinity Church, and then on to Währing Cemetery. *Der Sammler* reported 10,000, while Gerhard von Breuning doubled that number,

Fig. 3: *Beethoven's Funeral*. Watercolor by Franz Stöber.

and Schindler tripled it in his letter to Moscheles of April 4.[64] Military guards were called in to deal with the crushing crowds. In Franz Stöber's famous watercolor, Beethoven's coffin is overwhelmed by the throng—another indication of the magnitude of this day when schools were closed and the city lamented the loss of her premier artist.[65] (See Fig. 3.)

Participating in the event was a veritable Who's Who of the Viennese cultural and artistic elite, including leading singers and instrumentalists (such as Lablache, Schuppanzigh), composers (Hummel, Schubert, Seyfried, Kreutzer, Gyrowetz), literary figures (Grillparzer, Raimund, Castelli), publishers (Diabelli, Haslinger), and prominent officials who had worked with Beethoven. While accounts of the event mostly agree, they differ in some important respects.[66] The precise repetition of specific language in most of the published reports indicates knowledge of earlier sources, probably of some "Urtext" that was modified, corrected, and elaborated by later writers.[67] *Der Sammler* provided two lengthy versions of the event in the April 14 issue.[68] (They are included in their entirety as Appendix A.)

At three o'clock in the afternoon, eight members of the court orchestra carried the body out to the court, where priests blessed the coffin while sixteen vocalists sang the chorale "Rasch tritt der Todt den Menschen an" from Bernhard Anselm Weber's incidental music to Schiller's *William Tell* (1804). With the procession led by the crossbearer, four trombonists played two *Equale* (WoO 30, nos. 1 and 3), music Beethoven had written in 1812,[69] which alternated with a choral version fitted by Ignaz Ritter von Seyfried with words to the *Miserere* and *Amplius lava me*. The eight Kapellmeisters accompanied the coffin, borne by the orchestral musicians, and were followed by torchbearers. After them came family members and various dignitaries, as well as conservatory students. According to Gerhard von Breuning, the funeral march from Beethoven's Piano Sonata in A-flat Major, op. 26, was "intoned as the coffin rounded the corner of the Rothes Haus."[70]

All accounts agree that the crowd was so large that it took considerable time to reach the nearby Trinity Church. Inside was sung the *Libera me*, written by Seyfried as a supplement to Mozart's *Requiem* and on this occasion sung *a cappella*.[71] The coffin was then placed in a hearse drawn by four horses, and many mourners made the long walk to the cemetery, accompanied by some 200 carriages. The procession came to the parish church in Währing, where two priests blessed the coffin, and there was further singing of the *Miserere*, motets, and *Libera*.[72] As only clergy were permitted to speak on consecrated ground, the procession stopped at the gates of Währing Cemetery, where Heinrich Anschütz,[73] Germany's most prominent actor, read Grillparzer's celebrated oration, which began by invoking the pantheon of German genius of which only Goethe now remained:[74]

> We who stand here at the grave of the deceased are in a sense the representatives of an entire nation, the whole German people, come to mourn the passing of one celebrated half of that which remained to us of the vanished brilliance of the art of our homeland, of the spiritual efflorescence of the fatherland. The hero of poetry in the German language and tongue still lives—and long may he live. But the last master of resounding song, the gracious mouth by which music spoke, the man who inherited and increased the immortal fame of Handel and Bach, of Haydn and Mozart, has ceased to be; and we stand weeping over the broken strings of an instrument now stilled.[75]

Three laurel wreaths were placed on the coffin (the first one by Hummel) before it was covered with earth. It was now dusk. A memorial poem later composed by Baron Joseph Christian Zedlitz remarked that it was "as if two suns at one time were parting from the earth."[76]

Hundreds of printed copies of two poems written for the occasion were distributed to the mourners, although accounts differ about exactly when and where. Whether or not they were read aloud, Ignaz Franz

Castelli's *Bey Ludwig van Beethoven's Leichenbegängnisse* may have been given out at the Schwarzspanierhaus before the services began and Baron von Schlechta's *Am Grabe Beethoven's* later at Währing.[77] This confusion about such a minor detail is typical of the many inconsistencies in the accounts of this epilogue to Beethoven's biography: How many actually attended the funeral and who exactly participated? What music was performed, how and when? What happened once the procession reached the village of Währing? Drawing upon a wealth of published accounts, most nineteenth- and twentieth-century narratives of the events of March 29 paint a vivid picture without acknowledging any of the many discrepancies and missing information. While these particulars do not in themselves significantly matter, a general lack of concern for which version of events is most trustworthy and is best substantiated by the historical evidence points to the larger issue: the tendency to construct a compelling story at the expense of more nuanced and responsible analysis. Such problems plague any biographical investigation, although given the fact that so much of the information derived from Schindler, Seyfried, Rochlitz, and even Gerhard von Breuning has long been discredited, a more critical view generally seems warranted.

Honoring Beethoven

Once the traumatic and exhausting events of Beethoven's death and funeral had passed, the planning for and execution of more lasting tributes, memorials, and remembrances began in earnest. Immediately proposals emerged for a monument of some kind. While a physical structure was the prime concern, the language of reviews, letters, poems, and biographies talked of figurative monuments to Beethoven's memory in prose, poetry, and music, and often remarked that his own artistic achievement was in any case the greatest possible monument of all. The poems distributed at the funeral and the musical works heard on the occasion were soon issued to the public (see Tables 1 and 2, pp. 246–47 and pp. 248–49). Within ten days, the *Wiener Zeitung* was announcing Carl Czerny's *Marcia funebre sulla morte di Luigi van Beethoven*, which begins with a clear allusion to the funeral march of the *Eroica* Symphony (See Fig. 4). On April 9, Joseph Drechsler's *Bey Ludwig van Beethoven's Leichenbegängnisse*, a vocal setting of Castelli's funeral poem, was advertised in the same paper. Simon Sechter set the same text for four voices and piano, while August Swoboda used Schlechta's poem. In June, Haslinger published Seyfried's vocal settings of the *Equale* (WoO 30, nos. 1 and 3), including a detailed description of the funeral on the reverse of

Fig. 4: Title page of Carl Czerny's memorial composition honoring Beethoven, published by Anton Diabelli in April 1827. (Courtesy of the Gesellschaft der Musikfreunde.)

the title page. A note explained that this description was "inserted because several of the public papers contained erroneous and imperfect statements of the ceremony."[78] At the same time, Haslinger released Anselm Hüttenbrenner's *Nachruf an Beethoven* for piano.[79] (Some two years later Hüttenbrenner would compose a *Nachruf an Schubert* in memory of his close friend.)[80] Table 1 lists the musical compositions published in Beethoven's memory in Vienna soon after his death; other works would later appear in that city and elsewhere.[81]

Even more numerous than these published musical tributes were poetic ones.[82] Table 2 lists some of the poems that appeared within six months, mostly in newspapers or musical journals.[83] Although some were written by colleagues and collaborators of Beethoven (Treitschke, Kanne, Castelli), most were written by younger poets, the next generation of Viennese creators born in the 1790s and 1800s for whom Beethoven was a god.[84] The many poems inspired by Beethoven's death display a wide range of literary merit and thematic content. Some are generic musings on death that mention neither Beethoven's name nor specific compositions. While they tend to make some reference to music, such poems could have been written in remembrance of almost any relatively famous composer. The third verse of Castelli's poem, distributed at the service and set to music by Sechter and Drechsler, is typical:

Table 1
Memorial Compositions

Carl Czerny

Marcia funebre sulla morte di Luigi van Beethoven (composta da Carlo Czerny. Op. 146) 26 Marzo 1827 per il Piano-Forte solo, op. 146

April 1827; published in Vienna by Anton Diabelli; plate no. 2609 (no. 2610 is the same piece for piano duet)

Joseph Drechsler

Bey Ludwig van Beethoven's Leichenbegängnisse am 29ten März 1827 von J. F. Castelli. In Musik gesetzt für eine Singstimme mit Begleitung des Pianoforte von Jos. Drechsler

April 1827; published in Vienna by Anton Diabelli in commission; no plate number

Setting for voices and piano of Ignaz Castelli's poem

Ignaz Ritter von Seyfried

Trauer-Gesang bey Beethoven's Leichenbegängnisse in Wien den 29. März 1827. Vierstimmiger Männerchor, mit willkührlicher Begleitung von vier Posaunen, oder des Pianoforte. Aus Beethoven's Manuscripte zu dem obigen Gebrauche mit Text eingerichtet von Ignaz Ritter von Seyfried

No. 1 *Miserere*; no. 2 *Amplius lava me*

June 1827; published in Vienna by Tobias Haslinger; plate no. 5034

Vocal arrangements of Beethoven's *Equale*, WoO 30, nos. 1 and 3

Ignaz Ritter von Seyfried

Libera, welches bey Beethoven's Leichenbegängnisse vor der Einsegnung des entseelten Körpers, in der Kirche bey den P. P. Minoriten in der Alservorstadt in Wien, den 29. März 1827 von dem Sänger-Chor, welcher den Leichenzug begleitete, gesungen worden ist. Componirt, und zu obigem Gebrauche eingerichtet von Ignaz Ritter von Seyfried

June 1827; published in Vienna by Tobias Haslinger; plate no. 5035

Ignaz Ritter von Seyfried

Beethoven's Begräbniss. Gedicht von Jeitteles. Nach einer Composition des Verewigten: "Marcia funebre sulla morte d'un Eroe" für 4 Singstimmen mit Begleitung des Pianoforte eingerichtet von Ignaz Ritter von Seyfried

June 1827; published in Vienna by Tobias Haslinger; plate no. 5036

Table 1 continued

Anselm Hüttenbrenner

Nachruf an Beethoven in Akkorden am Piano-Forte von seinem innigsten Verehrer

June 1827; published in Vienna by Tobias Haslinger; plate no. 5039

Simon Sechter

Bei dem Leichenbegängnisse des Ludwig van Beethoven von J. F. Castelli

Spring/Summer 1827; published in Vienna by Ferdinand Kettner; no plate number

Setting for voices and piano of Ignaz Castelli's poem

August Swoboda

Am Grabe Beethoven's. Gedicht von Freyherrn C. von Schlechta. Vocal Quartett für zwey Tenore und zwey Bässe mit Piano Forte oder Guitarre Begleitung

Published in Vienna by the composer; no plate number

Setting for vocal quartet and piano of Franz Xaver Freyherr von Schlechta's poem

Ignaz Ritter von Seyfried

Trauerklänge bei Beethoven's Grabe. Vierstimmiger Männer-Chor, nach einer Original-Melodie des Verewigten. Die Worte von Franz Grillparzer

March 21, 1829; published in Vienna by Tobias Haslinger as a supplement to the *Allgemeiner Musikalischer Anzeiger*, No. 12 (21 March 1829)

Vocal arrangement of Beethoven's *Equale*, WoO 30, no. 2

Sources: Wiener Stadt- und Landesbibliothek, Musiksammlung; Österreichische Nationalbibliothek, Musiksammlung; Johann Baptist Geissler's "Sammlung aller Gedichte und Aufsätze, welche aus Anlass . . . 1828 gesammelt und der Bibliothek verehrt" in the Archive of the Gesellschaft der Musikfreunde (sig: 1938/32). Alexander Weinmann, *Vollständiges Verlagsverzeichnis: Senefelder, Steiner, Haslinger*, 3 vols. (*Beiträge zur Geschichte des Alt-Wiener Musikverlages* II/19, Munich, 1980); Alexander Weinmann, *Verlagsverzeichnis: Anton Diabellis & Co. (1824–1840)*, (*Beiträge zur Geschichte des Alt-Wiener Musikverlages* II/24, Vienna, 1985).

Table 2
Memorial Poems

Abbreviations

AGSLK	*Archiv für Geschichte, Statistik, Literatur und Kunst*
BAMZ	*Berliner allgemeine musikalische Zeitung*
FAMZ	*Allgemeine Musik-Zeitung zur Beförderung der theoretischen und praktischen Tonkunst* (Frankfurt am Main)
LAMZ	Leipzig *Allgemeine musikalische Zeitung*
TZ	*Wiener allgemeine Theaterzeitung*
WZKLTM	*Wiener Zeitschrift für Kunst, Literatur, Theater und Mode*
WZ	*Wiener-Zeitung*

Viennese publications

J. F. Castelli, *Bey Ludwig van Beethoven's Leichenbegängnisse am 29. March 1827*

Distributed at funeral; *Der Sammler* No. 39 (31 March 1827); set to music by Simon Sechter and Joseph Drechsler (see Table 1)

Franz Xaver Freyherr von Schlechta, *Am Grabe Beethoven's den 29 März 1827*

Distributed at funeral; set to music by August Swoboda (see Table 1)

Friedrich August Kanne, *Ludwig van Beethoven's Tod den 26 März 1827*
Brochure published by Tendler & von Manstein in Vienna (1827)

Paul Friedrich Walther, *Louis van Beethoven's Sterbetag*
TZ no. 40 (3 April 1827)

F[ranz] C[arl] Weidmann, *Am Grabe Beethoven's*
WZKLTM no. 40 (3 April 1827)

Heinrich Börnstein, *Fantasie an Beethovens Grabe*
TZ no. 41 (5 April 1827)

P[eter] A. Budik, *Auf Beethoven's Grab*
Der Sammler no. 43 (10 April 1827)

A[ndreas] St[umpff], *Auf Beethovens Tod*
WZKLTM no. 47 (19 April 1827)

A. v. M, *Beethoven im Sarge*
WZKLTM no. 49 (24 April 1827)

Franz Maria Freiherr von Nell, *Nachruf an Beethoven*
AGSLK nos. 50 and 51 (25 and 27 April 1827)

Table 2 continued

[Georg] Friedrich Treitschke, *Zu Beethoven's Gedächtniss*
WZKLTM no. 50 (26 April 1827)

Johann Gabriel Seidl, *In tumulum*
WZ no. 51 (28 April 1827)

F. H. Slavik, *Beytrag zu einem Cypressenkranz auf Beethoven's Grab*
WZKLTM no. 73 (19 June 1827)

[Friedrich] Ludwig Halirsch, *Beethoven's Requiem (Eine Vision)*
TZ no. 128 (25 October 1827)

German periodicals

Anselmus, *Beethoven ist gestorben* (1827)
BAMZ no. 15 (11 April 1827)

Heinrich Stieglitz, *Beethoven*
BAMZ no. 15 (11 April 1827), 115

[Friedrich de la Motte] L. M. Fouqué, *An Beethoven*
BAMZ no. 18 (2 May 1827)

Maximilian Löwenthal, *Nachruf an Beethoven*
Dresden Abendzeitung no. 122 (22 May 1827)

Wilhelm Christian Müller, *Beethoven*
LAMZ no. 20 (23 May 1827)

Johann Gabriel Seidl, *Beethoven*
LAMZ no. 22 (30 May 1827)
(spoken by Henrich Anschütz at the program given by members of the
Concerts spirituels on May 3, 1827)

Dr. [Alois] Ludwig Jeitteles, *Beethoven's Begräbniss*
FAMZ no. 13 (15 August 1827); set to music by Ignaz Ritter von Seyfried
(see Table 1)

Heinrich Stieglitz, *Zu Beethoven's Gedächtniss*
Dresden Abendzeitung, no. 169 (date unknown).

Sources: Hermann Josef Landau, *Erstes poetisches Beethoven-Album* (Prague,
1872); Ignaz Ritter von Seyfried, *Ludwig van Beethoven's Studien im Generalbass,
Contrapunkt und in der Compositionslehre* (Vienna, 1832); and Johann Baptist
Geissler's "Sammlung aller Gedichte und Aufsätze, welche aus Anlass . . . 1828
gesammelt und der Bibliothek verehrt" in the Archive of the Gesellschaft der
Musikfreunde (sig: 1938/32). Information on most of these poets can be found
in *Bio-Bibliographisches Literaturlexikon Österreichs von den Anfängen bis zur
Gegenwart*, ed. Hans Giebisch and Gustav Gugitz (Vienna, 1963).

Table 3
Selected Viennese Services in Beethoven's Honor and
Concerts Featuring His Music

March 26, 1827: Third Concert of Ignaz Schuppanzigh's Subscription Series
String Quartets by Mozart and Haydn
Beethoven, Piano Trio in G, op. 1, no. 2 (Josef Linke, cello; Carl Czerny, piano)

April 1: Fourth Gesellschaft Concert (E. v. Lannoy, conductor)
Beethoven, Symphony No. 1 in C Major
Rossini, Prayer from *Mosé in Egitto*
Leopold Jansa, Variations for Violin
Spontini, Overture to *Fernand Cortez*

April 1: Fourth Concert of Ignaz Schuppanzigh's Subscription Series
String Quartets by Mozart and Haydn
Beethoven, Trio in B-flat, op. 97 (Josef Linke, cello; Carl Czerny, piano)

April 3: Service at the Augustiner Hofpfarrkirche
Mozart, *Requiem*
Seyfried, *Miserere* and *Libera* (as heard at Beethoven's funeral)

April 5: Third *Concerts spirituels*
Beethoven, Symphony No. 6 in F Major
Vogler, Dies Irae, Sanctus, Benedictus from *Todtenmesse*
Beethoven, Kyrie from *Missa solemnis*
Castel, Overture to *Semiramis*

April 5: Service at the k.k. Pfarrkirche zu St. Carl
Cherubini, *Requiem* (Hummel conducting)

April 6: Concert by Cellist Joseph Merk
Beethoven, Overture to *Prometheus*
Works by other composers

April 6: Fifth Concert of Ignaz Schuppanzigh's Subscription Series
Beethoven, String Quartet No. 10 in E-flat, op. 74
Haydn String Quartet and Hummel Septet

April 7: Benefit Concert for Anton Schindler at the Josefstäder-Theater
Hummel, free improvisation on the Allegretto from Beethoven's
    Symphony No. 7 in A Major
Beethoven, Overture to *König Stephan*
Beethoven, Overture to *Die Ruinen von Athen*

April 16 (Easter Monday): Last Concert, Ignaz Schuppanzigh's Series
Schubert, Octet
Beethoven, *An die ferne Geliebte*
Beethoven, Piano Concerto No. 5 in E-flat, "Emperor," arranged for two
    pianos and string quartet (featuring Carl Czerny)

April 19: Fourth *Concerts spirituels*
Beethoven, Symphony No. 9 in D Major, first movement
Cherubini, Mass No. 2 in D

Table 3 continued

April 22: Concert of Franz Mennen, Blind Teacher at the Institute for the Blind
Beethoven, Overture to *Prometheus*
Works by other composers

April 22: Concert of Cellist Josef Linke
Beethoven, String Quartet in B-flat, op. 130 (using the new finale)
Beethoven, *Neue Liebe, neues Leben*
Beethoven, Piano Trio in C Minor, op. 1, no. 3 (Ignaz Schuppanzigh, violin; Carl Maria von Bocklet, piano)
Romberg, Divertimento

April 22: Concert of violinist Leopold Jansa
Beethoven, Overture to *Egmont*
Works by other composers

April 26: Service at the Augustiner Hofpfarrkirche Presented by the Gesellschaft der Musikfreunde
Cherubini, *Requiem*
Seyfried, *Miserere* and *Libera* (as heard at Beethoven's funeral)

May 1: Ignaz Schuppanzigh Concert at the k. k. Augarten-Saal
Beethoven, Symphony No. 4 in B-flat
Beethoven, Overture in C, op. 124
Works by other composers

May 3: Benefit Concert presented by Members of the *Concerts spirituels*; All Beethoven
Symphony No. 5 in C Minor
Poem by Johann Gabriel Seidl, recited by Heinrich Anschütz
Violin Concerto, first movement only, played by Joseph Böhm
Adelaide, op. 46, sung by Ludwig Tietze
Piano Concerto No. 3 in C Minor, op. 37, played by Carl Maria von Bocklet
Christus om Ölberge, op. 85, final chorus

Sources: Program collection, Archiv der Gesellschaft der Musikfreunde in Wien; *Chronologisches Verzeichniss aller auf den fünf Theatern Wien's gegebenen Vorstellungen vom ersten November 1826 bis letzten October 1827*, ed. K. Voll (Vienna, 1829); Leipzig *Allgemeine musikalische Zeitung*; *Der Sammler*; *Franz Schubert Dokumente 1817–1830. Erster Band. Texte. Programme, Rezensionen, Anzeigen, Nekrologe, Musikbeilagen und andere gedruckte Quellen*, ed. Till Gerrit Waidelich (Tutzing, 1993); Richard von Perger and Robert Hirschfeld, *Geschichte der k. k. Gesellschaft der Musikfreunde in Wien* (Vienna, 1912), pp. 285ff.

But lamenting must be for yourself alone!
For he who ranked so high in the holy domain
Can be held no longer to his earthly realm,
His spirit seeks rest in a loftier sphere.[85]

There are frequent allusions to Beethoven's deafness, solitude, and sufferings, and also to the power of an art that was not always comprehended during his lifetime but would be in the future. Consider the last verse of Schlechta's poem:

You, who lie here, freed from your pain and bonds,
You were the source, which I have named before!
So few understood your greatness,
Often praised, but more often misjudged.
Now all sing your honor in elevation,
You had to die, to die, so that you might live![86]

Some poems are quite specific about certain facets of Beethoven's life and death.[87] Those by Franz Carl Weidmann and Franz Maria Freiherr von Nell allude to the storm that raged the afternoon of his death ("Thunder was God's last word to you"). The one by Baron Joseph Christian Zedlitz describes the progress of the funeral service. Quite a few name individual compositions. Georg Friedrich Treitschke, who had revised the libretto of *Fidelio* in 1814, wrote a poem including the verse:

O works of His, resound as proof!
Prometheus-like, He brought you forth.
You *symphonies*—thus do heavenly spheres revolve—
You *song of holy mass*, full of dignity, majesty, power!
Fidelio and *Egmont* will glorify Him,—
Adelaide's sweet night of magic, too—
And also *our song "Germania"*! Gladly my heart
Dwells on the consecration He so richly bestowed.[88]

A lengthy poem was penned by the remarkable Friedrich August Kanne (1779–1833),[89] poet, composer, critic, editor of the *Wiener allgemeine musikalische Zeitung* from 1821–24, and a friend of Beethoven's—a true polymath. His *L. van Beethoven's Tod den 26 März 1827* appeared as a separate brochure published in Vienna by Tendler and von Manstein (1827).[90] Finally, a poem of higher literary merit, written at this time but only published seven years later, came from the pen of Johann Mayrhofer, the poet with whom Schubert lived for nearly two years and whose verses he set more often than those by any other poet save Goethe.[91] (Translations of the poems by Kanne and Mayrhofer are given in Appendices B and C.)

Beethoven's memory was, of course, honored as well through musical performances, both sacred and secular. In April, requiems by Mozart, Cherubini, and Abbé Vogler were heard in prominent churches. *Der Sammler*, among other publications, announced a memorial service:

Notice of Beethoven's Memorial Service

The observance of Beethoven's death will take place today, Tuesday the 3rd of April, at 11 A.M., in the Augustinian Court Chapel. Organized by a group of local art and music dealers, Mozart's Requiem and Beethoven's [own] funeral music will be performed.

On 5 April 1827 at 10 in the morning, in the Royal and Imperial St. Karl's Church, a solemn Mass for the dead will be held for the deceased composer Herr Ludwig van Beethoven.

Friends and admirers of the departed are respectfully invited to attend.

And two weeks later, *Der Sammler* announced:

Invitation
to the Requiem for Ludwig van Beethoven

The Gesellschaft der Musikfreunde will hold a performance of Cherubini's Requiem for Ludwig van Beethoven at the Augustinian Court Chapel on Thursday 26 April at 11 A.M. All members of the Society are invited to attend.[92]

Beethoven was most appropriately remembered with his own music, as the number of performances of his works increased dramatically during the remaining weeks of the 1826–27 musical season. Some compositions appeared on concerts whose programs had undoubtedly been planned well before his death, while in other cases performers must have added works in his honor. There were real obstacles to planning special concerts, for the season was drawing to a close, the availability of halls and musicians was limited to certain days when theatrical productions were not being held, and police permission was required before scheduling any such public events.[93] Table 3 (pp. 250–51) surveys the principal Viennese concerts that honored Beethoven or that offered his music during the remainder of the 1826–1827 season.[94] Some of these events were presented by individual performers, such as cellist Joseph Merk on April 6 and violinist Leopold Jansa on April 22. Also on April 22, Josef Linke, cellist in Schuppanzigh's Quartet, offered an all-Beethoven concert (or almost—a work by one of the Romberg cousins closed the program). Carl Maria von Bocklet, an excellent pianist closely associated with Schubert and highly praised by Chopin in 1831, joined with Schuppanzigh on this occasion. On April 7, a concert was presented for Schindler's benefit at the Josephstäder-Theater, where he had previously been orchestral director and where he was contractually entitled to the proceeds of an annual concert. Beethoven had hoped to write something for this event, but when it became clear he could not, he asked Hummel to participate. As A. B. Marx wrote in the *Berliner allgemeine musikalische Zeitung*, "Hummel, his heart broken, gave the master his hand and his word, and postponed his departure in order to fulfill his promise."[95] A great success, the concert included Hummel's improvisation on the most beloved orchestral movement of the time, the Andante of the Seventh Symphony, into which he evidently interspersed other melodies, including ones from *Fidelio*.[96]

Throughout the 1820s, Beethoven's works appeared frequently, far more than those of any other living composer, at the *Gesellschafts-Konzerte* organized by the Gesellschaft der Musikfreunde (or Musikfeinde—"enemies of music"—as Beethoven once irreverently called this august body). There were four concerts each season, and the First Symphony was performed at the final one of 1826–1827 (April 1). The following season, it programmed the "Pastoral" Symphony, the first two movements of the Ninth, and the Fifth.[97] Another regular series, the *Concerts spirituels*, offered the Sixth Symphony on April 5 and the first movement of the Ninth, presented "by request," on April 19. A special concert given by members of the *Concerts spirituels* on May 3, to raise money for a grave monument, was dedicated entirely to his compositions (see Fig. 5 on p. 256). The *Wiener Zeitschrift für Kunst, Literatur, Theater und Mode*, the *Wiener Zeitung* (May 1), and *Der Sammler* (May 3) announced the event:

Grave Monument for Ludwig van Beethoven

The members of the *Concerts spirituels*, willingly assisted by many of the notable artists of this capital city, have undertaken to present a musical-declamatory Academy on Thursday, 3 May of this year at 4 P.M. in the Landständische Hall, the proceeds of which are destined without deduction as a contribution to the erection of a monument to Beethoven at Währing Cemetery where his mortal remains rest. Only works of the deceased will be performed at the concert.

In doing so, they hope to inaugurate a series of similar events by others for the same purpose.

In any case, a committee will presently be assembled which, with the cooperation of the Royal and Imperial Court Counselor von Breuning, Beethoven's longtime friend, guardian of his nephew, and executor, will entrust the work to artistic hands so that by the fall of this year the monument can be erected.

Details concerning the works to be heard on this Academy, in which Professor Joseph Böhm, Carl Maria von Bocklet, Herr Ludwig Tietze, and Royal and Imperial Court Actor Herr Anschütz will participate, are announced on the placard.

Tickets of admission priced at 3 W.W. are to be had at Herr Tobias Haslinger's art and music shop on the Graben, No. 572.[98]

The concert opened with the Fifth Symphony. Anschütz recited a new poem written for the occasion by Johann Gabriel Seidl, a gifted young poet to whose work Schubert was increasingly drawn around this time.[99] Joseph Böhm performed the first movement of the Violin Concerto. (Presenting only one movement of a concerto or symphony was typical at the time.) Ludwig Tietze, a talented amateur tenor best known for his performances of Schubert Lieder, sang one of Beethoven's most popular compositions, "Adelaide," op. 46.[100] Bocklet next performed the opening allegro of the Third Piano Concerto, and the concert concluded with the final chorus from another favorite composition, the oratorio *Christus am Ölberge*, op. 85.[101]

Today we may think that insubstantial books thrown together after a celebrity's death are a postmodern consequence of the cult of personality and represent nothing more than the triumph of style over substance. Yet similar urges to capitalize on fame may have motivated some of the honors to Beethoven in 1827, especially biographical projects.[102] The first biography, a deplorable book by Johann Aloys Schlosser, rushed into print within months of the funeral,[103] begins with the observation: "Beethoven's death has been noted with more grief, in Germany and throughout Europe, than anyone else's in a long time. His art reached a level far above what others will attain. We therefore grieve not only because of our loss but also because there is no one able to take his place. Beethoven was not only a great artist but also a great human being; there is therefore a general desire for a biography."[104] No such work had materialized during Beethoven's lifetime, and misinformation about him was rampant.[105]

Schindler, who would himself ultimately write the most influential biography of Beethoven before those by Ludwig Nohl and Alexander Thayer began to appear in installments in the mid-1860s, tried at first to

Musikalisch - declamatorische
Akademie,

welche

Donnerstag den 3. May 1827, um 4 Uhr Nachmittags,

im n. ö. ständischen Saale

in der Herrngasse,

von den Mitgliedern der Concerts spirituels,

unter bereitwilliger Mitwirkung

ausgezeichneter Künstler,

gegeben werden wird,

und deren Ertrag, ohne Abzug,

als Beytrag zur Errichtung eines Grabmahles

für # Beethoven

bestimmt ist.

Vorkommende Stücke:

1. Fünfte große Symphonie in *C moll.*
2. Beethoven, Gedicht von Joh. Gabriel Seidl, declamirt von dem k. k. Hofschauspieler Herrn Anschütz.
3. Violin-Concert, erster Satz, vorgetragen von Hrn. Professor J. Böhm.
4. Adelaide, gesungen von Herrn Ludwig Titze.
5. Erstes Allegro aus dem Fortepiano-Concerte in *C moll,* vorgetragen von Herrn Carl Maria v. Bocklet.
6. Chor aus dem Oratorium: Christus am Oehlberge.

Sämmtliche Musikstücke von Beethoven's Composition.

Eintrittskarten zu 3 fl. W. W. sind in Herrn T. Haslinger's Kunst- und Musikalienhandlung am Graben Nro. 572, und am Tage der Aufführung bey der Kasse zu haben.

Für höhere Beträge wird auf Verlangen besonders quittirt.

Fig. 5: Placard for a Beethoven Memorial Concert on May 3, 1827. (Courtesy of the Gesellschaft der Musikfreunde.)

interest Friedrich Rochlitz, editor of the Leipzig *Allgemeine musikalische Zeitung*, in undertaking the project.[106] Schindler's letter to Moscheles on September 14 reveals his concern about the biographical component of Beethoven's legacy:

> In Prague, one Herr Schlosser has published a most miserable biography about Beethoven; here they are likewise announcing a subscription to one that, I hear, Herr Gräffer wants to write; and yet the biographer chosen by Beethoven is Court Counselor Rochlitz in Leipzig, for whom he gave Breuning and me very important papers. Now, however, the newly appointed guardian for Beethoven's nephew has given Breuning's papers to Herr Gräffer, which indeed is monstrous, but will not harm anything because they were for the most part family papers, and I have the most important ones in my hands.[107]

As Schindler states, Anton Gräffer, who worked for the Viennese publishing firm of Artaria & Co., was collecting information about Beethoven and attempting to interest potential subscribers in his project through a flyer distributed in September, as well as in notices published in various papers.[108] Responses from interested patrons were requested by November in the hope that the volume would be ready by March 1828, the first anniversary of the composer's death. Assisting in the effort for "a worthy biographical monument" was Jacob Hotschevar, the lawyer who had represented Johanna van Beethoven in the custody case over Karl van Beethoven and who had become Karl's executor after the death of Stephan von Breuning on June 4.[109] On September 20, Hotschevar issued an angry denunciation of Schlosser's competing biography, which he attacked as inaccurate and superficial, further objecting because the proceeds of that book were earmarked for a monument to Haydn, rather than to Beethoven.[110]

Requiescant in Pace

These biographical skirmishes took place just six months after Beethoven's death, at the start of a new concert season and the time of the official auction of Beethoven's estate.[111] Most important, Beethoven's tombstone was set in place at Währing Cemetery.[112] The simple design, bearing only the name BEETHOVEN, appeared in a print published by Haslinger (see Fig. 6). Grillparzer wrote another oration for the dedication ceremony, again delivered by Anschütz:

Six months have passed since last we stood on this same spot, lamenting and weeping—for we buried a friend. Now that we are gathered again, let us be calm and courageous—for we commemorate a victor. The river of impermanence has carried him off into the trackless ocean of eternity. Having shed his mortal raiments, he shines as a constellation in the heavenly night. From now on he belongs to history. May our words here be not of him, but of us.

We have caused a stone to be placed here. Perhaps as a memorial for him? Rather as a sign of truth for us. So that our grandchildren will know still where it is they should kneel, clasp their hands, and kiss the earth that covers his bones. The stone is simple, as he was in life. It is not large; the larger the stone, the more shameful the disparity with the man's worth. The name Beethoven stands upon it as the most glorious heraldic shield, at once the purple mantle of a duke and the headdress of a prince.

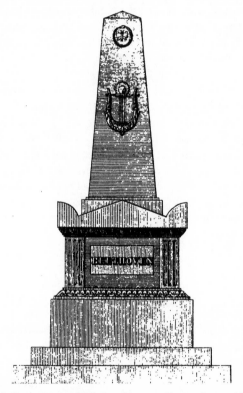

Fig. 6: *Beethoven's Gravestone at Währing Cemetery.* Engraving published by Tobias Haslinger.

A warm mantle; a regal headpiece! With this act the last duty has been fulfilled. And with this we say farewell forever to the man who was and assume the inheritance of the spirit that is and that will remain.

Rare are the moments of true enthusiasm in this spiritually bereft age. You, who are gathered at this place, step nearer to his grave. Fasten your gaze to the ground, direct all your senses together to that which you know of this man, and let the shudder of this act of gathering run through your bones like the frosts of this late season; carry it home like a fever, a healthy, saving fever; protect it and preserve it. Rare are the moments of true enthusiasm in this spiritually bereft age. Sanctify yourselves! He who lies here was an enthusiast. Aspiring after one thing only, caring for one thing, bearing up for one thing, sacrificing everything for one thing—thus did this man go through life. He knew neither spouse nor child, hardly a friend, few pleasures. If an eye offended him, he ripped it out and went onward, always onward to his goal. If, in this fragmented age, there is any sense for the whole within us, then let us gather together at his grave. This is why there have always been poets and heroes, singers and the divinely inspired: so that poor shattered men may be helped to raise themselves up, and to think upon their origin and their end.[113]

Six months later, performances of grief continued with events marking the first anniversary of Beethoven's death. On March 23, Josef Linke gave an all-Beethoven concert.[114] On March 26, the date of Beethoven's death, Schubert presented the only public concert of his career devoted entirely to his own works. Although not announced as a commemorative concert, two works on the program—the Piano Trio in E-flat, op. 100 (D929) and the song *Auf dem Strom* (D943)—subtly allude to the funeral march of the *Eroica* Symphony and seem intended as a secret homage to Beethoven.[115] Schubert, who had revered Beethoven above all other composers, undoubtedly experienced his death profoundly.[116] According to Hüttenbrenner, he and Schubert visited Beethoven about a week before he died, and Schubert's participation in the funeral is mentioned in all significant accounts. Both Schubert's music and career at this time reveal a renewed determination to assume a greater stature; professional musicians, publishers, critics, and the public increasingly recognized the thirty-year-old as more than just a composer of intimate Lieder, partsongs, dances, and keyboard music.[117] Indeed, it was precisely Beethoven's own performers, publishers, and critical supporters who helped to present and promote the more Beethovenian side of

Schubert—the composer of large-scale instrumental works. This, in part, was what his concert on the date of Beethoven's death in effect proclaimed. The union of Beethoven and Schubert in and around death would assume much greater importance in the years to come.

On March 29, 1828, the first anniversary of Beethoven's funeral, a ceremony was held at the gravesite in Währing at which the third of the *Equale* (WoO 30, No. 2) was sung,[118] this time to a short poem by Grillparzer:[119]

> You, to whom life gave no home or rest
> Now sleep in peace and quiet gloom.
> O, if our hymn can reach thy spirit blest
> Listen to thy sweet song, within the tomb!

At Währing Cemetery that afternoon was Marie von Pratobevera, a young aristocratic woman who left a vivid account two days later in a letter to her fiancé:

> The day was heavenly fair, the music most touching, and sung among the graves it could not fail to make a deep impression. I was surprised only that not more people were there, and also at the simple monument, made of common stone. It represents a pyramid, at the top of which hangs a very clumsy lyre, and at the base is just his name in gilt letters. I admit that I so much like the idea of making no verses on him, but merely to set down his name, and yet making him immortal thereby; but I do think the stone and the workmanship unworthy. But enough of graves and death: I must tell you of fresh and blossoming life, which prevailed at the concert of Schubert on the 26th March. Only compositions by *himself* were given and *gloriously*. Everyone was lost in a frenzy of admiration and rapture.[120]

There is a terrible dramatic irony in the way that Pratobevera equates Beethoven with "graves and death" and Schubert with "fresh and blossoming life," an unconscious free association that demonstrates how at least one contemporary audience member heard Schubert's concert on the twenty-sixth and experienced Beethoven's memorial three days after.

The promising young composer was himself dead eight months later and buried just a few feet away from the spot where Grillparzer's words were intoned for Beethoven that beautiful March afternoon. Ferdinand Schubert interpreted his younger brother's delirious cry from his deathbed, "This is not where Beethoven lies!" as a desire to be buried near to his hero.[121] The wish was granted, with Schubert lying three graves away under Grillparzer's notorious epitaph: THE ART OF MUSIC HERE ENTOMBED A RICH POSSESSION, BUT EVEN FAR FAIRER HOPES. Schubert, whose career was overshadowed by the older master's fame and greatness, gradually became recognized as his foremost contemporary. Even if their association in life was passing, their union in death has proved lasting.[122] The graves became favorite pilgrimage sites, as when Robert Schumann visited in the late 1830s and "gazed long on those two sacred graves, almost envying the person buried between them." Clara Wieck had already made a similar excursion, prompting a special request from her future husband: "Will you not pay a visit to our beloved Schubert and Beethoven? Take with you some sprigs of myrtle, twine them together in twos, and lay them on the graves. Whisper your name and mine as you do so—not a word besides. You understand?"[123]

The two composers did not rest in peace. At the time of Beethoven's burial there already was macabre but apparently justified concern for the safety of his body. Schindler wrote Moscheles on April 4 (as published at the time in the *Harmonicon*):

> Finally, I have to communicate to you a very extraordinary occurrence. Yesterday, the grave-digger of Währing came to announce to us, that an offer of a thousand florins, C.M., had been made to him, in a note, which he produced, if he would deposit the head of Beethoven in a certain place. The police is on the alert, and actively engaged in the investigation of this singular affair.[124]

As Haydn's head had been stolen two decades earlier, and interest in phrenology was on the rise, fear of such a plot was hardly unwarranted.[125] Gerhard von Breuning recalled that there was "a good deal of talk" about a reward for Beethoven's head, so much so that some people even considered "lowering the coffin in the reverse position, i.e., with the feet toward the outer wall," but that ultimately the "idea was dropped."[126]

For thirty-five years Beethoven and Schubert lay undisturbed, but by the mid-1800s the graves had fallen into an alarming state of disrepair.[127] On Tuesday, October 13, 1863 their caskets were exhumed, the remains measured and examined, the skulls photographed and plaster casts made, and then all finally replaced in metal coffins and reburied on October 22 (see Fig. 7).[128] The "scientific," popular, and private reports of the process are fascinating to read, not least because of the remarkable gendered comparisons made between the two.[129] Gerhard von

Fig. 7: Photograph of plaster casts of the skulls of Schubert, Haydn, and Beethoven.

Breuning, now a physician, observed the exhumation and remarked that "it was extremely interesting physiologically to compare the compact thickness of Beethoven's skull and the fine, almost feminine thinness of Schubert's, and to relate them, almost directly, to the character of their music."[130] As a prominent member of the Gesellschaft der Musikfreunde, Breuning was entrusted with Beethoven's head: "What stormy feelings passed through my mind evoking such powerful memories, as I had possession of that head for a few days, cleaned from it bits of dirt, took plaster casts of the base of the skull for Professor Romeo Seligmann, kept it by my bedside overnight, and in general proudly watched over that head from whose mouth, in years gone by, I had heard so often the living word!"[131]

Even after the refurbishing of their graves, the two were still not left undisturbed. Währing Cemetery was deconsecrated in the 1870s and today is a Schubert Park. In 1888, in an effort to centralize Vienna's many cemeteries into one location, the remains of the composers were transferred to the "Grove of Honor" of the aptly named Central Cemetery.[132] Lavish ceremonies, on June 21 for Beethoven and September 22 for Schubert, amounted to second funerals for both composers, allowing a Viennese population more than two generations removed from the events of 1827–28 to honor past glories in late-century performances of grief.

Other events throughout the nineteenth century, especially the erection of a monument in Beethoven's native Bonn in 1845 and the centennial festivities of 1870, afforded further opportunities to honor Beethoven in ways both respectful and celebratory—statues were dedicated; streets renamed; plaques placed on appropriate locations in Germany, Austria, Bohemia, and elsewhere; concerts and festivals held; and with the publication of the first collected edition, all (or almost all) of his music was at last available. The twentieth century found new ways to remember and praise, such as the recent edition of all (or almost all) his music on recordings. Paradoxically, as Beethoven's own time and culture recede ever further into history, technological advances can give the illusion of bringing them ever closer. Films offer what appears to be a realistic vision of Beethoven's milieu, while recordings provide access as never before to the actual sounds he created.

The impulse to learn more about Beethoven has also taken novel turns. Just as Vienna's Anthropological Society eagerly examined his skull in the 1880s so as to understand better the mechanisms of his genius and the causes of his sufferings, so today samples of his hair—of which, as we have seen, specimens abound—have been subjected to DNA testing; results are inconclusive at this time. Try as many Romantics, Moderns, and Postmoderns have, the shadow Beethoven cast on music history has made his continuing presence impossible to escape. For better or worse, the enduring effect of his life and death, of Beethoven as a model of what it means to be a creative artist, to live, to suffer, and to die for art, has yet to be transcended. The performances of grief known to Beethoven's world often seem very near.

APPENDIX A

Account of Beethoven's Funeral from *Der Sammler*
Translated by Scott Burnham

Der Sammler, April 1827, pp. 179–80

Beethoven's Burial

On the afternoon of March 29 the solemn funeral procession of our great Beethoven took place. A numerous group of devoted admirers and friends of the dearly departed gathered for the occasion. In addition to these, the sympathy of the entire population of this imperial city expressed itself in an extraordinary flood of people from all classes, who densely covered not only the square in front of the deceased's house but also the entire way from there to the parish church in the Alsergasse, the destination of the funeral procession. The crowd was so great that when the spacious courtyard of Beethoven's residence could no longer hold the throng, the gate had to be closed until the procession began. The coffin containing the body of the great composer had been placed on view in the courtyard. After the clergy arrived to perform their sacred office, those guests who had been invited to this ceremony—composers, singers, poets, actors, all in complete mourning, with flower-laden torches and nosegays on the arm—lined up around the bier, and the singers began intoning the *Miserere* composed by the deceased. The pious tones of this glorious composition swelled the still air with solemnity and majesty; the whole scene was imposing. The coffin with its richly embroidered pall, the clergy, the distinguished men who formed the last escort of their artistic kinsman, and the surrounding throng: all this made a most magnificent tableau. Now the coffin was raised; youthful singers took it upon their shoulders; six Kapellmeister (the Royal and Imperial First Court-Kapellmeister Eybler, the Royal and Imperial Vice Court-Kapellmeister Joseph Weigl, the Grand Ducal Saxony-Weimar Court-Kapellmeister Hummel, and von Seyfried, Kreutzer, and Gyrowetz) carried the white ribbons of the pall. The remaining escort formed themselves in front of, around, and behind the coffin, and in this fashion the solemn procession advanced through the numberless throng of people to the parish church. During the church service, the singers intoned the *Libera nos Domine*, which closed the ceremony. The coffin was now placed in the funeral carriage, equipped with four horses, which was led to the Währing Cemetery. There too a great crowd of people gathered to pay their last respects to the departed one. In the church's courtyard, the Royal and Imperial Court Actor Anschütz made some remarks in memory of Beethoven; his depth of feeling and masterly delivery moved every heart, and many a still tear from a noble eye honored the departed singer. That such an occasion did not lack for gifts of poetry is only natural. Castelli distributed a small poem at Beethoven's house, as did Baron von Schlechta at the graveyard. Deeply stirred by the emotion of this ceremony, everyone left the gravesite, which now embraced the earthly remains of this most highly venerated man. Soon a monument will be erected on this site, announcing to the wanderer what a loss art suffered with the passing of he who sleeps here. Already on April 3 local art and music dealers celebrated the memory of the great master through a performance, for the repose of his soul, of Mozart's Requiem. The Augustiner Court-Church was overflowing with pious visitors, who added their prayers for the same outcome. Lablache glorified this memorial service with his singing. On April 5 this memorial was repeated in the Karlskirche on the Wieden. The pain over the loss of this artist is felt generally in the musical public of all classes, and never has the recognition of this great genius been expressed in a more lively fashion as on this occasion. His name lives in luminous figures within the hearts of all friends of art. His fame will never be extinguished, no matter what progress music may make in the ages to come; he belongs to history, which assures every great man his place.

———

For those who are interested in the particulars of this sorrowful yet uplifting funeral celebration, we offer the following detailed account.

According to rough estimate, the uncommonly large gathering of onlookers numbered about 10,000. At three o'clock the coffin was placed on view in the courtyard; one-half hour later the clergy for the whole procession appeared. Before the procession got underway, the Court Theater singers Eichberger, Schuster, Cramolini, Müller, Hofmann, Ruprecht and Vorschitzky, along with Anton Wranitzky of the orchestra, sang a mourning song by B. Anselm Weber; then they carried the coffin on their shoulders into the church.

This was the order of the procession:

(1) The cross bearers. (2) Four trombonists (Weidl, Tuschke, and the brothers Böck), who played a refrain from the *Miserere*. (3) The Chorus Master Assmayer. (4) A Chorus, consisting of Tietze, Schnitzer, Gros, Sykora, Frühwald, Geissler, Rathmayer, Kokrement, Nejebse, Ziegler, Perschl, Leidl, Pfeifer, Weinkopf and Seipelt, who sang the *Miserere* alternately with the above named trombonists. The *Miserere* is an original melody by the deceased master written in a thoroughly noble, antique style; he composed it in 1812 in Linz for the resident Dome Kapellmeister Glöggl to perform as a trombone quartet on All Soul's Day. The tireless collector of so many autographs of this composer, Mr. Tobias Haslinger, possesses the autograph of this piece. Haslinger was quite involved with this funeral, even making significant offerings himself. Kapellmeister von Seyfried arranged the aforementioned quadricinium of brass instruments as a vocal chorus and set the words of the *Miserere* to it; this estimable memorial will soon be

published in this very format by Mr. Haslinger. (5) The high clergy. (6) The splendidly ornate coffin, carried by the aforementioned singers and escorted by Kapellmeisters Eybler, Hummel, Seyfried and Kreutzer on the right, Weigl, Gyrowetz, Gänsbacher and Würfel on the left, all bearing white cockades. (7) A row of torchbearers on both sides, among whom could be found Anschütz, Bernard, Blahetka, Jos. Böhm, Castelli, Carl Czerny, Signore David, Grillparzer, Konrad Graff, Grünbaum, Haslinger, Hildebrandt, Holz, Katter, Krall, Signore Lablache, Baron Lannoy, Linke, Mayseder, Mr. Meric (spouse of Mad. Lalande), Merk, Mechetti, Meier, Signore Paccini, Piringer, Radicchi, Raimund, Riotte, Schoberlechner, Schubert, Schickh, Schmiedl, Streicher, Schuppanzigh, Steiner, Weidmann, Weiss, Wolfmayer and many other friends of art and devoted friends of the departed. Everyone was dressed in black, with gloves of the same color and fluttering crepes on the left arm, except for the torchbearers, who had draped their torches with white sprays of lilies. And beyond these, one glimpsed in the slowly moving procession many distinguished notables, including Councillor Mosel, Councillor Breuning, childhood friend of the deceased and executor of his will, Beethoven's brother and sister-in-law, as well as the apprentices of the conservatory, the students of Mr. Drechsler, Kapellmeister at St. Anna, and so on, all of whom mourned a loss that a great portion of the civilized world felt with them. At the church, the benediction took place before the high altar, at which the abovementioned sixteen-voice choir sang a capella the *Libera me domine*, a vocal composition by Kapellmeister von Seyfried.—Many carriages followed the hearse, drawn by four horses to the Währing Cemetery. Before the grave was filled up, Mr. Haslinger drew forth three laurel wreaths, which his neighbor, Kapellmeister Hummel, lowered onto the coffin. The closest friends of the departed remained until the earth was leveled off. The place where Beethoven's mortal remains rest has already been privately purchased and will be graced with a monument made possible through contributions from several concerts.

APPENDIX B

L. van Beethoven's Death, 26 March 1827
Friedrich August Kanne

I.

Why do you howl, mighty storm, in the night?
Why do you break the branches in the forest?
Has strife awakened among the elements,
Making the foundations tremble and shake?
Why do you rage, storm,
Across the sea?
Why do you whip the waves
In terrible fury?
The cathedral trembles;
The river foams!
The waves, they rear over the banks
Where Vindobona's splendid walls
Form the peoples' sacred bond.
And yet again I hear sweet lilting
Like aeolian harps in the meadow.
And I see the white water's playful ruffle
Like mayflowers swaying in the meadow!
And again it sounds, like organs from
Within the rocks, from the chambers of death;
And again it lilts as in apple blossoms
That gently glow pink in the breath of May.

II.

Oh sacred nature, your voice sounds
As though I hear the mighty roar
Of sublime music which booms toward heaven
With terrible harmonious gushing
As though I heard the battle hymn's
Splendid sound
Where Vittoria's plain
Reverberates from the fall
Of the thunderous battle;
Where the victorious might
Of heroes rendered to dust the fetters
In which the people languished and wailed,
But fate was not deaf to their cry.

And again it sounds as though the friend called out
In the garden of spring lamenting "Adelaide."
O sweet sound from which my inner peace
So often built itself a house for its pleasure.
You, storm, I ask you, what are you saying?
What heartache would you like to confide to me?
The spirit that created these songs, he lingers
Here yet, where he heals many a wounded heart!

III.
And again the sound of a mighty storm!
Then the drops of fertile rain,
Then the form of the rainbow,
Announcing the blessing after the storms.
And as the beams'
Sacred edifice
Appears in the heavens
Like dew,
It sounds with power
And lovely splendor,
And sevenfold flows the harmonious stream
Like seven colors in beautiful unity,
Through the clouds onto the starry dome.

What do I sense? I know these sounds!
I often felt their beautiful magic,
In which Beethoven's genius in eternal beauty
Recreates the color prism's wonder anew!
The lovely jest often moved me to tears,
The quiet glow often awakened my longing!
And enveloped in the power of harmony
I was already on earth drunk with heavenly bliss!

IV.
Why do you roar in endless musical dialogue
Through the air, furious elements?
What is it that calls me out into open nature
With such mighty heartfelt striving?
Why do you sound, O nature, in battle hymns
Through which the great master's voice intones
In lovely lilts "Joy, beautiful spark of the Gods,
I enter your shrine drunk with ecstasy."

And again I hear trombones join in,
As when they carry the dead to their tombs,
Whereupon the symphonic choirs are stunned
And quickly change to soulful mourning,
Because even greatness by the whim of fate
Must tremble before death in the fullness of life;
Then it sounds forth from the choir:
"Beethoven's departing spirit hovers above the earth!"
Yes now I understand your angry commotion,
O elements, and your mighty roar!
With premonition I saw you taking fearful shapes,
O clouds, and quickly changing the sky.
It appeared as if the globe opened its dreadful crevices
To listen to the storms!
You spirits of nature, that's why you all screamed heavenward
With terrible thunderous roar!

V.
Does he endure, your favorite, who nourished his heart
With your beauty, appearing to succumb;
Whom you taught the omnipotence of music,
Who cried his secret bliss
Into your choral music when in thunderstorms
The anxious earth felt fear and trembling;
He who sucked in the springlike breath of creation
And sent it forth in floods of melodies!

Who looked into the blue of the sky,
Because there his eye learned secrets
Of how one creates the wonderworld of sound,
And must preserve and cherish depth and clarity,
So that the human heart beholds in tears,
And lifts itself up to the heavenly hosts;
So that heaven itself lives in the work
From which the master sucks the spirit's strength.

So you lament for him, whose song sounded
Powerful in millions of hearts?
Who earned immortality already here,
Whose name resounds beyond the oceans,
Who lifted himself in sacred art
To where never is heard an envious word;

Who created his world from the seven beams,
Whose splendor paints all the heavens.

VI.
Blessed world in which the workings of the arts
Create for man a spiritual ideal!
Blessed the land that preserves their fame
And ever renews their vitality!
Blessed the town that will not allow the fire
To die that summons the spirit;
Blessed the heart that stems from the Godhead
And is inflamed for the majesty of the arts.

Art lifts the human heart upward,
And soothes earthly grief and pain!
She stills the terrible turmoil of life's battles,
And calms the heart with glimpses of heaven!
The magic coat is woven of light,
Which borrowed its splendor from eternal suns!
O man, you know the path to eternity,
Because your spirit senses the eternal beautiful!

So grieve for him whom you adore,
Perhaps the physician's art will save him!—
O, if recovery were granted,
Then even distant friends' wishes would come true!
But if I was rightly informed
By the heavenly music I heard,
Then he died—because the sublime voice
Of nature's spirits spoke in ire!

VII.
Hark, hark! The storm rises anew!
The organs of creation sound!
Mountain and tower are shrouded in veils!
The clouds race and thunder.
The birds flutter
Fearful in the air!
Trombones join in,
The messengers of the grave!
And lovely and gentle,
As pure as silver,

I hear four voices
Playing in concert,
I hear Beethoven's sublime music—
As though the strings were wrapped in mourning gauze!

Then lightning strikes through the veil of clouds,
And suddenly thunder follows noisily,
The Danube trembles at the sound of spring's celebration,
And as flower buds awaken from the thunder,
And as the mountains stand bright before the eye,
Beethoven's spirit hurries heavenward!
Still! Still! The sound of bells hums in the air!
Hark! Hark! The trombones sound again!
That's how the world greets the dead in their graves,
Saying: "Someone precious descends from us today,
So that in the grave's cradle
He once more may dream his childhood's dream, and then fly
The sun's bright orbit, for whose beauty
He struggled here already, as master of sweet sounds!"

Notes by a friend of the dearly departed*

ɪ. Wellington's Victory at Vittoria. With the piece of this title, Beethoven expressed the feelings aroused in him by the representation of a battle.

ɪɪ. Adelaide, a poem by Matthison, written for voice and piano accompaniment by Beethoven. The masterpiece of German song.

ɪɪɪ. The Pastoral Symphony.

ɪv. The Septet.

v. From Schiller's famous "Ode to Joy," which appears as the closing chorus in Beethoven's ninth and final symphony.

vɪ. System of music notation.

vɪɪ. Schuppanzigh's quartet. This was the artistic group that removed the veil of prejudice that would have covered the rays of the unknown genius Beethoven at their first glimmering, after the death of Mozart. He [Schuppanzigh] was the one who first held the key to the solution of that wonderful riddle, namely, to the clear and lively contemplation of the masterpieces, and who obtained for the great man—from his own contemporaries—the recognition and appreciation that the chosen ones on this earth do not often enjoy during their lifetimes.

* This list of notes about the compositions and other things musical referred to in each numbered section of Kanne's poem was included in the original 1827 publication.

APPENDIX C

To Beethoven's Shades
1827
Johann Mayrhofer
Translated by Scott Burnham

Does Genius need the impoverished word,
That no sooner spoken already fades away?
His immeasurable impact lives on and on,
And time and space lose their power.

Whoever thinks of him, knowing what he made,
Feels stirred, moved, freed, in flight—
Feels how the spirit, bolstered by the tuneful call,
Pushes forward, striving.

Such that he tests his conscience with inward gaze,
Purifies himself, becomes truer, better,
And edifies himself with holy tones,
Unmoved by what's showy, or shallow.

You, O higher one, recognized and experienced
That which quickens deep in the breast,
Which kindles in the eye, ferments in the blood,
And, through Art, gloriously reconciled and transfigured it.

You rushed forth in powerful wrath,
In war and triumph like storm and flood,
Or again, like a still, pure spring,
Nourishing the tender realm of flowers.

Just as Spring prodigally bestows
Blooms by the millions—scents and colors, too—
Such wealth was yours; you gave it freely,
Willing, striving, creating, without rest!

We remain stunned, hardly able to survey
The plenty you have blessed us with;
You perished, like an overladen tree,
Under the burden of your own wondrous fruit!

Thus were you pushed down into your grave,
Your power to create now buried.
Yet grandchildren to come, renewed by your fruit,
Will bless—as we your sons do now—You!

NOTES

1. Funding for research on this essay, which is part of a larger study examining the deaths of Beethoven and Schubert and their aftermaths, was provided by a grant from the American Council of Learned Societies. Further assistance for research trips to Vienna came from the Austrian Cultural Institute and the State University of New York at Buffalo. I am grateful to Dr. Otto Biba and the staff of the Archive of the Gesellschaft der Musikfreunde in Vienna for assistance with locating materials and permission to reproduce some of them. I also wish to acknowledge the many helpful suggestions offered by Robert O. de Clercq, Christopher Hatch, Donald Wilson, Scott Burnham, Michael Lorenz, and Helena Sedláčkova Gibbs.

2. Elliot Forbes, ed., *Thayer's Life of Beethoven*, rev. ed. (Princeton, 1967), 1036 [hereafter Thayer/Forbes]. Beethoven had reminded the Society of its offer to give a concert for his benefit in London, and it decided not to delay sending the money as reports seemed so dire; see Beethoven's correspondence with Ignaz Moscheles, Sir George Smart, and Stumpff in *The Letters of Beethoven*, 3 vols. ed. Emily Anderson (London, 1961), Nos. 1550, 1554, 1555, 1559, 1563, 1566 [hereafter *Letters*]; also Schindler's request to Moscheles in *Letters to Beethoven and Other Correspondence*, 3 vols., ed. and trans. Theodore Albrecht (Nebraska, 1996), Nos. 460, 467; cf. Nos. 462–63, 468 [hereafter *Letters to Beethoven*].

3. *Letters*, No. 1550; *Letters to Beethoven*, Nos. 414, 435, 453, 462. According to a letter printed in the *Harmonicon*, "these works were his last joy" (5 [May 1827]: 87; *Letters to Beethoven*, No. 472).

4. *Letters*, Nos. 1560, 1562, 1564, 1569, 1570.

5. Recounted by Ferdinand Hiller, see *Beethoven: A Documentary Study*, ed. H. C. Robbins Landon (New York, 1970), p. 388 [hereafter Landon, *Beethoven*]; cf. *Letters to Beethoven*, No. 467.

6. *Letters to Beethoven*, Nos. 466, 479. Beethoven had repeatedly requested the publisher to send him the wine (*Letters*, Nos. 1553, 1558, 1561).

7. Many of those who visited are mentioned in Maynard Solomon, *Beethoven*, rev. ed. (New York, 1998), pp. 378–83.

8. April 4; first published in the *Harmonicon* 5 (May 1827): 85; for the full letter, see *Letters to Beethoven*, No. 477.

9. Almost all reports from individuals at the time, as well as the newspaper accounts and even memorial poems, mention the storm. Nicholas Slonimsky also checked the meteorological records for the day, see "The Weather at Mozart's Funeral," *Musical Quarterly* 46 (1960): 21.

10. According to the report in the Leipzig *Allgemeine musikalische Zeitung* [hereafter *LAMZ*], "At 5:50 Beethoven passed into eternal rest, painless, after an hour of sustained agony. At that moment Schuppanzigh was playing the incomparable adagio from his Piano Trio in G" (*LAMZ* 29, no. 17 [25 April 1827]: 289); my translation (unless otherwise indicated, all translations are my own).

11. Landon, *Beethoven*, 392; compare this statement (from a letter to Alexander Wheelock Thayer) with Hüttenbrenner's earlier oral account to Thayer on June 5, 1860, which is discussed later in this essay.

12. *Letters to Beethoven*, No. 477.

13. Carl Bär, *Mozart: Krankheit—Tod—Begräbnis* (Salzburg, 1966), pp. 119–36; H. C. Robbins Landon, *Haydn: The Late Years 1801–1809*, vol. 5 of *Haydn: Chronicle and Works* (Bloomington, 1977/1994), p. 388; *Letters to Beethoven*, No. 478.

14. See Christopher H. Gibbs, *The Life of Schubert* (Cambridge, 2000), pp. 170–73.

15. The literature on Beethoven's medical history is vast. See, for example, Anton Neumayr, *Music and Medicine: Haydn, Mozart, Beethoven, and Schubert*, trans. Bruce Cooper Clarke (Bloomington, 1994); Edward Larkin, "Beethoven's Medical History" in Martin Cooper, *Beethoven: The Final Decade 1817–1827*, rev. ed. (Oxford, 1985), pp. 439–66; and Hans Bankl and Hans Jesserer, *Die Krankheiten Ludwig van Beethovens: Pathographie seines Lebens und Pathologie seiner Leiden* (Vienna, Munich, Bern, 1987), all of which contain extensive bibliographies.

16. The first edition was published in Vienna in 1874, and a second edition in Berlin in 1907; English translation by Henry F. Mins and Maynard Solomon, *Memories of Beethoven: From the House of the Black-Robed Spaniards*, ed. Maynard Solomon (Cambridge, 1992) [hereafter *Memories*]. Although one might be skeptical that one so young would have had such access to the composer and retained such vivid memories, entries in Beethoven's conversation books confirm the extent of Gerhard's engagement.

17. For Wawruch's detailed account of May 20, 1827, see Friedrich Kerst, *Die Erinnerungen an Beethoven* (Stuttgart, 1913), vol. 2, pp. 210–15; translated in *Beethoven: Impressions by His Contemporaries*, ed. O. G. Sonneck (New York, 1926, 1967), pp. 221–26; abridged in Landon, *Beethoven*, p. 391. Schindler responded negatively to this report, *Beethoven As I Knew Him*, ed. Donald W. MacArdle (Mineola, N.Y., 1960), pp. 457–59.

18. In the *Gemeinnütziger und erheiternder Haus-Kalender für das oesterreichische Kaiserthum* (Vienna, 1830), lung disease was the leading cause of the 13,764 total deaths in Vienna in 1828 (2306), followed next by dropsy (1787); for more on the context of death at the time, see Christopher H. Gibbs, "Zu Schuberts Tod—Documente im Haus-Kalender," *Schubert durch die Brille* 24 (January 2000): 27–30.

19. There are differing accounts of when and how this happened, see Alexander Wheelock Thayer, *The Life of Ludwig van Beethoven*, ed. Henry Edward Krehbiel (New York, 1921) vol. 3, pp. 305–307 [hereafter Thayer/Krehbiel]; see also *Letters to Beethoven*, No. 479.

20. *Harmonicon* 5 (May 1827): 84–85; the letter also appeared in Moscheles's 1841 edition of Schindler's Beethoven biography (*The Life of Beethoven* [London, 1841], pp. 318–22). For a more accurate translation, together with extensive annotations, see *Letters to Beethoven*, No. 469; the original German is in *Ludwig van Beethoven: Briefwechsel, Gesamtausgabe*, 8 vols., ed. Sieghard Brandenburg (Munich, 1996), No. 2286.

21. *Letters to Beethoven*, Nos. 469 and 477.

22. The Währinger Ortsfriedhof was the newer private cemetery in the district and separate from the municipal Währinger Allgemeiner Friedhof. The former was consecrated in 1769 and closed in 1873.

23. Hüttenbrenner supposedly had visited Beethoven about eight days earlier with Schubert (Otto Erich Deutsch, *Schubert: Memoirs by His Friends*, trans. Rosamond Ley and John Nowell [London, 1958], pp. 66, 75, 76, 192), as well as on March 23 with Johann Baptist Jenger, but that time he was not admitted (Deutsch, "Die wiedergefundenen Bildnisse des sterbenden Beethoven," *Die Musik* 9 [1909]: 65). For biographical information about Hüttenbrenner, see Peter Clive, *Schubert and His World: A Biographical Dictionary* (Oxford, 1997), pp. 82–85; Carl Gottfried Ritter von Leitner, *Anselm Hüttenbrenner: Eine nekrologische Skizze* (Graz, 1868); and about his compositions, see Dieter Glawischnig, *Anselm Hüttenbrenner: Sein musikalisches Schaffen* (Graz, 1969).

24. Streicher to Stumpff, 28 March 1827 (*Letters to Beethoven*, No. 472) and Jenger's letter to Marie Pachler (Ludwig Nohl, *Beethovens Leben*, 3 vols. in 4 parts, 2nd ed., ed. Paul Sakolowski, (Berlin, 1909–1913), vol. 3, part 2, p. 539). His presence was later confirmed by Schindler, *Beethoven As I Knew Him*, p. 325; and Breuning, *Memories*, pp. 104–105.

25. The full letter is in Kerst, *Erinnerungen*, vol. 2, pp. 231–34; abridged translations in Paul Nettl, *Beethoven Encyclopedia* (New York, 1956), pp. 93–94; Thayer/Forbes, pp. 1050–51; and Landon, *Beethoven*, p. 392. Thayer's notes on the interview are reprinted in Henry E. Krehbiel, *Music and Manners in the Classical Period* (New York, 1898), pp. 204–206.

26. Ibid., pp. 204–206.

27. One reason Hüttenbrenner's general credibility has been questioned is because of his accounts of a visit to Beethoven he says he made with Schubert about a week earlier. He related this information in 1858 to Ferdinand Luib, a prospective biographer of Schubert, although it is unconfirmed by anyone else save Hüttenbrenner's younger brother Josef. Most Schubert and Beethoven biographers have accepted his story, although there is good reason to be skeptical; see Maynard Solomon, "Schubert and Beethoven," *Nineteenth-Century Music* 3 (1979): 114–25. Hüttenbrenner's knack for being the lone source for information about the deaths of great composers even extends to Mozart, who had died before Hüttenbrenner was born. In an 1825 memorial article honoring Salieri which he wrote for the *LAMZ*, he stated that Salieri attended Mozart's funeral (27, no. 48 [30 November 1825]: 797). While Salieri may have told him this years earlier, when Hüttenbrenner was his student, the information is unsupported by other accounts. Unfortunately, Hüttenbrenner burned his diaries in 1841, which makes confirming any of his accounts all the more difficult; see Otto Erich Deutsch, "Anselm Hüttenbrenners Erinnerungen an Schubert," *Jahrbuch der Grillparzer-Gesellschaft* 16 (1906): 107.

28. Landon, *Beethoven*, p. 392.

29. For texts of these documents and a penetrating discussion of their contents, see Solomon, *Beethoven*, pp. 144, 151–58, 207–46.

30. Beethoven addressed the letter, both at the opening and during the course of the text, to his "brothers Carl and   Beethoven." Three times in the letter he omitted Johann van Beethoven's name. For a discussion of possible reasons for this omission, see Solomon, *Beethoven*, pp. 155–58.

31. The pervasive importance of the image of the struggling, suffering, and isolated Beethoven for his general reception is traced in Hans Heinrich Eggebrecht, *Zur Geschichte der Beethoven-Rezeption* (Wiesbaden, 1972); see also Sanna Pederson's essay in the current volume.

32. Johann van Beethoven claimed that his brother died in his arms, and at least one published report of the time said he did (see below), but this is generally discounted; see Stephan Ley, *Wahrheit, Zweifel und Irrtum in der Kunde von Beethovens Leben* (Wiesbaden, 1955), pp. 40–42.

33. Breuning, *Memories*, 104; see also Johann Baptist Streicher's March 28, 1827, letter to Stumpff, which mentions Hüttenbrenner and "a painter" (*Letters to Beethoven*, No. 472). Johann Baptist Jenger's letter to Marie Pachler also places Teltscher there (Nohl, *Beethovens Leben*, vol. 3, part 2, p. 539). Two of the drawings show Beethoven, while the third (usually not reproduced) is of the empty bed and room. The drawings were thought lost for some eighty years; see Deutsch, "Die wiedergefundenen Bildnisse." Jenger, Hüttenbrenner, Schubert, and Teltscher were good friends—Teltscher made a famous triple portrait of the other three.

34. Stephan Ley has speculated that the maid may have been someone Hüttenbrenner mistook for Beethoven's sister-in-law; *Wahrheit, Zweifel und Irrtum*, 41–42; see also Alexander Wheelock Thayer, *Ludwig van Beethovens Leben*, ed. Hermann Deiters and Hugo Riemann (Leipzig, 1901–1911), vol. 5, p. 490 [hereafter Thayer/Deiters/ Riemann].

35. Krehbiel, *Music and Manners*, pp. 205–206; according to Krehbiel the "Mrs. Beethoven" here was the widow of Karl van Beethoven, and therefore this is an account given many years later by someone who had not herself known Beethoven.

36. The letter mentions Frau van Beethoven four more times, and is quite specific in identifying her as the wife of Johann; part of the problem may be that the letter is rarely quoted in full; see Kerst, *Erinnerungen*, vol. 2, pp. 231–34.

37. Solomon cites Thayer's account of Hüttenbrenner's oral report, which he calls "startling information . . . for Schindler had suppressed the identity of the woman in the room. Thayer could not believe that Johanna and Beethoven had been reconciled, and he apparently urged Hüttenbrenner to reconsider his testimony, whereupon Hüttenbrenner substituted Therese van Beethoven's name for that of Johanna." Although Solomon concedes there "can no longer be any certainty in this matter," he seems to want to believe in Johanna's presence; *Beethoven*, pp. 381–83. The most serious biographers before Solomon have all doubted that Johanna was present; Nohl, *Beethovens Leben*, vol. 3, part 2, p. 538; and the editors of German and English editions of Thayer (Thayer/Deiters/Riemann, vol. 5, p. 490; Thayer/Krehbiel, vol. 3, pp. 307–308; Thayer/Forbes, p. 1051).

38. Beethoven called himself Karl's "wirklicher leiblicher vater" in a letter to Johann Nepomuk Kanka (6 September 1816; *Letters*, No. 654). Susan Lund has speculated—wildly—that Beethoven was the actual father of Antonie Brentano's son Karl; "Beethoven: 'A True Fleshly Father'?" *The Beethoven Newsletter* 3.1 and 3.2 (1988): 1, 8–11 and 25, 36–40; see as well her *Raptus: A Novel about Beethoven* (Melbourn, Eng., 1995). A selection of reactions to and reviews of Rose's movie is given in *The Beethoven Journal* 10 (1995): 32–39.

39. The autopsy report is reprinted in Thayer/Forbes, pp. 1059–60.

40. Breuning, *Memories*, p. 106; *Letters to Beethoven*, No. 477. Concerning discrepancies about where the money was found, see the editor's note in Breuning, *Memories*, p. 140, n. 185; and Thayer/Forbes, pp. 1051–52.

41. *Letters to Beethoven*, No. 469.

42. *Letters to Beethoven*, Nos. 469, 472–73, 476, 477–78, 480, 485–86, 490–92.

43. *Letters to Beethoven*, No. 478.

44. *Letters to Beethoven*, Nos. 477, 485, 490; Stephan von Breuning responded to attacks in a letter to the Ausburg *Allgemeine Zeitung* (excerpted in Ludwig Nohl, *Beethoven Depicted by His Contemporaries*, trans. E. Hill [London, 1880], p. 367).

45. Schindler's letter to Moscheles of April 4 stated, "The Philharmonic Society has the honor to have buried this great man with their money, for without it we could not have done so respectfully" (*Letters to Beethoven*, No. 477, cf. 476). Schindler repeatedly flattered his English correspondents, as in a letter to Sir George Smart on March 31: "He lies next to the young Lord Ingestre, who drowned here last summer. And so it came to pass that he has something in common with an Englishman, even in his grave" (*Letters to Beethoven*, No. 476). In one letter to Moscheles, Schindler suggested that "a small portion" of the English money might be given to him, "for I really did not receive the least remembrance from [Beethoven]" (*Letters to Beethoven*, No. 477).

46. Landon, *Beethoven*, p. 390; cf. *Letters to Beethoven*, No. 490.

47. Ibid., Nos. 490, 492.

48. Supplement to vol. 97, part 1 (June 1827), 644.

49. Schindler reproduced this letter in facsimile in his *Beethoven As I Knew Him*, supposedly to prove "the authenticity of the death mask, and as an example of the handwriting of the friend who for so many years remained true and constant to the great composer" (pp. 329–32). Schindler may also have wanted to highlight his own role in arranging various matters. The letter is also given in *Letters to Beethoven*, No. 470; see also Kerst, *Erinnerungen*, vol. 2, p. 234.

50. Breuning, *Memories*, pp. 106–107; cf. Landon, *Beethoven*, p. 392; Thayer/Forbes, pp. 1052–53.

51. The caption reads "BEETHOVEN/ Den 28ten März an seinem/ Todtenbette gezeichnet/1827"; reproduced in *Ludwig van Beethoven: Gestaltung G. L. de Baranyai*, ed. Beethoven-Gesellschaft, Munich (Munich, 1970), No. 89.

52. *Letters to Beethoven*, No. 473.

53. "Erinnerungen an Beethoven," *Franz Grillparzer: Sämtliche Werke*, ed. Peter Frank and Karl Pörnbacher (Munich, 1964), vol. 3, p. 202; translated in Hamburger, *Beethoven: Letters, Journals, and Conversations*, pp. 273–75; and Sonneck, *Impressions*, p. 154; for a somewhat different account, see Breuning, *Memories*, p. 48.

54. The notice in the latter appeared on March 28, No. 72.

55. Vol. 29, no. 13 (March 28, 1827): 227–28; translated in *The Critical Reception of Beethoven's Compositions by his German Contemporaries*, ed. Wayne M. Senner, vol. 1 (Nebraska, 1999), pp. 99–100.

56. No. 38 (29 March 1827): 307–308 (trans. Scott Burnham). Streicher wrote to Stumpff in London on March 28 that Schickh had visited Beethoven around 2 P.M. on March 26 (*Letters to Beethoven*, No. 472). Schickh published one of Stumpff's poems (A. St., *Auf Beethovens Tod*) in his journal on April 19 (this is my identification—Stumpff had sent two other poems to Streicher on April 16; see *Letters to Beethoven*, No. 480).

57. No. 38 (29 March 1827): 148; Johann van Beethoven's own account claims that his brother died in his arms (Thayer/Forbes, p. 1051).

58. *Letters to Beethoven*, No. 469; Streicher sent a few strands of hair to Stumpff in London on March 28 (Nos. 472, 480).

59. Kerst, *Erinnerungen*, vol. 2, p. 235.

60. Landon, *Beethoven*, p. 396; see also Alessandra Comini, *The Changing Image of Beethoven: A Study in Mythmaking* (New York, 1987), p. 73.

61. Landon, *Beethoven*, p. 393; fuller entries from the Hartmann brothers' diaries are in Otto Erich Deutsch, *Schubert: A Documentary Biography*, trans. Eric Blom (London, 1946), pp. 621–23. Fritz Hartmann sent off some of his sample to Anna von Revertera (Walburga Litschauer, *Neue Dokumente zum Schubert-Kreis* [Vienna, 1993], vol. 2, p. 88).

62. *Memories*, 107–108. According to a report in the Dresden *Abendzeitung* in April, people flocked to see the body and "as they brought scissors with them, and cut off a great deal of his grey hair, the coffin was obliged to be closed as soon as possible. . . ." (quoted from Nohl, *Beethoven Depicted by His Contemporaries*, p. 358).

63. The American Beethoven Society recently acquired hair formerly owned by Paul Hiller and inscribed, "My father, Dr. Ferdinand v. Hiller, cut this hair from Beethoven's corpse on the day after his death, that is, on 27 March 1827 and presented it to me on 1 May 1883 as a birthday present. Cologne, 1 May 1883. Paul Hiller" (Ira Brilliant, "Beethoven Auction Report," *The Beethoven Journal* 10 [1995]: 67–68). Hummel's wife also clipped some hair during this same visit (Karl Benyovsky, *J. N. Hummel: Der Mensch und Künstler* [Bratislava, 1934], p. 154).

64. *Der Sammler*, no. 45 (14 April 1827): 180; Breuning, *Memories*, p. 108. The *Harmonicon* 5 (August 1827): 154; and Luigi Cramolini (in Kerst, *Erinnerungen*, vol. 2, p. 236) also place the number at 20,000; Schindler first stated 30,000 in his letter to Moscheles of April 4, 1827 (*Letters to Beethoven*, No. 477), which appeared in the *Harmonicon* (5 [May 1827]: 85–86), but in his biography of Beethoven he states 20,000 (*Beethoven as I Knew Him*, p. 325). The *Wiener allgemeine Theaterzeitung* gave the number 15,000 (12 April; cited in George R. Marek, *Beethoven: Biography of a Genius* [New York, 1969], p. 629). Baron Nikolaus von Zmeskall wrote to Countess Therese von Brunsvik that "never in the Austrian Empire had there been such a funeral as Beethoven's" and placed the number at 30,000, whereupon she wrote in her notebook: "If every one of them had

given one Gulden a year, the man would still be living" (Romain Rolland, *Beethoven: Les grandes époques créatrices* [Paris, 1966], p. 1324).

65. There are two illustrations of the funeral, signed "Stöber" and most likely by Franz Xaver Stöber (1795–1858), although possibly by his father Josef (1768–1852); for more information about these images, see Georg Poensgen, "Beethovens Begräbnis: Zum 125. Todestag des Meisters, 26 März," *Musica* 6 (1952): 96–99.

66. The participation of Karl's mother, Johanna van Beethoven, for example, is once again an issue; Solomon, *Beethoven*, p. 383.

67. The best known of these accounts appeared in Hermann Josef Landau's *Erstes poetisches Beethoven-Album* (Prague, 1872), which is abridged in Kerst, *Erinnerungen*, vol. 2, pp. 237–40; abridged translation in Landon, *Beethoven*, p. 394; and Sonneck, *Impressions*, pp. 226–29. This account is based on an "original report" from the time, but as the full version in Landau mentions memorial events that occurred as late as April 26, it would appear to date from well after the funeral and thus subsequent to accounts that had been published in *Der Sammler* and elsewhere. Thayer/Forbes includes a long description based on contemporaneous writings. Most important are receipts for funeral costs by Andreas Zeller, the director of ceremonies in the district, but the information is filtered through a much later article, published in 1925 in Vienna's *Reichspost*, by Robert Franz Müller, that appears to use newspaper accounts as well as the receipts (pp. 1052–55). The principal archival documents are discussed by Stephan Ley, "Urkundliches über Beethovens Beerdigung und erste Grabstätte," *Neues Beethoven-Jahrbuch* 10 (1942): 25–35 (reprinted in *Aus Beethovens Erdentagen* [Siegburg, 1957], pp. 207–16); and Hanns Jäger-Sunstenau, "Beethoven-Akten im Wiener Landesarchiv," in *Beethoven-Studien: Festgabe der Oesterreichischen Akademie der Wissenschaften zum 200. Geburtstag von Ludwig van Beethoven*, ed. Erich Schenk (Vienna, 1970), pp. 11–38. By June 1827, Ignaz Ritter von Seyfried and/or Haslinger apparently felt the need to correct some mistakes made in these earliest accounts and therefore gave a detailed description of the funeral, closely following much of the *Sammler* report, on the reverse side of the title page of Seyfried's vocal versions of the *Equale* heard at the funeral. The same account was published in Frankfurt's *Allgemeine Musik-Zeitung zur Beförderung der theoretischen und praktischen Tonkunst*, no. 13 (15 August 1827): 97ff. and reprinted in both the German editions and the English translation of Seyfried's *Ludwig van Beethoven's Studien im Generalbass, Contrapunkt und in der Compositionslehre* (Vienna, 1832), pp. 50–53; rev. ed. by Henry Hugh Pierson (Leipzig, 1853; rpt. Hildesheim, 1967), pp. 46–48; English translation by Pierson, *Louis van Beethoven's Studies in Thorough-Bass, Counterpoint and the Art of Scientific Composition* (Leipzig, Hamburg, New York, 1853), pp. 39–41. Seyfried's reliability may be questioned in certain matters because these "studies" were his own invention, as Schindler exposed in his biography (see *Beethoven as I Knew Him*, pp. 464–74). The Seyfried version was also the basis of the account that appeared in Moscheles's *Life of Beethoven* (London, 1841), pp. 330–35 (reprinted in *The Beethoven Newsletter* as "'Funeral Honors to Beethoven': Moscheles's Account of Beethoven's Funeral on March 29 and the Memorial Concerts of April 3 and 5, 1827," ed. Patricia Elliott, 8 [1993]: 22–25); Moscheles, of course, was not present, and this version is filled with inaccuracies.

68. No. 45 (14 April 1827): 179–80.

69. Othmar Wessely, "Zur Geschichte des Equals" in *Beethoven-Studien*, ed. Schenk, pp. 341–60. In an intriguing article, Daniel Jacobson and Andrew Glendening argue that Schubert, who as a torchbearer that day heard these *Equale* repeated again and again, was inspired to incorporate them into his haunting "Tenth" Symphony (D936A); see "Schuberts D.936A: Eine sinfonische Hommage an Beethoven?" *Schubert durch die Brille* 15

(June 1995): 113–26, but see also Brian Newbould, "Schuberts D.936A: Eine sinfonische Hommage an sich selbst?" *Schubert durch die Brille* 16/17 (January 1996): 123–29.

70. *Memories*, p. 109 (translation modified; it is not clear whether this was sung and/or played); cf. Thayer/Forbes, p. 1054. Haslinger published the march, transposed to A Minor, under the title *Beethoven's Begräbniss*. This sets a poem by Alois Jeitteles, who had written the text of *An die ferne Geliebte*. The contents of the poem, "Beethoven's Begräbniss," are appropriate for a procession, which further suggests that it may have been sung at the funeral (see Table 1).

71. Haslinger published the music in June under the title *Libera, welches bey Beethoven's Leichenbegängnisse vor der Einsegnung des entseelten Körpers, in der Kirche bey den P. P. Minoriten in der Alservorstadt in Wien, den 29. März 1827 von dem Sänger-Chor, welcher den Leichenzug begleitete, gesungen worden ist. Componirt, und zu obigem Gebrauche eingerichtet von Ignaz Ritter von Seyfried*, plate number 5035 (this is for voices alone). Haslinger also published Seyfried's *Libera zum Gebrauche bei Aufführungen des Mozart'schen Requiems*, plate number 5042–43. The *Miserere, Amplius*, and *Libera* appeared in the appendix of Seyfried's *Beethoven's Studien*.

72. The service in Währing is not mentioned in the *Sammler* report, nor in the account printed by Landau. The information given in Thayer/Forbes about the service in Währing apparently derives from a receipt from the Währing priest, Johann Hayek, which is dated March 28, thus the day *before* the event (p. 1055). According to the receipts published by Stephan Ley, the funeral in Alsergrund was "first class," but "second class" in Währing ("Urkundliches über Beethovens Beerdigung und erste Grabstätte": 31). In an autobiographical sketch that Schubert's older brother Ferdinand wrote in 1841, he states that he was the organist at the Währing church on this occasion (see Ernst Hilmar, "Ferdinand Schuberts Skizze zu einer Autobiographie," in *Schubert-Studien: Festgabe der Oesterreichischen Akademie der Wissenschaften zum Schubert-Jahr 1978*, ed. Franz Grasberger and Othmar Wessely [Vienna, 1978], pp. 94–95).

73. Breuning, *Memories*, p. 109; see also Alfred Kalischer, "Wie der Tragöde Anschütz mit Beethoven bekannt ward," in *Beethoven und Wien*, vol. 4 of *Beethoven und seine Zeitgenossen* (Berlin, n.d. [1909–1910]), pp. 210–14; and *Grillparzers Gespräche und die Charakteristiken seiner Persönlichkeit durch die Zeitgenossen*, ed. August Sauer (Vienna, 1905), vol. 2, pp. 326–27.

74. Grillparzer's oration acts out the controversy over Beethoven as a world figure or German nationalist, strongly in favor of the latter. According to Breuning, Grillparzer was upset at the time over the English gift to Beethoven, which was receiving so much attention in the press (*Memories*, p. 49).

75. *Sämtliche Werke*, vol. 3, pp. 881–83. The famous speech exists in slightly different versions and has been reprinted many times, for example, Landon, *Beethoven*, pp. 395–96; Thayer/Forbes, pp. 1057–58; Johann Aloys Schlosser, *Beethoven: The First Biography*, ed. Barry Cooper, trans. Reinhard G. Pauly (Portland, Or., 1996), pp. 113–18 and 179–81; Breuning, *Memories*, pp. 109–10 and 141–42; the last two sources discuss variants of the speech, as do the notes to Grillparzer, *Sämtliche Werke*, vol. 3, p. 1325. Grillparzer objected to its publication without his permission in the *Wiener allgemeine Theaterzeitung* and a Berlin periodical, and published a notice to that effect in the *Theaterzeitung* (19 June 1827); see *Sämtliche Werke*, vol. 3, p. 883.

76. The poem is reprinted in Landau's *Beethoven-Album*, pp. 160–61.

77. This is what *Der Sammler* reports, adding that both were read. Moscheles, who was not present, but whose translation of Schindler's Beethoven biography became widely known, states that they were read at the grave (*The Life of Beethoven* [London, 1841], p. 334). The account in Seyfried's *Beethoven's Studien*, which Haslinger printed on the verso

of the title page of the funeral music, states likewise. The contemporary account in Thayer/Forbes has them handed out at 3 P.M., but not read (p. 1053). Breuning states that they were distributed at the gravesite (pp. 110–12). Castelli's poem subsequently ran in *Der Sammler*, No. 39 (31 March 1827): 155; both were reprinted in Landau's *Beethoven-Album*, pp. 142–43. The Castelli poem appears in Breuning, who seems to have been mistaken about the poem by Johann Gabriel Seidl that he also includes, which was in fact written for a Beethoven concert given on May 3 (see the discussion below; Breuning *Memories*, pp. 110–12). Castelli's and Schlechta's poems are also found in both German editions of Seyfried's *Beethoven's Studien* (1832 and 1853).

78. Reprinted in the appendix to Seyfried's *Beethoven's Studien* (Vienna, 1832), pp. 50–53; (Leipzig, 1853), pp. 46–48; *Beethoven's Studies*, pp. 39–41.

79. The works by Seyfried and Hüttenbrenner were favorably reviewed in the *LAMZ* 29, no. 44 (31 October 1827): 749–50, and elsewhere.

80. Josef Hüttenbrenner mentioned both pieces years later, see Deutsch, *Schubert: Memoirs*, p. 190.

81. An incomplete list is given in *Thematisch-Bibliographisches Verzeichnis aller vollendeten Werke Ludwig van Beethovens*, ed. Georg Kinsky and Hans Halm (Munich, 1955), p. 471.

82. The largest collection of memorial poems, including ones that were not published at the time of Beethoven's death (Grillparzer, Mayrhofer, et al.) is Landau's *Beethoven-Album*. Many of these poems had appeared earlier in Haslinger's first edition (1832) of Seyfried's *Beethoven's Studien* (pp. 74–91); far fewer are included in the revised second edition from 1853 (pp. 46–48), and only a few poems are translated in the English edition, *Beethoven's Studies* (pp. 45–47). Both Seyfried and Landau most likely learned of these poems from a valuable collection in the Archive of the Gesellschaft der Musikfreunde, which was assembled in the 1830s by the archivist and librarian Johann Baptist Geissler; see "Sammlung aller Gedichte und Aufsätze, welche aus Anlass . . . 1828 gesammelt und der Bibliothek verehrt" (sig: 1938/32). A further poem, by Carl Philipp, appears in *Beethoven als Freund: Der Familie Wegeler-v. Breuning*, ed. Stephan Ley (Bonn, 1927), pp. 261–62. Landau, Seyfried, and the Geissler collection also include some prose tributes, epitaphs in Latin and German, and other relevant materials. A later memorial volume, which appeared in connection with the erection of the Bonn Beethoven monument in 1845, includes many poems, and even more music, that relate to Beethoven's death and grave; see *Beethoven-Album. Ein Gedenkbuch* (Stuttgart, 1846).

83. According to Leopold Hirschberg, Beethoven had not received public literary honors during his lifetime, although Clemens Brentano wrote some poems to Beethoven, and some others did appear; see *The Critical Reception of Beethoven's Compositions*, pp. 44–45, 79–80, 82–86. Beethoven did not receive a collection of poems comparable to the one celebrating Goethe in 1827; see "Beethoven in der Dichtung," *Die Musik* 10 (1910–1911): 339–55.

84. Background information concerning most of the poets listed in Table 2, including their dates, can be found in *Bio-Bibliographisches Literaturlexikon Österreichs von den Anfängen bis zur Gegenwart*, ed. Hans Giebisch and Gustav Gugitz (Vienna, 1963); and *Biographisches Lexikon des Kaiserthums Oesterreich*, ed. Constant von Wurzbach, 60 vols. (Vienna, 1856–1890).

85. *Der Sammler*, no. 39 (31 March 1827): 155; Seyfried, *Beethoven's Studien* (1832), p. 75; Landau's *Beethoven-Album*, p. 142; Breuning, *Memories*, pp. 110–112.

86. Seyfried, *Beethoven's Studien* (1832), pp. 85–86; Landau, *Beethoven-Album*, p. 143.

87. All of the poems mentioned here are included in ibid.

88. First published in the *Wiener Zeitschrift für Kunst, Literatur, Theater und Mode*, No. 50 (26 April 1827); reprinted in Seyfried, *Beethoven's Studien* (1832), pp. 86–87; and Landau, *Beethoven-Album*, pp. 166–67.

89. For information about Kanne, see Wurzbach, *Biographisches Lexikon*, 10: 438–43; and Hermann Ullrich, "F. A. Kanne: Ein verwildertes Genie des Wiener Biedermeier" (Vienna, 1970/1973); a copy of this unpublished monograph, available only in typescript, is in the archive of Vienna's Gesellschaft der Musikfreunde (145.18/152).

90. Reprinted in Seyfried, *Beethoven's Studien* (1832), pp. 80–85; and Landau, *Beethoven-Album*, pp. 127–32.

91. *Gedichte von Johann Mayrhofer. Neue Sammlung. Aus dessen Nachlasse mit Biographie und Vorwort*, ed. Ernst Freiherr von Feuchtersleben (Vienna, 1843), pp. 61–62; reprinted in Landau, *Beethoven-Album*, p. 180.

92. No. 40 (3 April 1827): 160; no. 49 (24 April 1827): 196.

93. The musical season usually started in late October and lasted until early May, with few concerts given in other months. As Vienna did not yet have a proper concert hall, theaters, taverns, and ballrooms were most commonly used, and this often led to scheduling difficulties, as did the lack of independent orchestras unconnected to theaters. Careful attention had to be paid to days when theaters were not allowed to present productions (*spielfreie Tage*), thus freeing up the locations and orchestras for concerts. These considerations were clearly on Schindler's mind as he planned memorial concerts (see *Letters to Beethoven*, No. 478). About the concert situation in Vienna at the time, see Alice M. Hanson, *Musical Life in Biedermeier Vienna* (Cambridge, 1985); Otto Biba, "Concert Life in Beethoven's Vienna," in *Beethoven, Performers, and Critics: The International Beethoven Congress, Detroit, 1977*, ed. Robert Winter and Bruce Carr (Detroit, 1980), pp. 77–93; and the still invaluable Eduard Hanslick, *Geschichte des Concertwesens in Wien*, 2 vols. (Vienna, 1869).

94. Christopher Reynolds's paper "Beethoven 1828," presented at the International Beethoven Conference at Harvard University, November 1–3, 1996, provides information about concerts in other cities.

95. Schindler, *Beethoven as I Knew Him*, pp. 389–90; cf. Thayer/Forbes, p. 1046; Breuning, *Memories*, p. 56.

96. Benyovsky, *J. N. Hummel*, pp. 155–56; *Wiener allgemeine Theaterzeitung*, no. 45 (14 April 1827); *LAMZ* 29, no. 22 (30 May 1827): 368–69.

97. Complete programs of the Gesellschafts-Konzerte are listed in Richard von Perger and Robert Hirschfeld, *Geschichte der k. k. Gesellschaft der Musikfreunde in Wien* (Vienna, 1912), pp. 285ff.

98. *Der Sammler*, no. 53 (3 May 1827): 212. Streicher was displeased with this announcement. As he explained in a June 9 letter to Stumpff, "A concert by dilettantes— because of a hasty advertisement as if this were only the beginning of a *series* of similar undertakings and because of the unfavorable time of the performance (4 o'clock in the afternoon)—had very little success." (*Letters to Beethoven*, No. 485)

99. Seyfried, *Beethoven's Studien* (1832), pp. 96–97; (1853), pp. 65–66; Landau's *Beethoven-Album*, pp. 188–89; English translation in Breuning, *Memories*, pp. 110–11; the *Harmonicon*'s report of Beethoven's funeral includes a poem which, although allegedly by Grillparzer and supposedly recited at the service, seems rather to be a free and abridged translation of Seidl's poem (5 [August 1827]: 154–55).

100. Tietze's accompanist is unknown, but it is interesting to note that Tietze performed this same song at a private party, attended by Grillparzer, three weeks earlier with Schubert accompanying. Indeed this is the only documented performance by the mature Schubert of the work of another composer. Tietze further appeared at public concerts with Schubert at the piano on April 22 and 29 and May 6, the most sustained number of pub-

lic performances Schubert ever gave. While it is unlikely that Schubert's participation in the May 3 memorial would have gone unnoticed—the pianist most likely was Carl Maria von Bocklet, who performed later in the concert—it is not inconceivable that Schubert accompanied his friend on this occasion as well.

101. This concert may not have been very successful, either artistically or financially. In addition to Streicher's disparaging remarks to Stumpff (*Letters to Beethoven*, No. 485), the review in the *LAMZ* suggests that the cost of 3 florins, the typical price of concerts at the time, affected attendance, which was low (vol. 29, no. 26 [27 June 1827]: 453). A letter from Johann Baptist Jenger states that only 300 attended (Nohl, *Beethovens Leben*, vol. 3, part 2, p. 547), while Georg August Griesinger states that the earlier church services, which were free, had been bursting (Landon, *Beethoven*, p. 393); see also *Letters to Beethoven*, No. 477.

102. The best overview of early biographical attempts is Clemens Brenneis, "Das Fischhof-Manuscript: Zur Frühgeschichte der Beethoven-Biographik," in *Zu Beethoven: Aufsätze und Annotationen*, ed. Harry Goldschmidt (Berlin, 1979), pp. 90–116.

103. Schlosser also wrote a biography of Mozart around the same time. Although dated "Prague 1828," the Beethoven book appeared in Vienna the previous summer and the preface is dated "June 1827."

104. Schlosser, *Beethoven: The First Biography*, p. 27.

105. *Der Sammler*, for example, tried to clear up the confusion concerning Beethoven's date of birth (no. 89 [26 July 1827]: 356), as did the *Wiener Zeitschrift für Kunst, Literatur, Theater und Mode* (no. 38 [29 March 1827]: 307–308). In addition to the letters of Beethoven, Schindler, and others that appeared in the *Harmonicon* and other periodicals, the text of the Heiligenstadt Testament was published in *LAMZ* 29, no. 17 (17 October 1827): 705–10; *Harmonicon* 6 (1828): 6; and elsewhere in the years immediately following his death.

106. *Letters to Beethoven*, No. 488.

107. *Letters to Beethoven*, No. 487; Beethoven had earlier wanted Karl Holz to be his biographer, but Schindler, who did not have good relations with Holz, apparently favored Rochlitz and may have been lying about Beethoven's approval of him as his ultimate choice for biographer.

108. Reprinted in Clemens Brenneis, "Das Fischhof-Manuscript in der Deutschen Staatsbibliothek," in *Zu Beethoven 2: Aufsätze und Dokumente*, ed. Harry Goldschmidt (Berlin, 1984), pp. 34–35. The *LAMZ* picked up the debate (30, no. 7 [13 February 1828]: 110–11).

109. Solomon and Brenneis both conjecture that Gräffer was collaborating with Karl Holz, who was in fact Beethoven's own choice for his biographer and had documentation to that effect; Solomon, "Beethoven's Tagebuch," in *Beethoven Essays* (Cambridge, Mass., 1988), p. 238; Brenneis, "Das Fischhof-Manuscript: Zur Frühgeschichte der Beethoven-Biographik," pp. 101–102.

110. Excerpts from Hotschevar's "Nachricht an Ludwig van Beethoven's Gönner, Freunde und Verehrer" (Report to Ludwig van Beethoven's Patrons, Friends, and Admirers) are given in Thayer/Deiters/Riemann, vol. 5, p. 500.

111. See Thayer/Forbes, pp. 1061–76; *LAMZ* 30, no. 2 (9 January 1828): 27–30.

112. The dates of the raising of the tombstone are given as November 4–10, in Grillparzer, *Sämtliche Werke*, vol. 3, pp. 1325–26, although the six-month anniversary fell on September 26. On September 14, Schindler wrote to Moscheles that the monument would be ready "very soon" (*Letters to Beethoven*, No. 487).

113. *Sämtliche Werke*, vol. 3, pp. 883–84 (trans. Scott Burnham).

114. The program consisted of the premiere of the String Quartet in F, op. 135, Variations in G on a Theme from *Judas Makkabäus*, WoO 45, *Der Wachtelschlag*, WoO 129,

and the Trio for Piano, Clarinet, and Cello, op. 11; the other performers included Carl Maria von Bocklet, piano; Joseph Friedlovsky, clarinet; and Ludwig Tietze, tenor.

115. See Gibbs, *The Life of Schubert*, pp. 147–48; and Rufus Hallmark, "Schubert's 'Auf dem Strom'" in *Schubert Studies: Problems of Style and Chronology*, ed. Eva Badura-Skoda and Peter Branscombe (Cambridge, 1982), pp. 25–46. I have explored the "secret program" of the trio in program notes for the 1997 Schubertiade at the 92nd Street Y in New York City, and for the Schubert Festival at Carnegie Hall (May 5, 1997); a more detailed study is forthcoming.

116. Schubert's close friend, Josef von Spaun, later recalled that Beethoven's "death shocked [Schubert] very deeply. Did he, perhaps, have a premonition of how soon he would follow him and rest at his side?" (Deutsch, *Schubert: Memoirs*, p. 137).

117. See Gibbs, *The Life of Schubert*; and John M. Gingerich, "Schubert's Beethoven Project: The Chamber Music, 1824–1828" (Ph.D. diss., Yale University, 1996).

118. Haslinger published the work as *Trauerklänge bei Beethoven's Grabe. Vierstimmiger Männer-Chor, nach einer Original-Melodie des Verewigten. Die Worte von Franz Grillparzer* in a supplement to the *Allgemeiner Musikalischer Anzeiger*, no. 12 (21 March 1829). Alfred Orel states that the *Equale* with words by Grillparzer had already been played when the tombstone was raised in November; see *Grillparzer und Beethoven*, p. 134, n. 115.

119. *LAMZ* 29, no. 19 (7 May 1828): 310–11; and *Wiener Zeitschrift für Kunst, Literatur, Theater und Mode*, no. 45 (12 April).

120. Otto Erich Deutsch, *Schubert: A Documentary Biography*, trans. Eric Blom (London, 1946), p. 760.

121. Ibid., p. 825.

122. See Christopher H. Gibbs, "'Poor Schubert': Images and Legends of the Composer" in *The Cambridge Companion to Schubert*, ed. Christopher H. Gibbs (Cambridge, 1997), pp. 36–55.

123. *On Music and Musicians*, ed. Konrad Wolff, trans. Paul Rosenfeld (New York, 1946), p. 107; and *Robert und Clara Schumann: Briefe einer Liebe*, ed. Hanns-Josef Ortheil (Königstein, 1982), p. 79.

124. *Harmonicon* 5 (May 1827): 86; *Letters to Beethoven*, No. 477; cf. Moscheles, *The Life of Beethoven* (London, 1841), vol. 2, p. 79.

125. Joseph Carl Rosenbaum, who stole Haydn's head, was interested in the theories of Dr. Franz Joseph Gall; see "The Diaries of Joseph Carl Rosenbaum 1770–1829," trans. Eugene Hartzell, ed. Else Radant, *Haydn Yearbook* V (1968), pp. 149–58; and Landon, *Haydn: The Late Years 1801–1809*, p. 388. For another example of the interest in phrenology, see Hegel's discussion in *The Phenomenology of Mind* [1807], trans. J. B. Baillie (New York, 1967), pp. 355ff.

126. *Memories*, p. 109.

127. Von Perger and Robert Hirschfeld, *Geschichte*, pp. 102–103.

128. Breuning, *Memories*, pp. 117–18; Theodor von Frimmel, *Beethoven-Studien: Beethovens äussere Erscheinung* (Munich, 1905), vol. 1, pp. 153–57.

129. *Actenmässige Darstellung der Ausgrabung und Wiederbeisetzung der irdischen Reste von Beethoven und Schubert* (Vienna, 1863); most of the text is reprinted in Bankl and Jesserer, *Die Krankheiten Ludwig van Beethovens*, pp. 89–95. For an interesting discussion of how the gendered descriptions continued, see David Gramit, "Constructing a Victorian Schubert: Music, Biography, and Cultural Values," *Nineteenth-Century Music* 17 (1993): 65–78.

130. *Memories*, p. 116. Wagner was fascinated by the issue. As he wrote in his 1870 Beethoven essay, "Though it has been an axiom of physiology that, for high mental gifts, a large brain must be set in a thin and delicate brain-pan—as if to facilitate immediate recognition of things outside us,—yet upon examination of the dead man's remains some

years ago it transpired that, in keeping with an exceptional strength of the whole bony skeleton, the skull was of quite unusual density and thickness. Thus nature shielded a brain of exceeding tenderness, that it might look solely within, and chronicle the visions of a lofty heart in quiet and undisturbed" (*Richard Wagner's Prose Works*, trans. William Ashton Ellis [London, 1898], vol. 5, p. 89). In the first substantial biography of Schubert, by Heinrich Kreissle von Hellborn, we are told that confronting Schubert's well-preserved skull, the "doctors and hospital attendants who were present were astonished at its delicate, almost womanly organization" (*Franz Schubert* [Vienna, 1865], p. 466; *The Life of Franz Schubert*, trans. Arthur Duke Coleridge [London, 1869, rpt. New York, 1972], 2: 152). See also Breuning's article "Die Schädel Beethovens und Schuberts" in the *Neue freie Presse* (17 September 1886), reprinted in *Aus dem Schwarzspanierhause* (Berlin and Leipzig, 1907), pp. 209–21.

131. *Memories*, p. 118.

132. The second disinterment is described in a report of Vienna's Anthropological Society; see *Bericht über die am 21. Juni 1888 vorgenommene Untersuchung an den Gebeinen Ludwig van Beethoven's gelegentlich der Uebertragung derselben aus dem Währinger Orts-Friedhofe auf den Central-Friedhof der Stadt Wien* (Vienna, 1888) and *Bericht über die am 22 September 1888 vorgenommene Untersuchung an den Gebeinen Franz Schuberts gelegentlich der Übertragung derselben von dem Währinger Orts-Friedhofe nach dem Central-Friedhofe der Stadt Wien* (Vienna, 1888); excerpts from the reports appear in Bankl and Jesserer, *Die Krankheiten Ludwig van Beethovens*, pp. 96–101; see also Karl Adametz, *Franz Schubert in der Geschichte des Wiener Männergesangvereines* (Vienna, 1938), pp. 49–58.

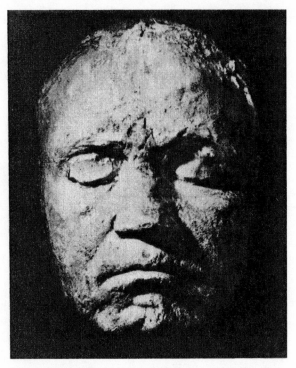

Fig. 1. Franz Klein, *Life Mask of Beethoven*, 1812, plaster, Beethovenhaus, Bonn.

The Visual Beethoven:

Whence, Why, and Whither the Scowl?

ALESSANDRA COMINI

Question: What did the French painter of Herculean horses Rosa Bonheur, the Italian Symbolist author and World War I aviator Gabriele d'Annunzio, and the Swedish dramatist August Strindberg have in common? *Answer*: A plaster copy of Beethoven's life mask on their walls.[1] Actually this grim, well-known image (Fig. 1) was not too unusual an object to encounter on display in homes at the end of the nineteenth century—a century that had witnessed the mythopoesis of the composer from suffering Promethean hero to triumphant demi-god, holding out, like Schopenhauer, the promise of redemption through art. But what binds these three particular Beethoven devotees from three different countries even more closely is the incorrect assumption that the scowling effigy was Beethoven's *death* mask. It is not difficult to understand how such a mistake (still prevalent today) could occur. The furrowed forehead, contracted brow, closed, sealed-over eyes, and tightly pressed downward pulling lips suggest not only the sleep but the frown of death, and Beethoven, the musical titan who from the age of twenty-five had fought a losing battle with deafness, looks appropriately pained—the way one would expect him to look in death, the way Bonheur, d'Annunzio, and Strindberg *wanted* him to look. And they were not alone in this desire.

The taking of life masks—as opposed to death masks—had found increasing popularity from the 1790s onward, thanks to the new interest in phrenology as indicator of character sparked by that proselytizing founder of the "science" of physiognomy, Johann Kaspar Lavater.[2] (Such famous persons as George Washington, Keats, Sarah Kemble Siddons, Beethoven, and Goethe submitted to the plaster procedure.) But the traditional procurement of a death mask, employed as far back as the wax casts of Roman times, was still by far the better known and more customary practice before the age of photography (as with Dante, Shakespeare, Schiller, Queen Louise of Prussia, Napoleon I, and Canova).

Hence to the uninitiated, the grimacing white or black Beethoven masks ubiquitously populating music and antiques shops during the age of Romanticism were generally presumed to reflect the unhappy composer's facial expression as ghoulishly immortalized in death. "Oh! *un infelice*," had been Beethoven's self-description to sympathetic visitors like Rossini, who later commented on the "indefinable sadness spread over his features."[3] No painted or engraved portrait of Beethoven had ever been able to convey this quality. Many sensitive observers responded to the human tragedy they believed implicit in the brooding plaster effigy. As late as 1910, for instance, the poet Rainer Maria Rilke penned this compassionate outburst upon seeing what he took to be Beethoven's death mask:

> The *mouleur*, whose shop I pass every day, has hung two masks beside his door. The face of the young drowned woman, a cast of which was taken in the Morgue because it was so beautiful, because it smiled, smiled so deceptively, as though it knew. And beneath it, his face, which did know. That hard knot of the senses tightly drawn together . . . the countenance of one whose ear a god had closed so that there might be no tones but his own.[4]

In responding to what he saw as the stamp of grief at being deaf imprinted upon Beethoven's morose mien, Rilke was merely following the lead of those who had known and observed Beethoven in life. Louis Spohr, the virtuoso violinist who had met the composer as early as 1812—the year the life mask had been made—and who saw him at regular intervals during the next four years, wrote after listening to Beethoven hammer obliviously on a gratingly out-of-tune piano: "I felt moved with the deepest sorrow at so hard a destiny. It is a sad misfortune for anyone to be deaf; how then should a musician endure it without despair? Beethoven's almost continual melancholy was no longer a riddle to me now."[5]

There exists a precious, first-hand insight into Beethoven's "almost continual melancholy" as it prevailed during that crucial year of the life mask, 1812. This was the year in which the forty-one-year-old composer, taking the cure at the Bohemian spa of Teplitz, wrote the famous three-part letter to his (unnamed) "Immortal Beloved." Beethoven's tortured declaration "Your love makes me at once the happiest and the unhappiest of men" is followed in the very next sentence by reason and resignation: "At my age I need a steady, quiet life—can that be so in our connection?"[6] The letter, discovered among the bachelor composer's papers after his death, is the only one known addressed to a woman in which the intimate "Du" form appears. It was also at Teplitz that Beethoven made the acquaintance of, and played for, Germany's living legend, Goethe. We have the poet's candid assessment: "His talent amazed me; unfortunately he is an utterly untamed personality, who . . . surely does not make it any the more enjoyable either for himself or others by his attitude. He is easily excused, on the other hand, and much to be pitied, as his hearing is leaving him."[7] In addition to the progressive deterioration of Beethoven's hearing, movingly announced as early as 1802 to his brothers in the famous Heiligenstadt Testament found along with the "Immortal Beloved" letter, the composer's general health in 1812 included chronic intestinal and stomach problems—thus his visit to the healing waters at Teplitz.

Let us now examine the circumstances surrounding the taking of Beethoven's life mask in 1812 against this background of heart and health troubles. Did the mask record the impress of physical and psychic suffering along with the topography of the composer's features? Could the relentless realism of a life cast penetrate to the character, matching the inner with the outer man, as the phrenologists believed? The commission to capture Beethoven's three-dimensional physiognomy for posterity came about at the request of his friend the piano maker Johann Andreas Streicher, who wanted to add his bust to those of other famous musicians already adorning the walls of his private concert hall. The task went to the Viennese anatomical sculptor Franz Klein, provider of plaster casts for the medical cabinet of the quirky Franz Joseph Gall, founder of Vienna's new science of the skull, cranioscopy, later known as phrenology. Klein's insistence on taking life masks from his sitters before modeling their busts had earned him the monitory nickname "Head Chopper" ("Kopfabschneider").

Beethoven was justifiably apprehensive. Taking a mold of the living face was not a pleasant procedure for the subject, who was made to recline on his back at an angle of about thirty-five degrees. In order to prevent adhesion of the wet gypsum, a lather of strong soap and water was applied to the hair. The face was then moistened with sweet-oil, protective shields placed over the eyes, and quills inserted into the nostrils so that the victim could breathe during the operation. Next the plaster was laid carefully upon the nose, mouth, eyes, and forehead, while the back of the head was pressed into a flat dish. The gypsum was then applied to those parts of the face still uncovered, cheeks and chin, and as soon as the mold hardened, it was removed, often with a single strong upward motion. Fearful that he was about to suffocate under the wet plaster while it was drying, Beethoven moved abruptly—the first take had ended in failure. But the result of the second attempt is a fascinating legacy. It exactly replicates not only Beethoven's living face, complete with pock marks (possibly from smallpox) and facial scars, but also his acute physical discomfort—for *this* is what the contracted brow and firmly clamped "scowling" mouth register. Not a metaphysician's melancholy of soul, but simply the claustrophobic apprehension of near suffocation![8] Nevertheless, subsequent image makers and musical interpreters (as different as Berlioz and Mahler) would seize upon the formidable impression of seriousness and intense concentration conveyed by Klein's austere life mask by as indicators of the suffering and triumph in both the musical and personal character of Beethoven.

Klein's follow-up bust, executed in plaster of Paris and painted to look like bronze, added a surround of unruly, "bristly" hair (Fig. 2), giving the sense of an imposing, massive head. Circling this life-size bust to obtain the informative profile view, we can note the slightly bulging forehead above the furrowed brow, the long, straight-across eyebrows, the pronounced philtrum—a vertical groove running from under the nose to just above the middle of the upper lip—and the muscular chin with its pronounced cleft. When one actually touches the bust, or the

Fig. 2. Franz Klein, *Bust of Beethoven,* c. 1812, bronzed plaster, Beethovenhaus, Bonn.

life mask upon which it is so meticulously based, this deep cleft can be felt to throw up a shell-like mound of flesh on either side. This strange configuration (remarked upon by many of Beethoven's friends) is the result of an overdeveloped mentalis muscle that raises the chin and pushes up the lower lip, thus adding to the apparent pouting aspect of Beethoven's facial expression. Furthermore, in modern dental terms, Beethoven had what is called a double protrusion: both upper and lower jaws and lips push forward. The low angle of the lower jaw definitively contributed to the habitual "stern" look upon which many contemporaries remarked and which appears as the main characteristic of the supposedly "tragic" life mask upon which so many printed, painted, and sculpted images of the composer were thereafter based.[9] Thanks to the then recent invention of lithography, these increasingly sullen, progressively leonine images received wide distribution throughout Europe and abroad.

One of the most lionizing and frequently reproduced of the portraits for which the composer agreed to sit (he usually vocally resented the time lost in posing for artists) was that by Joseph Karl Stieler, future creator of the Schönheitsgalerie in Munich—the display of portraits of thirty-six beautiful women who caught the appreciative and wandering eye of Bavaria's King Ludwig I. In the fall of 1819 the genial young painter miraculously coaxed three sittings from the preoccupied composer who was then working on the *Missa Solemnis*. The final product (Fig. 3) shows Beethoven at half-length in a grape arbor, pencil poised in mid air above a thick sheaf of music paper identified on the back as "Missa Solemnis." Beneath electrified hair Beethoven's lined forehead is high and broad and the eyebrows are vibrantly bushy and arched, transforming the level ones of Klein's mask. The "piercing" eyes (Rossini's term) are shown in thoughtful roving orbit, the flat pug nose of the life mask is flatteringly elongated, and the mouth is serious and tightly compressed, with long red lower lip protruding above muscular chin, the powerful jaw firmly set. All the elements dear to future iconographers are present in Stieler's heroizing conception: somber genius inspired by inner voices in the presence of nature, with long locks of hair writhing wildly in symbolic parallel to the seething turbulence of creativity. It would seem that Beethoven was not adverse to giving a nudge to the "whither" of his already famous scowl: he himself liked the portrait well enough to order copies to distribute as gifts to friends.

Verbal accounts and published descriptions of Beethoven not only corroborated but frequently amplified the image of tormented creator conveyed by such visual portraits. Here is one of the earliest, printed in 1809 and actually read (and scoffed at) by Beethoven himself. It is

Fig. 3. Joseph Karl Stieler, *Portrait of Beethoven,* 1819, oil,
Collection Walter Hinrichsen, New York.

written by the indefatigable musical journalist-composer and celebrity-
hunter Johann Friedrich Reichardt, who traveled from North Germany
to visit the lion in his Vienna lair. Biographers would jump on the last
sentence that credited melancholy with the inspiring of great works.

> At last I found him in his large, disorderly, lonely lodgings. He
> looked at first as gloomy as his apartment . . . . He is of a powerful
> temperament, his appearance practically Cyclopean, but really
> quite sincere, cordial, and good. . . . [He] has the unhappy,
> hypochondriac, melancholy notion in his head and heart that every-
> one here persecutes and despises him. His visibly stubborn nature
> may well frighten away many of the good-natured, gay Viennese.
> . . . It often grieves me deeply when I see this basically good, excel-
> lent man gloomy and suffering, although on the other hand I am
> convinced that his best, most original works can only be brought
> forth when he is in such headstrong, deeply sullen moods.[10]

And here is one of the last literary portraits published during Beethoven's lifetime, taken from Sir John Russell's journal of his travels on the continent, the first edition of which came out in 1824.

> Though not an old man, he is lost to society in consequence of his extreme deafness, which has rendered him almost unsocial. The neglect of his person which he exhibits gives him a somewhat wild appearance. His features are strong and prominent; his eye is full of rude energy; his hair, which neither comb nor scissors seem to have visited for years, overshadows his broad brow in a quantity and confusion to which only the snakes round a Gorgon's head offer a parallel.[11]

Russell was fortunate enough to hear Beethoven play and observed "how the music of the man's soul passed over his countenance. He seems to feel the bold, the commanding, and the impetuous, more than what is soothing or gentle. The muscles of the face swell, and its veins start out; the wild eye rolls doubly wild, the mouth quivers, and Beethoven looks like a wizard overpowered by the demons whom he himself has called up."[12] The litany of colorful attributes offered in these two reports could not fail to inspire maudlin interpretations of the visual Beethoven as gloomy, suffering, and sullen, with the shaggy hair and wildly rolling eyes of a man possessed.

Small wonder that the idolizing young Berlin critic Ludwig Rellstab who visited Beethoven in 1825—some thirteen years after the "scowling" life mask's debut—expressed surprise at *not* encountering the "powerful, genial savagery" he had observed in his portraits. The man did not look like the myth. "There was nothing expressing that brusqueness, that tempestuous, unshackled quality which has been lent his physiognomy in order to bring it into conformity with his works."[13] In this single sentence Rellstab deftly characterized the driving force motivating Beethoven's visual mythopoesis: the man should look like his scores. As the music thundered and scowled, so should its creator—thus the collective cultural unconscious. To the reverent visitor from Berlin the all too apparent reality was that of an ailing, now completely deaf Beethoven (fifty-five years old and with fewer than two more years to live): a "sick, melancholy sufferer."[14] Even the jealously possessive Anton Schindler, who from around 1820 had insinuated himself into Beethoven's life as indispensable secretary (and future biased biographer), removed his customary rose-colored glasses to report: "The illness [bouts of fever and diarrhea, paroxysmal stomach pains[15]] of 1825 dimmed the fire in [his] eyes so that, like so much of his internal

and external being which at that time had begun to undergo a meta-
morphosis, the strange look in his eyes was no longer to be seen."[16]

What did Beethoven really look like in the 1820s? Was he in truth
perpetually scowling? We have a fortuitously reliable answer in the final
documented (1823) oil portrait for which the composer sat (Fig. 4). This
glowering image is posterity's least favorite likeness; the least copied, the
least reproduced contemporary portrait of Beethoven. It is not the
image of genius. But it is certainly an image of Beethoven. It is the unro-
manticized work of that fanatical pursuer of reality, the Biedermeier
artist Ferdinand Georg Waldmüller, a superb genre and landscape
painter who excelled in portraiture as well. Known as the Austrian
Ingres, he combined photographic verisimilitude with rhythmical harmonies of precise form and subdued color chords. The courteous,
thirty-year-old painter was allowed only one sitting with the composer,
who took a sudden dislike to him and refused to let him return.
Schindler's account of the abortive meeting between Beethoven and his
adopted city's greatest portrait painter is revelatory in several ways:

> At the beginning of 1823 the publishing firm of Breitkopf and
> Härtel wanted to own a portrait of our master, and chose
> Waldmüller . . . to paint it. But there were obstacles. Beethoven felt
> the pressure of work, his eyes were giving him constant trouble,
> and he was almost always in a bad temper. After much wrangling,
> an appointment was made for the first sitting. Waldmüller's behav-
> ior on this occasion was reverential and far too self-effacing, a bear-
> ing Beethoven generally found most irritating. . . . No matter how
> much Waldmüller hurried with sketching the head and roughing
> out the portrait, the preoccupied master was impatient to get back
> to his work, and would repeatedly stand up, pace the floor irrita-
> bly, and go to his writing-table in the next room. The under layer
> of paint had not yet been completed when Beethoven made it clear
> that he could tolerate the procedure no longer. When the painter
> had left, the master gave vent to his spleen and called Waldmüller
> the worst artist in the world because he had made him sit with his
> face toward the window. . . . No further sittings took place and the
> artist completed the portrait from memory. . . .[17]

Schindler's repetition of Beethoven's naïve assertion that Waldmüller
was the world's worst painter because he made him sit facing a natural
light source is most informative. If anything, the impression given by the
Stieler portrait of an interesting, but second-rate talent at work is confirmed. Now at last Beethoven sat vis-à-vis an artist of superior gifts, and

that artist's utterly professional approach was found wanting—by a Beethoven who professed to detest flattery but was (unconsciously?) used to it in portraiture. Who else but the truth seeker Waldmüller, who did not hesitate to record the wart on the upper lip of one of his female sitters, had the gall to ask his pockmarked model to sit facing a window? How skilled the painter was at quickly grasping the minutiae of a human gestalt is exemplified in his observation of the disparate nostril openings so clearly indicated in the portrait (and observable in the life mask). Back in his studio the artist did not indulge in answering rudeness with documentation of his sitter's facial scars. What lodged in Waldmüller's memory however was the disgruntled aura radiated by the composer. The portrait fairly bristles with Beethoven's discontent. The incipient frown captured and immortalized in Klein's life mask is now pervasive and seemingly inveterate, while above the muscular chin the firmly clamped mouth with thrust-out lower lip maintains the scowling expression of the mask. The restless rolling of the eyes noted by Stieler is accurately recalled by Waldmüller, as are the narrow eyelids. The

Fig. 4. Ferdinand Georg Waldmüller, *Portrait of Beethoven*, 1823, oil, formerly possession of Breitkopf and Härtel, Leipzig (destroyed).

Fig. 5. Joseph Danhauser, *Death Mask of
Beethoven*, 1827, plaster, Historisches Museum
der Stadt Wien, Vienna.

eyebrows are impatiently arched but not nearly as massive as in the
Stieler portrait. This is the first and only painted image of Beethoven in
which the flat nose has not been subtly recast. The slightly sagging jowls
that now elongate the face (as in the death mask, see Fig. 5) are also rendered with unidealized fidelity. The artist's keen eye had noticed the
receding hairline of his fifty-two-year-old sitter as well as the silver-
streaked strands of long hair that now contrasted jarringly with the still-
dark eyebrows and red-flushed cheeks.

Waldmüller's frank, objective portrayal of an aging, splenetic
Beethoven was dismissed contemptuously as looking like that of a "venerable pastor"[18] by the hero-worshipping Schindler, who some five years
earlier had already commissioned his own private oil portrait—
unmatchable in his eyes. Schindler's commission showed Beethoven-
the-creator complete with mandatory flying hair, furrowed brow,
ludicrously sideward-rolling eyes, powerful nose and chin, and firmly
closed, determined lips.[19]

Beethoven's scowling-at-fate, suffering expression—commonly presumed to have been captured in the life ("death") mask, and slavishly
perpetuated in the visual arts—would be given compelling literary

propagation by Richard Wagner, whose self-identifying worship of the composer was to extend to an unusual appropriation of the visual Beethoven, as we shall see. He presented the world with a succinct verbal portrait of the composer in which deafness was the cause and a scowling visage the effect. Here he is in 1870 musing for the German reading public's benefit during the Franco-Prussian War on his fellow German's obdurate resolve in the face of adversity and on the resulting physical appearance: "So the expression of his face became spasmodic: the spasm of defiance holds this nose, this mouth at a tension that can never relax. . . . A musician without hearing!"[20]

Yet here is the knowledgeable Richard in a particularly empathic moment, as recorded by his devoted amanuensis and spouse Cosima in her nightly diary entry, remarking in wonderment: "Do you know that sometimes, when I have a musical thought, I catch myself with my mouth set just like Beethoven's in his death mask."[21] *Death* mask? Certainly Wagner had misspoken, thinking of the tightly compressed lips of the life mask, yet inadvertently referring to the death mask (Fig. 5), one of the few original copies of which he had seen in the possession of his illustrious father-in-law, Franz Liszt.[22] There is nothing of creative determination in this emaciated face, with its hollowed temples, sunken cheeks, and slack, drooping mouth—pathetic palimpsest of years of physical and emotional pain and of a protracted, terminal illness (cirrhosis of the liver). But so lodged in the universal conception of Beethoven as intensely concentrating, defiant genius was the life mask imago that even Wagner, in an unguarded moment, fell prey to confounding the two masks.

One of the Leipzig-born Wagner's earliest literary efforts, *Pilgrimage to Beethoven*, published during an impoverished and unhappy stay in Paris in 1840, had already provided posterity with an empathic and dramatic portrait of psychic cause and physical effect—why Beethoven's expression was habitually "gloomy and unfriendly."[23] The short story's hero is a penniless German musician, "R," from "L" (Leipzig, where else?) who walks to Vienna in fervent hopes of meeting the master and is successful to the point of becoming the recipient of a sermonette on the Ninth Symphony that (amazingly) anticipates his own music of the future, the music-drama. Wagner effectively conveys the personal impact of dealing with Beethoven's deafness: "At last in a hoarse voice he addressed me: 'You come from L—?' I was about to reply when he interrupted me by picking up a sheet of paper and pencil, which lay to hand. 'Use these,' he said. 'I cannot hear.' Of course I knew all about Beethoven's deafness and had prepared myself. But it smote my heart to hear that hoarse, broken voice say: 'I cannot hear.' To be poor and joyless, one's only solace one's sovereignty in the realm of sound, and have to say: 'I cannot hear.' In a flash I understood why Beethoven looked as he did: why the deeply careworn cheek, the somber angry glance, the tightly drawn defiant mouth."[24]

For Wagner it was not enough to write about the visual Beethoven. He yearned to possess his very own, "genuine" image of the great composer whose real and only spiritual heir he sincerely believed himself to be. A small likeness of Beethoven had graced his modest Zurich apartments as early as 1851[25] and by 1869, with his royal fan King Ludwig II patiently footing the rental bills for his composer-in-exile, he was at last in a position to provide his latest sumptuous home (Villa Triebschen overlooking Lake Lucerne[26]) with a worthy Beethoven icon—a portrait in oil. He knew exactly which portrait he wanted. On March 5, 1869, he wrote to the son of one of the founders of the Leipzig music firm Breitkopf and Härtel and asked whether the original of Waldmüller's "quite excellent" portrait of Beethoven, distributed by his firm as a print, was by any chance available "so that an exact copy of it might be made by a really skillful artist."[27] The artist Wagner had in mind was the Leipzig-based portrait painter Robert Krausse, who had already made a highly satisfactory copy. Härtel Jr. was encouragingly positive: "The portrait of Beethoven . . . is owned by me personally. . . . The picture was painted alla prima very quickly because Beethoven had little desire to sit for his portrait; it has not always been as favorably judged as by you. If you wish to have a copy made of it, it is at your disposal at any time."[28] By return mail Wagner took Härtel up on his offer, asking that he be allowed to give it to Krausse to copy and assuring his correspondent that the rapid execution of the picture was exactly what made it such a real portrait, free from all affectation, and superior to all other Beethoven portraits known to him. By May 13, Härtel was able to inform Wagner that Krausse had that day received not only the Waldmüller picture but also the "death mask, which I also own" (he must have meant the Klein life mask) in order to "control" the portrait results.[29] With not quite so much promptness this time, Wagner thanked Härtel, saying he hoped Krausse would not create an ideal portrait but rather a *true* portrait of the man.[30] To Krausse Wagner wrote encouraging but specific instructions to fix up—with great discretion—any technical faults that the "al prima" execution of the original might evince, to create the copy in the exact same size, and to keep the character of the original without making any essential changes.[31] On the second of July he was able to inform Härtel that the copy pleased him extraordinarily, and to the hardworking copyist he wrote his sincere thanks: "With this artistically executed copy I possess everything that I had wished to possess:

an unaffected, real portrait of Beethoven."[32]

Given Wagner's great satisfaction, an exact, perhaps even undifferentiatable, copy would certainly seem to be the result of this exacting commission. Let us compare the Krausse copy (Fig. 6) with the Waldmüller (see Fig. 4) to ascertain how faithfully it has preserved the "unaffected" character of the original. Even without the benefit of a color reproduction for Krausse's picture, it is clear that the copy could never be confused for the original. The eyeglasses of Biedermeier objectivity through which Waldmüller had viewed his model have been exchanged for the subjective spectacles of Romanticism with which both Krausse and Wagner unconsciously saw their Beethoven. What had originally attracted Wagner to this image of Beethoven—even if the least beloved by commercial mythographers—was that it demonstrated (for him) Beethoven's admirable poise and perseverance in the face of health troubles and advancing years, and not the tempestuous, perpetually youthful Beethoven, the manically "inspired" hero with tossed locks. (Wagner was already four years older than the subject of Waldmüller's portrait.) Nevertheless the titanic aspects of the man—his silver-streaked hair, incipient frown, pug nose, and compressed lips— have all been enhanced and exaggerated. Krausse clarified, as it were, the impress of suffering and mighty mental activity, aspects with which

Fig. 6. Robert Krausse, *Copy of Ferdinand Georg Waldmüller's 1823 Portrait of Beethoven*, 1829, oil, formerly Villa Wahnfried, Bayreuth.

Fig. 7. Johann Nepomuk Schaller, *Bust of Beethoven*, after 1827, before 1842, plaster, Bodleian Library, Oxford.

Wagner could readily identify. The lines of Beethoven's tightly set lips, cheeks, and chin are all just a shade more pronounced. The furrow between the now thicker and longer eyebrows is noticeably more prominent, and a curious feature that usually comes only with aging has actually been added to the eyelids—a slightly hooded aspect puffs out the originally narrow upper lids, dramatically contributing to the look of grim concentration illuminating Beethoven's features. And, in keeping with the forty-six years that had passed between Waldmüller's and Krausse's effigies, Beethoven's hair has become almost snow white. Wagner had never seen the original oil, only an engraving of it—a rendering less fierce than the Waldmüller prototype and one which also emphasized the contrast between the composer's silvering hair and his still dark eyebrows.[33] Cosima's diary records Richard's continuing pleasure in the scowling talisman which, along with images of Schiller, Goethe, Liszt, and Schopenhauer, eventually graced the *salon* of his final home, Villa Wahnfried in Bayreuth: "He is still delighted with the picture of Beethoven. 'That is how he looked, this poor man who gave us back the language men spoke before they had ideas . . . but this is also the reason why a musician such as he is a being for whom there is absolutely no place in society.'"[34] Wagner's transparent paralleling of himself with Beethoven concerning hardships and setbacks that threatened but never deviated musical purpose was confirmed by another reaction, faithfully preserved in Cosima's diary, concerning another Beethoven likeness which the couple chanced upon in Mannheim in 1872: "We see a very interesting picture of Beethoven which captivates R. enormously. 'Yes, that's how he looked; these eyes which see nothing and this mouth, showing all the stubbornness of a man whom nothing in the outside world can influence.'"[35]

Wagner's treasured oil "facsimile" of a morose, aging Beethoven is a fascinating instance of self-projection. It constitutes a unique milestone marking the "whither" of the visual Beethoven's (increasingly baleful) scowl. However it was in three-dimensional sculpture that Beethoven's mandatory grimace found its most unabashed expression. In conceiving their own Beethoven-in-the-round, sculptors displayed a marked preference for the composer's life mask as opposed to portraits. Thus it is hardly surprising that many of the memorial busts and public monuments which sprang up around Europe and elsewhere in honor of the dead composer fortified the public's expectation of a frowning titan with knit brows and pouting lips, intensely focused on his inner voices. Klein's bronzed plaster bust and the stern life mask upon which it was based seems mild by comparison with some of the posthumous effigies they inspired. Compare for example Klein's bust (see Fig. 2) with the one created by a fellow Viennese sculptor Johann Nepomuk Schaller for the London Philharmonic Society sometime after 1827 (Fig. 7). The double-breasted jacket of the prototype has been rejected in favor of drooping drapery. The curly locks have grown in length and number, thus "classicizing" Beethoven among Greek and Roman heroes. But this is a joyless hero, whose staring scowl charges and distorts his features.

Many imaginative carved and cast variations on the amplified scowl theme would follow during the course of the nineteenth century and into the next. The permutations are too numerous to discuss here,[36] but two flamboyant French contributions, stimulated by Berlioz's proselytizing of the concept of a "suffering" Beethoven[37] and the author Romain Rolland's "passional" interpretations of the composer's life whose mightiness of soul overcame all obstacles,[38] compete for acknowledgment. Auguste Rodin's bizarre portrait medallion of Beethoven, carved for the facade of the Brussels Royal Conservatory of Music in 1871–1877 (Fig. 8), accosts courageous students who would enter with a literally long-faced grimace (the forehead has grown in height, the chin mass has doubled in length). This is a jowled, old, and frazzled looking Beethoven; vitality has passed from the long, limp hair to the cloak that arches about the shoulders of this strangely realistic but pronouncedly remote image (fat cheeks, pointed nose with flared nostrils, small mouth). Rodin's contribution to the whither of Beethoven's scowl was massively outdone, however, by his student Antoine Bourdelle. Bourdelle, struck by what he believed to be his own remarkable physical resemblance to the composer, developed a lifelong obsession with the image of Beethoven, churning out more than forty-five sculpted and drawn ferocious-looking portraits of his idol from 1887 to the year of his death forty-two years later. The over life-size disembodied bronze head of 1901 (thirty inches high!) (Fig. 9) is characteristic of Bourdelle's dramatizing use of pitted and puffed surfaces to equate a ragged exterior with the tumult of his hero's inner life. Looking more like a severe burn victim than anything else, this *Grand Tragic Mask* is almost unbearable to look at, so swollen and distorted are the features, so raw and ruptured the hideous scowl. Both Rodin's and Bourdelle's poignantly personalized images of the composer are indebted to that French perception in Beethoven of absolute values and moral might—whether musical or personal—transmitted so eloquently and with such frequency by the apostles Berlioz and Rolland.

Turning from the fanciful extremes of Rodin and Bourdelle to the scrupulously literal in sculptured images of Beethoven, it is intriguing to observe how close to (and yet how far beyond) Klein's life mask the three major German monuments to Beethoven remained. A life-size memorial to its famous native son was dedicated in drowsy little Bonn with three days of musical performances (presided over by Liszt, who had already raised money for the project) in August of 1845. This haphazardly organized event surprised and overwhelmed the city fathers by attracting some five thousand visitors. It was a "nearly Europe-wide meeting" of musicians (Berlioz's phrase)—as well as Queen Victoria and her German husband Prince Albert, who watched the unveiling of the mysteriously shrouded statue from the only balcony overlooking the Münsterplatz. The young sculptor Ernst Julius Hähnel from Dresden was responsible for the monument destined for the square. He decided to show the historical Beethoven, dressed for a walk, arrested in midstride, with notebook and pencil in hand (Fig. 10). The bearing is upright and Beethoven stares ahead, his features concentrated in the well-known frown. Still, the "known" Beethoven—the earthling with his metal-buttoned frock coat—seems to have confounded the sculptor, presenting him with the problem confronting all icon makers, that of transforming the temporal into the eternal. (A modest pedestal, about the height of Beethoven's figure, would help somewhat.) Striving for contemporary accuracy while attempting heroic universality, Hähnel clutched at the cliché of wrapping his figure in a voluminous mantle, meant to create the desired impression of a classical, timeless cloak. At the moment of its unveiling, this static bronze hybrid—half-paragon, half-pedestrian with its sullen expression designed to be seen from below writ large with exaggeratedly knit brows and protruding pouting lips—was discovered to have its back to the expectant royal visitors on the balcony! So much for the city fathers' attention to detail.

Vienna's answer to the Bonn memorial (characteristically late: thirty-five years, to be exact, and with Liszt's fundraising assistance once again) was unveiled in 1880, one hundred and ten years after Beethoven's birth. The sculptor entrusted with the ambitious three-dimensional monument, mandated to outclass Bonn's homage, was the Bavarian Kaspar Clemens Zumbusch, provider of the large bronze bust of Ludwig II fronting Villa Wahnfried, and creator of several marble portrait busts of his friends Wagner and Liszt. Three-and-a-half decades of additional mythopoesis had helped shape Zumbusch's concept: *his* Beethoven would not be period-bound or accessible as though on a walk; *his* Beethoven would be awesome. And indeed it is (Fig. 11). Placed on top of a towering smooth granite porphyry pedestal and flanked below by Prometheus and Nike (symbolizing the two supposed poles of Beethoven's music, struggle and triumph), ringed by nine putti personifying the nine symphonies (the ensemble design rising to twenty-two feet), the Vienna Beethoven is grave, formidable, and imposing. He sits,

Fig. 8. Auguste Rodin, *Portrait Medallion of Beethoven*, 1871–1877, facade of the Royal Conservatory of Music, Brussels.

Fig. 9. Antoine Bourdelle, *Beethoven Grand Tragic Mask*, 1901, bronze, Bourdelle Museum, Paris.

Fig. 10. Ernst Julius Hähnel, *Beethoven Monument*, 1845, bronze, Bonn.

with no visible support, his features wrapped in the familiar frowning concentration suggested by Klein's life mask (Zumbusch had procured a copy), yet enhanced by additional wrinkles in the brow, prominently arching eyebrows, broad, down-thrust mouth, and protruding set chin. He scowls; he is sad; but he is not incapacitated. Like Michelangelo's *Moses*, of which Zumbusch in fact owned photo-graphic reproductions, the contrap-posto of Beethoven's turning torso emits a sense of "action in repose." How different from Hähnel's burgher-of-Bonn conception! How the guests at the Vienna unveiling shivered at the *terribilità* of Zumbusch's towering (over eight feet tall) titan! A close look at the face (already cast in 1878) shows that this terribilità has also visited Beethoven's mighty locks of hair. The eyes fairly glower in their challenging stare. (Brahms, who had long kept a treasured bust of Beethoven mounted on the wall of his Vienna apartment, enthusiastically acquired a small replica of the colossal Zumbusch figure.[39]) It was the pained, scowling face of Zumbusch's Beethoven that elicited the greatest praise from critics, even in its initial bronzed plaster model: "Seldom have I seen a sculpted work of such gripping simplicity, so vigorous in mood and so powerfully effective. . . . The history of the genesis of an entire symphony can be read in the deeply ground features, how he suffered as he created. This face tells us this, this face upon the forehead of which is unmistakably imprinted the mark of suffering genius."[40]

No future three-dimensional image of Beethoven could match the Zumbusch monument as far as evoking and augmenting the interpre-tive nuances resident in the Klein life mask. The original scowl of phys-ical discomfort had metamorphosed categorically into an obligatory expression of spiritual suffering. Yet an apotheosis was at hand that would surpass both the Hähnel and Zumbusch renderings. The unlikely author of this sculptural accomplishment was Max Klinger, son of a

Fig. 11. Kaspar Clemens Zumbusch, *Figure of Beethoven*
for the *Beethoven Monument*, 1878, bronze, Vienna.

wealthy Leipzig soap manufacturer. An ultra-German bourgeois
schooled in comfort and culture (the family grand piano graced his large
Leipzig atelier), he was nonetheless visited by and communicated visions
of suprareal intensity in his riveting work. (His hallucinatory 1881 cycle
of prints about a young man's sexual daydreams upon finding a
woman's glove anticipated Freud's exploration of taboo subjects, and
would inspire future artists from Kubin to De Chirico to Dali.) A talented
amateur pianist possessed of a brooding and melancholy temperament,
Klinger had discovered the "dark" side of Beethoven for himself. While
producing widely admired polychromatic marble femmes fatales
(Salome, Cassandra), he began to search out the marble quarries of
Europe in answer to an inner command—the compulsion to realize a

haunting vision of Beethoven that had come to him unsolicited at the piano one evening during a sojourn in Paris fifteen years earlier. "It was as clear, and the colors as pronounced, as are very few things: the pose, the clenched hand, the red mantle, the eagle, the throne, the drapery folds—even the gold throne arms (Fig. 12)."[41]

A throne! This no sculptor had yet provided Beethoven. Klinger, who was equally at home in graphics, painting, and sculpture, soon conceived an audacious plan to mix mediums by carving his Beethoven and accompanying eagle in marble, while casting in bronze the throne with its symbolic relief commentaries. Years passed before a foundry was found willing to attempt the one-piece casting of such a majestic adjunct. Thereupon Klinger set to work fashioning five angel heads to be carved in African ivory with wings of agate, jasper, and antique glass for the throne's inner face. The outcome of the casting (done in Paris in 1901) exceeded all expectations. The entire ensemble, complete with gold, mosaic, and precious-stone inlay soon stood on public display in Klinger's studio, where photographs[42] of the multi-piece work-in-

Fig. 12. Max Klinger, *Beethoven Monument*, 1902, various colored marbles, ivory, precious stones, polished gold, and bronze, Gewandhaus, Leipzig. Detail at right.

progress show a copy of Klein's life mask carefully installed alongside the marble figure of Beethoven. Klinger's seventeen-year labor of love offered German monumental sculpture an authoritative direction: the employment of precious, mixed, and contrasting mediums and the use of polychromy to create a single *Gesamtkunstwerk*—overwhelming in effect and tactilely sensuous. What Wagner had done with his music-drama, Klinger proposed to achieve with sculpture. Beethoven's introduction of voices into a symphony had been an innovation of far-reaching consequence; Klinger's combining of marble and bronze would constitute a knowledgeable and provocative salute to the composer's daring departure. (Indeed, critics of the day would refer to the polychromatic ensemble as "Max Klinger's Ninth Symphony.")

If deification is implicit in the godlike throne and mountain peak setting, it is verified in Klinger's marble figure of Beethoven. Gone are the pencil and notebook of Hähnel's Bonn statue; absent is the generalized but still recognizably nineteenth-century clothing of Zumbusch's Vienna monument. Klinger's Beethoven is stripped to the waist in heroic and timeless nudity. He is presented as an *immortal*. This is no longer Beethoven the man, nor even Beethoven the musician. This is Beethoven the enthroned genius. The tone hero has been promoted from Promethean striver to Zeus-like creator. An amber-eyed empyrean eagle, attribute and companion of the king of the gods, he who alone can ascend to Olympian heights, stares in awe at the new Zeus. Removed from the world, Beethoven is occupied in the divine work of creative thought—his figure inclines forward, his legs cross, and his fists ball within each other as if in extreme determination.

The focal point of Klinger's cogitating Beethoven—despite or perhaps because of all the accouterments of cliff, eagle, throne, and angel heads—is the face, and it is to this face (indicated by a pointing angel on the far right) that the beholder's attention returns time and again. Clearly and carefully based on the Klein life mask, it picks up dramatically on one aspect previously neglected or "corrected" in other Beethoven monuments—the blanked out eye sockets, (which in the original mask were protected by shields). Following tradition, Klein's bronzed plaster bust (see Fig. 2) had provided his subject with stylized open eyelids and eyeballs, the frontally staring pupils of which had been lightly indicated. (Drawing on accrued mythopoesis, Schaller's posthumous bust would emphasize the upward-roving pupils, see Fig. 7). Klinger had initially thought to set Beethoven's eyes with opals or amber—but he decided the effect would be too specific, too pronouncedly a portrait effigy and not sufficiently an image of genius. In the end the eyes were left quite blank; not even the pupil holes were drilled. The result was tremendously effective: it "spiritualized" the face. Although an enthroned apotheosis of Beethoven had distanced him from the world, Klinger 's desire to convey the composer's compassion for that world, to suggest the great humanity expressed in his music, was an important factor in the sculptor's final conception of the white marmoreal features. The rumpled hair seems to reverberate to a throbbing behind the high forehead, and the downward pull of Beethoven's lips imparts an expression that is tinged with spiritual grief, effectively transcending the "whence" of the life mask's scowl of physical discomfort.

Klinger's transcendent Beethoven monument—his three-dimensional Ninth Symphony—had come at the right time. It was first exhibited in Vienna in 1902 in collaboration with Gustav Klimt, who painted an accompanying Beethoven frieze with allegories referring to Schiller's *Ode to Joy*, and Gustav Mahler, who reorchestrated the fourth movement of the Ninth for brass and wind instruments and conducted the Vienna Opera chorus at the exhibition on opening day. The enthralled public was caught up in a multiple spectacle that inundated the senses and swayed the emotions through its seductive suggestion of a national mystique. At the close of the nineteenth century—Beethoven's century—a subliminal longing for deliverance from the materialistic present had overtaken industrialized Europe. In Germany and Austria this disenchantment with modern life was coupled with nostalgic remembrances of Germanic cultural greatness. A weary society was predisposed to welcome a cultural champion from the past. Who, then, better than Beethoven, the composer whose hard-won musical language spoke directly to souls of victory over sorrow, triumph over suffering? Here at the turn of the troubled century—poised to explode into two world wars—was the long-awaited redemption through art. And although the whither of Beethoven's scowl in the new century would crop up in transmogrifications as far-removed from Klinger's apotheosis as the touching homage of Schroeder, Charlie Brown's little sidekick, who keeps a bust of the frowning composer on his tiny piano, the universal yearning for heroes and salvation has remained unchanged.

NOTES

1. Bonheur's copy of the Klein life mask was prominently placed on the wall near one of the windows of her large studio at By (where it can still be seen today); d'Annunzio's copy was given the place of honor in his crowded music room at Villa Vittoriale (now a museum) on Lake Garda and was crowned with a laurel wreath in a characteristic touch of Italian effusiveness; Strindberg's copy was reverently installed in his last apartment at Drottninggatan 85 in Stockholm (preserved as a museum.) Here in his final years the world-weary playwright would slowly play through Beethoven sonatas on his upright piano (scrupulously skipping the scherzos). Above him the "death" mask hung flanked by two candles. Today, his piano, candle holders, and a plaster cast of Beethoven's face—still misidentified as "Beethoven's death mask"—are all in place. (Strindberg's original white copy was stolen and has been replaced by a black one.) The Swedish playwright in particular required his Beethoven be tragic: "Joy was never my thing, so I find his Ode to Joy banal, which Beethoven can be when he tries to be happy." As quoted in Michael Meyer, *Strindberg: A Biography*, (New York, 1985), p. 446.

This is not the forum for delving into the myth-making vicissitudes inspired by Beethoven's physical appearance as recorded in his life and death masks, contemporary portraits, and posthumous monuments. I was able to pursue the intriguing topic at length in my book, *The Changing Image of Beethoven: A Study in Mythmaking* (New York, 1987), a volume originally intended purely as an investigation of Beethoven's iconography, but ultimately dedicated to exploring the *interior* image of Beethoven held by all those who contributed to his mystique, especially those composers, performers, artists, writers, and critics who consciously engaged with him as a musical or moral force in their own lives. This present essay on Beethoven's "scowl" has afforded me the welcome opportunity to focus upon just one aspect of the visual Beethoven—the two plaster casts taken of his face, one in life, the other in death—and to trace the resulting, often conflated metamorphoses in art and in later interpretations of Beethoven's character and music.

2. The prolific Swiss writer Lavater (1741–1801) taught that character could be read in the formation of the face and body. His exclamatory-style treatise *Physiognomical Fragments for the Promotion of the Knowledge and Love of Mankind* (1775–78, 1802) had a tremendous impact on artists and scientists and went through many editions in the original German, with translations into French and English.

3. Beethoven's remark of 1822 was quoted by Rossini to Wagner in 1860, as reported by Edmond Michotte, see Herbert Weinstock, trans., *Richard Wagner's Visit to Rossini (Paris 1860) and An Evening at Rossini's in Beau-Sejour (Passy) 1858* (London, 1992), pp. 52, 44.

4. Rainer Maria Rilke, *The Notebooks of Malte Laurids Brigge* (1910), trans. M. D. Herter Norton (New York, 1949, 1964), pp. 70–71.

5. See O. G. Sonneck, ed., *Beethoven: Impressions by His Contemporaries*, (New York, 1926, 1967), p. 100.

6. As given in Alexander Wheelock Thayer, *Life of Beethoven*, ed. Elliot Forbes (Princeton, 1970), p. 534.

7. Goethe, letter to his musician friend Carl Friedrich Zelter, ibid., p. 537.

8. This feeling of approaching suffocation was common to others who submitted to the plaster procedure, and varying expressions of tenseness or patience being tested can be discerned in other life masks of the period (for example Goethe, whose austere living features were recorded twice in plaster, in 1807 and again in 1816, and the genial Danish sculptor Bertel Thorvaldsen, in 1810), but in no individual did the hint of discomfort pre-

served in gypsum approach that of Beethoven's dramatic (and dentally predetermined, see text below) scowl. The nineteenth-century American sculptor William Wetmore Story was of the opinion that the more mobile and variable the face, the more a mask loses, but the more set and determined the character and expression, the more perfect the life mask's reproduction of the subject's essence. Despite testimony to the contrary concerning the mobility of Beethoven's facial features, it was the latter, "determined" characterization as applied to Beethoven's "visibly stubborn nature," (see Reichardt' s description in text below) and hence "set" countenance in life that seemed to be mirrored in the life mask, and which certainly prevailed in subsequent portraits of the composer.

9. Since Beethoven's twenty-ninth year painters and sculptors had asked to portray him, and publishing houses had issued lithographic and engraved pictures of his likeness. The composer's years in Vienna commenced and ended with the firm Artaria's commissioning artists to sketch his portrait for reproduction and commercial distribution. For a full discussion and illustration of these disparate images see especially Chapters Two and Three in my book, *The Changing Image of Beethoven.*

10. Albert Leitzmann, ed., *Ludwig van Beethoven: Berichte der Zeitgenossen, Briefe und persönliche Aufzeichnungen,* 2 vols. (Leipzig, 1921), letter of December 10, 1808, pp. 102–103 (translation mine).

11. Sonneck, *Beethoven: Impressions,* p. 114.

12. Ibid., p. 116.

13. Ibid., p. 180.

14. Ibid.

15. A convincing argument that Beethoven's chronic intestinal complaints fit the diagnosis of Crohn's disease is presented in Anton Neumayr's interesting *Musik und Medizin: Am Beispiel der Wiener Klassik* (Vienna, 1900, 1987), pp. 182–84.

16. Anton Felix Schindler, *Beethoven As I Knew Him* (1840; rev. and enl. eds., 1845 and 1860), ed. Donald W. MacArdle; trans. Constance S. Jolly (New York, 1972), p. 455.

17. Ibid., pp. 453–54.

18. Ibid., p. 454.

19. Schindler's private, demoniac portrait of Beethoven was created by his young friend the amateur artist, singer (friend of Schubert), and later professional actor, Ferdinand Schimon (for a color reproduction see Plate 3 in my book, *The Changing Image of Beethoven,* where there is also a fuller discussion of this particular myth-making icon, pp. 40–42).

20. Richard Wagner, *Beethoven* (1870), trans. Edward Dannreuther, 3d ed. (London, n. d. [1800?]), pp. 49–50 and p. 54.

21. Cosima Wagner, *Cosima Wagner's Diaries,* trans. Geoffrey Skelton (New York, 1978–1980), vol. 2, p. 116, entry of July 18, 1878.

22. The youngest artist ever to approach the mortal Beethoven, the twenty-one-year old Viennese Josef Danhauser would be the one to take his death mask. While waiting for a barber to come and shave Beethoven's face so the plaster could be laid, Danhauser also made two drawings of the dead man which he worked up into oil sketches—one of the composer's face, the other of his hands. The original death mask passed into the possession of Josef's brother Carl, who lived to be eighty (1891), and a very fine copy of the mask was presented by Josef as a unique gesture of homage to Liszt after a Vienna concert appearance in 1840. Liszt kept the precious relic always and it was installed in a place of honor in both of the Weimar houses where he spent so large a part of his later life and where Wagner had several occasions to study it. A photograph taken of the aged Liszt (c. 1880) seated at his writing table in the Hofgärtnerei house shows the Beethoven death

mask behind him on the wall to the far left, crowned with a wreath to diminish the austere impact of the sunken cheeks and missing cranium (removed during the autopsy to determine the reason for Beethoven's deafness).

23. Robert L. Jacobs and Geoffrey Skelton, eds. and trans., *Wagner Writes from Paris* ... (New York, 1973), p. 77.

24. Ibid., p. 78.

25. As we learn from a letter to Liszt dated December 14, 1851; see Francis Hueffer, trans., *Correspondence of Wagner and Liszt*, 2d ed., rev. 1897 (New York, 1973), vol. 1, p. 182. I believe this image to be the small steel engraving in a heavy gold frame that can still be seen today at Villa Triebschen (now a museum) along with other similarly framed engraved images of Gluck, Haydn, and Mozart in Wagner's selective portrait gallery of worthy predecessors.

26. For a chronological tour of Wagner's many residences and their multiplying cultural icons and family portraits see my essay "The Visual Wagner: Environments, Icons, and Images" in Peter Ostwald and Leonard S. Zegans, eds., *The Threat to the Cosmic Order: Psychological, Social, and Health Implications of Richard Wagner's Ring of the Nibelung* (Madison, Conn., 1997), pp. 25–56.

27. This and other pertinent letters in the exchange between Wagner and Härtel are given in Ludwig Volkmann, "Das Beethoven-Bild im Haus Wahnfried und seine Entstehung," *Allgemeine Musikzeitung* 66, no. 17 (April 28, 1939): 271–75, letter of March 5, 1869 (translation mine).

28. Ibid., p. 272, letter of March 16, 1869.

29. Ibid.

30. Ibid., letter of June 15, 1869.

31. Ibid., p. 273, letter of May 4, 1869.

32. Ibid., pp. 272, 274.

33. This engraving, by an anonymous artist, is reproduced in my book, *The Changing Image of Beethoven*, p. 187, Fig. 98.

34. Wagner, *Cosima Wagner's Diaries*, vol. 1, p. 119.

35. Ibid., vol. 1, p. 558.

36. In the New World, the German-American sculptor Henry Baerer was responsible for ever more grim Beethoven busts presented to New York and Brooklyn public parks during the 1880s and 1890s.

37. Berlioz's passionate and discerning contribution to a vaulted image and interpretation of Beethoven is documented at length in my book, *The Changing Image of Beethoven*, pp. 226–251.

38. The subject of Beethoven occupied Rolland all his life: a sweepingly successful 1903 life of Beethoven, written when French readers in need of spiritual regeneration responded to his call to breathe the breath of heroes, was followed by two serialized monuments, one a scholarly seven-volume study (unfinished, 1928–45), the other a ten-volume *roman fleuve, Jean-Christophe* (1904–12). Rolland's ecstatic portrait of Beethoven presents the composer seizing destiny by the throat—a universal inspiration, belonging to all peoples.

39. For more on Brahms's Beethoven, refer to my book, *The Changing Image of Beethoven*, pp. 305–14, and for a tour of Brahms's Vienna apartment, see my article "The Visual Brahms: Idols and Images," *Arts Magazine* 54, no. 2 (October 1979): 123–39.

40. Written by a critic for the *Allgemeine Zeitung* of February 10, 1874, as quoted in Maria Kolisko, *Caspar von Zumbusch*, Vienna, 1931, p. 54, n. 1 (translation mine).

41. As quoted in Gerhard Winkler, *Max Klinger 1857–1920* (Leipzig, 1970), p. 55 (translation mine).

42. One of these informative photographs is reproduced in my book, *The Changing Image of Beethoven*, Fig. 199, p. 379. The conceptual development of Klinger's monument, the complex meaning of the allegorical reliefs on the throne, and the circumstances of its installation at the fourteenth exhibition of the Vienna Secession, with the participation of Gustav Klimt and Gustav Mahler, are discussed at length in Chapter Six of this book.

Beethoven and Masculinity

SANNA PEDERSON

"He is the most virile of musicians; there is nothing—if you prefer it, not enough—of the feminine about him." On the hundredth anniversary of Beethoven's death in 1927, Romain Rolland proclaimed Beethoven's masculinity and rejected the Romantics' association of the composer with feminine qualities. Rolland extolled Beethoven's very unfeminine physical attributes: "the musculature is powerful, the body athletic; we see the short stocky body with its great shoulders, the swarthy red face, tanned by sun and wind, the stiff black mane, the bushy eyebrows, the beard running up to the eyes, the broad and lofty forehead and cranium, 'like the vault of a temple,' powerful jaws 'that can grind nuts,' the muzzle and the voice of a lion."[1]

Although more recent scholarship is not so impressed by Beethoven's physical characteristics,[2] no one has doubted his exemplification of masculinity. Indeed, his status as "the most virile of musicians" has been revisited in sexuality-oriented Schubert scholarship, with the difference that this quality is not celebrated but instead condemned. This shift in perspective is pushed to its extreme in Lawrence Kramer's 1997 book *After the Lovedeath: Sexual Violence and the Making of Culture.* Kramer uses Robert Schumann's review of Schubert's Great C Major Symphony to exemplify the absolute authority of Beethoven's masculinity:

> In relation to Beethoven, Schumann wrote, Schubert was indeed a feminine composer, but in relation to all other composers he was masculine enough. Beethoven, in this reading, is a violent figure, or a figure—a personification—of violence: one who feminizes others but who can never himself be feminized. . . . In this hypervirile role, Beethoven stands as the embodiment of musical culture itself: stern, unyielding, commanding, his name the name of the father.[3]

Kramer subscribes to the general view of Beethoven as "the embodiment of musical culture," but gives it a negative valuation. Rather than the personification of Western civilization's highest values, Beethoven is called the personification of violence, with the source of his repressive and coercive power identified as his masculinity. Kramer uses a psychoanalytic approach to arrive at the same conclusion as Susan McClary, who in her 1991 book *Feminine Endings* singled out the recapitulation of the first movement of the Ninth Symphony as "one of the most horrifyingly violent episodes in the history of music."[4] McClary's pronouncement in particular has been received as a polemical feminist attack on the aesthetic experience of absolute music, which has been judged as one of Western civilization's most rarified and precious achievements.[5] Kramer and McClary, as leaders of the "New Musicology" of the 1990s, established gender and sexuality as central categories for musical interpretation that were more critical than affirmative of established masters and masterpieces. In the wake of their work and others, the subject of Beethoven and masculinity has been transformed from a polemical critique by outsiders into a mainstream issue that aligns musicology's approach to gender and sexuality with that in other humanistic academic disciplines. Now that the topic itself is accepted as legitimate, we can consider how to go about the immensely complex task of incorporating the categories of sex and gender into the historical understanding of Beethoven and his music.

This essay is concerned with how Beethoven's "hypervirile role" as the most masculine composer relates to his position at the center of the classical music canon as its greatest composer. I suggest that the definition of masculinity as formulated during Beethoven's lifetime contains a contradiction that enforces an image of Beethoven simultaneously as specifically masculine and as ungendered, universal. I propose two historical factors responsible for the notion of Beethoven's unsurpassable masculinity: first, Beethoven's association with politics and the public sphere; and second, the understanding of his music in narrative terms. To begin, it is necessary to define what I mean by "masculinity."

Defining Masculinity

"It seems that every man and his dog is writing a book on masculinity," comments sociologist John MacInnes at the beginning of his important 1998 book *The End of Masculinity*.[6] The recent spate of academic, semischolarly men's studies, and popular self-help books address what they call an increasingly critical situation for men. However, MacInnes contests the idea that this crisis is recent, arguing that

> the briefest historical survey will show that masculinity has always been in one crisis or another. . . . This is because the whole idea that men's natures can be understood in terms of their "masculinity" arose out of a "crisis" for all men: the fundamental incompatibility between the core principle of modernity that all human beings are essentially equal (regardless of their sex) and the core tenet of patriarchy that men are naturally superior to women and thus destined to rule over them.[7]

Following the influential feminist political theorist Carole Pateman, MacInnes locates the emergence of the modern political concept of gender in seventeenth-century contract theory. In contesting a natural or divine order of society, contract theorists such as Thomas Hobbes and John Locke argued that all human beings are born equal and that all relationships should be understood as the result of voluntary social contract rather than a natural right of certain groups or individuals to dominate others. Although they did not want to go so far as to champion women's rights, the contract theorists made it very difficult for themselves to justify the unequal positions of men and women in society. They wanted to avoid not only conceding to their opponents' argument of natural right but also the full implications of their own theory. One consequence of this stalemate, MacInnes claims, was the invention of the modern concept of gender. In order to avoid patriarchalist assumptions, the contract theorists accepted that a woman was born equal to other individuals. However, they maintained there *was* something that prevented her from assuming equal rights with man in society, and this something was her *gender*, her socially constructed femininity.

Because the concept "gender" is contingent on the social construction of sexual difference, it has usually been considered a progressive concept and also one crucial to feminism. But MacInnes argues that, on the contrary, gender "was invented to *defend* the fact of sexual inequality on the basis that it *was* socially constructed . . . and thus was consistent with a modern society which claimed to have left patriarchy behind."[8] In MacInnes's view, masculinity is a concept that only makes sense historically, as something that enabled patriarchy to disguise itself and hold on during the transition to a universal society.

The social upheaval of the period of the French Revolution accelerated this transition; the theory of gender gained significance accordingly.

During Beethoven's lifetime in Germany, both anonymous writers for encyclopedias and magazines as well as distinguished philosophers put their minds to the problem of how to reserve the rights of man to a much more narrow group than the phrase implied. There was an intense effort to come up with a satisfactory theory that could effectively prescribe the relationship between men and women in society. One explanation involved formulating the essential characteristics of the sexes. "Geschlechtscharaktere" were "the mental characteristics which were held to coincide with the physiological distinctions between the sexes."[9] This German encyclopedia entry from 1815 provides one such description:

> Thus in the male form the idea of power prevails, in the female more the idea of beauty. . . . The male spirit is more creative, having greater effect on the outside world, more inclined to strive, to process abstract subjects, to form wide-ranging plans; of the passions the swift, volatile ones belong to the man, the slow, secretive, inward ones to the woman. The man is eager, loud in his desires, the woman knows quiet longing. The female is confined to a small intimate circle; she has more patience and perseverance in small tasks. The man must acquire, the woman seeks to preserve, the male with force, the female with her virtue or her wiles. The former belongs to bustling public life, the latter to the quiet domestic circle. The man works by the sweat of his brow, and exhausted, requires repose; the woman is always busy, always active. The man will oppose his very fate and even when laid low remains defiant; the woman willingly bows her head and finds comfort and help in her tears.[10]

This article schematically attributes to man all the qualities that make him suited to the public sphere and portrays woman as destined for domesticity by her character traits. It formulates the "idea" of male and female, connects the idea to the way male and female minds work, and then links these mental characteristics to male and female behavior and actions. This reasoning provided Germany with an argument for maintaining patriarchal authority in the wake of revolutionary social and political change. An additional notion that is only implicit in this article but is increasingly put forward in the nineteenth century is the complementary nature of the sexes. The way both male and female with their different functions came together for reproduction was extrapolated to give a basis to the complementary domestic and public spheres of society.

The characteristics of the sexes were classified not only in encyclopedias but also in idealist philosophy; the notion was extended as far as possible, including into intellectual and aesthetic classification systems, as part of the idealist philosopher's goal to decipher the world as a unified whole, rationally planned by nature. The all-encompassing nature of this project provides the necessary context, I think, for understanding a subsidiary issue of Beethoven's masculinity, the gendering of sonata form.[11] In his extremely influential *Kompositionslehre* of the 1840s, A. B. Marx described the gendered themes of sonata form as a masculine *Hauptsatz* and a feminine *Seitensatz*. Scott Burnham has noticed the contradiction that the themes are designated primary and subsidiary, but at the same time are called equal; he asks: "so what kind of relationship is this, anyway?"[12] This equal but unequal relationship is characteristic not only of this description of sonata form, but more generally of the description of the relation of the sexes in the aftermath of the French Revolution, and, according to MacInnes, the very definition of gender. It manifests the same contradiction embodied in the phrase "all men are created equal," a phrase ambiguous about whether it really refers only to men.

Burnham emphasizes that for Marx, even if the masculine part is more important, the feminine part is indispensable because the two parts must come together to form a perfect whole. According to Marx, "each theme is a thing apart until both together form a higher, more perfected entity."[13] Burnham quotes an essay by Wilhelm von Humboldt to corroborate the importance of the complementarity of the sexes. Humboldt describes two polar opposites that together form a perfect unity, with love as the force that brings them together:

> The powers of both sexes operate with equal freedom, and thus one can regard them as two beneficial agents, from whose hands Nature is granted her final perfection. They are sufficient to this sublime calling, however, only when their spheres of activity complement and embrace each other—and the inclination which serves to endear each to each is Love. Thus Nature obeys the same divinity to whose care the prescient wisdom of the Greeks consigned the ordering of Chaos.[14]

Burnham uses this quotation to counter the argument made by Susan McClary that sonata form is gendered in order to represent and affirm male domination.[15] While not elaborating on Humboldt's words, Burnham seems to imply that if sonata form was once understood as analogous to the relationship between the sexes, this does not make it an unequal power relationship but rather a love relationship. Indeed, that is how Humboldt and others presented it, and that is why they needed the theory of sex characteristics in order to explain why a loving, uncoercive marriage of equals must always simultaneously be the subjugation of wife to husband. According to Humboldt, that is the way Nature in her wisdom ordered it.

A similar discussion of marriage at this time can be found in the philosopher J. G. Fichte's theory of natural right. Fichte emphasized that women and men were equal since both were rational human beings: "Has woman the same rights in the state which man has? This question may appear ridiculous to many. For if the only ground of all legal rights is reason and freedom, how can a distinction exist between two sexes which possess both the same reason and the same freedom?"[16] But his declaration of obvious equality did not prevent him from insisting that "the conception of marriage involves the most unlimited subjection of the woman to the will of the husband."[17] In order to reconcile nature and reason *and* maintain the status quo of women in society, Fichte argued that women exercise their rights when they give up all their rights to their husbands, because that is what nature intended.[18]

Both Fichte and Wilhelm von Humboldt are important figures in the history of the concept of gender. In 1795 Humboldt initiated a controversy involving Germany's most illustrious writers with two essays that appeared in his friend Friedrich Schiller's journal *Die Horen*. "Über den Geschlechtsunterschied und dessen Einfluß auf die organische Natur" ("On the differentiation of the sexes and its influence on organic nature") and "Über die männliche und weibliche Form" ("On masculine and feminine form") characterized the polarity and complementarity of the sexes.[19] Schiller expressed some of Humboldt's ideas poetically in "Die Würde der Frauen" ("The Dignity of Women") and "Das Lied von der Glocke" ("Song of the Bell"), which portrayed the divided, striving nature of man that could only be healed and made whole again by the serene nature of woman. These writings were met with hilarity and derision by the renegade group at philosophers at Jena, who prided themselves on putting their radical Romantic philosophy into practice in their unconventional personal relationships. Schiller's poems were ridiculed in essays and fragments that appeared in the Schlegel brothers' periodical the *Athenäum*. The whole dispute culminated with Friedrich Schlegel's scandalous novel *Lucinde*, which advocated the switching and blending of sex roles.[20] Although the Jena Romantics' concept of masculine and feminine proved too provocative to constitute a viable alternative at the time, it galvanized their philosophical opponents.[21]

Humboldt's writings show particularly clearly the contradiction that the sexes are equal, yet not equal. And although he emphasizes complementarity—together the parts form a more perfect whole—he also argues that man both forms one part of the whole and simultaneously transcends the limitations of being an incomplete part. In the essay "Über die männliche und weibliche Form," he describes the appearance of male and female bodies, using the Greek gods as examples, in order to define masculinity and femininity. After enthusiastically cataloging the female charms of the goddesses, he turns to describing the appearance of masculinity, then hesitates as he tries to explain why masculinity cannot be treated the same way as femininity:

> Now, in masculine beauty there should be apparent an equivalent character of masculinity. But there is the peculiar difference that masculinity is not so much observed as such when it is present, but rather missed when it is not. Intrinsic sexual characteristics are less obvious in the masculine figure, and it is hardly possible to single out an ideal of pure masculinity in an individual configuration, such as can be done for femininity in the figure of Venus. A first glance at the male and female body shows us that the specific sexual characteristics of the male are less dispersed, less closely connected with the rest of the bodily structures. In the case of the female body, nature with unmistakable care has poured all the parts, whether they designate its sex or not, into a single mold and even made its beauty dependent upon this arrangement. In the male body, nature permitted herself a greater freedom; it allowed its beauty considerable independence of its sex, and was content to indicate sex with a single stroke, as it were, not bothering about its harmonious union with the rest of the body.[22]

Humboldt elaborates on the idea that the visible physical differences of the sexes reveal how sex is the essence of woman but only a part of man:

> Women seem to be permitted to a very high degree to give in to their sexual natures, whereas men must at a very early stage sacrifice a great deal of theirs to other human values. But this too is affirmed by the great freedom his figure shows from the limitations of sexuality. For the male body can reveal the highest degree of masculinity without reminding one of the exigencies of sex, whereas the careful observer of the female body is always made conscious of it, however delicately the femininity seems to be contained and spread out. The male bodily structure seems to accord with one's expectations of the human body, and it isn't partiality on the part of men toward men that makes the male body the rule, as it were, from which the female deviates. Even the least

prejudiced observer must admit that the female body more closely incorporates the specific ends of nature, namely to reproduce her kind, but the male more the universal aim of all life, namely to conquer mass by form.[23]

Humboldt illustrates vividly here the long-standing and widespread identification of males with culture and females with nature.[24] Humboldt reduces woman to the body, to the function of reproduction, while distancing man from the body and conferring on him something said to be a "more universal aim of life" than reproduction, the abstract task of conquering mass by form.[25] The implication is that to be masculine is to be more free and independent from the body in all its mortality. He seems unaware of the paradox this brings him to: man sacrifices his sexuality in order to achieve his masculinity. From this point of view, it is certainly not difficult to understand why Beethoven would be considered quintessentially masculine—just think of all the sacrifices he made in order to concentrate on expressing abstract values through music. If "giving in" to sexuality is a feminine characteristic, it makes sense how Beethoven's renunciation of the Immortal Beloved, for instance, could actually enhance his masculinity.

Humboldt's reasoning casts light on another distinctive feature of our understanding of Beethoven's masculinity. This is his idea that the male body is the rule from which the female deviates and that "masculinity is not so much observed as such when it is present, but rather missed when it is not." Beethoven can appear ungendered and his qualities universal. The most obvious example of this is the way we understand sonata form, which, based on his pieces, becomes the rule from which other composers deviate. However, once put in the context of another composer, that composer's lack of masculinity appears while Beethoven's universality reveals itself as masculinity.[26] The question then arises: why does Beethoven always appear more masculine than any other male composer? Psychoanalytic approaches such as Kramer's can uncover the structure of this scenario, and perhaps explain the force that makes it convincing. On the other hand, psychoanalytic explanations skim over determining historical factors and continue to mystify the power of masculinity. I propose to begin understanding Beethoven's masculinity historically by investigating how, relative to other composers, Beethoven is more associated with the public sphere and politics.

The Masculine Sphere of Politics

That Beethoven would be associated with politics is not surprising, since he was exactly the right age to be affected directly by the upheavals of the French Revolution. But he alone has persisted as the musical symbol of European politics up to the present, the most vivid recent example being the performance of the Ninth Symphony in 1989 to commemorate the fall of the Berlin Wall.[27] His music can be appropriate for any political situation: Ulrich Schmitt and David Dennis have documented how effectively Beethoven's music has been used to promote a militaristic politics and enthusiasm for war.[28] Yet *Fidelio* and the Ninth Symphony have been used equally effectively in celebrating the end of war and the prospect of peace and freedom.

It has often been argued that Beethoven's music embodies the republican spirit of the French Revolution—*liberté, égalité, fraternité*. It is also assumed that these values correspond to our own contemporary ideals, which explains why his music has functioned so well to express our political values. But did Beethoven really stand for freedom, brotherhood, and equality?[29]

In a basic way, Beethoven's *Freiheit* can be considered the equivalent of *liberté* and of a freedom that is the opposite of imprisonment. At the end of Act One of *Fidelio*, for example, political prisoners sing a chorus expressing their longing for *Freiheit*, to be released from prison.[30] *Brüderlichkeit* corresponds to and even surpasses the concept of *fraternité*. Maynard Solomon judges that the last movement of the Ninth Symphony, with its repeated declaration "Alle Menschen werden Brüder," "celebrates the principle of fraternity; indeed, [Beethoven] succeeds in creating the most universal paradigm of fraternity in world culture."[31] Our contemporary ideal of fraternity, however, has been shaken by its exposure in recent times as the bond specifically between men. Carole Pateman has questioned "why fraternity, rather than another term, should be used as a synonym for community."[32] She argues that the concept of fraternity is part of the ideology of "the sexual contract"—that women are precluded from any discussion of the equal rights of man because of the assumption of a more basic contract that gives men the right to rule women. Beethoven's strong association with the concept of fraternity enforces our perception of his masculinity because fraternity means membership in an exclusively male society; but because fraternity can also mean all-embracing community, it simultaneously covers over this male identification with universal mankind.

The feminist critique of the concept of fraternity perhaps as yet poses little threat to the elation of hearing "Alle Menschen werden Brüder." On the other hand, the problem of the lack of a Beethovenian idea corresponding to *égalité* has been acknowledged. As Solomon puts it: "Liberty and fraternity—but not equality. It is on the issue of equality that Beethoven parts company with the slogans of the French Revolution and the eighteenth-century utopian *philosophes*."[33] Solomon quotes the composer as declaring in 1798: "*Power* is the moral principle of those who excel others, and it is also mine."[34] This remarkable statement and many others clearly indicate that Beethoven did not subscribe to the idea that "all men are created equal," even when only men were indicated. Historically, however, this has not prevented the Ninth Symphony and the image of Beethoven from being enlisted as the symbol of universal equality.[35]

In short, the identification of Beethoven with these revolutionary values may break down on closer inspection, but something stronger than the facts overrides these particulars. Certainly, what we call "the music itself" or the aesthetic effect is a factor in the persistence of Beethoven as the musical image of the ideal political state. But taking a historical perspective shows that there is another reason, which has to do with how the relationship between music and politics has developed since Beethoven's time.

Music, like woman, helped define the political sphere in the nineteenth century by being specifically excluded from it. This exclusion was ambiguous. On the one hand, it meant that woman and music did not figure in the "real" world of power struggles: important conflicts with the prospect of decisive triumph or devastating defeat were not possible in these spheres. On the other hand, neither did woman and music take part in the real world of boring, meaningless work and ruthless striving for its own sake that furthered the evolution of a completely rational and efficient but unfulfilling and ultimately inhuman society. As early as the 1815 encyclopedia entry quoted above, woman functions not only as the counterpart to, but also as an escape from the public world of politics. The love, warmth, and quiet of domestic life emanating from feminine qualities were understood to mitigate the coldness of public life. Closer to nature than man to begin with and protected in the home, woman seemed unaffected by the accelerated alienation of civilization from the natural world. With the seemingly limitless advances in science and technology in the nineteenth century, all the more value was placed on woman as a source of natural humanity in an increasingly inhuman world of men. The complementary relationship revealed itself as compensatory. Music was treated analogously because of what was thought of as its irrational and emotional nature. It too seemed to elude disenchantment, and therefore to provide a refuge from rationality. This was the situation of music in the second half of the nineteenth century which Carl Dahlhaus termed "neo-romanticism."[36]

Although music and woman were valued, they were still for the most part kept in their domestic role as a temporary escape, rather than as a viable alternative to the man's public world. Music took on feminine faults as well as virtues, especially in the second half of the nineteenth century.[37] With the aesthetic turn toward realism, music seemed to lose ground in the struggle to be considered a progressive form of art. In this context the importance of Beethoven's masculinity grew; it became a talisman that was used to ward off accusations that music had nothing to do with the real world. To give a brief example: As part of the 1848 revolutions, proposals for a musical reorganization that would make music more accessible and a more integral part of people's lives were formed by liberal and revolutionary musicians. Put on the defensive by anti-romantic allegations that music was merely an escapist, irresponsible, and feminizing pastime of the upper classes, these reformers pointed to Beethoven as their sole proof that music could play an important role in the public sphere. The liberal Leipzig *Neue Zeitschrift für Musik,* under attack by the conservative *Allgemeine musikalische Zeitung* for trying to bring a political dimension into music, played what it considered its single ace when it declared: "Beethoven was a democrat not only in his life, but also in his music; he was filled by the spiritual powers of his time and attested to them in his works."[38] In their view, no contemporary composer actually involved in mixing music and politics during the 1848 revolutions (such as Wagner) came even close to Beethoven in demonstrating how music could play an important public role. For the most extreme critics who had no patience with art at all, even Beethoven could be vulnerable to the charges of irrelevance and escapism. As Ulrich Schmitt comments, "The pleasure in revolutionary music was easier and above all less dangerous than concrete political activity. One needed merely to sink oneself in Beethoven's symphonies and be lost for a few hours in sweet dreams of freedom, equality and fraternity."[39] But Beethoven's masculinity survived, even though it was manifested only in music, because his heroic confrontation with fate put him in a category apart from other musicians.

Beethoven's Heroic Narrative

Beethoven was not the only composer of music celebrating freedom and brotherhood during the Napoleonic Wars; this element alone does not account for his masculinity. The other factor I want to discuss concerns his association with the archetypal narrative of overcoming, of struggle and triumph. Hans Heinrich Eggebrecht has designated the notion of overcoming a central, perhaps the central idea to be gleaned from the history of Beethoven reception.[40] This narrative applies equally to Beethoven's life and his music; it functions to impose unity on his life and works. As A. W. Ambros declared in 1865, "We consider his works as commentary on his life . . . his life as commentary on his works."[41]

Overcoming requires movement past an obstacle, and this very basic definition constitutes the formal and temporal structure of the heroic narrative. In his book *Beethoven Hero*, Scott Burnham describes the story portrayed by Beethoven's heroic style by invoking "the necessity of struggle and eventual triumph as an index of man's greatness, his heroic potential."[42] "Man" is not specifically identified in this narrative, nor is the time and place of his struggle. The story is so purified of particularity that "it is always the same, or nearly so: something (someone) not fully formed but full of potential ventures out into complexity and ramification (adversity), reaches a *ne plus ultra* (a crisis), and then returns renewed and completed (triumphant)."[43] Such an abstract structure can accommodate sonata form as well as the basic quest narrative or adventure story.

Is there any specific content to this archetypal narrative? In a letter from 1815, Beethoven wrote: "We mortals with immortal spirits are born only to suffering and joy, and one could almost say that the most distinguished among us obtain joy through suffering."[44] Burnham comments, "it would be hard to imagine a more direct transcription of the popular view of the meaning of Beethoven's heroic style."[45] The document that has provided the main material for the narrative content is the Heiligenstadt Testament, in which Beethoven described the obstacle of deafness and his determination somehow to overcome this unavoidable fate. The Fifth and Ninth Symphonies, above all, have been interpreted in its light.[46] What happens between the tormented minor opening and the triumphant major ending varies depending on the interpreter, but the basic message of overcoming prevails.[47]

Burnham emphasizes that this heroic narrative should be understood in context, as part of the age of Goethe and Hegel, a time when the idea of *Bildung*—self-formation, education—was expounded novelistically by Goethe in *Wilhelm Meisters Lehrjahre* and philosophically by Hegel in

Phänomenologie des Geistes.[48] Wilhelm von Humboldt again figures prominently here as a theorist of *Bildung*. A founder of the University of Berlin, Humboldt argued for the importance of an education that allowed an individual to realize himself as a person, as opposed to a training for a specific task. Humboldt envisioned humanistic education as providing the skills for the personal struggle to achieve a unified and complete sense of oneself in the face of an increasingly specialized and mechanized society.[49] This is the story of achieving status as an autonomous, free individual realizing one's potential from within, instead of being formed from outside by society's utilitarian aims.

It may not be particularly controversial to argue that the idea of *Bildung* and the archetypal narrative of overcoming inform our basic understanding of the meaning of Beethoven's music; but to link it to gender may seem more tenuous. Why should a narrative of overcoming necessarily mark the music as masculine? Shouldn't the struggle to realize one's potential be a true universal of humanity? Historically, the answer is no: for the nineteenth century, the corollary of the philosophical construction of the process of becoming a man declares that woman does not become; she *is*. A woman's life does not involve becoming, does not have a narrative, because she does not grow intellectually or spiritually. The issue is more complex in novelistic representation; whether one can speak of a female *Bildungsroman* is currently a subject of vigorous debate.[50] But the German philosophical tradition that is so important for the understanding of Beethoven is particularly strong in denying women their own *Bildung*.[51] In a now notorious passage from *The Philosophy of Right*, Hegel remarked, "Women are educated—who knows how?—as it were by breathing in ideas, by living rather than by acquiring knowledge. The status of manhood, on the other hand, is attained only by the stress of thought and much technical exertion."[52]

The idea that man had to exert himself while woman merely had to keep breathing was thought to be verified by the roles of man and woman in sexual intercourse.[53] Humboldt expounded the active/ passive distinction in the essays on the sexes discussed above: "Everything masculine shows more self-activity [*Selbstthätigkeit*], everything feminine more passive receptivity"[54]; man is "energy" and woman is "existence" (*Daseyn*).[55] Humboldt's formulation of this distinction was only the beginning of a long tradition in German philosophy. In the generation after Hegel, Ludwig Feuerbach reformulated Humboldt's definition of the sexes bound together by love into the aphorism: "What is love? The unity of thinking and being. Being is the woman, thinking the man."[56]

In sum, the German tradition that valorizes Beethoven's narrative of overcoming has a tradition of viewing woman as an unchanging, eternal essence, as the polar opposite of the dynamically striving and achieving man. Theoretically, the notion of the attainment of selfhood, of growing up and realizing one's potential, is not necessarily gendered; it can be understood to apply equally to males and females. But historically the *Bildungs*-narrative has been shaped by the complementary notion of the unchanging nature of woman. Like the ideology of equality and fraternity, it helps perpetuate Beethoven's universality while simultaneously enforcing his masculine image.

I have argued that masculinity, defined politically, is a way of legitimating male domination in a modern world which recognizes that all people are born equal. The reason why Beethoven is assumed to be the most masculine of composers is that what he and his music stand for is precisely the same ideology that tries to attain universal society in theory while maintaining male domination in practice. But Beethoven reception is also part of a historical evolution that has come to recognize the negative as well as positive aspects of masculinity. McClary and Kramer continue in the tradition of this historical narrative when they contend that Beethoven's masculinity is problematic, something they recognize as previously having been unequivocally affirmed. Understanding these arguments as part of a historical dialectic can help avoid collapsing gender categories into merely evaluative judgments. A feminist approach to this topic does not necessarily aim to vilify or celebrate Beethoven. Rather, as part of the debate of how to interpret the meaning of Beethoven and his music, it can expose the gendered history of the so-called universal concepts that have secured his legacy. This approach will help us to understand what keeps Beethoven at the center of the canon, as well as the forces that are unsettling his position.[57]

My thanks to Richard Taruskin, Lloyd Whitesell, and the editors for their comments.

NOTES

1. Romain Rolland, *Beethoven the Creator,* trans. Ernest Newman (New York, 1929), pp. 27–28. The quotation comes from the chapter "Portrait of Beethoven in His Thirtieth Year," which was first written for the centenary of Beethoven's death in 1927 and which also appeared in *Romain Rolland's Essays on Music* (New York, 1948).

2. We now know, for instance, about the "pustular facial eruptions," the "uneven circumference" of the nostrils, and other unflattering details. See Alessandra Comini's discussion of the life mask taken of Beethoven in 1812 in *The Changing Image of Beethoven: A Study in Mythmaking* (New York, 1987), p. 33; also, her essay in this volume.

3. Lawrence Kramer, *After the Lovedeath: Sexual Violence and the Making of Culture* (Berkeley, Los Angeles and London, 1997), pp. 4–5.

4. Susan McClary, "Getting Down Off the Beanstalk: The Presence of a Woman's Voice in Janika Vandervelde's *Genesis II,*" in *Feminine Endings: Music, Gender, and Sexuality* (Minnesota and Oxford, 1991), p. 128.

5. For a defense of absolute music and counterattack on McClary, see Pieter C. van den Toorn, *Music, Politics, and the Academy* (Berkeley, Los Angeles and London, 1995).

6. John MacInnes, *The End of Masculinity: The Confusion of Sexual Genesis and Sexual Difference in Modern Society* (Buckingham and Philadelphia, 1998), p.1.

7. Ibid., *End of Masculinity,* p. 11.

8. Ibid., *End of Masculinity,* p. 12.

9. Karin Hausen,"Family and Role-Division: The Polarisation of Sexual Stereotypes in the Nineteenth Century—an Aspect of the Dissociation of Work and Family Life," in *The German Family: Essays on the Social History of the Family in Nineteenth- and Twentieth-Century Germany,* ed. Richard J. Evans and W. R. Lee (London, 1981), p. 51.

10. "Daher offenbart sich in der Form des Mannes mehr die Idee der Kraft, in der Form des Weibes mehr die Idee der Schönheit. . . . Der Geist des Mannes ist mehr schaffend, aus sich heraus in die Weite hinwirkend, zu Anstrengungen, zur Verarbeitung abstracter Gegenstände, zu weitausehenden Plänen geneigter; unter den Leidenschaften und Affecten gehören die raschen, ausbrechenden dem Manne, die langsamen, heimlich in sich selbst gekehrten dem Weibe an. Aus dem Mann stürmt die laute Begierde; in dem Weibe siedelt sich die stille Sehnsucht an. Das Weib ist auf einen kleinen Kreis beschränkt, den es aber klarer überschaut; es hat mehr Geduld und Ausdauer in kleinen Arbeiten. Der Mann muß erwerben, das Weib sucht zu erhalten; der Mann mit Gewalt, das Weib mit Güte oder List. Jener gehört dem geräuschvollen öffentlichen Leben, dieses dem stillen häuslichen Cirkel. Der Mann arbeitet im Schweiße seines Angesichtes und bedarf erschöpft der tiefen Ruhe; das Weib ist geschäftig immerdar, in nimmer ruhender Betriebsamkeit. Der Mann stemmt sich dem Schicksal selbst entgegen, und trotzt schon zu Boden liegend noch der Gewalt; willig beugt das Weib sein Haupt und findet Trost und Hilfe noch in seinen Thränen." *Conversations-Lexikon oder Handwörterbuch für die gebildeten Stände,* vol. 4, 3d ed. (Leipzig/Altenburg, 1815), p. 211. Translated in Hausen, "Family and Role-Division," p. 54. The original German can be found in the German version of Hausen's essay, "Die Polarisierung der 'Geschlechtscharaktere'—Eine Spiegelung der Dissoziation von Erwerbs- und Familienleben" in *Sozialgeschichte der Familie in der Neuzeit Europas. Neue Forschungen,* ed. Werner Conze (Stuttgart, 1976), p. 366.

11. See McClary's introduction to *Feminine Endings,* pp. 9–17.

12. Scott Burnham, "A. B. Marx and the gendering of sonata form," in *Music Theory in the Age of Romanticism,* ed. Ian Bent (Cambridge, 1996), p. 182.

13. Quoted in ibid., p. 165.

14. Wilhelm von Humboldt, "Über den Geschlechtsunterschied und dessen Einfluß auf die organische Natur," quoted in ibid., pp. 185–86.

15. Besides McClary's *Feminine Endings*, see her "Constructions of Subjectivity in Schubert's Music," in *Queering the Pitch: the New Gay and Lesbian Musicology*, ed. Philip Brett, Elizabeth Wood, and Gary C. Thomas (New York and London, 1994), pp. 205–33.

16. J. G. Fichte, *Grundlage des Naturrechts nach Principien der Wissenschaftslehre* (1796); trans. as *The Science of Rights* by A. E. Kroeger (London, 1970), p. 439.

17. Ibid., p. 417.

18. For a detailed analysis of this contradiction in Fichte's theory, see Karen Kenkel, "The Personal and the Philosophical in Fichte's Theory of Sexual Difference," in *Impure Reason: Dialectic of Enlightenment in Germany*, ed. W. Daniel Wilson and Robert C. Holub (Detroit, 1993), pp. 278–97.

19. For commentary on this controversy, see Volker Hoffmann, "Elisa und Robert oder das Weib und der Mann, wie sie sein sollten. Anmerkungen zur Geschlechtercharakteristik der Goethezeit," in *Klassik und Moderne: Die Weimarer Klassik als historisches Ereignis und Herausforderung im kulturgeschichtlichen Prozeß*, ed. Karl Richter und Jörg Schönert (Stuttgart, 1983), pp. 80–97. See also Ursula Vogel, "Humboldt and the Romantics: Neither *Hausfrau* nor *Citoyenne*—The Idea of 'Self-Reliant Femininity' in German Romanticism," in *Women in Western Political Philosophy: Kant to Nietzsche*, ed. Ellen Kennedy and Susan Mendus (New York, 1987), pp. 106–26.

20. For a recent interpretation of Friedrich Schlegel's notion of androgyny, see Catriona MacLeod, *Embodying Ambiguity: Androgyny and Aesthetics from Winckelmann to Keller* (Detroit, 1998), pp. 66–90.

21. A good introduction to the complexities of understanding the Jena Romantics' approach to gender can be found in Lisa C. Roetzel, "Feminizing Philosophy," in *Theory as Practice: A Critical Anthology of Early German Romantic Writings*, ed. Jochen Schulte-Sasse et al. (Minneapolis and London, 1997), pp. 361–81.

22. "Gleich sichtbar muss nun zwar in der hohen männlichen Schönheit die Männlichkeit seyn; nur zeigt sich hier der sehr merkwürdige Unterschied, dass die letztere nicht sowohl, wenn sie da ist, leicht bemerkt, als, wo sie fehlt, vermisst wird. Der eigentliche Geschlechtsausdruck ist in der männlichen Gestalt weniger hervorstechend, und kaum dürfte es möglich seyn, das Ideal reiner Männlichkeit eben so, wie in der Venus das Ideal reiner Weiblichkeit, zuvereinzeln. Schon bei dem ersten Anblick beider Gestalten wird man gewahr, dass der Geschlechtsbau bei der männlichen bei weitem weniger mit dem ganzen übrigen Körper verbunden ist. Bei der weiblichen hat die Natur mit unverkennbarer Sorgfalt alle Theile, die das Geschlecht bezeichnen, oder nicht bezeichnen, in Eine Form gegossen, und die Schönheit sogar davon abhängig gemacht. Bei jener hat sie sich hierin eine grössere Sorglosigkeit erlaubt; sie verstattet ihr mehr Unabhängigkeit von dem, was nur dem Geschlecht angehört, und ist zufrieden, dieses, unbekümmert um die Harmonie mit dem Ganzen, nur angedeutet zu haben. "Über die männliche and weibliche Form," in *Wilhelm von Humboldts Werke*, vol. 1 ed. Albert Leitzmann, (Berlin, 1903; rprt. Berlin, 1968), pp. 342–43. Translation by Marianne Cowan in *Humanist Without Portfolio: An Anthology of the Writings of Wilhelm von Humboldt* (Detroit, 1963), p. 363.

23. "Obgleich diess im Ganzen auch bei den Weibern der Fall ist, und in der Heftigkeit des Affects die lieblichsten Züge der Weiblichkeit erlöschen, so ist doch hier die Gränze weiter gesteckt, und es ist den Weibern in einem hohen Grade ihrem Geschlecht nachzugeben verstattet, indess der Mann das seinige fast überall der Menschheit zum Opfer bringen muss. Aber gerade diess bestätigt aufs neue die grosse Freiheit seiner Gestalt von den Schranken des Geschlechts. Denn ohne an seine ursprüngliche

Naturbestimmung zu erinnern, kann er die höchste Männlichkeit verrathen; da hingegen dem genauen Beobachter der weiblichen Schönheit jene allemal sichtbar seyn wird, wie fein auch übrigens die Weiblichkeit über das ganze Wesen mag verbreitet seyn. Schon von selbst stimmt der männliche Körperbau fast durchaus mit den Erwartungen überein, die man sich von dem menschlichen Körper überhaupt bildet, und nicht die Partheilichkeit der Männer allein erhebt ihn gleichsam zur Regel, von welcher die Verschiedenheiten des weiblichen mehr eine Abweichung vorstellen. Auch der partheiloseste Betrachter muss gestehen, dass der letztere mehr den bestimmten, der männliche dagegen den allgemeinen Naturzweck alles Lebendigen ausdrückt, die Masse durch Form zu besiegen." Humboldt, "Über die männliche," p. 344. Trans. in ibid., pp. 364–65.

24. The apparent universality of this assumption is discussed in Sherry B. Ortner's "Is Female to Male as Nature Is to Culture?" in *Woman, Culture and Society* (Stanford, 1974), pp. 67–87.

25. Humboldt uses the terms "mass" and "form" in this essay solely to apply to the appearance of the body. Form conquers mass by the way the man's body (his "mass") appears formed, in the sense that it is highly defined, angular, hard; "it shows all its outlines plainly." See "Über die männliche," pp. 344–45; *Humanist Without Portfolio*, p. 365.

26. Analyzing the many ways the universal-masculine conflation pervades musicology, Suzanne Cusick wonders: "Can there be a universal that excludes the concept of gender?" See her "Gender, Musicology, and Feminism," in *Rethinking Music*, ed. Nicholas Cook and Mark Everist (Oxford and New York, 1999), p. 473.

27. Less dramatic but perhaps equally significant is the choice of the "Ode to Joy" theme as the "European Anthem" of the European Union. See Caryl Clark, "Forging Identity: Beethoven's 'Ode' as European Anthem," *Critical Inquiry* 23 (Summer 1997): 789–807.

28. Ulrich Schmitt, *Revolution im Konzertsaal: Zur Beethoven-Rezeption im 19. Jahrhundert* (Mainz, 1990); and David B. Dennis, *Beethoven in German Politics, 1870–1989* (New Haven and London, 1996).

29. Dennis summarizes Beethoven's own political views in *Beethoven in German Politics*, pp. 22–31; for a more detailed look, see Thomas Sipe, *Beethoven: Eroica Symphony*, Cambridge Music Handbook (Cambridge, 1998).

30. Rudolf Bockholdt offers a more complicated definition by arguing that Beethoven owed his idea of *Freiheit* primarily to Kant, who defined freedom paradoxically (and some say perversely) as submitting to duty. See Bockholdt's "Freiheit und Brüderlichkeit in der Musik Ludwig van Beethovens," *Beethoven zwischen Revolution und Restauration*, ed. Helga Lühning and Sieghard Brandenburg (Bonn, 1989), pp. 77–107, especially pp. 84–90.

31. Maynard Solomon, "The Ninth Symphony: A Search for Order," in *Beethoven Essays* (Cambridge, Mass., and London, 1988), p. 30.

32. Carol Pateman, *The Sexual Contract* (Stanford, Calif., 1988), p. 79.

33. Solomon, "Beethoven's *Magazin der Kunst*," in *Beethoven Essays*, p. 203.

34. Ibid., "Beethoven and Schiller," p. 212. Not only did Beethoven believe that some people were better than others owing to their ambition, abilities, and achievements, but he also seemed to believe in inherited worthiness, as in the superiority of the aristocracy. See ibid., "The Nobility Pretense," pp. 43–55.

35. See Dennis, *Beethoven in German Politics*, pp. 89–105 and Andreas Eichhorn, *Beethovens Neunte Symphonie: Die Geschichte ihrer Aufführung und Rezeption* (Kassel, 1993), p. 326.

36. Carl Dahlhaus, "Neo-romanticism," in *Between Romanticism and Modernism: Four Studies in the Music of the Later Nineteenth Century*, trans. Mary Whittall (Berkeley, Los Angeles, and London, 1980), pp. 1–18.

37. I trace how music took on feminine traits which then came to be viewed negatively in the area of German philosophical aesthetics in my "Romantic Music under Siege in 1848," in *Music Theory in the Age of Romanticism*, pp. 57–74.

38. "Beethoven war Demokrat nicht nur im Leben, auch in seiner Kunst, er war erfüllt von den geistigen Mächten seiner Zeit und beglaubigte dies in seinen Werken." Ernst Gottschald, "Ein Prophet des Stillstands und zwei Artikel der Allg. musik. Zeitung," *Neue Zeitschrift für Musik* 29 (1848), 299. For the background to this attempt to politicize music, see Chapters 5 and 6 of my dissertation, "Enlightened and Romantic German Music Criticism, 1800–1850" (University of Pennsylvania, 1995).

39. Schmitt, *Revolution im Konzertsaal*, p. 249.

40. Hans Heinrich Eggebrecht, *Zur Geschichte der Beethoven Rezeption* (Laaber, 1994), p. 71.

41. A. W. Ambros, *Das ethische und religiöse Moment in Beethoven*, cited by Eggebrecht, *Zur Geschichte*, p. 35.

42. Scott Burnham, *Beethoven Hero* (Princeton, 1995), p. xiv.

43. Ibid., *Beethoven Hero*, p. 3.

44. Letter to Countess Erdödy October 19, 1815, cited in Eggebrecht, *Zur Geschichte*, p. 40. Beethoven made many similar declarations in his letters and notebooks, particularly around this time period.

45. Burnham, *Beethoven Hero*, p. xvi.

46. On the Heiligenstadt Testament and the Ninth, see Eichhorn, *Beethovens Neunte*, pp. 249–55.

47. The *Eroica* symphony manages to portray this without the minor to major shift; Burnham's *Beethoven Hero* explores the many ways this symphony has been understood to depict the basic narrative of overcoming.

48. See especially Burnham's chapter 4, "Cultural Values: Beethoven, the *Goethezeit*, and the Heroic Concept of Self," pp. 112–46.

49. See William Rasch, "*Mensch, Bürger, Weib*: Gender and the Limitations of Late Eighteenth-Century Neohumanist Discourse," *The German Quarterly* 66.1 (1993): 20–33, especially pp. 23–25 for a summary of Humboldt's views on the importance of education in enabling the individual to encounter on his own terms the demands of society.

50. The problems with the idea of a female *Bildungsroman* begin with the difficulty in defining the *Bildungsroman* itself. Susan Fraiman summarizes the secondary literature in her chapter "Is There a Female 'Bildungsroman'?" in her book *Unbecoming Women: British Women Writers and the Novel of Development* (New York, 1993), pp. 1–31. As Fraiman's title indicates, she is against placing novels by Jane Austen, Charlotte Bronte and George Eliot in the same category as Goethe's *Wilhelm Meister*. Lorna Ellis's *Appearing to Diminish: Female Development and the British "Bildungsroman," 1750–1850* (Lewisburg, 1999) counters Fraiman's arguments with an emphasis of the similarities between the development of male and female protagonists. For an example of how this debate is playing itself out in German studies, see Todd Kontje, "Socialization and Alienation in the Female 'Bildungsroman,'" in *Impure Reason: Dialectic of Enlightenment in Germany*, ed. W. Daniel Wilson and Robert C. Holub (Detroit, 1993), pp. 221–41.

51. In her anthology of philosophical writing on women, Annegret Stopczyk comments depressingly that "I have not found a single thinker in the entire German philosophical tradition who, like the French Fourier or the English Mill, seriously and fundamentally questioned the historical actuality of the dependence of woman on man." Annegret Stopczyk, *Muse, Mutter, Megäre. Was Philosophen über Frauen denken* (Berlin, 1997), p. 260.

52. G. W. F. Hegel, *Hegel's Philosophy of Right*, trans. T. M. Knox (London, 1952), p. 264 (addition to paragraph 166). This is the same ill-fated paragraph in which Hegel claims that "the difference between men and women is like that between animals and plants" and that "when women hold the helm of government, the state is at once in jeopardy."

53. See Hausen, "Family and Role-Division," p. 55.

54. Humboldt, "Ueber den Geschlechtsunterschied," p. 319. For a more detailed look at how Humboldt based his theory of the characteristics of the sexes on the male and female roles in the sexual act, see Rasch, *"Mensch, Bürger, Weib,"* especially pp. 25–28.

55. Humboldt, "Ueber den Geschlechtsunterschied," p. 333.

56. "Was ist Liebe? Die Einheit von Denken und Sein. Sein ist das Weib, Denken der Man." Ludwig Feuerbach, letter to Bertha Löw, cited in Stopczyk, *Muse, Mutter, Megäre*, p. 142.

57. See my review of Burnham's *Beethoven Hero*, "The Beethoven Ethic and the Masculine Imperative," forthcoming in *Women and Music* 3.

The Search for Meaning in Beethoven:

Popularity, Intimacy, and Politics in Historical Perspective

Leon Botstein

I. The Consequences of Popularity

It is difficult to remove the myriad inherited images and constructs of Beethoven from attempts to reformulate a potentially valid historical representation of what the composer intended, what his musical texts mean, and what they ought to sound like. No other composer in the canon of instrumental concert music has been subject to such intense uninterrupted scrutiny with so little consensus and so much disagreement. Late-twentieth-century scholarship has made this circumstance itself an object of research.[1] Historians and theorists in each succeeding generation have offered assertions and arguments in an effort to "rescue" Beethoven from facile and philistine popularity. Beethoven's posthumous dominance—the unrivaled place he and his music have occupied in nineteenth- and twentieth-century European culture—has been the cause of the problem.

There are three distinct phases in the history of the controversy surrounding Beethoven's posthumous popularity. The first began with the dissemination of expectations that can be classified under the rubric of Romanticism. These were first articulated in the late eighteenth century by Tieck and Wackenroder, but came to the fore most eloquently in the case of Beethoven with E.T.A. Hoffmann's analysis of the Fifth Symphony. The second phase began in the mid 1850s and culminated in the dominance of Wagner's reading of Beethoven. It was the Wagnerian view of Beethoven that received the greatest currency during the last decades of the nineteenth century and exerted the strongest influence on composers and critics born after 1860.[2] The third phase occurred at the fin de siècle with the advent of the self-conscious musical modernism of Mahler and Strauss and carried forward into the interwar years.

The debate over Beethoven is not only a matter of academic interest. The fin-de-siècle revision of the Wagnerian view of Beethoven resulted, for example, in radical changes in performance practice. (This is especially true for the generation of Artur Schnabel and Arturo Toscanini, who helped make the anti-Wagnerian views of Felix Weingartner[3] appear normative.) And the anti-romantic modernism of adherents of the second Viennese School, particularly as reflected in the work of Rudolf Kolisch, has further influenced the antirhetorical formalist bias in the way post–World War II performers and audiences have approached Beethoven.[4]

The dispute over meaning in Beethoven's instrumental music has centered on a single issue: whether or not it has "extramusical" significance. While audiences, critics, composers, and performers have heard a wide variety of such meanings in the music with uncanny regularity, others have vociferously rejected this notion, citing instead the autonomy of music and the self-referential logic of its materials. Authorities from Carl Czerny on have suggested that a certain narrative is inherent in the music, and that some representational logic served as an impetus for Beethoven in the act of composition. Other eminent supporters of the idea that Beethoven's music "means" something, including Berlioz and Wagner, have taken a less historical or biographical approach. They have been content rather to trust their perceptions and reactions to the music, arguing for parallels between what they hear and particular emotions, plot lines, images, and ideas,[5] and assuming that the public, through its own independent experiences with the music, would find their claims credible. Both in the popular imagination and among cognoscenti, Beethoven became a moralist, thinker, novelist, poet, and psychologist with whom the individual listener could legitimately engage, on terms that were hardly musical or aesthetic, at least from the opposing point of view.

The fascination with Beethoven's life and his symbolic status as the quintessential modern "free" artist helped sustain the plausibility of hearing in Beethoven's music some sort of commentary on life and human destiny. It is a paradox that from 1815 on Beethoven became, on the one hand, the composer easiest to listen to and, on the other, a composer held up as unusually difficult, complicated, and profound. For Schlosser, Beethoven's first (and now discredited) biographer,

Beethoven was not only the heroic figure of freedom and originality, but the modern composer most comparable to Johann Sebastian Bach. Schlosser predicted that those with a superficial music education and tied to conventions would have difficulty liking or understanding Beethoven.[6] In the 1830s Mendelssohn thought the audience "loves Beethoven . . . because they think one must be a connoisseur in order to love him; very few of them experience any actual joy in it. . . . Beethoven's symphonies are like exotic plants to them, they don't really have to look at them, but they're a curiosity. . . ."[7] Indeed, opponents of the view that Beethoven's music "means" something beyond music itself have held to the idea that Beethoven places great demands on some sort of "pure" musical perception, that the imputing of emotional and philo-sophical meanings to Beethoven trivializes the greatness of his music and the character of aesthetic perception and judgment in music. In this interpretation, Beethoven's becoming popular (on so-called extramusical grounds) during the mid nineteenth century rendered a true under-standing of his achievement nearly impossible. From 1830 on, the controversy over Beethoven became a debate over the trajectory of edu-cation and culture, the consequences of the spread of literacy, the stan-dards of musical literacy, and, by implication, modernity.[8]

Much of the debate has concentrated on instrumental works with extramusical titles or close biographical connections such as the "Eroica" or "Pastoral" symphonies, the piano sonatas with subtitles, or other works with a long history of extramusical commentary, such as the Fifth Symphony (famously analyzed by E. T. A. Hoffmann in 1810) and the Seventh Symphony (associated almost constantly with the dance). If, however, one considers a work without the burden of an immense criti-cal literature—the Symphony No. 4, op. 60 (1806), for example—one can locate the central issues most readily. Is the introduction to the first movement merely an original extension of conventions brilliantly exploited by Haydn, or is something quite different at work? What does one make of Beethoven's use of B-flat minor, the subsequent implication of B minor, his harmonic traversal through G major, C major, D minor, before finding his way abruptly to the dominant of what then turns out to be the tonic that arrives finally after the start of the Allegro vivace? In this sequence of events B-flat major is smuggled in at m. 29 and m. 30 in the context of D minor, with no real clue that it will become the tonic.

When one looks at the way the introduction and the initial motivic material are laid out, particularly in relationship to the subsequent Allegro, one can readily understand why listeners might find both nar-rative and emotional meaning in the music. The rhetorical, fragmentary presentation of the first violins suggests a mood, or the elements of an emotion or plot. The introduction seems to tell a story, as does the transition in the first movement to the recapitulation, where fragmentation becomes reminiscence in a startling context in which the tonic is anticipated by a pedal point B-flat timpani sounding enharmonically A sharp.[9] There is the startling use of unisons and registration. There are sudden shifts in dynamics, punctuations of a placid and ominous-sounding, mysteriously static framework. Beethoven's characteristic use of sforzandi and abrupt fortissimo interventions juxtaposed against pianissimos can be heard as something more than musical inspiration.

Beethoven was celebrated for the humor in his music, so how does the listener reconcile the last movement with the first? And if one throws into the mix the second movement (noting that the first movement Allegro, the second movement, and the last movement possess nearly the same underlying rhythmic pulse as defined by the 1817 metronome markings), it's not hard to see why even the first generations of post-1827 Beethoven enthusiasts concluded that the coherence and structure of the work as a whole possesses a significance beyond its musical substance. The use of rhetoric in the second movement and the interplay of figuration and materials related to other movements (e.g., mm. 26–41, 81–105, both sections that prefigure Schubert) only further this suspicion. The work is governed, in a manner different from Mozart or Haydn, by a desire to communicate content—something other than musical originality or aesthetic novelty as defined by prior examples of symphonies. The undeniable aspects of intensity and compression, as well as the formal ingenuity and use of surprise—when considered in the light of Beethoven's distinctive handling of orchestral color and massing of sound—all make the suggestion of a so-called extramusical meaning seem apt.[10] Even today we continue to respond with empathy to those who have argued that Beethoven went beyond the traditions of affective expression, philosophical allusion, and the use of formal rhetorical conventions associated with eighteenth-century practice, particularly the models of Beethoven's teacher Christian Gottlob Neefe.

The conviction that more was at stake in Beethoven than music alone influenced performance traditions during the late nineteenth and early twentieth century and suggested linkages between the interpretation of Beethoven and specific ideological commitments well outside of the narrow frame of musical politics. Wagner helped give Beethoven's reception a wide political significance. But beginning with the early twentieth century, the political implications became less obvious than they had been when Wagner wrote his seminal 1870 essay on Beethoven. Gustav Mahler for example, who cited Wagner as an authority in defense of his reading and reorchestrations of the Ninth Symphony against the critical outrage expressed by Schenker and Robert Hirschfeld, had little use for the cultural-political appropriation of Beethoven by Wagner and his followers.[11]

Nevertheless, from the moment of the composer's death the controversy over meaning in Beethoven's music was inextricably tied to historical developments having to do with who was listening to and playing Beethoven, which Beethoven in particular, and why. Beethoven became associated with progress, modernity, individuality, complexity, and therefore the advance of culture in history. In the aphorisms from "Master Raro's, Florestan's and Eusebius' Journal of Poetry and Thought," Robert Schumann noted in the early 1830s, that

> [I]t is foolish to say that we cannot understand the music of Beethoven's last period. And why? Is his last music too difficult for comprehension . . . is the contrast of thoughts too bold? . . . Music is the latest of the arts to have developed; her beginnings were the simple moods of joy and sorrow (major and minor). Indeed, the less cultivated man can scarcely believe that there exist more specialized emotions, whence his difficulty in understanding the more individual masters such as Beethoven. . . .[12]

The interplay between popularity and the construct of meaning in Beethoven was revisited eloquently at the end of the nineteenth century by Richard Strauss. Strauss agreed to become the general editor of a series of small volumes directed at the general public and entitled "Die Musik." The very first volume, published in 1903, was a small book on Beethoven by August Göllerich, who would become famous posthumously for his massive work on Anton Bruckner. In the introduction to the Beethoven volume and the entire series, Strauss wrote that all art is "a cultural product." Strauss, following a Wagnerian line of thought, took Schumann's view a step further and argued that music was the last of the arts to be taken seriously as an integral aspect of cultural history. Strauss attacked a formalist view of music and argued that just like literature and painting, music had to be understood beyond the realm of a "game-like formalism." Instead, "the immediate connection between life and culture has been demonstrated by the history of our great composers and their greatest masterpieces in an incontrovertible manner." The choice of Beethoven for the first volume was Strauss's own, and an explicit defense of his notion of meaning in music. He thought the choice appropriate because "Beethoven is precisely that great figure on whose connection to culture in general both friend and foe can most easily agree." Strauss hoped that by illuminating the grounds for

Beethoven's popularity—the complexity and contrast of the thoughts and emotions conveyed by the music—he could pave the way for the broadening of appreciation and comprehension about more controversial and less well-known subjects in music.[13]

Strauss's disingenuous description of a critical consensus he knew did not exist was prompted by the fact that in the popular imagination there was agreement: Beethoven was the most popular composer among the swelling fin-de-siècle musical public because he was understood as communicating thought and emotion—the difficulty of his music notwithstanding. The explicit purpose of Heinrich Schenker's 1912 monograph on the Ninth Symphony was to break the back, so to speak, of the programmatic interpretation of Beethoven and the supposition of an extramusical logic that Schenker identified with Wagner's influence. The corruption of the understanding of Beethoven had run parallel to a debasement of musical standards. The monumental scope and polemical intensity of Schenker's work on Beethoven can be traced as well to the success of Mahler's Vienna performances of the Ninth Symphony, performances which stood squarely in the tradition of an anti-formalist, extramusical interpretation. In Schenker's view, the popularization of Beethoven among the mass of amateurs and professionals had been achieved at the expense of any understanding of its true character. Hans Pfitzner made the very same point in 1920, when he attacked the prominent Berlin critic Paul Bekker for furthering a tradition of making Beethoven "all too easy" for the lay public.

A half century later, Harry Goldschmidt declared once more that the popularization of Beethoven in the nineteenth and twentieth centuries had led to three catastrophic consequences. The first was an inappropriate "standardization" in Beethoven performance practice, particularly in the selection of works in the standard repertory, wherein a large percentage of Beethoven's music was neglected in favor of a very few so-called masterpieces. The second was a trivialization and a lowering of standards in the understanding of Beethoven. The third and most egregious misuse of the extraordinary popularity of Beethoven and his music was as a justification for a rigid hostility to new music and an intolerance towards innovation in contemporary musical composition.[14] To Goldschmidt, Schenker was a classic case in point, since he had little use implicitly for modernism and had held up Brahms as the last great figure in musical history. The formalist celebration of Beethoven was self-contradictory. Exaggerated affection for a composer hailed as a revolutionary, as the first and greatest exponent of aesthetic freedom and originality, was effectively blocking appreciation of new music and a continuing tradition of radical change.

The sustained conflict between exponents of a formalist reading and those who argued for the centrality of an extramusical logic and significance can therefore be understood as a displacement, albeit thinly veiled, of a controversy over standards of musical taste, the character and consequences of the spread of musical literacy, and therefore the proper way of building and sustaining an audience for music. By the time Strauss wrote his introduction, Beethoven had been successfully appropriated as a figure whose work had reached a mass audience in large measure because of the popularization of the Wagnerian view of Beethoven as musical dramatist. Strauss, Mahler, and Bekker all believed that this wide appreciation of Beethoven did not constitute a corruption of cultural standards, that the public listened to Beethoven in a way that corresponded to the composer's intentions and to the internal logic of the music itself. The extramusical was not an inappropriate imposition, but an integral part of the composer's achievement, of the logic of composition. The validity of the notion of the "extramusical" was cast into doubt.

When Goldschmidt expressed his concern about a lowering of standards, he focussed on the reductive way in which Beethoven's personality and achievements were understood, not on the fundamental premise of extramusical significance. The object of his attack was "the standard picture of Beethoven," perhaps most strikingly visible in Abel Gance's highly sentimental 1927 film *Beethoven*. Goldschmidt, unlike Schenker or Pfitzner, believed (as did Bekker) that the complexity and variety of connections between Beethoven's music and life—the poetic logic, rhetoric, and the realistic representation of life through music—were being overlooked.

The formalist, anti-Wagnerian biases expressed by as diverse an amalgam of figures as Eduard Hanslick, Schoenberg, Pfitzner, Schenker, and Adorno were all informed by the conviction that the post–Wagnerian manner in which Beethoven was widely understood effectively destroyed the capacity for any authentic musical understanding in the modern public. The way Beethoven was heard had undermined the power of all music and rendered music appreciation a commercial mass phenomenon. By subordinating the autonomy of music (in their view the actual source of Beethoven's greatness), post-Wagnerians had made music's future a prisoner of their purpose and transformed music into a medium dependent upon ordinary emotions and meanings. At stake was the validity of the habit of listening described by Romain Rolland in the first part of *Jean-Christophe*. The young hero listens for the first time to the *Coriolan* Overture:

The boy knew neither Coriolan nor Beethoven, for though he had often heard Beethoven's music, he had not known it. He never bothered about the name of the works he heard. He gave them names of his own inventions, while he created pictures and little stories for them. . . . Beethoven was fire—now a furnace with gigantic flames and vast columns of smoke; now a burning forest, a heavy and terrible cloud, flashing lightning; now a wide sky full of quivering stars, one of which breaks free, swoops, and dies on a fine September night setting the heart beating. Now the imperious ardor of that heroic soul burned him like fire.[15]

The debate over Beethoven was not only about the approach of the listening public and the mass of amateurs who sought to learn to play Beethoven's piano music guided by instructions by A.B. Marx and Carl Reinecke; it revealed concern about the presumed abuse of the example of Beethoven by composers.[16] The debate was not limited to the late-nineteenth-century rivalry between the aesthetics of Wagner and Brahms. Consider two more obscure examples. The overlay of extra-musical meaning associated with the "Moonlight" Sonata, which plays a prominent role in Gance's film (and has now been disavowed even by those who consider extramusical programs a key to understanding Beethoven), led John Field in 1836 to use that sonata as an explicit model in his E-minor Nocturne No. 10. The ostinato triplet figure beneath the melodic line is designed to make the connection directly for the listener. What better model for a novel miniature form of solo piano music defined explicitly by the notion of a nighttime reverie than Beethoven's sonata?[17] A similar pattern is audible in the climax of Hans von Bülow's Lisztian tone poem, *Nirvana*.[18] Although the symphonic fantasy is essentially monothematic, near the end the development of the material turns, somewhat abruptly, into a direct evocation of the first movement of Beethoven's Symphony No. 5 in C minor. The extramusical logic of Bülow's tone poem was the composer's representation of the then quite fashionable fascination with the Hindu and Buddhist notion of the ultimate exit from the limits of ordinary existence and the emancipation from passion and reality. What better way to communicate this triumphant moment than a shameless association with the most famous rhetorical gesture in instrumental music, one closely allied in the public imagination with the idea of fate? Bülow's tone poem was published in 1881. In 1887, the most successful guide to musical literature in the German language, written by Hermann Kretzschmar, described Beethoven's opening motive and its elaboration as the picture of a "struggle" of the human soul, depicting the confusion and pain of life and death.[19]

The perception of Beethoven as a composer intent on communicating emotions and ideas was fueled by a clichéd image of the composer and his life. Although the convention of using reductive accounts of the lives of great artists to illuminate their achievement predated Beethoven (it can be dated from Vasari and was most widely exploited in the nineteenth century in music by La Mara),[20] interest in Beethoven's biography during the nineteenth century was marked by a particular fascination with his personality, human qualities, and struggles. Schlosser declared that Beethoven had been as great a man as he had been an artist.[21] It is an irony of history that Beethoven's posthumous reception, supported in part by the fascination with the biographical, made even the late works widely accessible. Still, suspicion remained acute that the use of biography to render the music comprehensible was based on false premises. The myth surrounding Beethoven the man and the concomitant celebration of the monumental achievement and heroic struggle fulfilled, as Scott Burnham has argued, a set of cultural expectations that helped define the very act of listening to music. The conflicting efforts to explain Beethoven helped shape the character of the formal analysis of normative structures in music.[22]

II. Beethoven and the Construct of the Intimate, 1830–1870

A significant dimension of later twentieth-century scholarship on Beethoven has focussed on the historical Beethoven. Both through biography and the close readings of musical texts, scholars have been eager to establish Beethoven's intentions. The composer's creative process and the extensive array of his verbal comments have been brought to bear on the issue of the music's meaning.[23] Whether based on biography or a presumed normative assessment of the internal workings of particular pieces, the search for the "authentic" Beethoven has shed considerable light on how Beethoven's music might be understood either as absolute or as programmatic music. The reception of the Sixth Symphony, the "Pastoral," is a fairly reliable gauge. Those who view it as an exception comparable to "Les Adieux" or the "Tempest" sonatas have been inclined to place it on the periphery. These are the same critics who take a less than charitable view of *Wellington's Victory* and other so-called minor works, especially ones with a clearly narrative intent. For others like Schumann, who believed that all of

Beethoven can be understood as possessing or having been guided by so-called extramusical meaning or content—poetic, historical, biographical, and political—the "Pastoral" Symphony becomes emblematic and *Wellington's Victory* no embarrassment.[24]

The twentieth century has seen considerable revision of the once commonplace association of Beethoven with subsequent musical Romanticism. The notion that Beethoven was decisively influenced by his Bonn teacher Neefe has helped locate the programmatic element in Beethoven within an eighteenth-century pre-romantic tradition of rhetoric and the correspondence between sound and affect. For those who consider Beethoven to have been motivated by formal musical considerations, the ideals of musical Classicism are equally in the foreground. Before the mid 1850s, however, the discontinuities between Beethoven and his immediate predecessors Mozart and Haydn seemed relatively unproblematic. Beethoven was the innovator who broke through the limitations of Classicism without abandoning them. He fulfilled the logic of Classicism by extending the expressive power inherent in the traditions of instrumental music bequeathed to him. His achievement of fulfilling and transforming classical style defined as well as limited the options available to the early romantic generation born around 1810, particularly Berlioz, Mendelssohn, and Schumann. The achievement of Beethoven appeared to open up the ways in which instrumental music might more overtly engage the individual's intimate self. This notion is perhaps best understood in the use the young Robert Schumann made of Beethoven's example and legacy. As Liszt observed in 1837:

> It is obvious that things which objectively belong to exterior perception alone cannot in any way offer music a connection. The least talented student of landscape painting will be able to recreate a view more accurately with just a few strokes of the pen than a musician who has the entire apparatus of the finest orchestra at his disposal. But at the moment when they enter into a relationship with the life of the soul and, if I may say so, are subjectivized, those same things will turn into ruminations, into ideas, into something that elevates the spirit: do they not have a unique relationship to music? And would not music be able to translate them into its own secret language? If the imitation of the quail and the cuckoo in the Pastoral Symphony is considered by severe critics as child's play, does one have to infer that Beethoven has done an injustice by relating to the soul the same impressions that a joyous rural life, a beautiful landscape, a rural celebration interrupted by a storm, can evoke?[25]

The notion that Beethoven legitimated the use of instrumental music explicitly as a vehicle for a "secret" and highly personalized, if not private language for dreams and ideas was accepted without much question until the mid 1850s. The debate then took a different turn, as a result of the polemics surrounding the New German School of Liszt and Wagner. The split between that camp and the individuals who wrote the infamous manifesto of 1860 to which Brahms appended his signature, defined the trajectory of a widening debate over the meaning and example of Beethoven. Liszt had already claimed Beethoven as a source of inspiration and a model for a new mode of programmatic instrumental composition. The divisions between a formalist and a programmatic reading became more extreme as an emphasis on epic and drama became dominant through the influence of Wagner and the example not of Liszt's early piano music, but of his orchestral tone poems. As Beethoven was integrated into competing constructs of a teleological history of music, one progressive and the other which ought not be deemed conservative but rather philosophically neo-Classical (espousing transhistorical norms for music), the appeal to a historical link between Beethoven and traditions of rhetoric and expressiveness characteristic of C. P. E. Bach satisfied neither camp. But the legacy of the connection of Beethoven to a tradition of intimate discourse survived, particularly in Brahms, whose debt to Schumann remained lifelong and who had lost, by the mid 1860s, any taste for the widening polemical exchange between Wagner and his supporters and anti-Wagnerians.

The historical question that bears closer scrutiny, however, is only tangentially connected to the historical Beethoven, or to the history of reception as seen primarily through the work of theorists and critics. What was the role of music after 1827 within the larger cultural discourse? How did music function and what were the sources of its popularity? Music in Europe, particularly German-speaking Europe, had become a significant component of public culture through the many civic institutions of music and widening amateur participation. In 1832 Felix Mendelssohn, writing to his teacher (and Goethe's friend) Zelter, expressed amazement and dismay that in Frankfurt amateurs "knew all of Beethoven's" piano music, and "by heart" at that, and that the contemporary audience "loves Beethoven uncommonly" and perhaps all too enthusiastically, to the exclusion of older music.[26] How Beethoven and his music were perceived by the public during the first half century after his death can perhaps be best expressed by citing Friedrich Nietzsche's characterization of the composer's particular role in musical culture. Nietzsche reiterated in a general manner Liszt's view of Beethoven's contribution in creating an instrumental music that might function as a secret if not dangerous language of inner thoughts and sensibilities. In 1874 he wrote:

> . . . it was only with Beethoven that [music] began to discover the language of pathos, of passionate desire, of the dramatic events which take place in the depths of man. Formerly the objective was to give expression in sound to a mood, a state of determination or cheerfulness or reverence or penitence; by means of a certain striking uniformity of form, through protracting this uniformity for some time, one wanted to compel the listener to interpret the mood of the music and in the end to be transported into it himself. . . . Beethoven was the first to let music speak a new language, the hitherto forbidden language of passion: but because his art had grown out of the laws and conventions of the art of ethos, and had as it were to try to justify itself before them, his artistic development was peculiarly difficult and beset with confusions. An inner dramatic event—for every passion takes a dramatic course—wanted to break through a new form, but the traditional scheme of the music of moods set itself in opposition and spoke against it almost as morality speaks against the rise of immorality.[27]

Although Nietzsche's view is influenced by his assessment of Wagner's achievement and place in history vis à vis Beethoven, he downplays the epic-dramatic intent and the monumental in Beethoven. He characterizes Beethoven as the inventor of music as the language of personal experience. Nietzsche was both a musician and a composer whose music sought to be expressive, though its vocabulary and materials remained decidedly pre-Wagnerian and pre-Lisztian.[28] His music reflected a very high but not uncommon conventional level of literacy and taste. For Nietzsche, Beethoven had not so much succeeded in communicating emotion per se, or states of minds and moods (the classical ideal of expressiveness), to render a general state specific (as Schumann had suggested in the early 1830s): he had made instrumental music individual, personal, and historical. Beethoven's music did not communicate a generic sensibility or a static mood but rather an active desire and passion within each individual, something precise and particular and temporal. The events of the "Pastoral" Symphony were appropriated by the listener not as generalized moods or even Beethoven's own feelings, but as a unique template of subjectivization that could be adapted by the listener into his or her own experience of pathos. In its very structure Beethoven's instrumental music could be personalized by the listener. This departure from uniformity and standardization of mood made the new language "forbidden" and "immoral." In the specific moment of an individual's life, desire and passion, for Nietzsche "the inner dramatic event," could be linked to particular events in the mind of an individual. Instrumental music went beyond theory and metaphysics.

The mid-century fascination with Beethoven's love life and artistic struggles confirmed the suspicion that one could hear in Beethoven's music an adequate expression of and response to the intensity of feeling triggered by a real and unique life experience. Most startling, the music was able to do this within a framework of inherited formal expectations. The notion, therefore, that conflict and contradiction with respect to these expectations could be found in Beethoven's music did not become a drawback. Indeed, as Nietzsche understood, difficulty and confusion were integral to pathos and deep passion. This perception of Beethoven justified the ambivalence if not discomfort that many of Nietzsche's contemporaries encountered in dealing with the late works.[29] Beethoven's achievement, for Nietzsche, vindicated his own critique of the novel and contemporary prose. Beethoven's music was not musical prose, in the sense of Wagner. Neither was it a formalist poetry. Yet as a kind of poetry it confronted the boundaries of form, inspiring a persistent recurring reinterpretation as passionately experiential and personal.

Nietzsche's perception of the nature of the mid-century allure of Beethoven, his offering a quite dangerous "hitherto forbidden" experience of emotional intensity within the artificiality of the musical moment, can be buttressed by Soren Kierkegaard's 1843 essay on repetition.[30] Kierkegaard does not explicitly discuss the experience, or rather the illusion, of repetition in music. The significance of repetition in Beethoven had already been discussed in the 1830s by Liszt, who wrote that

> from the standpoint of the public, repetition is indispensable for the understanding of thought, and from the perspective of art it is almost identical with advancement of clarity, structure, and effect. Beethoven, whom nobody could accuse of poverty of creative ability or lack of ideas, is one of the composers who relied most heavily on this technique.

Liszt had particularly in mind the repeats in the Scherzo of the Seventh Symphony.[31]

The hallmarks of Beethoven's instrumental style, including his handling of repetition, the use of harmony and rhythm (which for Guido Adler was his greatest contribution to Romanticism[32]), the compression of motivic materials, and the intensification of their development distorted the conventions of form and symmetry of Classicism and gave his music its distinctive surface and structure. Using the opaque materials of instrumental music—which initially signalled abstraction and the absence of visual or verbal meaning to mid-nineteenth-century audiences—Beethoven created a powerful secret language of emotion whose meaning could not be decoded with certainty for one individual by another. Beethoven had written instrumental music that not only defied censorship by the state, but created an impregnable secure space of intense private emotional experience. Music after Beethoven held out the promise Mendelssohn cherished—the capacity to communicate in a manner even more precise than words were able to do. In 1837 Mendelssohn expressed the hope that the music in *Paulus* would "become something important and personal for every member of the community."[33] Nietzsche's 1874 observation echoed the idea expressed in a letter Mendelssohn wrote in 1842 that words were ambiguous but music not. He observed:

> The thoughts which are expressed to me by music that I love are not too indefinite to be put into words, but on the contrary, too definite. And so I find in every effort to express such thoughts, that something is right but at the same time, that something is lacking in all of them; and so I feel, too, yours. This, however, is not your fault, but the fault of the words which are incapable of anything better. If you ask me what I was thinking of when I wrote it, I would say: just the melody as it stands. And if I happen to have had certain words in mind for one or another of these songs, I would never want to tell them to anyone because the same words never mean the same things to different people. Only the song can say the same thing, can arouse the same feelings in one person as in another, a feeling which is not expressed, however by the same words. . . . Words have many meanings, but music we could both understand correctly.[34]

The crucial point is the paradox that an evident clarity of words masks their impotence to be clear and communicate, just as the ambiguous surface of music masks not only the clarity and precision of communication, but the evidence of its own success. Beethoven, as the discoverer of the language of pathos and the exemplar of the way in which music could be subjectivized, created a novel instrument of intimate experience and secret thinking. This fact explains Mendelssohn's 1832 observation that his contemporaries displayed an extreme passion for Beethoven's symphonies and quartets, but denigrated those of Mozart and Haydn.

Like other nineteenth-century observers of music, Kierkegaard was keenly aware of the process of reading, and of the relationship of author to reader. With the spread of musical literacy after 1830, the parallels (and divergences) between reading and listening become relevant, since the evolution of ordinary literacy and musical literacy possessed comparable trajectories. Reading, like the experience of music, was held in suspicion by early-nineteenth-century observers as not only subversive in the political sense, but psychologically dangerous in a manner rendered famous in literature by Stendhal and Flaubert.[35] Kierkegaard concludes his "venture in experimenting psychology" with a letter to the reader who he claims grasps "the interior psychic states and emotions" communicated by a text.[36] As Kierkegaard observed in his journals, his interest in repetition was fueled by his desire to understand consciousness. Consciousness contained a relation "whose connection was a contradiction." The ideal sphere and external reality collide in the fact of consciousness. The most significant event of that collision is the experience of repetition, since the consciousness of repetition presupposes that which has occurred in reality before.[37]

Like Nietzsche, Kierkegaard posits an ancient/modern contrast. For Nietzsche, music before Beethoven communicated ideal states—permanent sensibilities—which, as he put it, "the Greeks called ethos"; this Nietzsche contrasted with the pathos around which Beethoven's music created room for expression.[38] For Kierkegaard, the Greeks stressed recollection. But in modernity, repetition had supplanted recollection: "Repetition and recollection are the same movement, except in opposite directions, for what is recollected has been, is repeated backward, whereas genuine repetition is recollected forward." Kierkegaard observed that repetition, where at all possible, makes the individual happy, whereas recollection creates unhappiness. The mature individual requires courage to will repetition. Hope for Kierkegaard is cowardly, and recollection an act of youth. "Recollection is a discarded garment that does not fit, however beautiful it is, for one has outgrown it. Repetition is an indestructible garment that fits closely and tenderly, neither binds nor sags." God willed repetition for Kierkegaard. The experience of repetition is "actuality and the earnestness of existence."[39]

Kierkegaard is aware that there is in fact no actual repetition. He also dismisses music as a means to achieve aesthetic repetition (Kierkegaard's objective) on account of the pre-reflective immediacy of response it requires. Nonetheless, in a moment of time we encounter something, whether by seeing or hearing, and explain it to ourselves as a repetition. Repetition, therefore, is an act of will which moves along with thinking in the present moment, in time; the character of temporal experience becomes transformed. Not surprisingly, Kierkegaard preserves his highest praise for that exceptional individual who "grows weary of the incessant chatter about the universal and the universal repeated to the point of the most boring insipidity."[40] The exceptional individual is not satisfied with languishing on the surface of universal ideas; he thinks the universal with intense passion. For Kierkegaard that exception can be the man of faith, or perhaps even the poet who creates in the specific moment the experience of recollection moving forward, i.e. repetition, because it has the "blissful security of the moment."[41]

If we apply this analysis to the experience of hearing music by Beethoven as understood by Liszt we gain insights into the startling success of Beethoven's music with the European public at mid-century. The tension Nietzsche identified between the composer's discovery of music as the language of passion, and his concomitant adherence to classical form, resulted in a music which, more than any of its predecessors, permitted the listening individual to experience repetition in Kierkegaard's sense. The structure in Beethoven's music (e.g., the relationship of exposition to development and recapitulation), the manner of variation and transformation and the character of the musical materials themselves, including the aspects of rhetoric and gesture, inspire the listener to experience a very particular intensity within the artificial dynamic temporal moment created by the inherited forms of, for example, the sonata and symphony. The abstract character of this instrumental music, its absence of visual and linguistic instruments of "exterior perception" (in Liszt's sense), allows listeners to repeat, so to speak, an intensity of their own emotion and passion forward in time. They are not left on the plane of vague permanent states or universals, or pushed back to mere recollection. Listening to Beethoven, in other words, creates an illusion of immediacy, particularity, and intimacy, combined with the sense of personalization.[42] The enthusiasm for Beethoven that Mendelssohn witnessed may have been more than mere pretense to connoisseurship. In Beethoven's music, the universal and the particular collided with an intensity that provided the listener with the sense of ecstatic realism. Beethoven's music gave the individual the Kierkegaardian experience of happiness; it gave him "time to live" rather than the sense that he could "sneak out of life" because he has realized that he has forgotten.[43]

The way the experience of listening to Beethoven was described during the mid nineteenth century justifies, I believe, the suggestive parallel between Kierkegaard's understanding of the psychology of the experience of repetition and Beethoven's music. A very late and retrospective summation of the commonplaces associated with the reception of Beethoven in the nineteenth century can be found in Guido Adler's

1927 centenary essay, "Beethovens Charakter." Adler credits Beethoven with "commanding the entire scale of human feelings."[44] His music communicates understanding through the mirroring of contradictions and contrasts in real experience. Even when it achieves an ethical purpose and takes on a moralizing function, the music communicates particularity without abstraction. The secret for Adler lies not only in the simplicity of the musical materials and the revolutionary range of their transformation and juxtaposition. Adler anticipates Goldschmidt's claim that in Beethoven there is more than merely the heroic and monumental, but also the lyric and ephemeral. For Adler Beethoven was no titan; he was rather a flawed, complicated human being whose emotions and experiences were no different from those who cherished his music. The magic was that Beethoven communicated the inner complexities of life in music, as Nietzsche suggested, within the framework of Viennese Classicism; the conflict between conventional constraint and expressive freedom was essential to the music's achievement. Adler took issue with the image of Beethoven popularized by Max Klinger's 1902 monumental sculpture as the idealized representation of a godlike, larger-than-life presence.[45] His Beethoven was merely a human being, uniquely capable of revealing his weaknesses and aspirations in his music.

Although Adler's characterizations of Beethoven's music and character and his influence came at the end of the Wagnerian era of Beethoven reception, his summation more closely paralleled the mid-century view. What Beethoven's music—and not Wagnerian music drama—could offer a listener was the opportunity for him or her to adapt the surface and content of instrumental music to his or her own experience, without words or pictures. The debate over whether Czerny or other contemporaries were accurate in suggesting that Beethoven wrote with and against ideas, stories, and other extramusical frameworks, has to be understood in the context of a century of reception in which listeners acted as if he had. Listeners may not have grasped Beethoven's particular narrative (as for example the Orpheus legend in the second movement of the Piano Concerto No. 4), but they experienced a parallel intensity of Nietzschean pathos and Kierkegaardian repetition without prompting. An unlikely but telling witness of this pattern of reception was the young Eduard Hanslick.

This brings us to the beginning of the great divide between the formalist approach and the programmatic interpretation. Credit is usually given to Hanslick for setting the terms of the discourse regarding the absolute character of music and reversing the trajectory of early romantic ideas about the nature of music. His 1854 tract *On the Musically Beautiful* has remained the locus classicus of a radical formalism. In that work Hanslick confronts directly the attempt to defend a programmatic reading of Beethoven by referring to the composer's creative process. Hanslick argues that in the end only the musical impression and the musical determinants give a work coherence, and therefore aesthetic value. Music for Hanslick cannot represent specific feelings. Therefore it must not be considered a language. Hanslick's intent in the 1854 tract is to posit a proper and idealized habit of listening, one adequate to the unique aesthetic character and form of music. Music becomes elevated and distant from vulgar and sentimentalized listening. Hanslick's intent is as much social as it is philosophical. As in Schumann's distinction between great art and the philistine, Hanslick took on the "wrong" kind of listeners, the half educated and the half cultured, who cherished the intimate experience offered by Beethoven's music.[46]

If one, however, looks at Hanslick's views from the late 1840s and early 1850s, a somewhat milder, more differentiated, and less rigid picture emerges. The uneasy balance that Nietzsche identified in Beethoven between old forms and a new language is reflected in an assertion from March 1848, written in the midst of the same crucible of revolution that helped shape the views on music and its future espoused by Wagner, Hanslick's arch enemy. In 1848 Hanslick did not view Beethoven's achievement as a triumph of formalist autonomy: "The works of great composers [*Tondichter*] are more than mere music; they are mirror images of the philosophical, religious, and political world views of their time. Does not the proud majesty and the tormented skepticism of German philosophy suffuse the late works of Beethoven. . . ."[47] In a review written in April 1849 of *Christus am Ölberge,* Hanslick wrote:

> For Beethoven the divine grew out of the human; he perceived in it the proud transcendence of matter by spirit. He unleashes a downpour of all exterior and internal adversities of life on the human being; the battle is heated, but the divine in man fights its way triumphantly and emerges phoenix-like from the ashes of passion. The two symphonies, in C minor and D minor respectively, illustrate this process most clearly and beautifully. The triumphant finale of the former, the transfigured adagio of the latter, are the most sublime of monuments of Beethoven's true religiosity, i.e., of his belief in a supra-worldly eternal spirit (*Urgeist*) and of the belief in his own connection with it. In life he believed in God and loved Him with all the power of his great and lonely heart. . . . Where religion was shown as being exterior to the human being it remained foreign and distant. Thus it is that there is no other composer who expressed a greater treasure trove of subjective

religion in his work, and who still did so little for its objective glorification.[48]

These views parallel those of Liszt and Strauss. They correspond to the perceptions of Nietzsche and Kierkegaard. The real and the ideal collide, and the particular and the universal work against one another. In Beethoven the human experience is at the center, the abstract and the metaphysical emerge out of the particularities of ordinary life. Writing in 1851, Hanslick notes that Beethoven was the first to express humor through music by using extreme contrasts that "tore open a chasm, thus dividing the ideal and the real, the world and the beyond."[49] Hanslick evokes Kierkegaard's characterization of the intensity of the moment of aesthetic consciousness in which the real and the ideal confront one another.

Nonetheless, in the early 1850s Hanslick's views began to shift. Perhaps because of the cultural politics of the post-1848 era, he began to abandon his earlier views not only about Beethoven, but about the nature of music. In 1853 he sketched an argument in which he made a distinction between the objective work of art and the subjective moment of creation. In this sketch he made a transitional concession. Beethoven, for example, might have intended to express emotions and ideas, but what emerges is an objective work of beauty. The listener's emotional response becomes an affective reaction which may be generically the same (e.g. that of pride or melancholy), but it is not the emotion that brought the composer to write the work. Hanslick creates a category of "aesthetic contemplation" based only in the work itself and nothing exterior to it that is a higher form of listening than the imputation of extra-musical meaning or the adaptation of the musical experience into one's personal circumstances and life.[50]

By 1854 Hanslick had clearly divorced himself from his own, earlier response to Beethoven. He expressed extraordinary hostility to a mode of listening in which "people surrender themselves so completely to the elemental in art that they are not in control of themselves . . . this is not to the credit of that art and is still less to the credit of those people." In defense of this position, Hanslick tries to deny the evident meaning of Beethoven's remark that music should "strike fire in the soul." For Hanslick music was definitely not a language, and thus not an instrument of either emotion or ideas.[51] It should therefore not come as a surprise that in 1856 he wrote a scathing denunciation of the last movement of the Ninth Symphony. It was a work of "an unfortunate darkening of the mind"; it was an example of "artistic confusion," a "painful raging of an

imagination which, though still great, is sick to the very core." In aesthetic terms, the finale was not beautiful. It was, indeed, unmusical.[52]

The conventions and expectations associated with listening to
Beethoven before the mid 1850s are confirmed not only by witnesses
within the confines of musical culture. Historical developments in the
arts do not run parallel in any neat manner. Hanslick's rejection of the
notion of music as a language in the early 1850s was a direct attack on
two literary and philosophical traditions dating from the late eighteenth
century that had become widely popularized. The first was the eighteenth-century notion that music was the ideal language of nature. The
second, closely associated with Tieck, Wackenroder, Schlegel, Novalis,
and, last but not least, Jean Paul and E. T. A. Hoffmann, was the idea
that for the reader and author poetic language and the experience of
poetry demanded that language and poetry achieve a status akin to
instrumental music. Music, as Barbara Naumann has argued, functioned during the late eighteenth century as a linguistic model for the
development of poetry. Listeners to music who were avid readers of
poetry and philosophy, formed part of their expectations about the
experience of music from their encounter with literary Romanticism.
The composer who most profoundly fulfilled these expectations for
instrumental music developed through an engagement with romantic
poetry, particularly Novalis, was Beethoven.[53]

Another more direct confirmation of the susceptibility of Beethoven to
a mode of listening in which the imposition of narrative and the extramusical seem at no way at odds with the "essence" of Beethoven comes
from the visual arts. Moritz von Schwind, Schubert's close friend,
sketched and completed a painting on oil and canvas entitled *Eine
Symphonie* between the years 1848 and 1852. It was intended for the
music room of the opera singer Karoline Hetzenecker, whom Schwind
had previously depicted in her role as Leonore in *Fidelio*.[54] Without any
sense of contradiction or irony, Schwind chose as musical inspiration for
his depiction of the symphony per se not a Beethoven symphony, but the
choral melody from Beethoven's Choral Fantasy op. 80. The painting is
divided into four sections, mirroring the four movements of a symphony.
Schwind saw no contradiction in painting the allegory of a Beethoven
symphony—an idealized form of instrumental music—using op. 80, a
choral work in a single movement; in addition to "Symphony," he originally thought of entitling the painting "Quartet." An idealized four-
movement form of Beethovenian instrumental music remained
Schwind's subject and the inspiration for the painting. The melody of op.
80, he argued, rather than the words, justified its use in this manner.[55]

Fig. 1. *Eine Symphonie*, by Moritz von Schwind, sketched in 1848–49, painted in 1852, Munich, Kgl. Neue Pinakothek; Oil on canvas, H. 1.65 meters; W. 0.97 meters

Designed as a "Beethoven wall" in a music room, the bottom panel of the painting depicts a rehearsal of op. 80 in which everyone is engaged, either actively or by listening. This panel then generates the centerpiece, the second movement of the painting, entitled by Schwind "Andante or Adagio." The music inspires a biographical, retrospective fantasy having to do with the love life of Karoline Hetzenecker. The painting of the love story sets the seduction within the natural landscape (appropriately for the contemporary celebration of Beethoven's affinity for nature.) The repose and intimacy of the second movement were crucial to Schwind. But even more significant was that in this second movement/panel, Beethoven focuses the viewer's gaze on side illustrations with smaller parallel depictions of the four seasons, night and day, that is, the passage of time, change, and reoccurrence. The particular reverie centering on a moment of love and attraction is framed visually by the general, and vice versa. This panel reaffirms Kierkegaard's notion of the collision of the real and the ideal, of the necessity to render the universal intensely passionate and particular. The second movement narrative of the lovers meeting in nature is followed by a third movement/panel, the scherzo, in which the formal declaration of love is presented. On either side are depictions of recollected events, a masked ball, a small concert, and a variety of mythological interpolations. Schwind mirrored the structure of a scherzo by making the images of the masked ball the bookends of the panel; if one looks at this panel in musical terms, one can see two AB structures organized as mirror images of one another, with the more languid, relaxed trio at the center.

The fourth and closing movement/panel, which is above the scherzo, is an Allegro presto. Appropriately, it shows the couple on their way after their wedding—a perfect example of Kierkegaard's notion of repetition as recollection moving forward. The coach travels left while two passing friends on foot move to the right, having just greeted the couple. The final movement is also surrounded by images, this time of mythological scenes—once again offering the viewer a specific event framed by generalized universals. Schwind, imitating the character of Beethoven's instrumental music, utilizes the illusion of an architectural niche to locate the specific within the general. The Schwind painting confirms Nietzsche's characterization of Beethoven's achievement as the creation of a new language of pathos working in tension with classical norms. In Schwind's case, he invented a neoclassical architectural framework that contains references from St. Cecilia to Greek mythology. Inside of it, Schwind's romantic realism predominates.

This painting depicts internal ruminations about life experience as inspired through sound. What triggers the painter's fantasy narrative of his heroine's (or the viewer's) life is Beethoven's music. The first and largest frame, which relates the present-time experience of making music, generates the subsequent scenes of past and future. It implies for Schwind that the participants in the first panel might be generating their own narrative fantasies of personal experience. Schwind had no doubts about how Beethoven's music functioned for his contemporaries (identifiable in the first panel are Franz Lachner, Schubert, and two of Beethoven's aristocratic female friends, Gallenberg and Brentano). Whether by intention or imputation, Beethoven's music provided a framework for the past relived, for aesthetic repetition, including personal subjective narration, fantasy, and extramusical significance. Meaning was located not, as in opera or vocal music, in the text, but in the character and progress of sonata-form music itself.[56]

III. Beethoven and the Politics of Cultural Symbolism: 1912–1936

In the early twentieth century the debate over Beethoven focussed not on intimate and personal experience, but shifted to its political significance and symbolism. As has been observed, there was meaning embedded in the use of the two German words used to describe Beethoven, "Komponist" and "Tondichter." The latter is not merely an archaic form associated with the romantic literary movement of the late eighteenth century, the "Sturm und Drang." The same can be said for the vocabulary prevalent in early-twentieth-century discourse regarding cultural decline. Max Nordau helped popularize the pseudo-scientific concept of degeneration, "Entartung."[57] Although he was aware of its use, in the culminating moment of the debate over the meaning of Beethoven and the significance of Beethoven reception, in 1920 Hans Pfitzner raised the rhetorical question whether "the new aesthetics of musical impotence" was not a "Verwesungssymptom."[58] Degeneration describes an evolutionary process from health to illness; "Verwesung" more directly denotes the decay and putrefaction of the diseased or already dead.

The occasion for Pfitzner's polemic was Paul Bekker's book on Beethoven, which first appeared in 1911.[59] For Pfitzner, as for Hanslick in 1854, the struggle was over the very nature of the public understanding of music. To Pfitzner, Bekker had reduced a unique art form characterized by specifically musical inspiration and notions of beauty to a mere intellectual game. This trivialization was best indicated by Bekker's claim that what lay behind each work by Beethoven was a poetic idea not, as Pfitzner would have had it, musical inspiration and thinking. To Pfitzner, this claim was part of a pernicious contemporary trend to intellectualize and rationalize music—the supremely non-rational art. It was bad enough to find this attitude pronounced in the work of younger modernist composers or in the theories of Busoni, but to see it influence the interpretation of the greatest composer's work was too much to bear. In Bekker's hands Beethoven's music had become little more than a translation of ideas and pictures into sound. Pfitzner accused Bekker of falsifying Beethoven not only in order to make the music accessible to the masses, but to promote through musical sound a certain set of Enlightenment ideals and an overarching humanism.

Pfitzner argued in 1920 (and after) that the greatness of the German tradition of music, and particularly of Beethoven, rested in a pre-rational if not irrational gift for thinking musically. The denial of this plain truth was the sign of a new, dangerous musical impotence on the part of contemporary composers, critics, and audiences. Bekker and his allies were concealing the absence of the requisite predisposition—the spontaneous, aesthetic gift and their lack of true native talent for music—behind rational arguments. It was a travesty to think that the greatest of all composers, and certainly of all German composers of instrumental music, had been inspired and guided by ordinary thinking and musings easily described in language.

For Bekker, Beethoven was a "Tondichter" who, unlike Wagner, did not illustrate. Beethoven derived his fundamental principles of musical form from a sort of pseudo-Platonic range of ideas that then took a poetic shape. Impressions from the outside, complex ideas, and inner feelings and convictions all explained Beethoven's music, not only his style, but the very structure of each work. Bekker reduced Pfitzner's quintessential "Erzmusikant" (instinctive natural musical being) to the status of a mere poet. In so doing, he subordinated music to a world inappropriately accessible to every literate and educated though unmusical individual.[60]

Pfitzner's conclusion corresponds to Hanslick's mature position. Writing nearly seventy years apart, both argue for the autonomy of music, for its independence from the linguistic and the visual. Both are concerned about the simplification and falsification of the criteria for the adequate judgment of music. There, however, the similarity ends. Hanslick's position can be usefully compared to that of Theodor W. Adorno, namely that even if the popularization of Beethoven constituted a corruption, it was at least theoretically possible to communicate widely the proper way of listening to music.[61] For Pfitzner, however, there is an unbridgeable divide between musical and unmusical people.

The social and political implications were not thinly veiled. Like Wagner, Pfitzner felt that Jews and their highly intellectualized cosmopolitan allies lacked a rooted musicality. They were incapable of creating music, and cloaked their incapacity by seducing the audience with elaborate extramusical characterizations of music. Ironically, this argument echoed Wagner's own critique of Hanslick, to whose arguments Pfitzner was profoundly indebted. The enemies, as in Wagner's day, were modernity's culture enthusiasts and their journalists—a world dominated by a rootless elite, a prime example of which was Paul Bekker.

As Pfitzner correctly pointed out, Bekker's argument was based on the conviction that Beethoven could be widely understood precisely because there was a parallelism between his musical forms and a comprehensible trajectory of poetic ideas. Beethoven was the pivotal figure in the history of music because through an appreciation of his music, the audience for music could, indeed, become universal. Beethoven had transformed music, once a purely aristocratic entertainment, into an accessible medium communicating values and beliefs. Because Beethoven's music could be viewed as advocating notions of universal equality, freedom, morality, and justice, his music had to be, as Strauss had argued in 1903, more than about itself. For Bekker as for Adler, Beethoven was not a revolutionary, but a conservative who had been influenced by Neefe. Beethoven's achievement was to take, as Nietzsche had argued, a static and amorphous parallelism between music and feeling characteristic of the eighteenth century, and turn it into a disciplined "spiritual collaboration" between sound and thought. For Beethoven, Bekker wrote, "musical hearing is experienced, and composition is, in its own language, the very same as the writing of poetry." ("Ihm ist Musikhören ein Erleben, und komponieren gilt in seiner Sprache dasselbe wie dichten.")[62] Bekker thus rejected Pfitzner's notion of musical inspiration as privileged.

Two facets of Bekker's argument particularly infuriated Pfitzner. First, Bekker claimed that the intellectual and spiritual "poetic program" of a work could be revealed through an internal analysis of each work of music itself. Thus Bekker's programmatic reading of Beethoven, unlike Wagner's, was not an imposition or an excursus on the music. The form the music took itself revealed the flow and character of ideas. Bekker's interpretive strategy was strangely formalistic, even if he strengthened his argument with an awareness of Beethoven's debt to eighteenth-century rhetoric and aesthetics, and by using Beethoven's own descriptions and comments and the observations of contemporaries. The explicit evidence of intentionality, an articulated biographical connection, or Beethoven's claim about what he was doing—was not necessary, even if it could be helpful. Bekker believed that the "content of a work of music [*Tondichtung*] is the result of the realization of musical affect."[63] The recognition of the musical meaning resulted in the revelation of its spiritual content through its particular use of musical means. In this way, Bekker sought to counter the suspicion first articulated by Hanslick and supported by later theorists that programmatic readings of Beethoven did not derive from an analysis of the music itself.

The second galling aspect of Bekker's argument was that Beethoven's spiritual agenda was in effect a manifesto for "freedom." For Bekker, the result of the totality of Beethoven's music was, "[F]reedom in the artistic, political, and personal, freedom of will, of action, of belief, freedom of the entire individual in all his doings, be they internal or external; that is the message Beethoven delivers and to which he gives symbolic expression in his heroes, in drama and poetry." Beethoven, for Bekker, was the musical equal of Kant, Fichte, Humboldt, Stein, Schiller, and Goethe.[64]

Bekker reversed the direction of the nineteenth-century habit of particularizing the perception of an inherent narrative in Beethoven. Beethoven's music now became the incarnation of the philosophical and metaphysical rendered personal. Bekker secularized the views of Schleiermacher. For the latter, music allowed the individual to confront and deepen faith. For the former, Beethoven's music transformed abstract ideas into a personal credo. Beethoven's poetic musical ideas were moral claims, and possessed a distinct public ideology, one which from the perspective of post-World-War-I Germany was unmistakably allied to the critique of nationalism, the rejection of race thinking (and therefore Wagnerian ideology), and the defense of democracy. For Bekker, subjective appropriation and intimacy as such were no longer on center stage. Beethoven's moral and spiritual influence was. It could be renewed for each generation precisely because of the abstract substance of instrumental music itself. Bekker defined Beethoven as communicating the highest sphere of truth as understood in terms of the divided line in Plato's *Republic*. The key difference of course was that for Plato only an elite could grasp the truth at its highest level. In Beethoven's hands, however, the very metaphysical character of the ideas was translated into a music that could appeal to the mass of modern listeners. Beethoven's greatness consisted of a democratized Platonism achieved through musical perception. Music became rational and democratic, where in Pfitzner it was the non-rational, exclusive possession of an elite and of a distinct race.

In a subsequent and more condensed recapitulation of his views, published in the late 1920s, Bekker responded to Pfitzner's criticisms. He wrote, "[music] is no longer sonority pure and simple; it contains abstract ideas. Beethoven did not write music to preconceived ideas, but the ideas and the music went inseparably together. . . . But an attempt is being made at present to deny that Beethoven's music bore any relation to ideas, to deny, that is, its essentially ideal character. . . . [I]n his particular type of ideas, Beethoven is the great child of a great imaginative era—an era in which the gods and heroes of idealism throve, an era which believed in man as a spiritual being, in freedom and brotherhood, in the joy and divine inspiration, in the everlasting peace and happiness of mankind."[65]

To deny that the "idea" functioned as the constructive and dynamic principle behind the form of Beethoven's instrumental music was comparable, claimed Bekker, to denying that in Michelangelo's "Moses" the idea of Moses was not an inherent quality of the work. Given the prominence of the Jewish question at the time, Bekker's choice of this analogy was pointed.

The most original feature of Bekker's otherwise derivative description of Beethoven's intellectual commitments and personality was that he justified his argument through a detailed analysis of works in the canon of Beethoven's instrumental music. Borrowing from the priority accorded instrumental music by Hanslick and his adherents, Bekker argued that instrumental sound had the capacity of "interpreting the abstract" in a manner that went far beyond what the voice could do. Music with words could not emancipate itself from particularity. The impact of Beethoven on modern audiences could be explained by the fact that his music, using sound alone, was capable of spreading and communicating abstract principles and ideas that transcended their historical and specific extramusical origins, both linguistic and visual.

Heinrich Schenker's monograph on the Ninth Symphony, dedicated to the "memory of the last master of German composition, Johannes Brahms," was published in 1912, one year after Bekker's book appeared. It was inspired by a commission for a series of lectures to the Association of Music Critics in Vienna, which Schenker never gave.[66] In contrast to Hanslick, Schenker argued that even the last movement of the Ninth Symphony could be understood exclusively in terms of "purely musical laws" and "musical logic—logic in the absolute sense, understood as completely separate from program or text." The movement was a triumph "*in spite*" of Schiller's text.[67]

The coherence between Pfitzner and Schenker seems initially uncanny, particularly their focus on German musical traditions. The preface to the 1912 monograph is a tirade against poorly trained performers, the greed of musical commerce, and the laziness of the public.

The only way to understand Beethoven, and to perform him properly, is to understand "the laws of tonal life." Unfortunately, in Schenker's view, theorists and historians from Wagner on had "made the approach to tonal art easier for laymen." Musicians themselves succumbed to using shortcuts in their own preparation. Schenker believed that he was living in an age of "intellectual robber-barony." [68] The world of music was now filled with unproductive noise justified by the cult of individuality and personality. The criteria for distinguishing between good and bad music had disappeared. Modern listeners and performers no longer understood the language and grammar of music. Schenker explained the structure of the Ninth, a work commonly viewed as possessing an extramusical significance and content, through a massive analysis which made no reference to extramusical meanings. The key difference between Schenker and Pfitzner was the former's emphasis on the rational processes of tonality and musical form; Pfitzner's notions of irrational inspiration would have been irrelevant to Schenker.

In the post-World War I era, the polemic of Hans Pfitzner against the extramusical analysis of Beethoven espoused by Paul Bekker revealed a clear divide along pro- and anti-modernist lines. Yet Schoenberg's views on Beethoven were much closer to Schenker's and Pfitzner's than they were to Bekker's, even though his and Schenker's political sentiments were opposed to Pfitzner's.[69] Pfitzner and Schenker shared contempt for most contemporary music; Bekker was an ardent defender of Mahler and Schoenberg. However, among modernists and their adherents, Schoenberg and his advocate Adorno sided with the anti-programmatic side, albeit in different ways. If Pfitzner's obsession was the corrupt public perception of Beethoven and the essence of music, Schenker's concern was for the dominant performance practices that cheapened Beethoven. The political implications of both the programmatic and formalist arguments of the 1920s in terms of the cultural politics of the inter-war era and the rise of Nazism were not straightforward. Some formalists believed that music, construed as autonomous, could function as a progressive political instrument just as Bekker hoped Beethoven's poetic content would. Those committed to a programmatic reading could be characterized as either understanding Beethoven as quintessentially German in a post-Wagnerian sense, or construing, as did Adler and Bekker, the extramusical essence of Beethoven as a universalizing force against tyranny and hatred. Bekker inverted the Wagnerian tradition of reading Beethoven against Wagnerian politics.

The evolution of the musical public from the participatory amateurism of the 1830s to the concert going and radio listening audience had resulted in a shift in the debate over meaning in Beethoven. The popular enthusiasm for Beethoven became significant as a force not in the private sphere of life experience but in a political struggle over ideological allegiances.

Arnold Schering's contributions to the Beethoven literature in the 1930s for example were more akin to Bekker, though his politics made him an explicit ally of Pfitzner. In fact, Schering went to great lengths to discredit Bekker in his sophisticated and carefully detailed book on Beethoven, *Beethoven und die Dichtung*, published in 1936 well after the Nazi's seizure of power. Schering, hiding behind the veneer of scholarly criticism, dismissed Bekker and his neo-Platonic notions. Instead Schering argued for a very explicit, historically and biographically based literary programmatic underpinning for a series of Beethoven's works.[70] Schering rejected the early romantic tradition of attributing vague meanings to Beethoven, the mid-century habit of favoring personal subjective extramusical responses, as well as the legacy of arbitrary neo-Wagnerian impositions. Closely argued interrelationships between specific works of literature and music in Beethoven existed; often they were hidden and had to be revealed through painstaking research and analysis.

Yet Bekker was not the main enemy for Schering. Where Pfitzner saw a corrupting and foreign intellectualizing in Bekker's theory, Schering, who shared with Pfitzner a sympathy for the Nazi regime, considered Bekker merely misguided and undisciplined. The real enemy for Schering was the anti-programmatic view of Beethoven espoused by Heinrich Schenker. The false intellectualizing of Beethoven had resulted in a cold, reductive formalistic analysis of Beethoven that only rootless intellectuals could appreciate.[71]

* * * *

In the post-World War II era the contrasts in the understanding of Beethoven do not suggest consistent cultural and political parallels. Consider, for example, the contrast between Theodor W. Adorno and Harry Goldschmidt.[72] The post-war triumph of a formalist reading of Beethoven located in views about the self-contained logical immanence of music and its elements cannot be lined up neatly along ideological lines. The efforts of modern scholars such as Owen Jander or Hartmut Krones to revive a line of analysis compatible with the work of Bekker, Schering, and Goldschmidt do not appear to indicate a consistent position in terms of ideological controversies beyond the realm of music strictly defined.[73] At the same time, the evolution of the early-twentieth-century movement dedicated to overturning a sentimental, romantic, or Wagnerian view of Beethoven has continued. The success of period instrument performances over the last twenty years has made this plain.[74]

From the perspective of the beginning of the twenty-first century, we seem no closer to resolving the question of what Beethoven's music is all about, or explaining why it continues to hold its special sway over the public. In the post-World War II era, the most convincing among the proponents of the significance of the extramusical was Harry Goldschmidt, whose emphases lay on the role of prosody and rhetoric.[75] But like Bekker, Goldschmidt's particular notion of the connection between Beethoven's music and aesthetic realism was guided by ideological considerations directly in opposition to Schenker's. He displayed no contempt for the mass public.

The great strides made in recent decades on illuminating questions concerning the historical Beethoven have had the perhaps unintended consequence of diminishing Beethoven's accessibility in the sense defined by Nietzsche and other mid-nineteenth-century observers. Period instrument performances and the precise linkage in Beethoven to specific eighteenth-century rhetorical conventions and to extramusical programs may have deterred today's audience from trying to hear Beethoven as audiences were accustomed to doing so in the years between Beethoven's death and the mid 1850s. A valid intimate personal connection seems harder to forge. At the same time, the debate over meaning in Beethoven no longer possesses powerful political significance. Bekker's views seem hopelessly naïve in view of the successful Nazi appropriation of Beethoven. The performance by Leonard Bernstein of the Ninth Symphony marking the fall of the Berlin Wall (with its altered text) represented a hollow echo of Bekker's idealism. Such gestures only serve to lend credence to the formalist view.[76]

New generations of listeners who wish to widen the range of their own response might be well advised to make a distinction between understanding the historical Beethoven and continuing the insights gleaned from the heritage of reception. The unusual susceptibility of Beethoven's music to nearly contradictory readings and responses has been an integral part of what the music is. The tension and ambiguity suggested by Nietzsche may explain how listeners are able to find in Beethoven meaning that goes well beyond the traditions of the heroic and monumental. As Hanslick before 1854 and Strauss in 1903 suggested, Beethoven achieved a unique balance between the command of music as a self-contained formal process and as the extension of an eighteenth-century commitment to music as a medium with meanings beyond the formally musical. Whether through uses of tonality, rhetoric, gesture, sonority, verse meter, ideas, or, as Czerny claimed, narrative structures, Beethoven succeeded in creating instrumental music that has offered succeeding generations an unparalleled opportunity for the experience of the Kierkegaardian moment of repetition.

Likewise, contemporary performers of Beethoven should not hide behind the veil of objective scholarship to suppress a search for new strategies. Whether Beethoven sought to write music designed to engender emotions, ideas, and ideals in the listener or not, the perception of articulate extramusical meaning and significance in Beethoven may be something to encourage. The music's rhetorical, emotional, and moral power need no longer be understood as extramusical; these attributes may have become permanently inseparable from the musical texts and their sounding presence. This fact may explain the unique place occupied by Beethoven's instrumental music for over two centuries. Our task may be to sustain the music's unusual capacity to renew its allure and elude not only the historical patina of its origins, but the evident traces of subsequent interpretation.

NOTES

1 See Elisabeth E. Bauer, *Wie Beethoven auf den Sockel kam. Die Entstehung eines musikalischen Mythos* (Stuttgart and Weimar, 1992); Scott Burnham, *Beethoven Hero* (Princeton, 1995); and Hans H. Eggebrecht, *Zur Geschichte der Beethoven Rezeption* (Laaber, 1994).

2. See Klaus Kropfinger, *Wagner and Beethoven. Richard Wagner's Reception of Beethoven*, trans. Peter Palmer (Cambridge, 1991).

3. See Felix Weingartner, *On the Performance of Beethoven's Symphonies*, trans. Jessie Crosland (New York, 1906).

4. See Rudolf Kolisch, *Tempo und Charakter in Beethovens Musik*, Musik-Konzepte 76/77 (Munich, 1992). For an English translation of this text, see the *Musical Quarterly* 77 (1993): 90–131 and 268–342.

5. For Richard Wagner, see especially his "Beethoven" essay of 1870 (in *Richard Wagner's Prose Works*, vol. 5, trans. William Ashton Ellis [London, 1896; repr. New York, 1966]), as well as his other writings on Beethoven; for Hector Berlioz, see *A Critical Study of Beethoven's Nine Symphonies*, trans. Edwin Evans (London, n.d.).

6. See Johann A. Schlosser, *Ludwig van Beethoven. Eine Biographie desselben, verbunden mit Urtheilen über seine Werke* (Prague, 1828), p. 92. An English translation, by Reinhard G. Pauly and edited by Barry Cooper, appeared under the title *Beethoven. The First Biography* (Portland, Oregon, 1996).

7. Letter to Zelter of February 15, 1832, in *Felix Mendelssohn: A Life in Letters*, ed. Rudolf Elvers, trans. Craig Tomlinson (New York, 1986), p. 178.

8. See Leon Botstein, "Listening through Reading: Writing on Music and the Concert Audience," *Nineteenth-Century Music* 16, no. 2 (1992): 129–145.

9. Samples of narrative explanations for the Fourth Symphony can be found in R. von Elterlein, *Beethoven's Symphonies Explained*, trans. F. Weber (London, n.d.), pp. 47–51;

Philip H. Goepp, *Symphonies and Their Meaning* (Philadelphia and London, 1902), pp. 87–110; and Berlioz, *Beethoven's Nine Symphonies* (op. cit.), pp. 53–57.

10. These are internal descriptive justifications for the presence of ideas in the instrumental music.

11. Mahler's performance of the Ninth Symphony took place on February 18, 1900 at a benefit concert, the so-called Nicolai Concert, and was repeated four days later. Mahler's response to the critics was distributed at the second concert. Cited in Henry-Louis de La Grange, *Gustav Mahler. Vienna: The Years of Challenge (1897–1904)*, pp. 235ff. Hirschfeld's review, "Die neunte Symphonie," appeared in the *Neue musikalische Presse*, 25 February 1900, pp. 64–65. For Schenker's review of a repeat performance, also at a Nicolai Concert, in 1901, see "Beethoven Retouché" in *Heinrich Schenker als Essayist und Kritiker. Gesammelte Aufsätze, Rezensionen und kleinere Berichte aus den Jahren 1891–1901*, ed. Hellmut Federhofer (Hildesheim and Zurich, 1990), pp. 259–268.

12. Robert Schumann, *On Music and Musicians*, ed. Konrad Wolf, trans. Paul Rosenfeld (New York and London, 1964), pp. 41 and 45.

13. Richard Strauss, "Einleitung," in August Göllerich, *Beethoven*, "Die Musik," vol. 1 (Berlin, 1903), pp. i–iv.

14. See Harry Goldschmidt, *Die Erscheinung Beethoven* (Leipzig, 1974), pp. 20–22.

15. Romain Rolland, *Jean-Christophe*, trans. Gilbert Cannan, 3 vols. (New York, 1910), vol. 1, p. 97.

16. See A.B. Marx, *Anleitung zum Vortrag Beethovenscher Klavierwerke* (Regensburg, 1912); and Carl Reinecke, *Die Beethoven'schen Clavier-Sonaten. Briefe an eine Freundin* (Leipzig, n.d.).

17. John Field, Nocturne No. 10 in E Minor (1836), in Field, *Nocturnes and Related Pieces*, ed. Robin Langley (London, 1997), pp. 34–36.

18. Hans von Bülow, *Nirwana*, Orchesterfantasie op. 20 (Munich 1881) from rehearsal letter Aa (piu animato) to Bb.

19. See Hermann Kretzschmar, *Führer durch den Konzertsaal*, Part I: *Symphonie und Suite* (Leipzig, 1887), p. 89.

20. La Mara, aka Marie Lipsius (1837–1927), came from a family of well-known Leipzig intellectuals and was a friend of Liszt and the Wagner family. She was the author of a large number of books and articles on musical subjects, among them the highly successful series "Musikalische Studienköpfe," on the lives of the composers Schumann, Liszt, and Chopin.

21. See Schlosser, *Ludwig van Beethoven*, p. v.

22. See Burnham, *Beethoven Hero*, particularly pp. 66–111 and 162–168.

23. For the best Beethoven bibliography and work list, see Klaus Kropfinger's article on Beethoven in *Die Musik in Geschichte und Gegenwart, Allgemeine Enzyklopädie der Musik*, ed. Ludwig Finscher, Personenteil (Kassel, 1999), vol. 2, pp. 670–943. Another excellent review of the extensive Beethoven literature can be found in Maynard Solomon's revised edition of his *Beethoven* (New York, 1998), pp. 492–518. Also instructive in this context are the work of Hartmut Krones, *Ludwig van Beethoven. Werk und Leben* (Vienna, 1999); George Barth, *The Pianist as Orator. Beethoven and the Transformation of Keyboard Style* (Ithaca and London, 1992); and Konrad Küster, *Beethoven* (Stuttgart, 1994).

24. See Goldschmidt, *Erscheinung*, p. 23. On the "Pastoral," see the provocative reading in Roland Schmenner, *Die Pastorale: Beethoven, das Gewitter und der Blitzableiter* (Kassel, 1998).

25. Franz Liszt, *Gesammelte Schriften*, (Leipzig, 1881; repr. Hildesheim and Wiesbaden, 1978), vol. 2, p. 104.

26. Elvers, *Mendelssohn*, p. 175.

27. Friedrich Nietzsche, "Richard Wagner in Bayreuth," in Nietzsche, *Untimely Meditations*, trans. R.J. Hollingdale (Cambridge, 1983), pp. 240ff.

28. For examples of his compositions, see Friedrich Nietzsche, *Der musikalische Nachlaß*, ed. Curt Paul Janz (Basel, 1976).

29. Karl Goldmark, for example, recalls his teacher Gottfried Preyer, who like Albrechtsberger in Beethoven's day was in charge of music at St. Stephen's Cathedral and served for a time as director of the Conservatory, saying, in the late 1840s, that in his Ninth Symphony, Beethoven "showed himself no longer quite clear in his mind." Karl Goldmark, *Notes from the Life of a Viennese Composer*, trans. Alice Goldmark Brandeis (New York, 1927), p. 113.

30. See Soren Kierkegaard, "Repetition. A Venture in Experimenting Psychology," and "Selected Entries from Journals and Papers Pertaining to 'Repetition'," in Kierkegaard, *Fear and Trembling. Repetition*, ed. and trans. Howard V. Hong and Edna H. Hong (Princeton, 1983), pp. 125–231 and 274–330. I take issue with Adorno's 1933 reading of the relevance of Kierkegaard's aesthetics to music. See Adorno, *Kierkegaard. Construction of an Aesthetic*, ed. and trans. Robert Hullot-Kentor (Minneapolis, 1989), pp. 19–22. I want to thank Joan Retallack and Daniel Berthold-Bond for their suggestions concerning Kierkegaard.

31. Liszt, *Gesammelte Schriften*, vol. 2, p. 103. See also Alan Walker, *Franz Liszt. The Weimar Years, 1848–1861* (New York, 1989), p. 322.

32. Guido Adler, *Beethovens Charakter* (Regensburg, 1927), pp. 17ff.

33. Letter to Julius Schubring of July 14, 1837, in *Felix Mendelssohn: Letters*, ed. G. Selden-Goth (New York, 1973), p. 269.

34. Letter to Marc-André Souchay of October 15, 1842, in *Felix Mendelssohn: Letters*, p. 314.

35. Consider the role of reading in Stendhal's *The Red and the Black* (1830) and Gustave Flaubert's *Madame Bovary* (1856).

36. Kierkegaard, "Repetition," p. 231.

37. Kierkegaard, "Selected Entries," pp. 274ff.

38. Nietzsche, "Richard Wagner in Bayreuth," p. 240.

39. Kierkegaard, "Repetition," pp. 131–33.

40. Kierkegaard, "Repetition," p. 227.

41. Kierkegaard, "Repetition," p. 132.

42. The use of music, particularly Beethoven's, as a medium for intimate appropration was perhaps most strikingly described already in 1837 by Balzac in the small novel *Gambara*. He noted that "Beethoven has extended the boundaries of instrumental music and no one has followed him in his flight"; for Balzac, Beethoven in the C-minor Symphony revealed nature in its entirety and all its detail. The protagonists celebrate Beethoven in contrast to Rossini and stress the organic unity of his instrumental forms, whose handling of detail and structure can be compared to the novels of Walter Scott. For Balzac, music had advanced so that it is the art "that penetrates deepest into the soul. . . . You see only what the picture shows you, you hear only what the poet says to you; music goes far beyond: does it not shape your thought? Does it not arouse the torpid memory? . . . [A] phrase transmitted . . . develops as many different poems; to this one a woman appears long dreamed of; to that one, I know not what bank along which he has strolled . . . this woman recalls a thousand feelings that tortured her during an hour of jealousy; and other things of the unsatisfied desires of her heart, and paints with the rich colors of the dream an ideal being . . . another imagines that she will realize some desire that very evening . . . music alone has the power of restoring us to ourselves;

while other arts give us defined pleasures." Honoré de Balzac, *Gambara*, trans. Thomas Walls and G. B. Ives (Philadelphia, 1899), pp. 26, 36ff.

43. Kierkegaard, "Repetition," p. 131.

44. Adler, *Charakter*, p. 20.

45. Adler, *Charakter*, pp. 20–22, 24. For Klinger's statue, see for example Marian Bisanz-Prakken's essay, "Die Beethovenfigur von Max Klinger," in her book, *Gustav Klimt. Der Beethovenfries* (Salzburg, 1977), pp. 13–17.

46. See Eduard Hanslick, *On the Musically Beautiful. A Contribution towards the Revision of the Aesthetics of Music*, ed. and trans. Geoffrey Payzant (Indianapolis, 1986).

47. Eduard Hanslick, *Sämtliche Schriften. Historisch-kritische Ausgabe*, vol. 1, part 1: Aufsätze und Rezensionen 1844–1848, ed. Dietmar Strauß (Vienna and Cologne, 1993), p. 157.

48. Hanslick, *Sämtliche Schriften*, vol. 1, part 2: Aufsätze und Rezensionen 1849–1854 (Vienna and Cologne, 1994), pp. 65ff.

49. Hanslick, *Sämtliche*, vol. 1, part 2, p. 164.

50. Hanslick, *Sämtliche*, vol. 1, part 2, pp. 234ff.

51. See Hanslick, *Beautiful*, p. 61.

52. Hanslick, *Sämtliche*, vol. 1, part 3: Aufsätze und Rezensionen 1855–1856 (Vienna and Cologne, 1995), p. 326.

53. See Barbara Naumann, *"Musikalisches Ideen-Instrument": Das Musikalische in Poetik und Sprachtheorie der Frühromantik* (Stuttgart, 1990) especially pp. 74–89; Barbara Naumann, ed., *Die Sehnsucht der Sprache nach der Musik. Texte zur musikalischen Poetik um 1800* (Stuttgart and Weimar, 1994), pp. 245–73; and Peter Schleuning, *Die Sprache der Natur. Natur in der Musik des 18. Jahrhunderts* (Stuttgart and Weimar, 1998), pp. 127–37, 194–99, 210; and Schmenner, *Die Pastorale* (op. cit.), pp. 1–24, 91–107.

54. See Otto Weigmann, ed., *Schwind. Des Meisters Werke in 1265 Abbildungen* (Stuttgart and Leipzig, n.d.), p. 261.

55. See Ulrike Olbrich, "Moritz von Schwind und die musikalische Bilddichtung," in *Moritz von Schwind. Meister der Spätromantik*, exhibition catalogue (Karlsruhe and Leipzig, 1997), pp. 76–84.

56. For a critical confirmation of this representation of how Beethoven's instrumental music was heard at mid century, see the brilliant but skeptical judgment of pure instrumental music and the success of Beethoven in G.G. Gervinus, *Händel und Shakespeare. Zur Ästhetik der Tonkunst* (Leipzig, 1868), pp. 144–80.

57. See Max Nordau, *Entartung*, 2 vols. (Berlin, 1893).

58. See Hans Pfitzner, *Die neue Aesthetik der musikalischen Impotenz. Ein Verwesungssymptom?* (Munich, 1920). On the Pfitzner-Bekker controversy, see an extremely pro-Pfitzner position in Walter Abendroth, *Hans Pfitzner* (Munich, 1935), pp. 402–405, and the more balanced but still pro-Pfitzner approaches in B. Adamy, *Hans Pfitzner* (Tutzing, 1980), pp. 102–109; John Williamson *The Music of Hans Pfitzner* (Oxford, 1992); and Johann Peter Vogel, *Pfitzner. Leben Werke Dokumente* (Zurich, 1999), pp. 127–129.

59. See Paul Bekker, *Beethoven* (Berlin, 1912). Two examples of the extensive popularity of Beethoven in the early twentieth century are the annual Beethoven-Kalendar (Berlin-Liepzig) publications (e.g. *Beethoven-Kalendar für 1907*) and the set of essays and illustrations in a special 1920 edition of the journal *Moderne Welt* entitled "Beethoven Festschrift," vol. 2, no. 9 (Vienna, 1920), designed to celebrate the 150th anniversary of the composer's birth.

60. See Pfitzner, *Die neue Aesthetik*, p. 16. It is important to remember that Pfitzner elaborated further his notion of musical inspiration at the height of success of the Third Reich in a small tract *Über musikalische Inspiration* (Berlin, 1940).

61. See Theodor W. Adorno, "Analytical Study of the NBC 'Music Appreciation Hour,'" *Musical Quarterly* 78, no. 2 (1994): 325–377.

62. Bekker, *Beethoven*, pp. 80ff.

63. Bekker, *Beethoven*, p. 78.

64. Bekker, *Beethoven*, pp. 89ff.

65. Bekker, *The Story of Music. An Historical Sketch of the Changes in Musical Form* (New York, 1927), pp. 191–93.

66. See Heinrich Schenker, *Beethoven's Ninth Symphony. A Portrayal of Its Musical Content, with Running Commentary on Performance and Literature As Well*, ed. and trans. John Rothgeb (New Haven and London, 1992).

67. Schenker, *Beethoven's Ninth*, p. 225.

68. Schenker, *Beethoven's Ninth*, pp. 10, 18, 26.

69. Consider, for example, the manner in which Schoenberg treats examples from Beethoven in both the *Harmonielehre* (Vienna, 1911, beginning of Chapter 14) and in the posthumously published *Fundamentals of Musical Composition*, eds. Gerald Strang and Leonard Stein (New York, 1967, in the discussion of the piano sonatas and the larger sonata-allegro form), pp. 120–21 and 199–213.

70. See Arnold Schering, *Beethoven und die Dichtung. Mit einer Einleitung zur Geschichte und Ästhetik der Beethovendeutung* (Berlin, 1936; repr. Hildesheim and New York, 1973), pp. 121 passim.

71. See Schering, *Beethoven und die Dichtung*, pp. 13–118.

72. Compare, for example, Goldschmidt's *Erscheinung* with Adorno's *Beethoven. Philosophie der Musik. Nachgelassene Schriften*, vol. 1, ed. Rolf Tiedemann (Frankfurt, 1993). We could, however, construct a parallel between two forms of mid-century Marxist thought using both authors.

73. See Owen Jander, "Beethoven's 'Orpheus in Hades': The *Andante con moto* of the Fourth Piano Concerto," *Nineteenth-Century Music* 8, no. 3 (1985): 195–212; Jander, "The Prophetic Conversation in Beethoven's 'Scene by the Brook'," *Musical Quarterly* 77, no. 3 (1993): 508–559; and Krones, *Ludwig van Beethoven*, esp. pp. 1–102.

74. The parallel between analytic strategies and performance practices is not always obvious. See for example a brilliant and imaginative discussion of this issue in Nicholas Cook, "The Conductor and the Theorist: Furtwängler, Schenker and the First Movement of Beethoven's Ninth Symphony," in *The Practice of Performance. Studies in Musical Interpretation*, ed. John Rink (Cambridge, 1995), pp. 105–25. See also Schenker's diary entry of November 4, 1929, in Hellmut Federhofer, ed. *Heinrich Schenker. Nach Tagebüchern und Briefen in der Oswald Jonas Memorial Collection* (Hildesheim and Zurich, 1985), pp. 250ff. It is oddly critical of Artur Schnabel's playing and interpretation.

75. See Goldschmidt, *Erscheinung*, esp. the chapter on "Vers und Strophe in Beethovens Instrumentalmusik," pp. 25–48.

76. See Leon Botstein, "Why Music in a Time of War?" *New York Times*, 3 March 1991.

INDEX

.

Index

Subject Index

Notes on the Contributors

Leon Botstein is president of Bard College, where he also serves as the Leon Levy Professor in the Arts and Humanities. He is the author of *Judentum und Modernität* (Vienna, 1991) and of a forthcoming study, *Music and Its Public: Habits of Listening and the Crisis of Modernism in Vienna, 1870–1914.* The editor of *The Compleat Brahms* (New York, 1999) and of *The Musical Quarterly,* he is music director of the American Symphony Orchestra and has recorded extensively for Telarc, Arabesque, CRI, and Vanguard.

Scott Burnham, Professor of Music at Princeton University, is the author of *Beethoven Hero* (Princeton, 1995; paperback reprint, 2000) and translator of A. B. Marx, *Musical Form in the Age of Beethoven* (Cambridge, 1997). He recently revised the article "Beethoven" for the forthcoming new edition of *The New Grove Dictionary of Music and Musicians* and is now at work on a project entitled "Mozart, Schubert, and the Music of Romantic Subjectivity."

Reinhold Brinkmann is the James Edward Ditson Professor of Music at Harvard University. His main areas of research are the history and aesthetics of music from the late eighteenth to the twenty-first century. Most recent publications include: *Late Idyll. The Second Symphony of Johannes Brahms,* (Cambridge, Mass., 1997, paperback), and *Schumann und Eichendorff* (Munich, 1997). With Christoph Wolff, he is the editor of *Driven Into Paradise: The Musical Migration From Nazi Germany To the United States* (Berkeley, 1999).

Alessandra Comini is University Distinguished Professor of Art History at Southern Methodist University in Dallas. An amateur flutist and an authority in the field of musical iconography, she is the author of several books about the art and artists of Vienna including several on Egon Schiele, as well as *The Changing Image of Beethoven: A Study in Mythmaking* (1987). Her many reviews, essays, and articles appear in national and international publications, and she is a regular contributor to *Stagebill.* Her lively revisionist work in the history of women artists was acknowledged in 1995 by the Women's Caucus for Art's Lifetime Achievement Award.

Christopher H. Gibbs, Assistant Professor of Music at the State University of New York at Buffalo, edited *The Cambridge Companion to Schubert* (Cambridge, 1997) and is the author of *The Life of Schubert* (Cambridge, 2000). He received the ASCAP-Deems Taylor Award in 1998 and currently holds a fellowship from the American Council of Learned Societies to write a book on the connections between Beethoven and Schubert in and around their deaths.

William Kinderman is Professor of Music at the University of Victoria. Two of his books on Beethoven were recently reprinted (*Beethoven* and *Beethoven's Diabelli Variations*, issued together with his acclaimed CD of that work with Hyperion Records). Kinderman recently received a Killam Research Grant in support of his editorship of the new *Beethoven Sketchbook Edition* for the University of Nebraska Press, and he is also currently writing a study of Beethoven's creative process.

Lewis Lockwood is the Fanny Peabody Professor of Music at Harvard University. His work on Beethoven includes the book *Beethoven: Studies in the Creative Process* (Cambridge, Mass., 1992) and numerous essays and reviews. He is currently preparing a critical biography of Beethoven and further studies of individual works and their compositional origins.

Nicholas Marston is Reader in Music at the University of Oxford, and a Fellow of St Peter's College; he is currently also Chairman of the Faculty Board of Music. His publications include *Beethoven's Piano Sonata in E, op. 109* (Oxford, 1995) and *Schumann: Fantasie, op. 17* (Cambridge, 1992). He is a co-author of *The Beethoven Compendium*, ed. Barry Cooper (London: Thames & Hudson, 1991), and has published work on Beethoven, Schumann, Schubert, and Heinrich Schenker in many leading musicological journals.

Sanna Pederson has published articles relating Beethoven and German music to nation building, historiography, and anti-romanticism. She is currently working on a book called *Musical Romanticism and Cultural Pessimism: the Impact of the Revolutions of 1848 on German Musical Thought*. She is visiting assistant professor of music at Wesleyan University.

Elaine Sisman is Professor and Chairman of the Music Department at Columbia University. The author of *Haydn and the Classical Variation* (Cambridge, Mass., 1993), *Mozart: The 'Jupiter' Symphony* (Cambridge Music Handbook, 1993), and editor of *Haydn and His World* (for the Bard Music Festival in 1997, Princeton University Press), she specializes in music, aesthetics, and the history of ideas in the eighteenth and nineteenth centuries, and has published on Beethoven and the meanings of *pathétique* and *fantasia* (in *Beethoven Forum*, of which she is co-editor) and on his "musical inheritance," the classical style (in *The Beethoven Companion*, ed. Glenn Stanley, Cambridge, 2000). She is at work on a study entitled "C. P. E. Bach, Beethoven, and the Labyrinth of Melancholy."

Glenn Stanley has edited *The Cambridge Companion to Beethoven* (Cambridge, 2000) and written articles on historiography and German music criticism for the forthcoming edition of *The New Grove Dictionary of Music and Musicians*. He is currently working on the chapter about *Parsifal* for *The Cambridge Companion to Wagner*, as well as a large-scale study of the symbol theory and music criticism of Arnold Schering.

Michael P. Steinberg is Professor of Modern European History at Cornell University and Associate Editor of *The Musical Quarterly*. He is the author of *Austria as Theater and Ideology: The Meaning of the Salzburg Festival* (Cornell, 1990; second edition, with a new preface, 2000) and the forthcoming *Listening to Reason: Music and Subjectivity in the Long Nineteenth Century*.